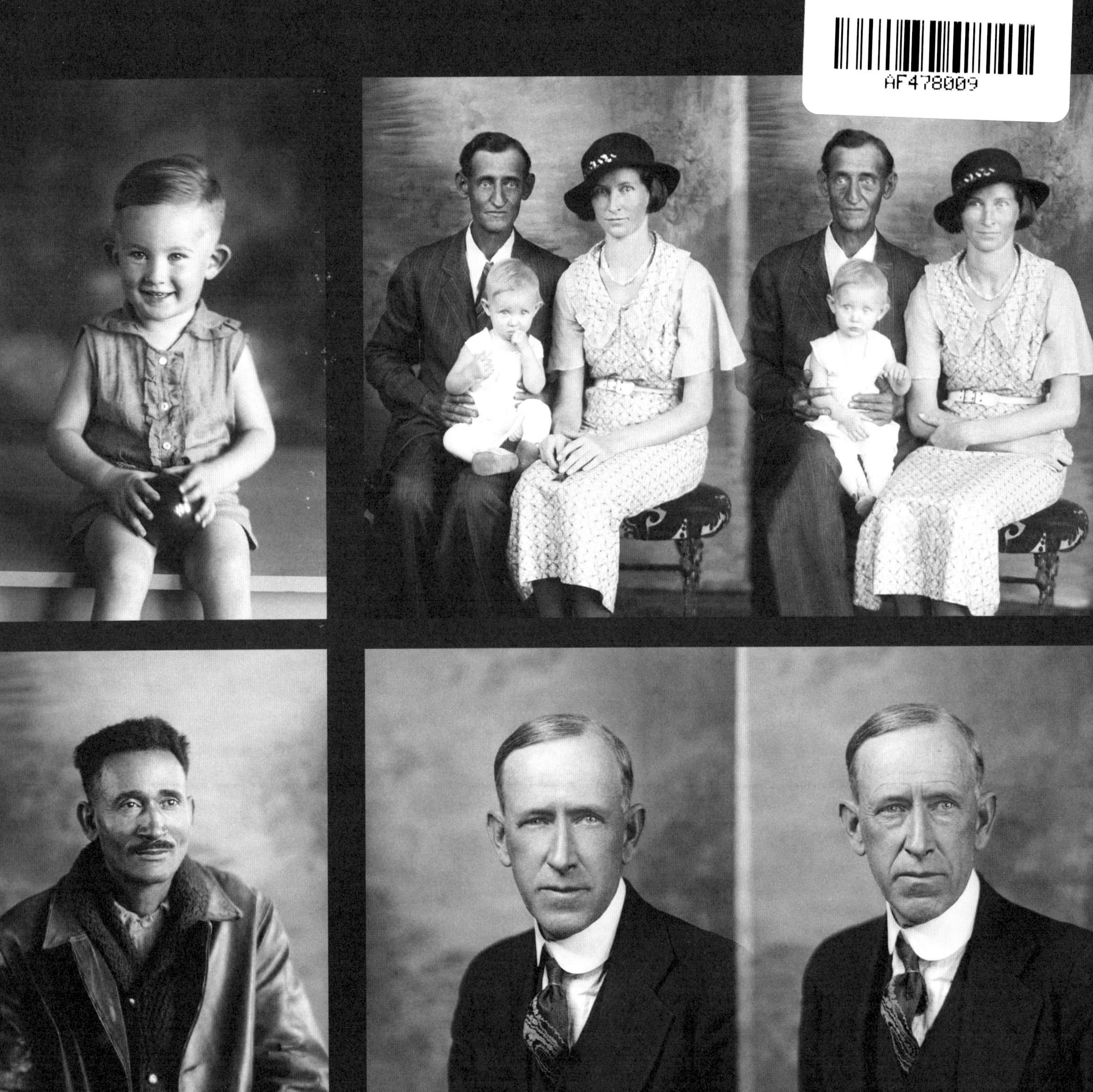

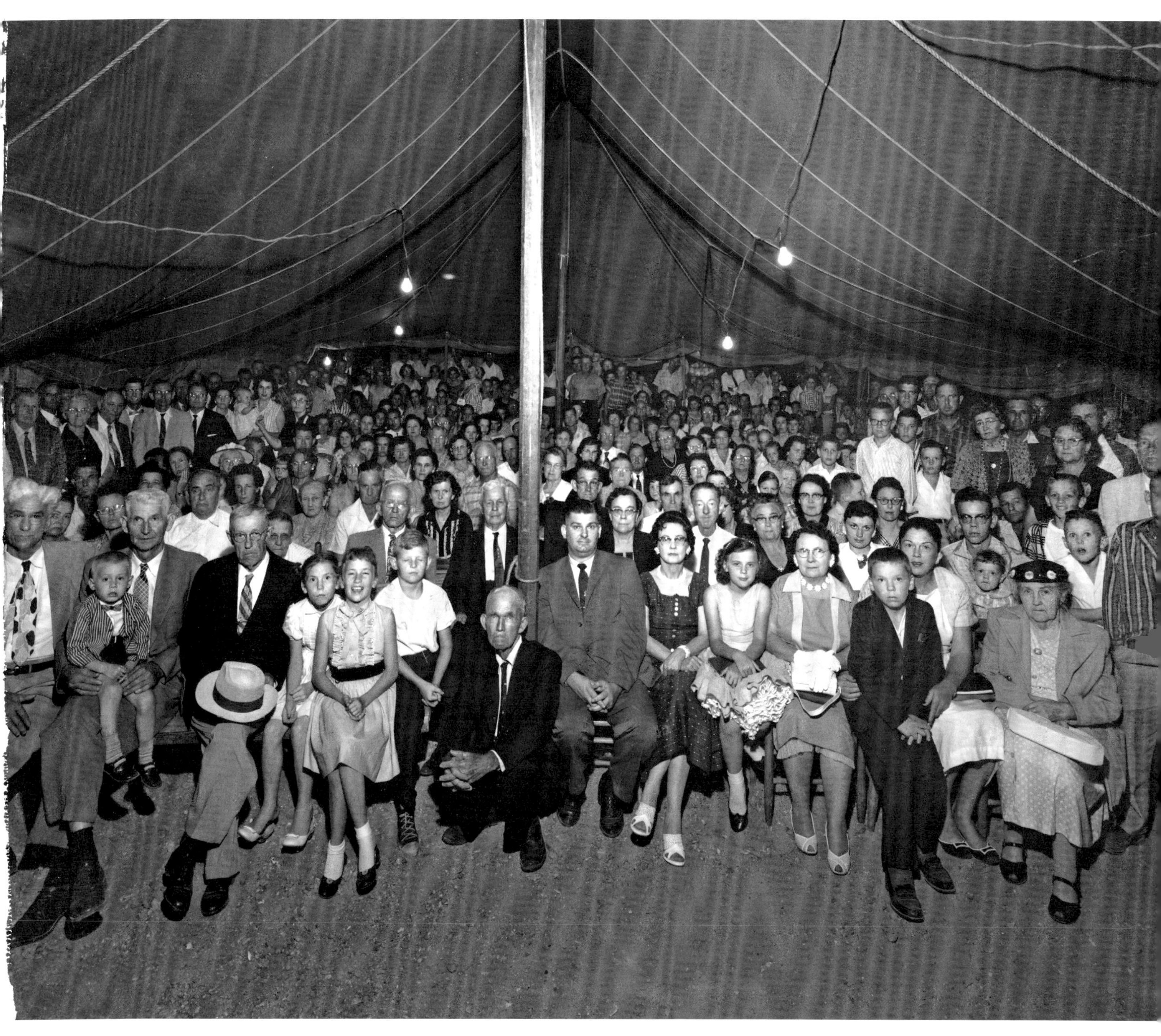

Church of Christ tent revival, circa 1955. Oliver Murray, preacher, seated to right of tent pole.

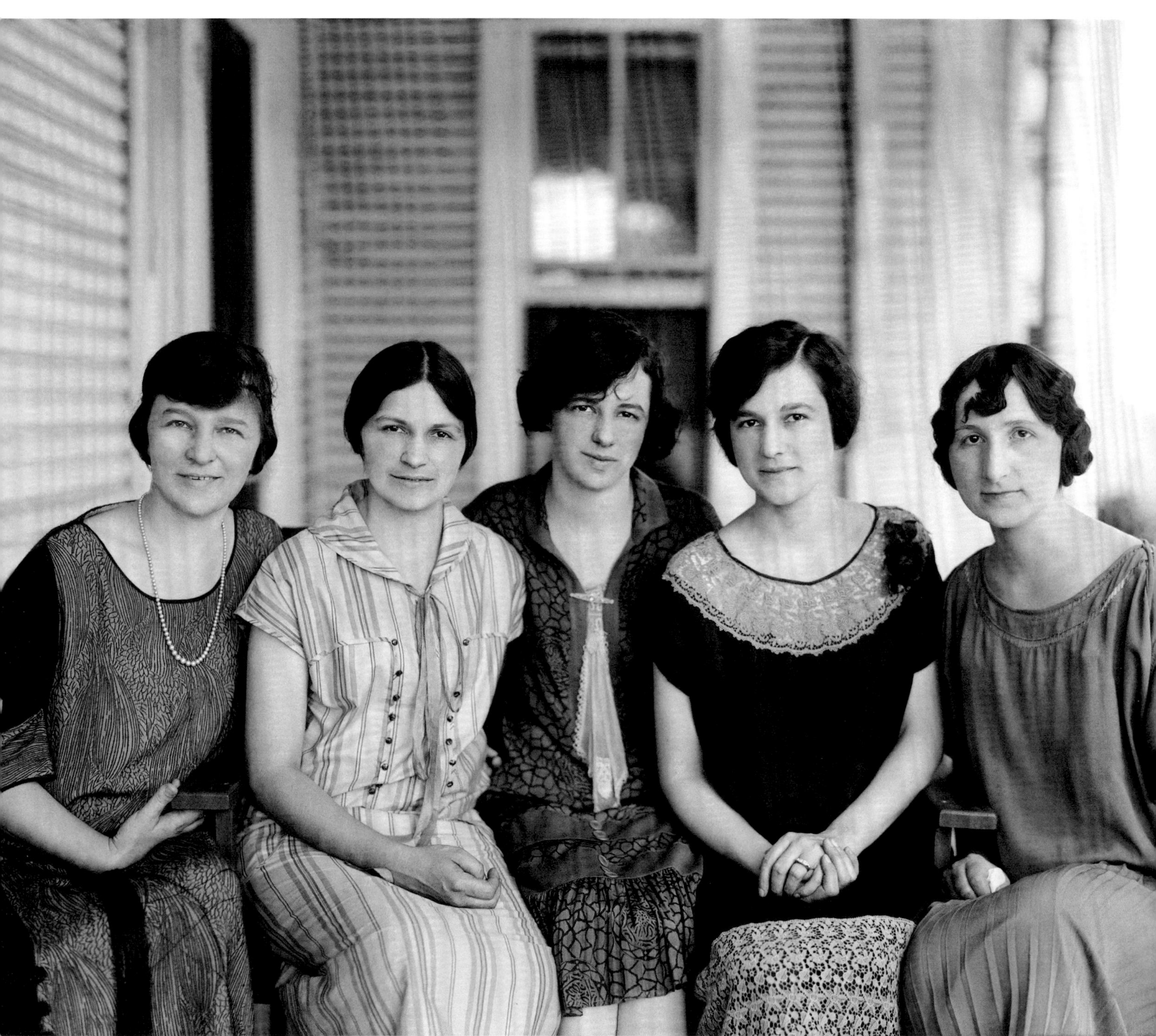

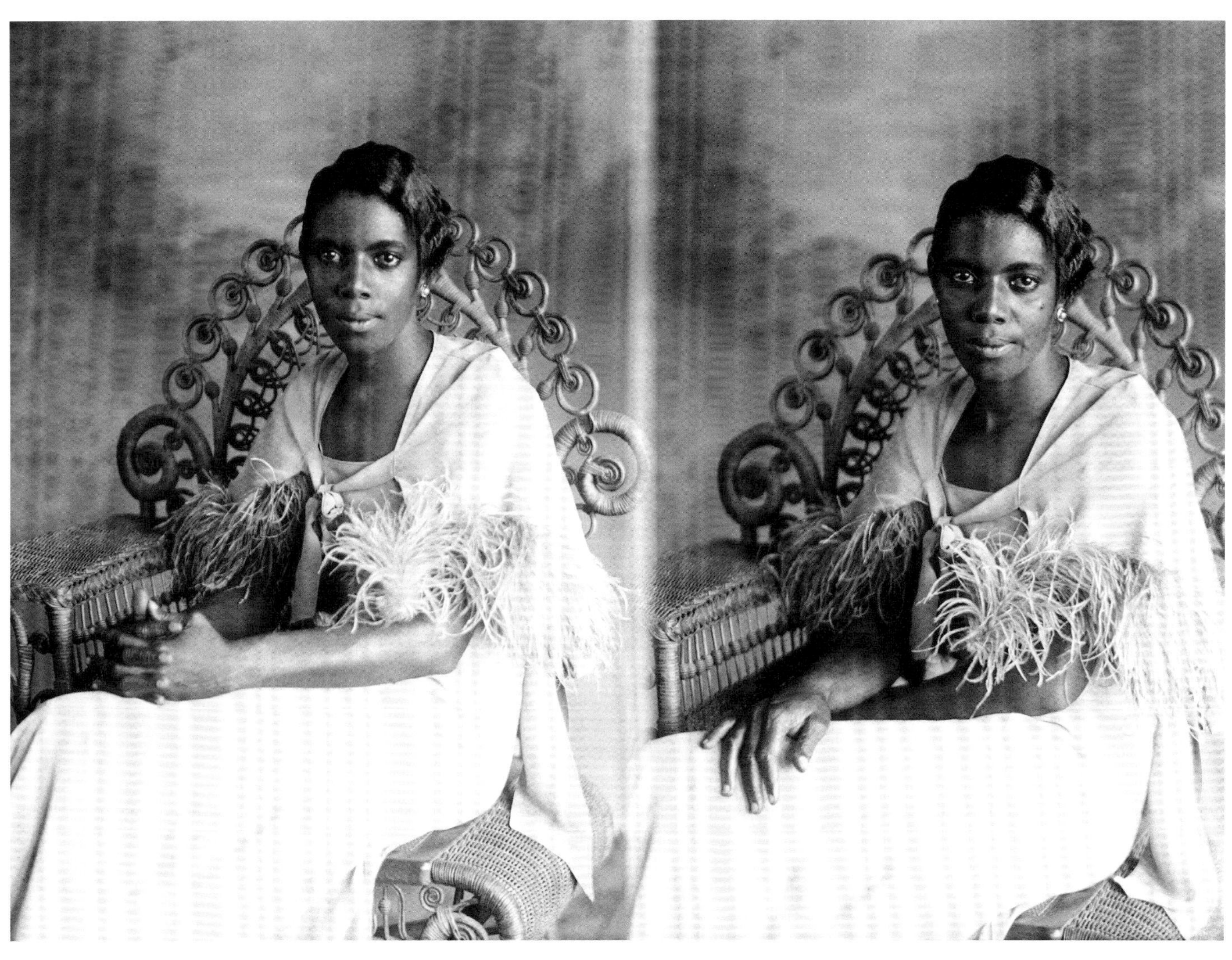

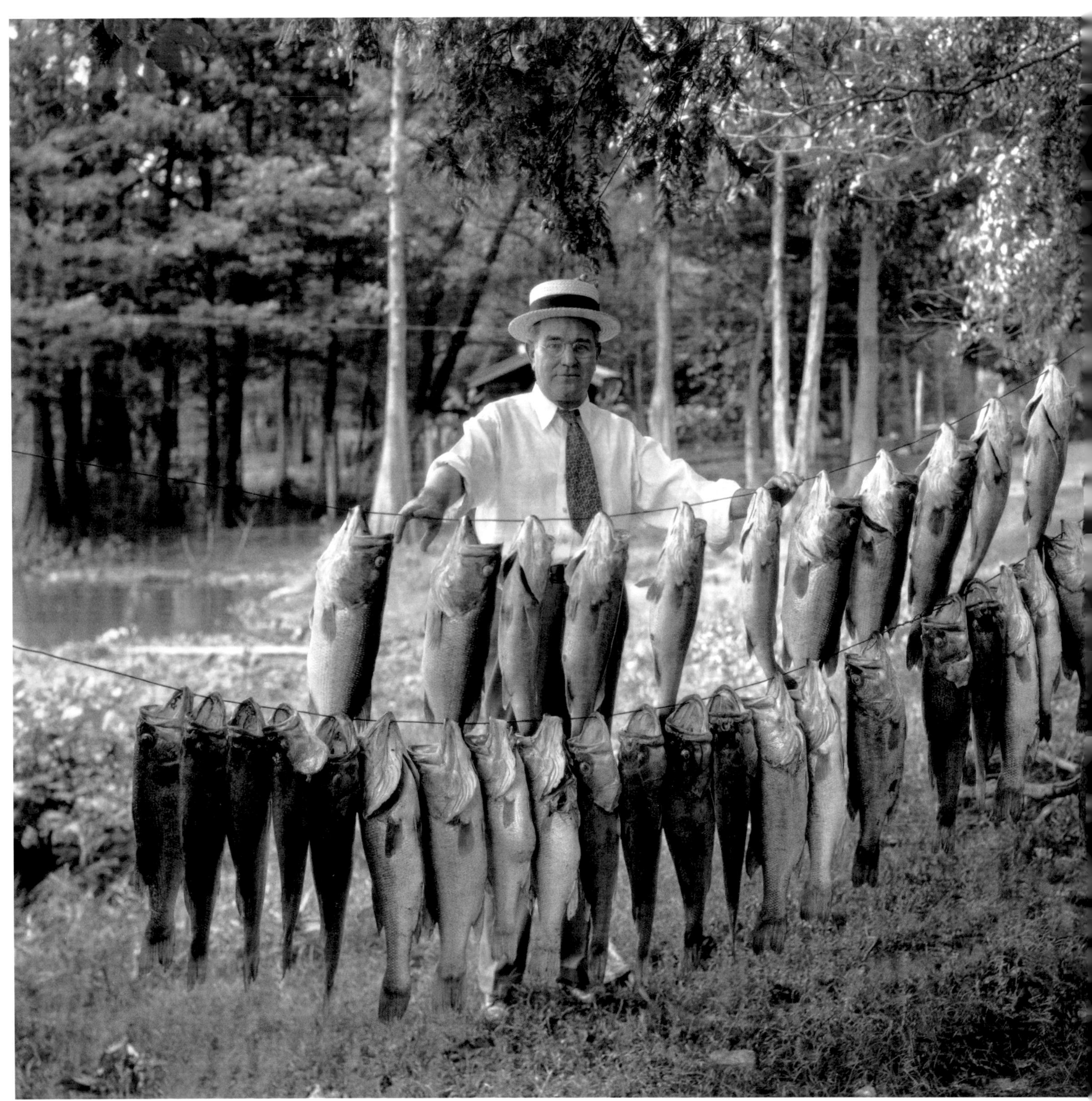

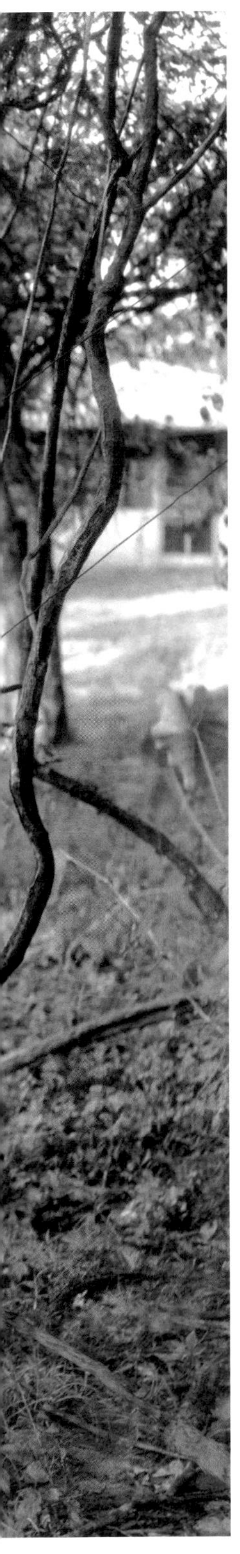

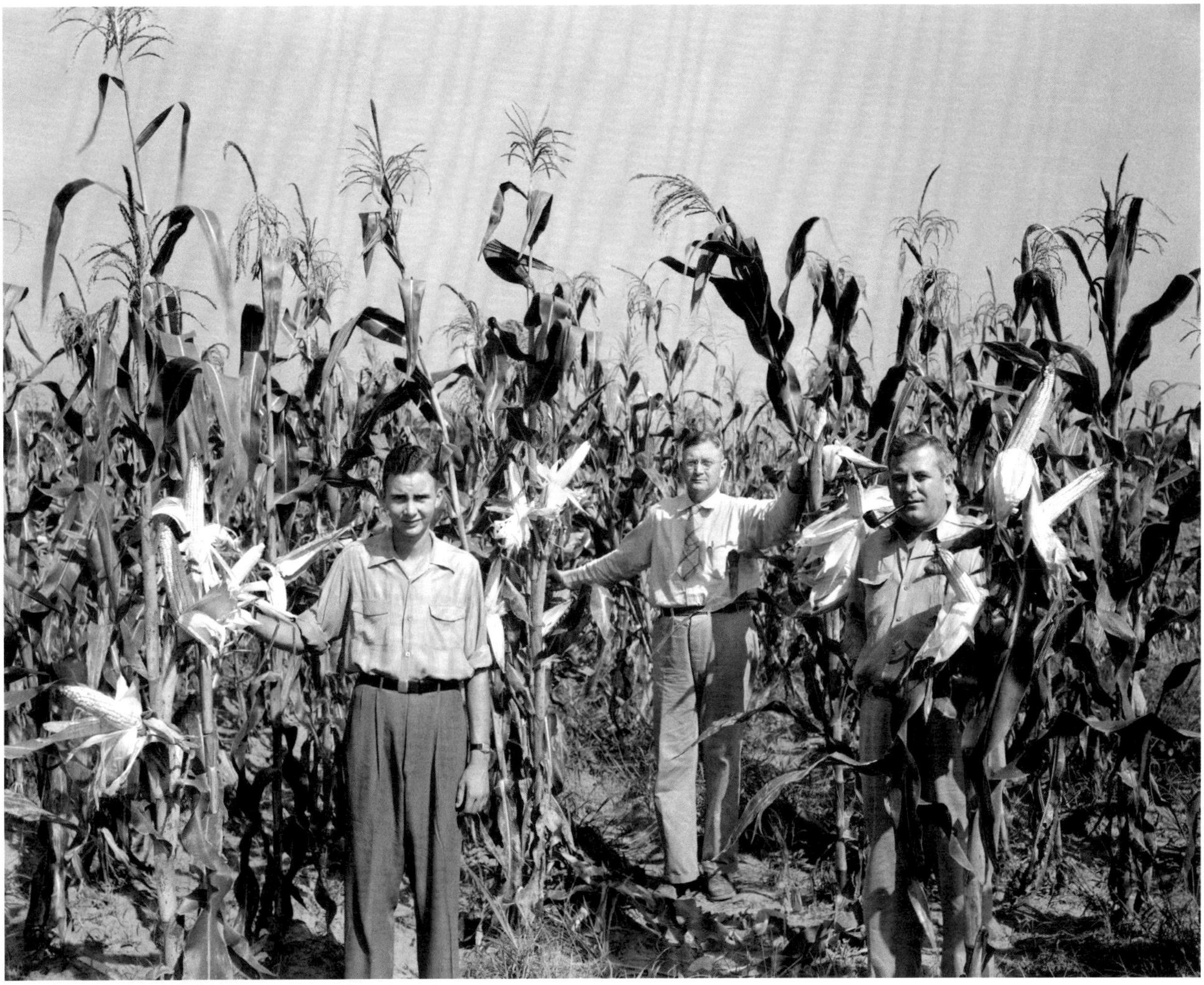

Businessman Thomas J. Locke Jr. at his lake retreat, zoo, and lodge, south of Friendship Cemetery, by the Tombigbee River, August 18, 1934.

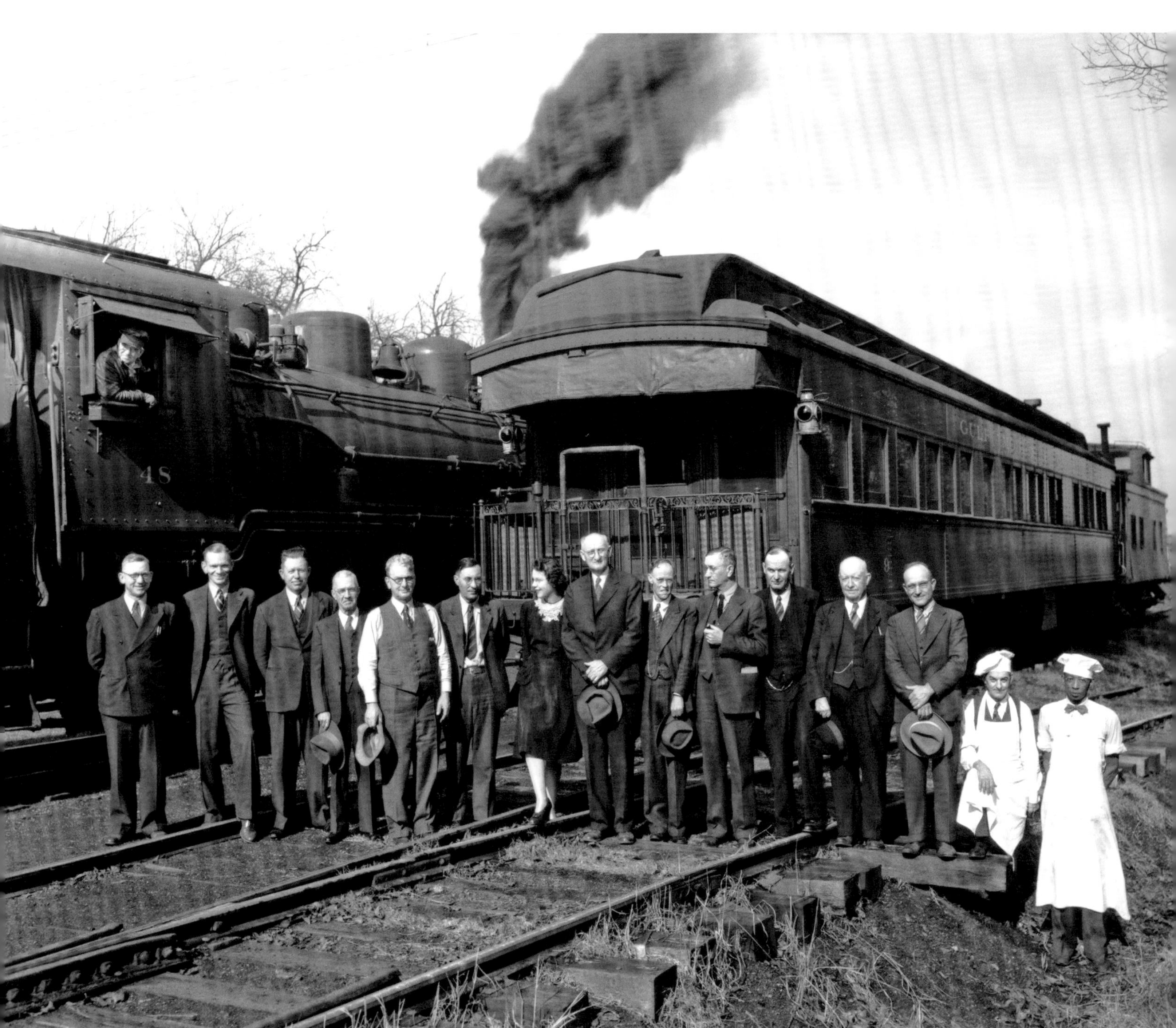
48

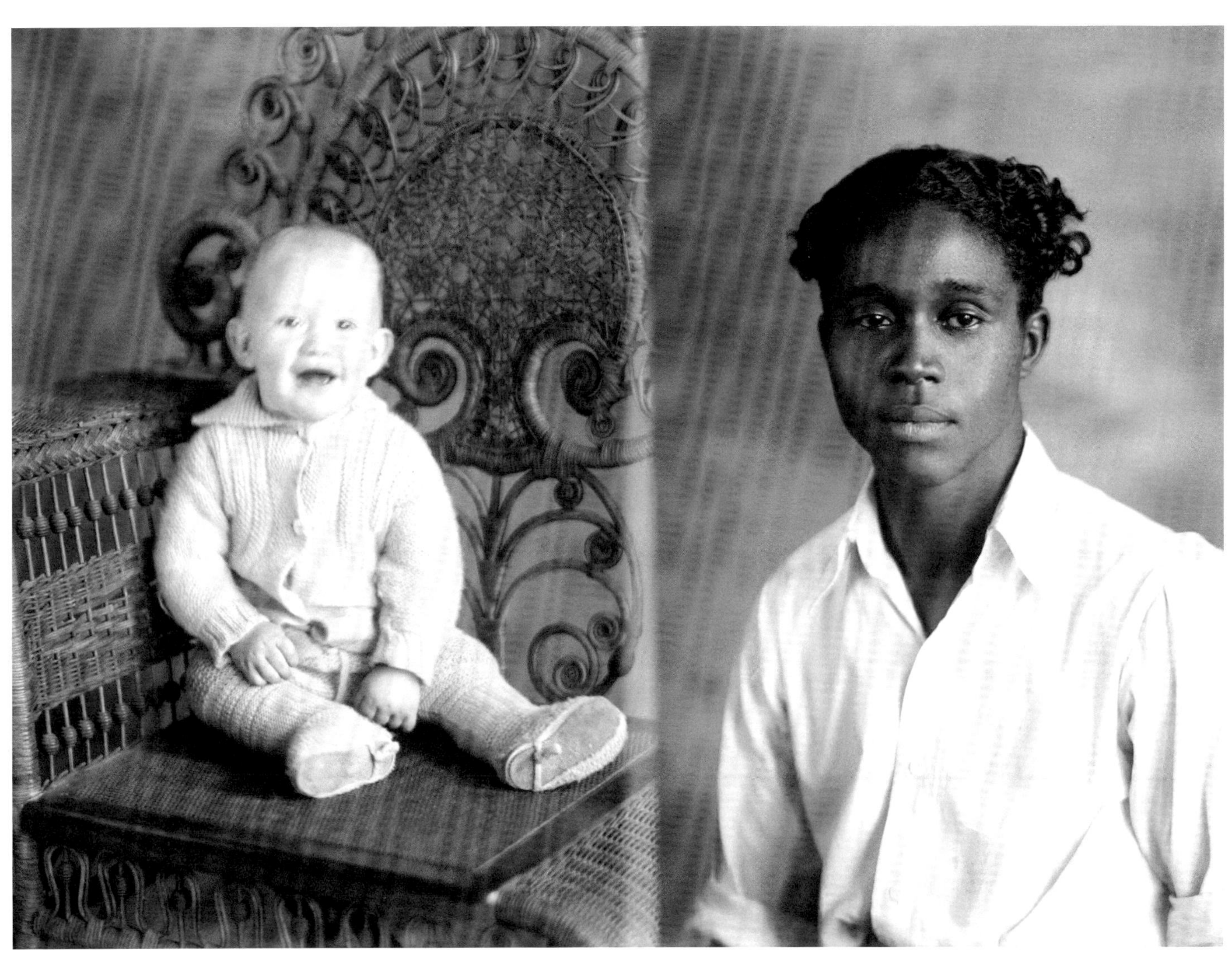

Girl with live canebrake rattlesnake, circa 1920s–30s.

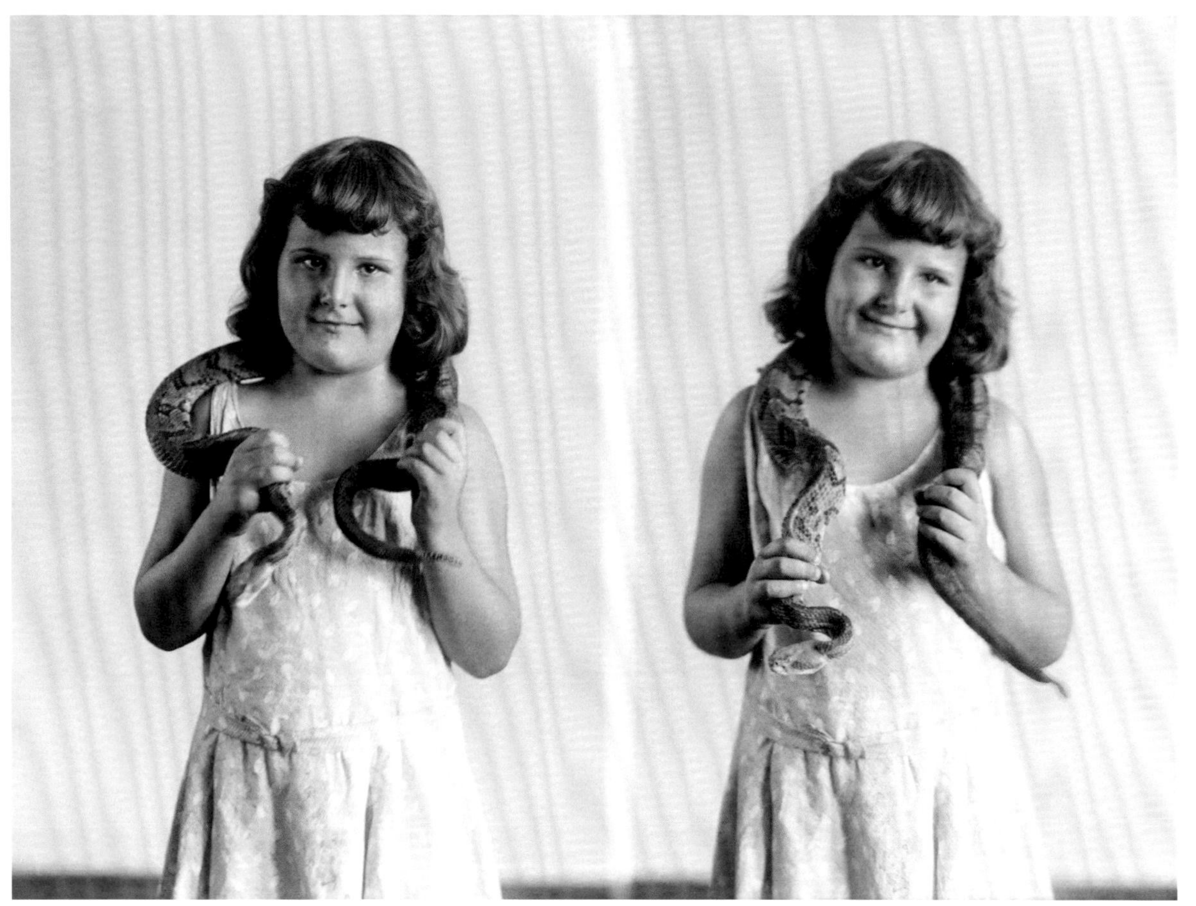

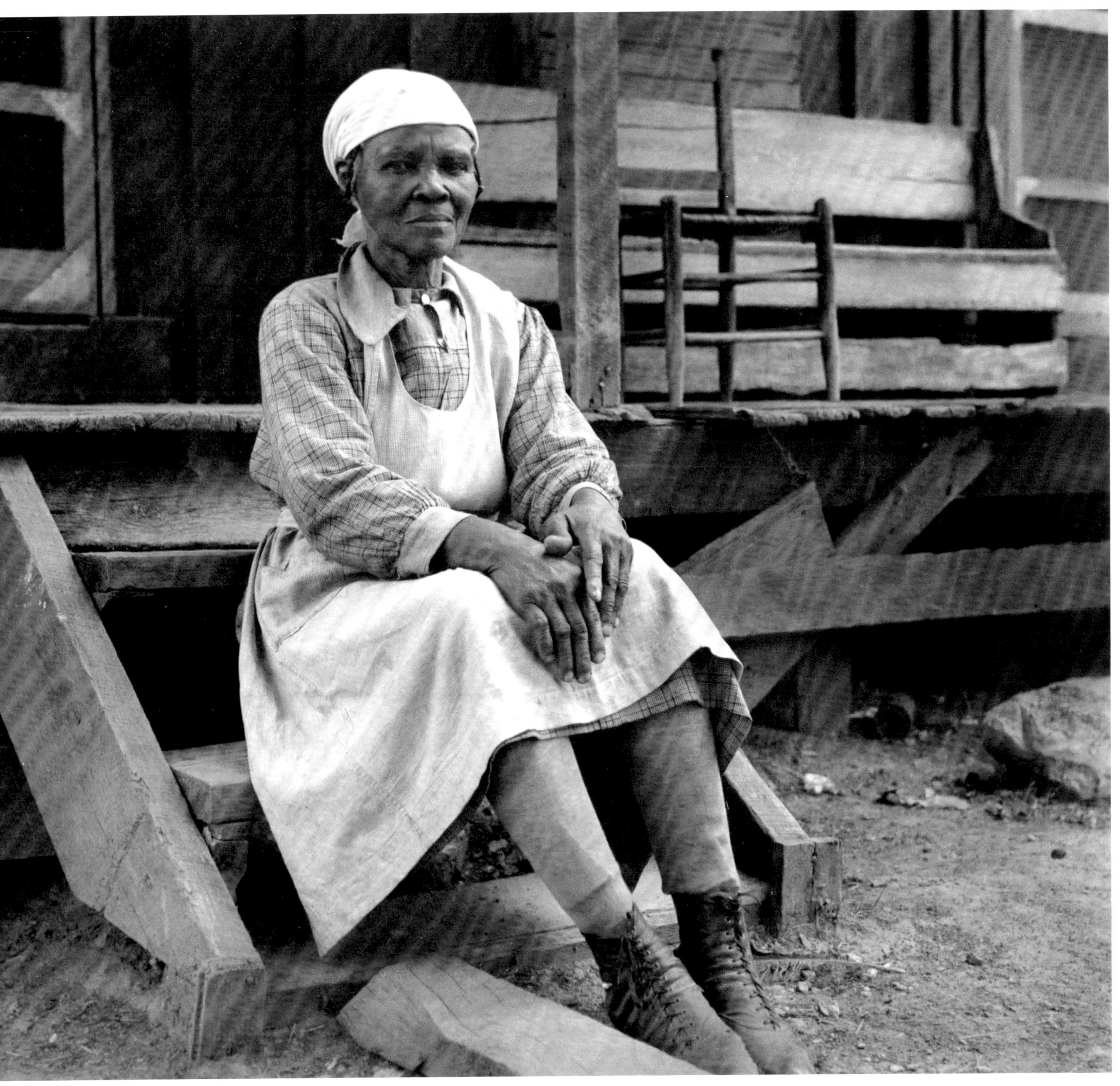

Boy with bloodied nose.

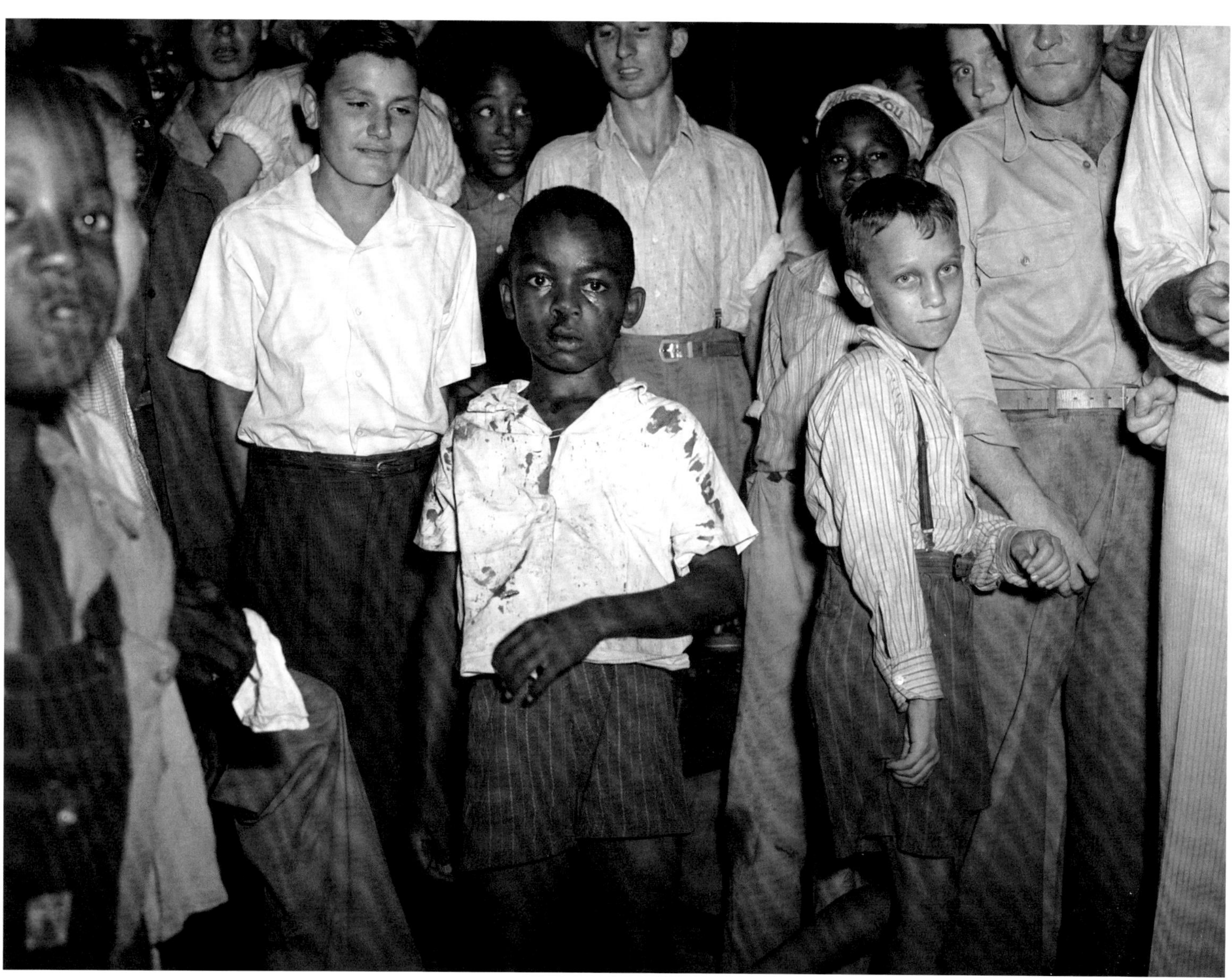

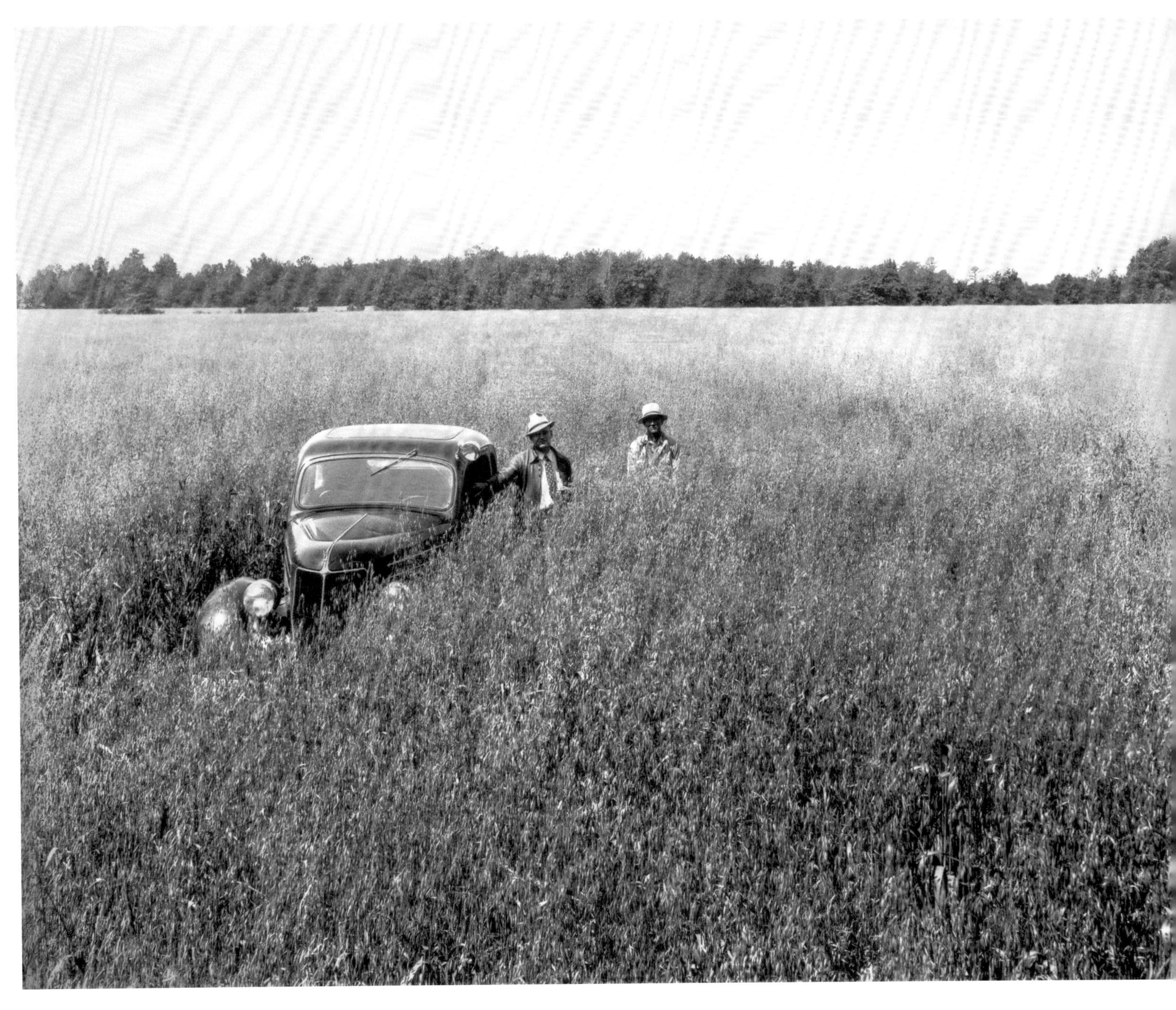

Florist and nurseryman Herman Owen (at left) *with his 1937 Ford V8 and an unidentified man in a field of oats, circa 1938–39.*

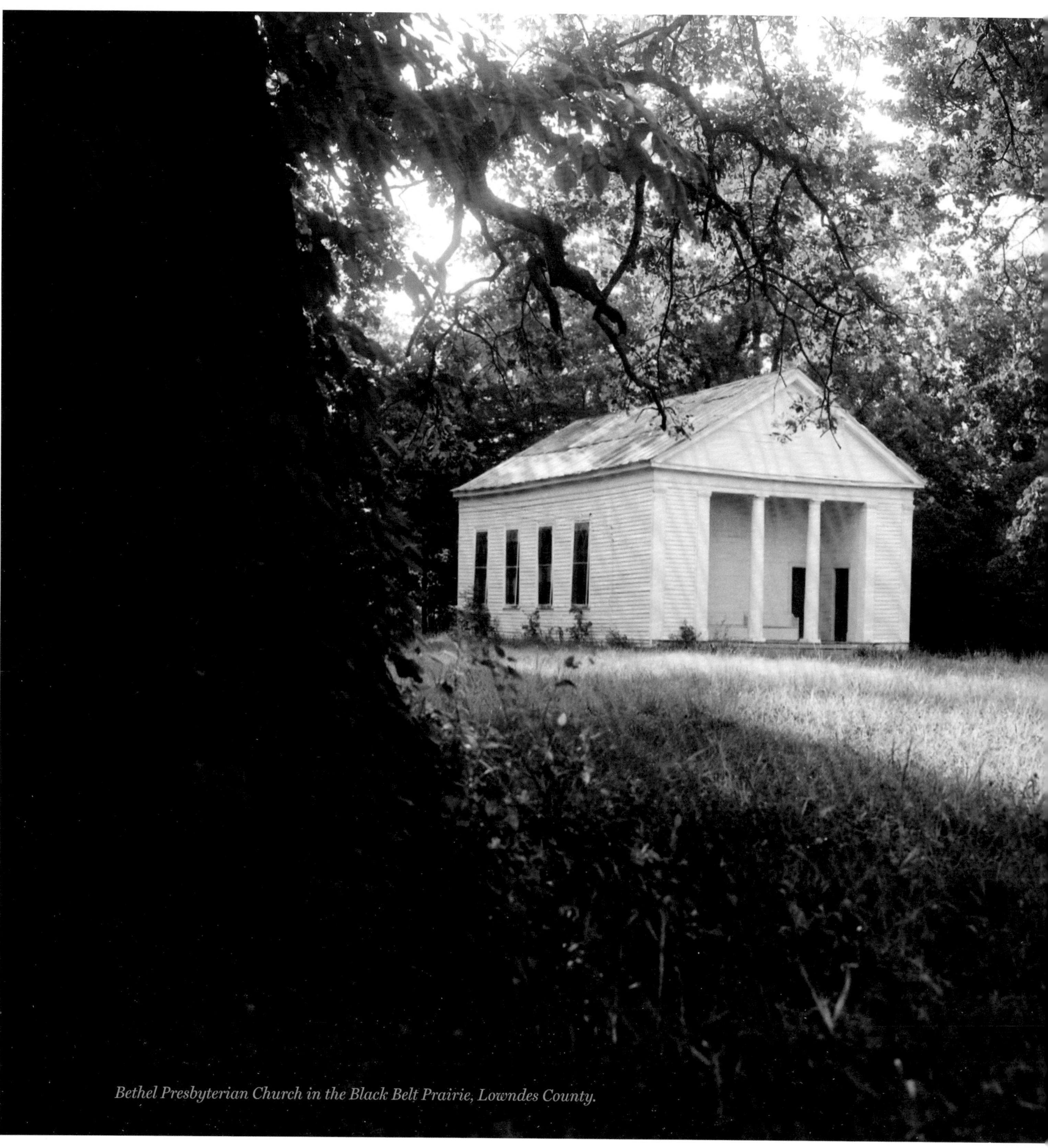

Bethel Presbyterian Church in the Black Belt Prairie, Lowndes County.

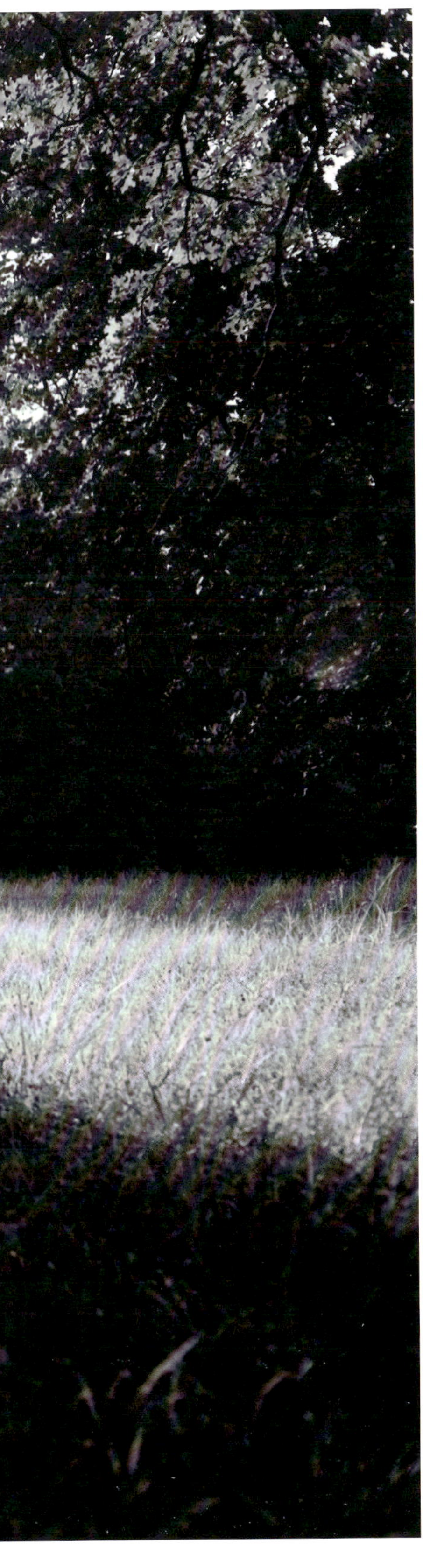

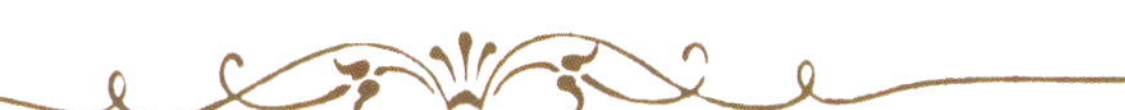

O. N. Pruitt's POSSUM TOWN

Photographing
TROUBLE & RESILIENCE
in the American South

Berkley Hudson

Published in association with the
Center for Documentary Studies at Duke University
by the University of North Carolina Press,
Chapel Hill

The Martha and Spencer Love Foundation, as a longtime champion of civil rights, welcomes this book's helpful perspective on race relations in the American South.

Manufactured in Canada
Designed and set by Kim Bryant in Miller and Acie types
The University of North Carolina Press has been a member of the Green Press Initiative since 2003.

Cover illustration courtesy of the Pruitt-Shanks Collection, Southern Historical Collection, Wilson Library, University of North Carolina at Chapel Hill

Library of Congress Cataloging-in-Publication Data
Names: Hudson, Fraser Berkley, author.
Title: O.N. Pruitt's Possum Town : photographing trouble and resistance in the American South / Berkley Hudson.
Other titles: Documentary arts and culture.
Description: Chapel Hill : The University of North Carolina Press ; [Durham, North Carolina] : Published in association with the Center for Documentary Studies at Duke University, 2021. | Series: Documentary arts and culture | Includes bibliographical references and index.
Identifiers: LCCN 2021038334 | ISBN 9781469662701 (cloth ; alk. paper) | ISBN 9781469662718 (ebook)
Subjects: LCSH: Pruitt, O. N., 1891–1967. | Documentary photography—Mississippi—Columbus. | Photographs as information resources. | Photographs—Social aspects. | Photographs—Psychological aspects. | Photographers—Mississippi—Columbus—Biography. | Columbus (Miss.)—Social life and customs—Pictorial works. | BISAC: PHOTOGRAPHY / Photoessays & Documentaries | HISTORY / United States / State & Local / South (AL, AR, FL, GA, KY, LA, MS, NC, SC, TN, VA, WV)
Classification: LCC TR820.5 .P73 2021 | DDC 770.9762/973—dc23
LC record available at https://lccn.loc.gov/2021038334

DOCUMENTARY ARTS AND CULTURE
Edited by Alexa Dilworth, Wesley Hogan, and Tom Rankin of the Center for Documentary Studies at Duke University

In a time when the tools of the documentary arts have become widely accessible, this series of books, published in association with the Center for Documentary Studies at Duke University, explores and develops the practice of documentary expression. Drawing on the perspectives of artists and writers, this series offers new and important ways to think about learning and doing documentary work while also examining the traditions and practice of documentary art through time.

Center for Documentary Studies at Duke University
documentarystudies.duke.edu

To Pruitt's photographic subjects
and to their families

And especially to the memory of my parents,
Russell Hudson Sr. and Eva Byrd Fraser
Hudson, and my brothers, Russell Jr., Don,
and Carroll—whose photographs live forever
in the archive of Otis Noel Pruitt

SUQUA TOMAHA OR POSSUM TOWN

Original inhabitants of northeast Mississippi, the Choctaw and Chickasaw, called the white settlement located between Luxapalila Creek and Tombigbee River by the name of Suqua Tomaha. *This translates as Possum Town, a nickname for Columbus, Mississippi. This early nineteenth-century name derived from the local trading post's wizened-looking manager, Spirus Roach. His face reminded people of a possum's.*

CONTENTS

EDITORS' NOTE

Alexa Dilworth, Wesley Hogan, and Tom Rankin
Editors, Documentary Arts and Culture Series

O. N. Pruitt's *Possum Town: Photographing Trouble and Resilience in the American South* embodies the capacity of a single archive to speak powerfully about race, class, historical memory, and the lasting resonance of images. Berkley Hudson's careful, relentless investigations into Pruitt's forty years of photographing provide not only a record of the life of a single Mississippi community in the twentieth century but also a window on the long and shifting meaning of photographs through and across time. Pruitt's compelling body of work, along with Hudson's associated narratives of Columbus, Mississippi, and the surrounding county, stand as a visual record and expression of wider truths about the cultural history of the American South. There is both privilege and tragedy in this kind of documentary remembrance; ordinary and mundane scenes coexist alongside ones of extraordinary violence. As with other titles in our Documentary Arts and Culture series, this book presents the work of a photographer who was engaged in one locale for an extended period of time and who was deeply familiar with many of the people and places he photographed. While Pruitt was a commercial photographer, often hired to photograph people as they wanted to be seen, he also never went far without a camera, seemingly forever attuned to the possibilities of photographing. Though Pruitt left little articulation of his overall intent, it is through the depth of documentation created by his persistent and layered vision—in the studio and beyond—that we witness an unfolding documentary view that speaks to the complexity and multiplicity of voices within O. N. Pruitt's photographic vision and archive.

O. N. Pruitt's POSSUM TOWN

Photographs are better at raising questions than answering them; they can reveal what you do not understand, and also what you take for granted.

—Photographic historian
Barbara Norfleet, writing in
The Champion Pig

A PHOTOBIOGRAPHY OF A TIME AND PLACE

Although this is neither a memoir nor fully a cultural, oral, social, or visual history, a combination of these elements is present. Above all, this is a "photobiography" of a time and a place called Mississippi. It offers an introduction to the photographs of Otis Noel Pruitt, a white man working in the Jim Crow era of racial segregation of the early to mid-twentieth century.

The images were selected from among 88,000 negatives. They represent a range of photographic categories: floods of biblical proportion, portraits of people in Sunday-go-to-meeting clothes, traveling troupes of entertainers or locals devising their own diversions, family reunions, postmortem photographs, and more. Nonetheless, this selection is limited. "Expressive power," to use photographic historian Deborah Willis's concept, serves as the guiding principle here—whether a photograph emanates an aesthetic beauty or the palpable shock of an execution or lynching. The sequence is purposeful: from sublime to intriguing and perplexing, from the harshness to the grace of everyday life.

O. N. Pruitt was unusual for a white photographer in the American South because he photographed many aspects of Black life when a rage for racial order persisted. So far, this project has found a broader representation of the lives of white citizenry than Black life. African Americans are depicted in formal church portraits or baptisms, as subservient to white employers, or in street scenes where racial segregation is manifest. Yet Pruitt also photographs them in his studio or in their homes, and these settings might have offered Black subjects a greater degree of autonomy in how they were photographed.

The process of looking is deeply personal. Specialists such as folklorists, historians, photographers, and documentarians can see things differently from one another. So can ordinary viewers. Some want more words and analysis. Some want more pictures and fewer words. For certain of these Pruitt photographs, details are lacking; captions are not always provided. Regardless, the visual record is powerful, often enabling readers to supply their own captions.

On the point of written text with photographs, in *Let Us Now Praise Famous Men* (1941), James Agee wrote that if he could, he would not have written any words to accompany the pictures that Walker Evans made when the two went to Hale County, Alabama, in 1936 to document the Great Depression for *Fortune* magazine. Instead, Agee said he would have substituted "fragments of cloth, bits of cotton, lumps of earth, records of speech, pieces of wood and iron, phials of odors, plates of food and of excrement." Essays and descriptions that accompany these Pruitt photographs do concern themselves with an era that historians such as Yale's C. Vann Woodward referenced in *The Strange Career of Jim Crow*. Likewise, the photographs speak to twenty-first century life illuminated by Mississippi authors such as Jesmyn Ward, John Grisham or Kiese Laymon. In some instances, the pictures offer evidence for what Nobel Laureate author William Faulkner of Mississippi in 1950 called "the human heart in conflict with itself."

More than three decades have passed since four white boyhood friends and I banded together to save the Pruitt Collection from the dustbin of history. We marveled at what we discovered: photographs representing an intangible treasure for our community. We underestimated the work required to preserve, research, archive, and manage the collection. Nevertheless, we were committed to bring to public light these visual stories of trouble and resilience.

LISTENING TO PICTURES

In the Mississippi house of my boyhood, a red brick, three-bedroom place on South Fourth Street in Columbus, framed photographs lined the walls of a long hallway.

Here were pictures of family gatherings of Thanksgiving, Christmas, and birthdays, many taken at my grandmother's house. She lived around the corner in a rambling, two-story Victorian filled with Pekingese and antiques. At that house, a man named Mr. Pruitt would come to make pictures that ended up in our hallway. Anywhere from fifteen to twenty-five of us would arrange ourselves in rows: cousins, brothers, sisters, aunts, uncles, and above all, the matriarch who paid for the picture, Lillian Pearl Walker Fraser, my grandmother, an eccentric woman called Gaddy—short for Gad-about, because she loved to drive her baby blue Lincoln Continental.

Pruitt was the picture man for our family and town in northeast Mississippi. To paraphrase poet Williams Carlos Williams's description of photographs by Walker Evans, Pruitt's photographic eye was straightforward and puritanical. He photographed the Sanitary Laundry and Dry Cleaning, run by my maternal grandparents ("When clothes are dirty, dial Six-Thirty"). He photographed my father's Main Street Service Station ("Don't Cuss. Call Russ"), with its separate "Clean Restrooms Inside" for "gentlemen," "ladies," and "colored."

Outside the station, he would make pictures of my daddy and the men who worked with him. Among them were two Black men, George Aaron, known as Bobby Sox, and John Henry. Today, at that same spot where they pumped gas and washed cars stands the Tennessee Williams Welcome Center. It is a Gothic Victorian, two-story house that once was the rectory of St. Paul's Episcopal Church. In 1911, Thomas Lanier Williams, who would become a Pulitzer Prize–winning playwright, was born in Columbus and lived in the rectory. How that house came to be moved from St. Paul's around the block is a story for another day. But in 1952, when Tennessee Williams returned to visit Columbus, Pruitt did photograph him.

I do not attribute this to Pruitt, but in high school I became a photographer and writer for, then editor of, my school newspaper. In the early 1970s, as a student journalist at the University of Mississippi and then at Columbia University, I became interested in Pruitt's photographs. I was making lots of pictures, sometimes with photographers Birney Imes and Mark Gooch, two boyhood friends. I even photographed at the Lowndes County jail—still segregated by race in 1972 when I wrote a college magazine story about the "Groundhog Hotel," so-called because prisoners could dig out and escape.

As part of visual excursions with my friends, we visited photographer Calvin Shanks, a beanpole of a white man with curly brown hair and a cigar often in the side of his mouth. Shanks had been Pruitt's assistant until 1960, when Pruitt retired and Shanks bought the business, located up one flight of creaky wooden stairs at number 413 ½ Main Street. One day Shanks showed us the trove of negatives taken over four decades by Pruitt. The negatives smelled to high heaven, but we realized that these were the pictures of our childhood, families, friends, and neighbors—white and Black in black and white.

We asked Shanks if he would sell the negatives to us. He said he wanted to hold onto them, for now.

Years passed. Shanks died in 1981. Eventually, Shanks's family sold most of the photographic equipment and negatives to Bill Frates, a photographic hobbyist who admired Pruitt's pictures of trains. For a few years, Frates maintained the collection in his Main Street store, where he and his mother sold everything from refrigerators and stoves to shotguns, fishing rods, and knitting supplies. But, like Shanks, he never found time to deal with the voluminous set of pasteboard boxes and wooden crates chock-full of smelly negatives. Eventually, in 1987, Frates agreed to sell us the negatives; we bought a remaining few from the Shanks family. By then, two other Columbus boyhood friends, Jim Carnes and David Gooch, joined our project.

Twenty-five years later, with the vagaries of weather and time taking a toll on the negatives, we decided that the best home for the collection would be Wilson Library at the University of North Carolina at Chapel Hill, a foremost repository of items from the American South. We then estimated the number of negatives: 48,726

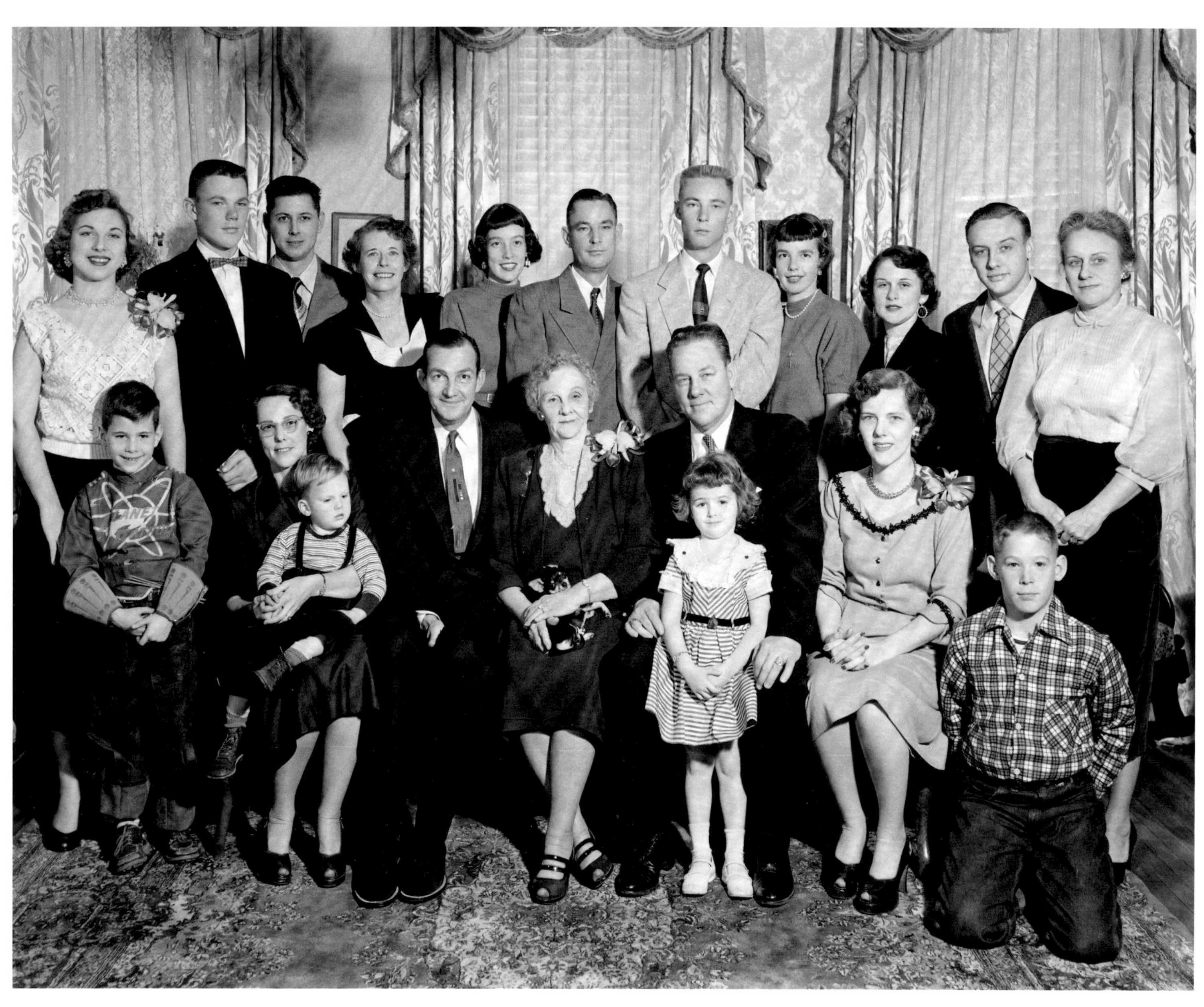

Fraser family with author Berkley Hudson in mother's lap (front row).
Matriarch Gaddy Fraser (center). *Third Street South, Christmas Day 1953.*

from Shanks and nearly double that from Pruitt, 88,657, including close to 2,000 glass plates, from bygone era of photography greater than film.

To research and to tell a visual story of one's own people—friends, family, and townspeople—can be difficult. Yet that is the task to which I set myself. The stories embedded here do not simply belong to me. I pay attention to the caution offered by contemporary Atlanta artist Jamaal Barber, whose work connects to the first time Africans were brought in chains to the Virginia coast 400 years ago. Barber writes, "I want to discuss the black American experience, but it is not my story to tell alone." Likewise, I alone cannot tell the stories of Pruitt's photographs. That requires a collective effort of reflection and conversations among all kinds of people with all kinds of backgrounds and beliefs. As part of that process, I do not desire to tell anyone specifically what to think; rather, I want to suggest what to ponder or, perhaps, to dream.

In 1921, when a physician, James McElroy, gave a celebratory speech during the centennial of Columbus, he spoke of a recent dream. In heaven, he saw a man in chains. The doctor asked St. Peter, "Since this is heaven, not hell, why is this man in chains?" St. Peter replied, "That man is from Columbus. Were he not chained, he would escape to Columbus—because that town was far better than even heaven." That said, Mississippi has no monopoly on heaven or hell. The Pruitt photographs reveal how this patch of earth embodies paradise and purgatory. The images not only offer representations of faces and bodies, of machines, buildings, and animals, of shapes, textures, light, and shadows, but they also give visual voice to quiet as well as turbulent histories not seen in other ways.

Sometimes I feel like that man chained in heaven: no place is finer than Columbus. I love to walk through neighborhoods described by the 1930s Federal Writers' Project, whether passing by antebellum or postbellum mansions in the style of Federal, Gothic, Victorian, Greek Revival, or Georgian. I love to walk up the wooden, unpainted stairs of a dogtrot house where lived "hewers of wood, drawers of water." To drive at sunset on gravel roads through the black, flat prairie west of the Tombigbee is a delight. In juke joints or country stores or swamps, I've discovered surprises, be they people, plants, or rocks on a riverbank, or turtles, deer, fish, raccoons, and turkey vultures. Pruitt documented this world.

While there may be no place more wonderful than Mississippi, no place may be more baffling or terrible. As a Columbus resident during my first two decades, I experienced, in my privileged white male way, the pain of being a witness to racial segregation and to what scholar Susan Gubar calls the "spirit murder" of Black and white people alike.

To survive, Black writer Frantz Fanon has said, Black people must wear a mask when they are around white people. Throughout my boyhood, my family employed a Black maid named Lula Bell Gardner Dillard. Herself a mother of eight, she cared for me and often when my mother was busy with the United Daughters of the Confederacy, the bridge club, the garden club, the sewing circle, the Women's Missionary Union, or the Daughters of the American Revolution.

We called her Lula Bell or just Bell. She called my mother Mrs. Hudson and my Daddy Mr. Hudson. This nomenclature defined the relationships, based on race, in my household, town, and the world as I knew it. My mother helped Lula Bell and her family move to better homes: from a wooden shack with a well and outhouse to a federal housing project of brick duplexes and eventually to a brick home that she would own. One of her sons would marry a woman who would become among the first Black members of the Columbus City Council. Historian Grace Hale, in *Making Whiteness: The Culture of Segregation in the South, 1890–1940*, describes the fraught relationships such as the one my family had with Lula Bell, how that shaped us. I did not go to school with Blacks until my junior year in high school when, thirteen years after the *Brown v. Board of Education* decision of 1954, Mississippi complied with the law of the land.

This upbringing permeates how I see these photographs. My English and Scotch-Irish ancestors, who include slaveholders, arrived in Mississippi in the early nineteenth century by way of Georgia, North Carolina, and Virginia. Some ancestors fought for the Confederate States of America. At least one, Lt. John P. Sanders, is buried in Columbus's Friendship Cemetery. In 1840s Georgia, one of my great-great-uncles, Elijah Hudson, owned a plantation; his will listed that he had enslaved workers.

My Mississippi great-grandfather, James A. Hudson, was a mercantile businessman. Active in Columbus politics, in the late 1800s he served on the city council and school board. He ran unsuccessfully for mayor. Once a member of the police department, he worked in leadership roles. People called him Captain Hudson, or Cap'n, using a common honorific for white men. At the time of his death in 1928, he was a Lowndes County justice of the peace. It would be naive not to realize this was a consequential job in maintaining the racial, religious, gender, and class status quo. It also would be naive, as cultural historian Joel Williamson taught me, to think that my great-grandfather was nothing more than a beastly enforcer of what scholars today would call the "hegemonic panopticon" of the white establishment. As a meditation on how this contributes to my lifelong opportunities, I have gold-framed oil paintings in my living room, one of my great-grandfather Hudson and one of my great-grandmother Olivia Saunders Hudson. They were painted in 1883, at the time of their wedding in Columbus, by one of my great-great-uncles, an itinerant portraitist in Mississippi and Alabama.

In these paintings and in Pruitt's photographs, I search for clues of everyday graces. I listen for the voices from a town where Pruitt took pictures, so people could put them on mantles, walls, and in family albums, or so they could publish them in newspapers, magazines, or books. James Agee long ago evoked what I feel looking at Pruitt's pictures: "This was my right home, right earth, right blood … so keen, sad, precious a nostalgia as I can scarcely otherwise know: a truancy into the sources of my life."

If this sounds sentimental, it may be.

During my growing-up years, long before I read Eric Lott's *Love and Theft* (1993) detailing the history of minstrelsy, blackface was common. Two of my fellow white classmates at Stephen D. Lee High School—named for a hometown

Confederate general hero who was very remotely related to the *other* general, Robert E. Lee, blacked up for their performances as servants in Moss Hart's *You Can't Take It with You*. In my lead role as Grandpa Vanderhof, I was oblivious to the insult of blackface to our two Black classmates who worked on the play.

That same spring of 1969, I was a member of the Pilgrimage "royal court" of high school seniors, "presented" debutante-style at a pageant and ball, and overseen by a king and queen. Then, the Pilgrimage ball was whites-only, and "Dixie" was played. Blackface characters appeared in pageant plays harkening to antebellum days. First begun in 1940 to foster tourism, the Pilgrimage involves tours of antebellum homes, once as many as 100 of them, unscathed by the Civil War. Even as a Cub Scout, I had participated in the Pilgrimage. Our mothers made us Confederate gray uniforms with gold braids. As we hosted tourists at Wisteria Place, we wore hats bearing the Confederate "Stars and Bars."

Now, the Pilgrimage has evolved to become more inclusive in its perspectives about slavery and the Confederacy's Lost Cause ideology. For several decades, the Pilgrimage has incorporated "Tales from the Crypt," set in Friendship Cemetery with high schoolers performing monologues based on the lives of Black and white people from a century and more ago. A similar project now culminates with a performance in a Black cemetery, Sandfield Cemetery. Challenging audiences to consider a more complete understanding of the community's history, both are nationally recognized projects of the statewide magnet high school, the Mississippi School of Mathematics and Science in Columbus.

WORKING WITH THE PRUITT IMAGES, I've found connections to my life—unknown, unconscious, or purposefully hidden. With this project, I learned heartrending stories I wish someone had told me long ago. From the photographs, I learned about executions and lynchings that my mother and father knew about but never mentioned. I learned about baptisms in the 1920s and 1930s in the Tombigbee River where Black and white church groups gathered in a measure of biracial Christian harmony. As children, my mother and my uncles went to these on Sunday afternoons near their home and a few blocks from where I one day would live.

In this research, I found no diaries and few letters by Pruitt or about him. His motivations for making certain photographs remain enigmatic. What we have are his photographs. To a degree, these represent his consciousness and that of his subjects. Although I interviewed his grandson Thomas Caldwell in Ohio, and I knew Pruitt when I was a boy, I could not interview him or his wife, Lena. They died long ago; he in 1967, she in 1976. However, I interviewed people who worked for him, including my uncle, Merle Fraser Sr., who as a youth worked in Pruitt's studio. One of my colleagues, Jim Carnes, interviewed Pruitt's daughter, Irene, especially about Pruitt's taking a photograph of two bodies after a lynching.

That this book deals, in part, with a lynching and executions must bring scrutiny. These are gruesome photographs to be treated with sensitivity. I have worked to uncover what I could about the people who were lynched and executed. I continue to search for their families, though in some cases I have found that, generations later, they have no interest in speaking publicly. Likewise, I have worked, to no avail, to find white families of the people who conducted the lynching or those who executed the men. Once, three decades ago, a white man in his nineties told me he knew the names of the killers, but he wouldn't disclose them. Hearing such things, I reflected on how stories of racist brutality from the last two centuries live on to this day, passed down among families and friends, whether Black or white. Still, my task remains to provide a context for *all* the Pruitt images.

When Pruitt was in his heyday, in 1938, and when to be a photographer was perhaps equivalent of being a twenty-first-century internet entrepreneur, the poet-physician William Carlos Williams reviewed a New York photographic exhibition of Walker Evans at the Museum of Modern Art. In the *New Republic*, Williams wrote of Evans's work, some of it from the American South, "The pictures talk to us. And they say plenty."

Likewise, the Pruitt images talk to us—*they say plenty*.

O. N. PRUITT

An Insider Photographer

Otis Noel Pruitt was born on September 11, 1891, on a farm in south central Mississippi. By age nineteen he was working in his uncle's mercantile store and had married his girlfriend, Lena. Pruitt became interested in photography when he began photographing their son and daughter. As a sideline, he used a Brownie 122 camera to photograph timberland for landowners who wanted to market acreage to potential buyers from the Pennsylvania Dutch Country. Pruitt's uncle, however, grew weary of the smells of the chemicals that Pruitt used in the store to develop film and make prints. By 1915 Pruitt had left the store for full-time photography. To extend his photographic knowledge beyond self-instruction, Pruitt studied for a year in 1916 at the Illinois School of Photography, focusing on courses in X-ray and general photography. Then, he returned to central Mississippi and opened a photography studio in Newton.

Eventually, he headed north to Columbus to work for Henry Emil Hoffmeister, a German immigrant who, beginning in 1900, had developed there a thriving business as a studio and commercial photographer. By 1921 he had bought out his employer, vowing "to continue the same high-class work which has characterized the Hoffmeister Studio."

The original studio was on the second floor of a brick building on the south side of Main Street. Hoffmeister had installed northern skylights, which provided even lighting without shadows, ideal for portraiture. Pruitt stayed there until a combination of a fire and difficult financial times in the mid-1920s prompted him to move to an upstairs studio across the street. During that time, he had a Black assistant, Amzi, whose last

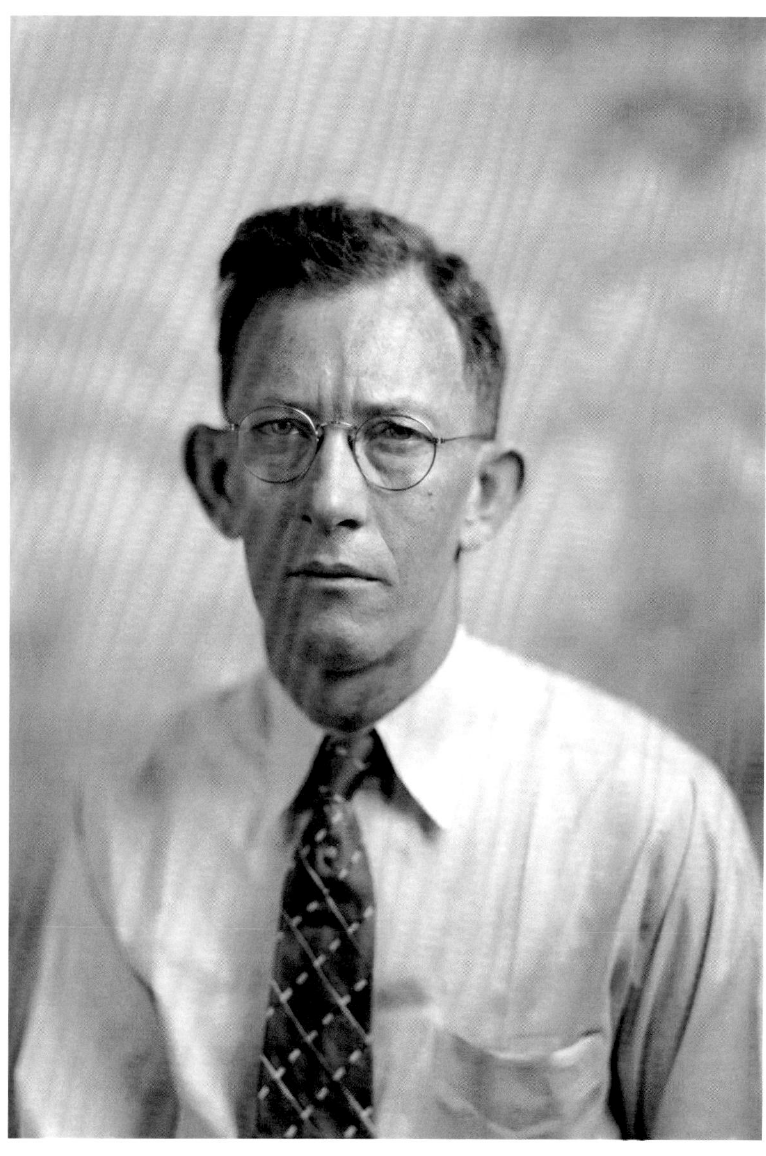

O. N. Pruitt.

name is lost to history. For a while, Amzi lived in a structure behind Pruitt's house, but eventually, like hundreds of thousands of other Mississippi Blacks fleeing Jim Crow oppression and violence, he moved to Chicago.

For his postage stamp of soil of Lowndes County, Mississippi, where race, class, and gender mattered greatly, Pruitt was a de facto documentarian. He took pictures throughout Mississippi and nearby Alabama, but he focused on the crossroads town of Columbus, the county seat. His studio, in the words of his advertising brochure, "pictured many phases of the life of Columbus and Columbians." By photographing the familial and communal, the sacred and profane, Pruitt shows us a range of community life filtered through his perspective, that of a white man in a highly segregated society made up primarily of Anglo-Americans and African Americans. After World War II, Pruitt hired as his assistant a white man and war veteran named Calvin Shanks. In the studio's front, they made portraits, using risers, props, and drapery for backdrops. In the back, behind rows of hanging negatives, they developed film. Marjorie Baugh Doster, who as a child was a regular Pruitt subject and whose father was Pruitt's cigar-smoking companion, recalled that the studio was filled with "clotheslines full of negatives drying."

Throughout his life, Pruitt was a familiar fixture in the town where almost everyone addressed him by his last name or added the honorific "Mr." Eventually, he became a part of the white male Columbus power structure. Dark-haired and wiry, Pruitt had a feisty personality, friendly face, and ears that stuck out. He routinely wore a business suit, white shirt, dark tie, and dress hat. He was gregarious and known for practical jokes. Although he was a devoted member of the Barraca Sunday school class at the First Methodist Church, he told "smutty jokes." He bought Roi-Tan cigars by the box and, though not a heavy drinker, sipped a glass of Mogen David wine before bedtime. "My grandfather was a perfect example of somebody that probably never worked a day in his life," Thomas Caldwell, Pruitt's grandson, told me in 2001. "He thought that photography was fun." Pruitt loved to hunt and fish and even built his own fishing pond. "He didn't care about much of anything other than photography ... and going fishing.... He did not take care of the business end of it. My grandmother did all of that, pure and simple. She did all the billing, all the collecting."

Like the traditional craftsperson who makes clay pots, or white oak baskets, or fiddles, Pruitt produced his craft in exchange for money; his studio was very much a business on which he and his family depended. "He'd photograph anything," said Rachel Shute, who worked for Pruitt as a retoucher in the 1930s and 1940s. "Most of the time Mr. Pruitt got paid.... Mrs. Pruitt always was very much on his coattails—demanding money." It is hard to decipher, however, whether he was paid for all of his photographs. As was a common practice in the Depression-era South, he sometimes bartered in exchange for his work, accepting vegetables, fruits, fish, or poultry in payment. In other instances, he photographed for the sheer love of picture-taking, regardless of whether people paid him.

During Pruitt's era, besides Hoffmeister and Shanks, there were other local white photographers with studios, including Edward N. Hanna, Carl Brown, Roy Gring and son Gordon Gring, John Odom, and Joe Sarcone, in addition to a Black photographer, George Brown. A distinguishing practice of Pruitt, however, was not only his omnivorous photographic approach but his unflinching documentation of trouble: death portraits of children or a makeshift morgue of Black bodies after the 1936 tornado in nearby Tupelo. Law enforcement officials and insurance companies would commission him to document homicide victims, train and automobile wrecks, and fires. At times, Pruitt's photographs would appear in the local *Commercial Dispatch*. On occasion, they were distributed nationally via the Associated Press or ACME Newspictures or used as illustrations in books and magazines. Sometimes Pruitt was summoned to testify before juries, his photographs offered as evidence. As with those made by other photographers in small towns across America, Pruitt's photographs were as likely to appear in newspaper advertisements as in the news pages.

One critical element in Pruitt's photographs is the potent reality of the racial divide. During the time he photographed, Mississippi was at the center of what historian Joel Williamson calls a "crucible of race." As a white man, Pruitt photographed Blacks and whites inside and outside his studio. The complexity of Black-white relationships appears in concrete ways, in how he staged his photographs, including placement of subjects according to race, gender, and social status, and in how the subjects presented themselves before the camera.

The setting or subjects of some of Pruitt's photographs reflect racial, class, and gender perspectives deeply embedded in the dominant white community. The most prominent, wealthiest, and whitest subjects appear at the image's center. In other cases, there is scant evidence of differentiation among subjects. Regardless, Pruitt moved authoritatively as a photo-eye, documenting rich and poor, Black and white, male and female, young and old.

Research on Pruitt's life and of a sampling of thousands of his images suggest that as a photographer he fluctuated between liberal and conservative viewpoints. In practice, he mirrors each. Although his work often reveals a white conservative viewpoint, he supplied vital images for the Black community, including making pictures for the president of the Mississippi National Association for the Advancement of Colored People (NAACP). He photographed Blacks in and out of his studio. In that era and within the Black community, writes social critic bell hooks, photographs served the important role of revealing "a sense of how we looked when we were not 'wearing the mask,' when we were not attempting to perfect the image for a white supremacist gaze." Before integration, she notes, Blacks struggled "to create a counter-hegemonic world that would stand as visual resistance, challenging racist images." A crucial part of that resistance was the display of photographs in southern Black homes.

When Pruitt photographed Blacks in their churches and homes, away from the white community, the subjects appear more open. In essence, they helped to determine how they ultimately would look. This was happening in a town where, until even the early 1970s, "colored only" or "whites only" signs were posted in public places. Indeed, Pruitt was unusual as a white hometown photographer in the segregated South photographing African Americans. (Hugh Mangum [1877–1922] in North Carolina, Paul Kwilecki [1928–2009] in Georgia, Florence Mars [1923–2006] in Mississippi, and Joe Hardy Shipp [1914–78] and son Ronnie Shipp [1952–2003] in Tennessee were other white photographers who in differing ways photographed Black and white alike.) Of course, as a white man Pruitt easily could move in both worlds, unlike African American photographers of the time. He could invite Blacks to his studio to photograph them or go into their homes to take their pictures. And for everyone, Black or white, fortunate enough to own a camera, he provided the service of developing film and printing pictures. Regardless, the Pruitt images—whether of African Americans, whites, or other racial groups, and whether taken in the studio, street, home, school, or church, or on the farm—have their own dynamic of pose, gaze, object, and subject. For many of his subjects, Pruitt's camera was the first one they had ever seen up close; his were the first photographs made of many of them.

Although Pruitt was a fine photographer, he was by no means an artist or documentarian on the level of twentieth-century photographers such as Walker Evans, Dorothea Lange, Eugène Atget, Gordon Parks, William Eggleston, or August Sander. Other than that year spent in Illinois at photography school, Pruitt essentially was an unlettered man educated in rural, racially segregated primary and secondary schools in Mississippi. He was not an avid reader or an intellectual. It is not clear what he knew of the wider world of photography as an art form. He spent most of his life in Columbus and did not travel much, as illustrated by his perfect attendance record at Kiwanis Club meetings for nineteen years in row.

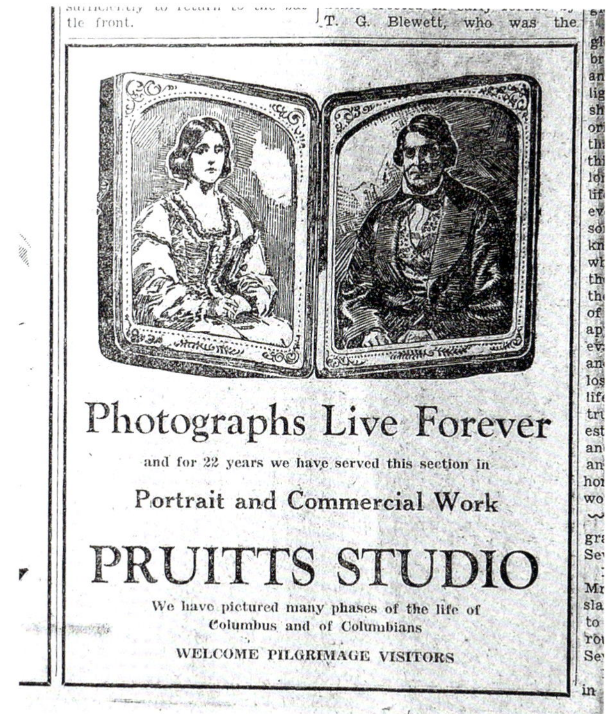

Advertisement in the Commercial Dispatch *for Pruitt's studio with reproduction of nineteenth-century daguerreotype, April 4, 1941.*

Still, the aesthetic of the Pruitt images reveals an accomplished photographer. Above all, however, is the content. He was in the right place at the right time.

Stories unfold whenever a single Pruitt photograph is given a close reading. If you look at one photograph, you may find the image compelling in its own right, defying categorization. This can include ones in the local newspaper or the studio portraiture that was his bread-and-butter. These photographs function like pottery shards from an archaeological dig that tell one tale but point to others; when seen in fullness, the stories form a mosaic, grounded in a past time and place yet continuing into today. His photographs capture scenes of the ordinary graces of everyday life, ethnic identity, and race relations as well as brutal power, full of excruciating suffering. His photograph of a 1935 lynching of two Black farmers served the purposes of white racial radicals when it was made into a postcard. However, two decades later, during the civil rights era, the image was used on a poster to foster support for those advocating voting rights for Blacks in Mississippi. Since then, the photograph has appeared in documentary films about racial violence and Black history.

PHOTOGRAPHIC CURATOR ANNE TUCKER, in writing about the photography of Brassaï, who worked at the turn of the twentieth century in France, said something that could describe Pruitt. "[Brassaï] sought neither to judge nor to change, but to fathom the living arrangements of the world." Pruitt's photographs very much "fathom the living arrangements" of the American South, the raw and the sublime. He documented life for those around him then, and for us today, if we listen to the pictures.

Only in recent decades have scholars begun to consider the work of small-town photographers such as Pruitt. Beginning in the 1970s and 1980s historians began to focus more on ordinary folk and culture specific to a local place and people. "Photography," noted John Szarkowski, photography curator at New York's Museum of Modern Art, "has learned about its nature not only from the great masters, but also from the simple and radical works of photographers of modest aspiration and small renown." One of those is Otis Noel Pruitt.

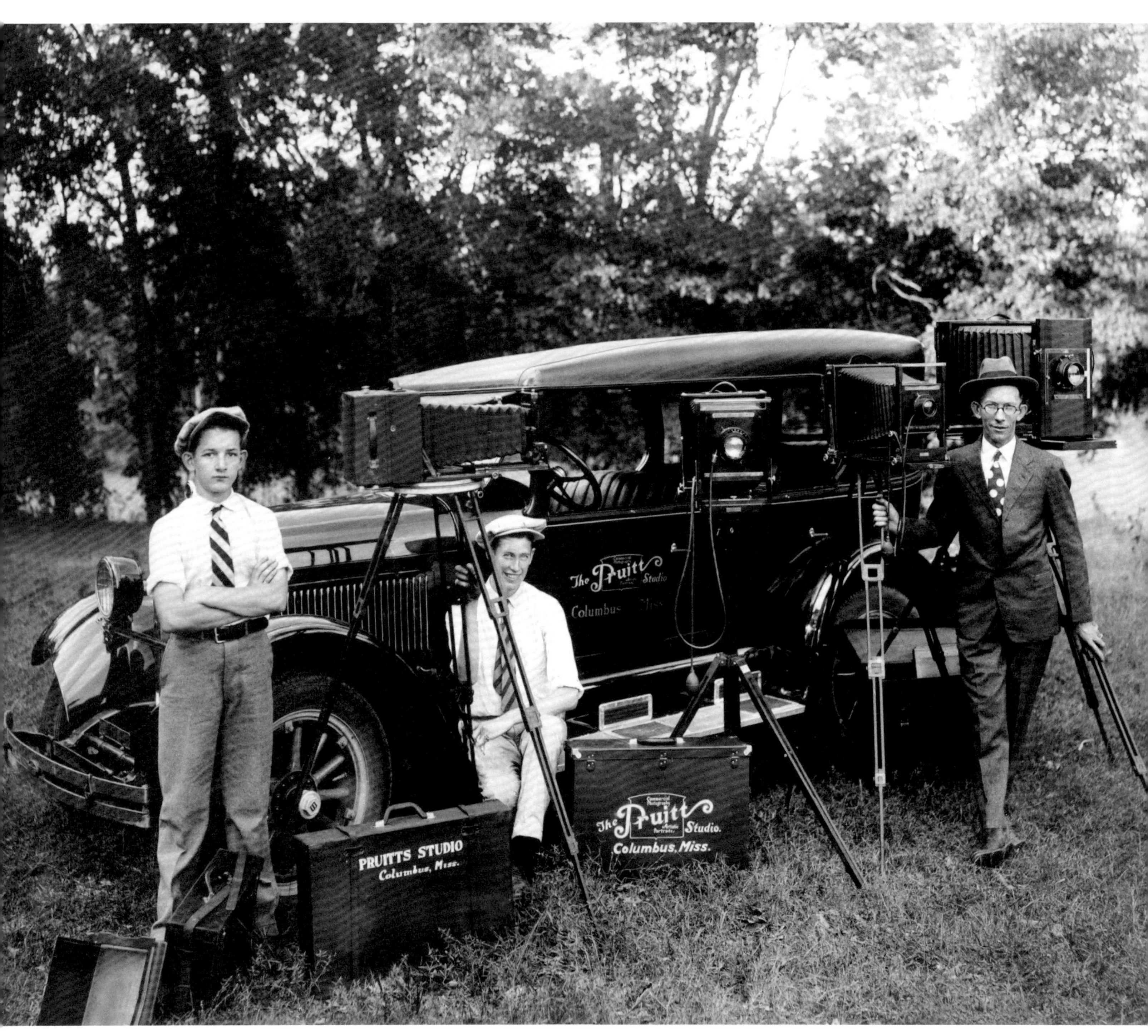

O. N. Pruitt (right) with son Lambuth (left) and Pruitt's brother Jim. Lambuth later worked as a photographer in Jackson as did Jim in nearby Starkville, circa 1925.

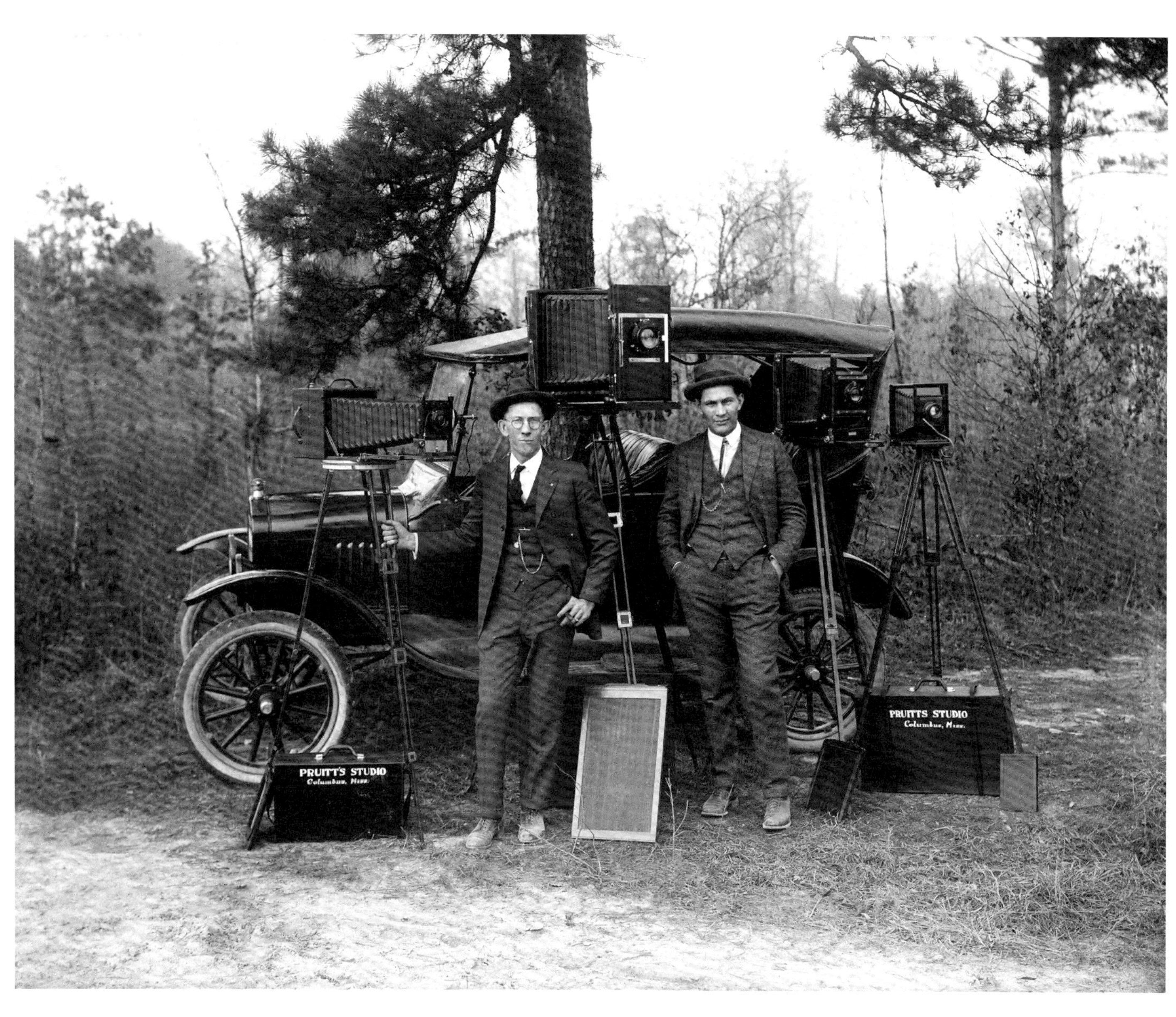

O. N. Pruitt (left) *and unidentified man with car and photography equipment, circa early 1920s.*

O. N. Pruitt by artesian well, Lake Norris Fishing Club, circa 1920s. Artesian wells once flowed freely in northeast Mississippi.

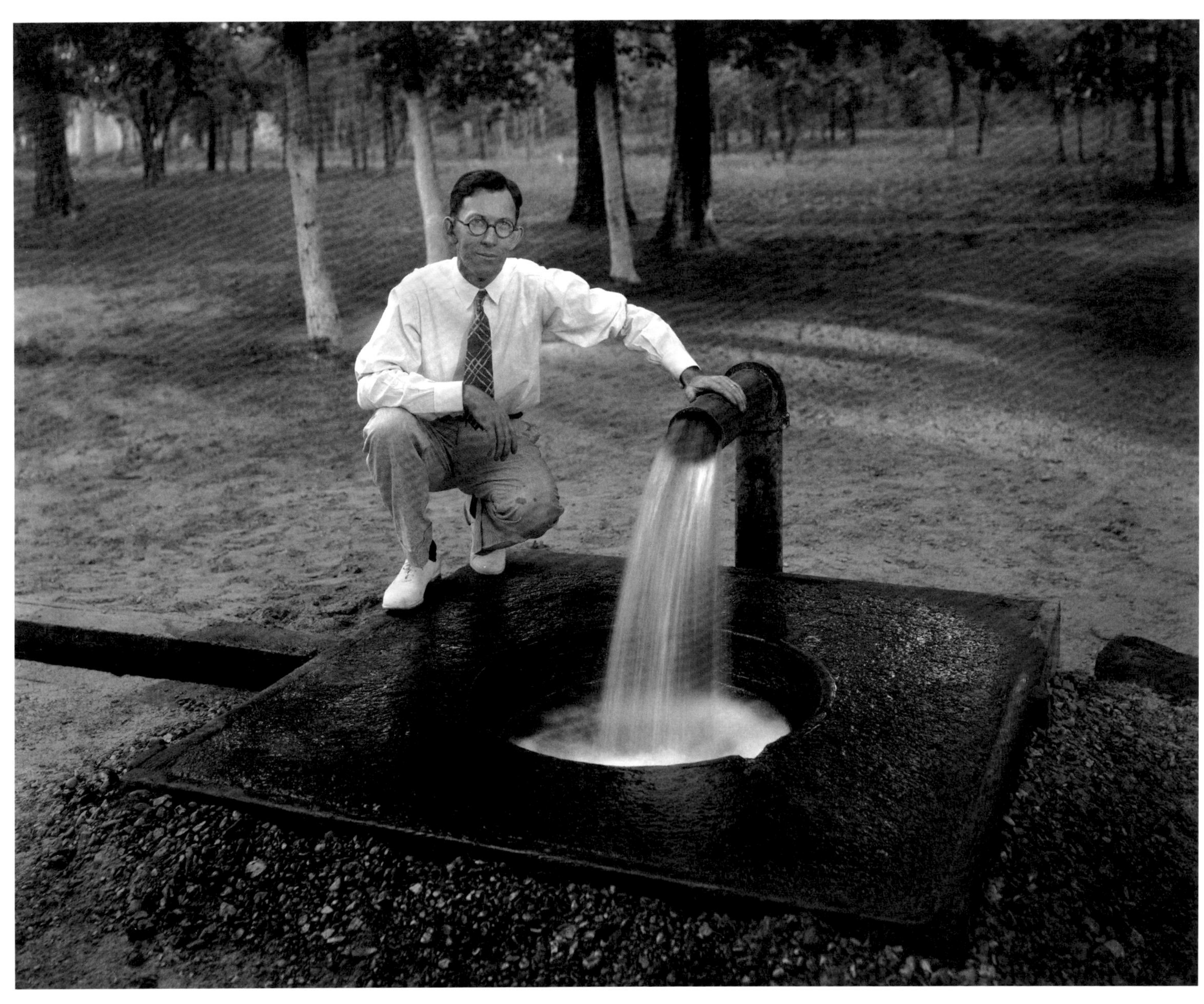

(opposite) *Studio portrait of O. N. Pruitt with twelve-gauge shotgun and squirrels, circa 1925. Pruitt loved to hunt and fish and built his own fishing lake.*

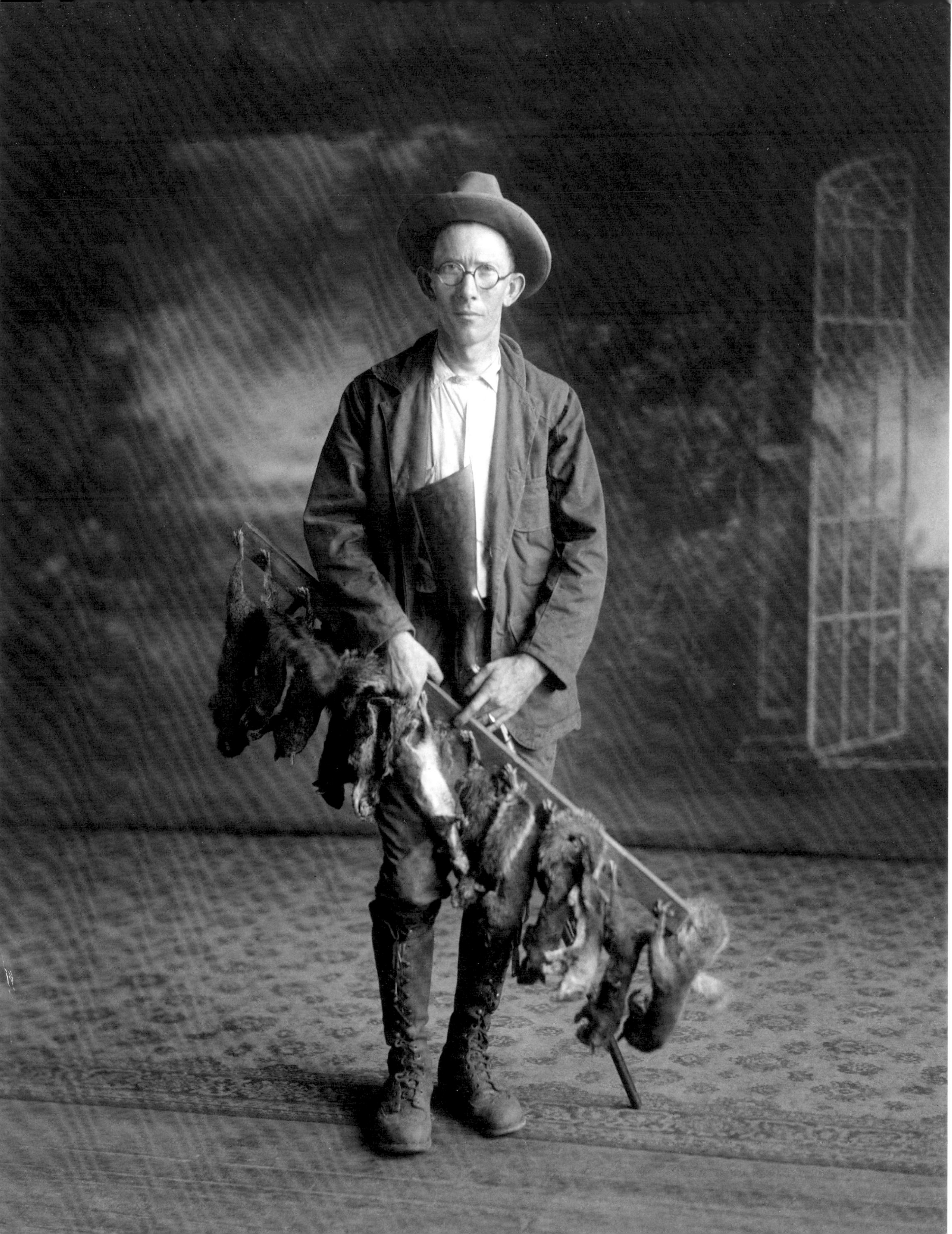

BY THE FLOW OF THE INLAND RIVER

When Pruitt first came to Columbus, its boundaries were confined on the west by the coffee-colored Tombigbee River and on the east by the equally muddy Luxapalila Creek, two Edenic waterways. The Alabama border was ten miles due east. The intersection of Main and Market Streets, five blocks east of the Tombigbee, was downtown, where Pruitt had his studio. Two- and three-story brick buildings with grocery, drug, dry goods stores, restaurants, and churches formed the downtown, its streets unpaved until 1921. One block north of Main and Market, the red brick Lowndes County Courthouse, built before the Civil War, rose above the landscape. A 1912 marble monument to Confederate soldiers of Lowndes County anchored the courthouse lawn.

Reminiscent of William Faulkner's character Gavin Stevens, who declared that in the South "the past is never dead; it is not even past," Columbus was wedded to its history. The legacy of slavery, the Civil War, and Reconstruction permeated every aspect of life. That past consisted not only of Pruitt's era but also the era of "the Redemption," as conservative whites referred to their 1877 reclamation of the legislative seats they lost during Reconstruction. It dated from the "War of Northern Aggression" to the "Flush Times" of the antebellum days of the slave and cotton economy, when Mississippi was one of the wealthiest states in America, and to Columbus's founding in 1821 and its naming for explorer Christopher Columbus, and to the establishment of the Mississippi Territory at the turn of the nineteenth century.

During Pruitt's boyhood, Mississippi endured social, demographic, and economic tumult.

Cotton prices, which had been as high as twelve cents a pound in the early 1880s, at one point dropped to five cents a pound in the 1890s, not enough for anyone to make a profit or earn a living. At this time radical whites embarked upon an unprecedented reign of terror and a campaign of disenfranchisement. White supremacy and racial segregation laws locked a stranglehold on people of every color, taking the worst toll on people with the darkest skins.

Historians C. Vann Woodward and Neil R. McMillen summarized the factors that led to this: enduring economic poverty and agricultural depression in the South, scientific racism that gained credence not only in the South but also throughout America and Europe, social Darwinism, and the Populist movement. The racial intolerance these factors fueled throughout the nation was made worse in Mississippi, McMillen has written, by "a growing Yankee readiness to accept a 'southern solution' to the race problem." Thus began the Great Migration of Blacks fleeing the South's Jim Crow laws. The 1890 census for Lowndes County recorded 21,036 Black residents compared to 6,009 white residents, 71 percent compared to 29 percent. Yet by the time Pruitt established himself in Columbus just over two decades later, the town was becoming essentially a half-Black, half-white community of 10,000 residents, although overall Lowndes County, population 27,632, was two-thirds Black and one-third white. By then, Columbus nonetheless was growing as an agricultural market center for cotton, lumber, floral plants, honey, dairy cows, beef cattle, and tombstones. The Federal Writers' Project in 1937 described Columbus as "a city in which there is room to breathe." The federal Works Progress Administration (WPA) guide masked poverty and suffering with this description:

> A comfortable old-tree shaded town, the streets are broad, the sidewalks wide, lawns are spacious, and houses are set apart . . . characteristic of the lavish ante-bellum period in which they were built. It is the junction of the Old South with the New, with gracious lines of Georgian porticos forming a belt of mellowed beauty about a modern business district. . . .
>
> The same leisurely atmosphere of spaciousness is carried into "Northside," the Negro section of town. Here approximately 45 percent of Columbus's population lives in low-roofed, red frame houses that are festooned with wisteria and shaded by umbrella chinaberry trees and tall, brightly colored sunflowers. A majority of the Negro men find work with white families rather than with industries, or are delivery boys, taxi drivers, and filling station helpers. The Negro women who work are employed almost entirely as domestic servants. In their section of town, they have their own stores, cafes, hotels and recreational center.

In the 1930s, some years after she attended Mississippi State College for Women in Columbus, Eudora Welty photographed for the WPA. Welty, who won the 1973 Pulitzer Prize in fiction, wrote in *Eudora Welty Photographs* (1989), "Poverty in Mississippi, white and black, really didn't have too much to do with the Depression. It was ongoing. Mississippi was long since poor, long devastated." Clyde Edgerton captured this common bond of poverty in a half-serious, half-joking essay accompanying another book of photographs from the American South. In *Picturing the South: 1860 to Present,* Edgerton reports on nonelites as if he were an anthropologist looking back from the twenty-second century:

> The Cornbread Eaters—the largest group of Southerners, 1900–1930, were divided into dark-skins and light-skins. The dark-skins suffered indignity, pain, horror, and inhumanity as a consequence of light-skinned racial hatred. The light-skins suffered, but generally not as a result of direct, unabridged evil. Each day almost all of the Cornbread Eaters made and ate a bread made of cornmeal, salt, and water. They also had in common: fried fatback, buttermilk, non-taxed whiskey, hot weather, vegetable gardens, chickens, blackberries, dogs, extended families, several taboos, certain similar language habits and religious practices, and little or no political or economic power.

Cornbread Eaters—both white and Black—are the subjects of many a Pruitt photograph. Likewise, so are wealthy and powerful white people.

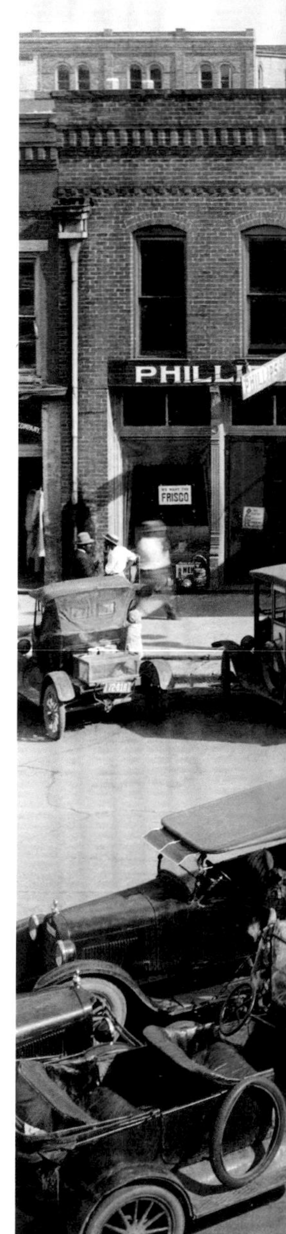

A farmers' hay market where pigs, chickens, and sorghum and cane syrup were sold, Main Street at Fourth Street intersection, circa 1927.

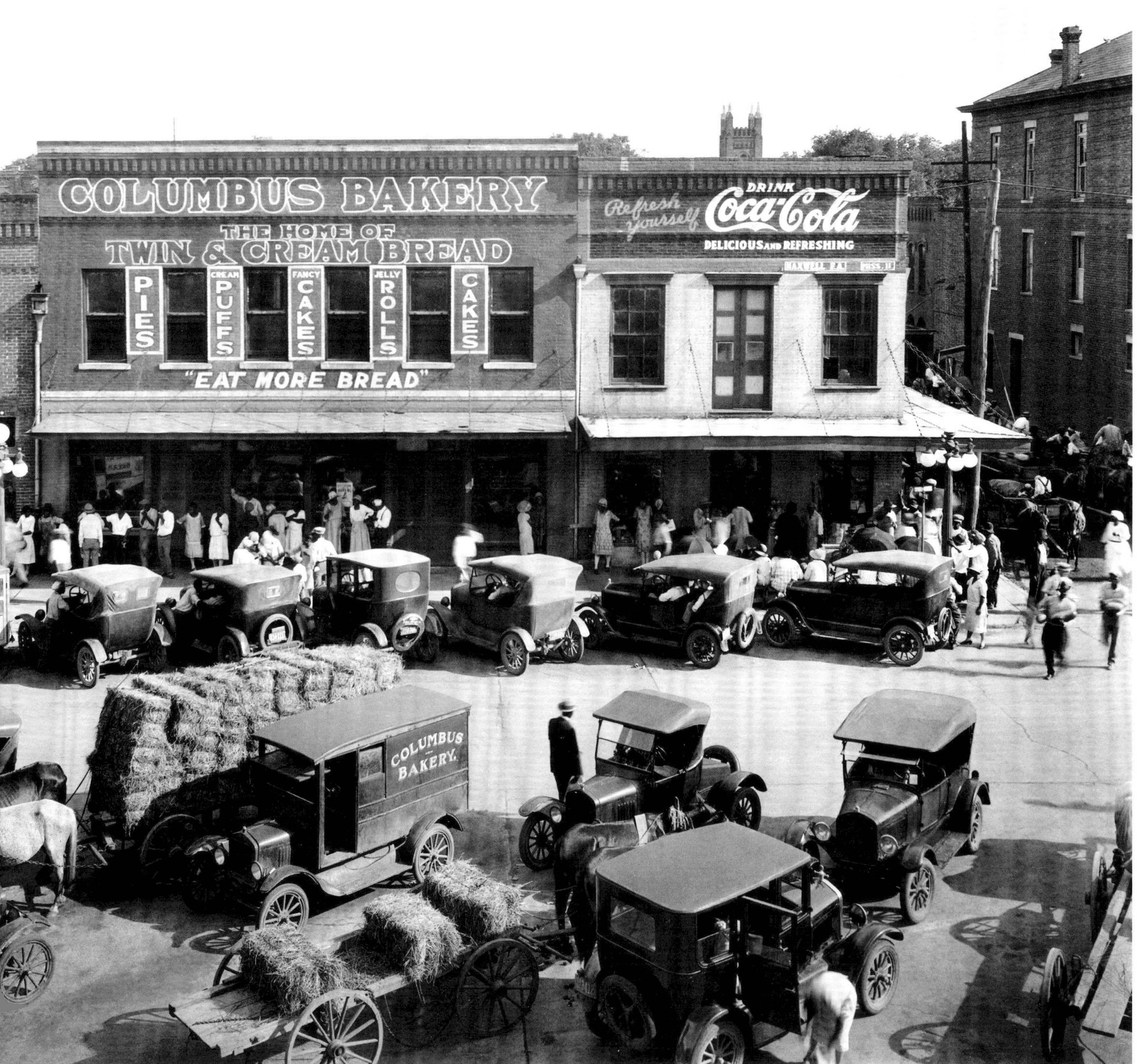
COLUMBUS BAKERY
THE HOME OF
TWIN & CREAM BREAD
PIES
CREAM PUFFS
FANCY CAKES
JELLY ROLLS
CAKES
"EAT MORE BREAD"
Refresh yourself
DRINK
Coca-Cola
DELICIOUS AND REFRESHING
COLUMBUS BAKERY

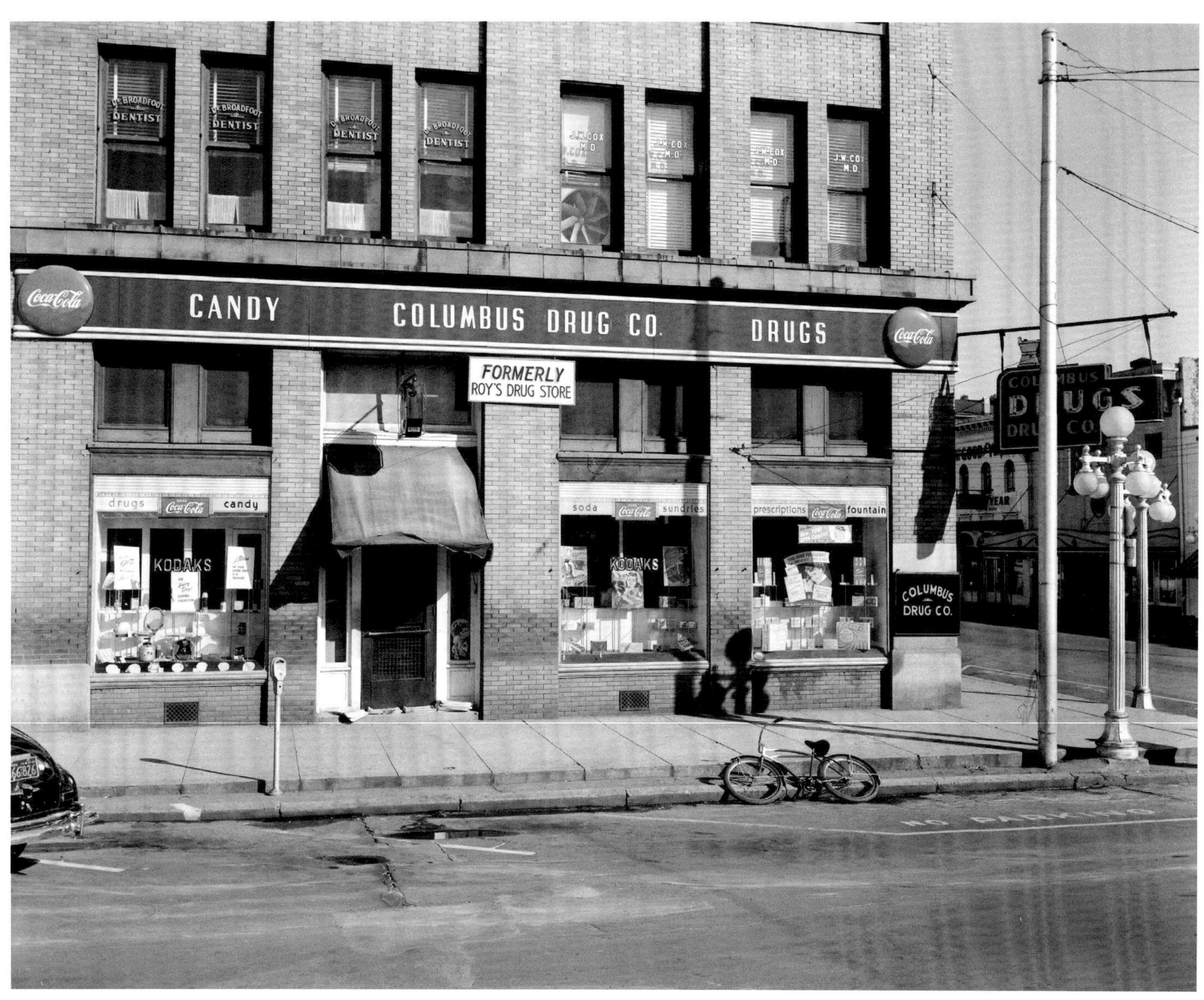

Main Street northwest corner at intersection with Market Street, late 1940s.

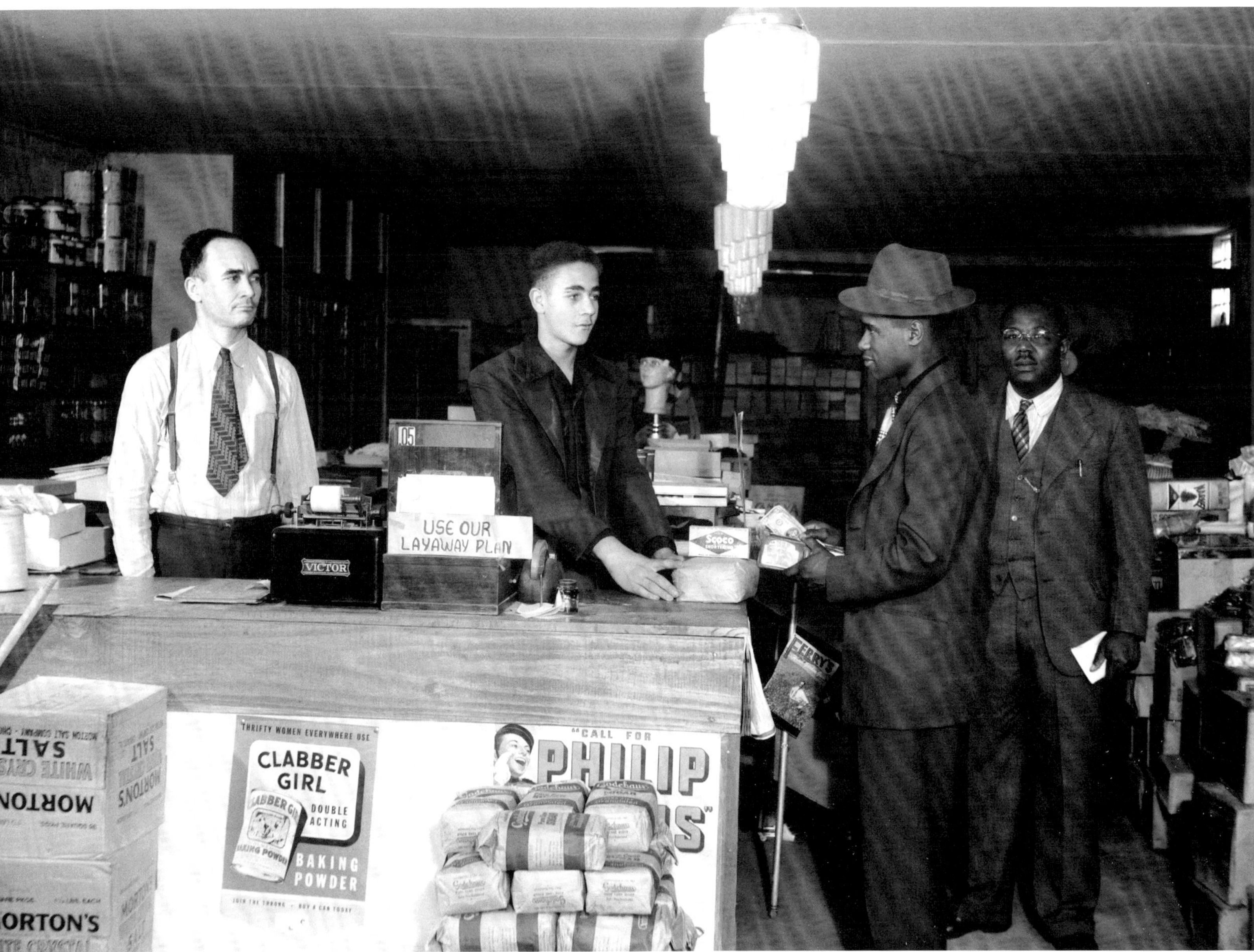

.05
USE OUR
LAYAWAY PLAN
VICTOR
FERRY'S
THRIFTY WOMEN EVERYWHERE USE
CLABBER GIRL
DOUBLE ACTING
BAKING POWDER
"CALL FOR
PHILIP
MORTON'S

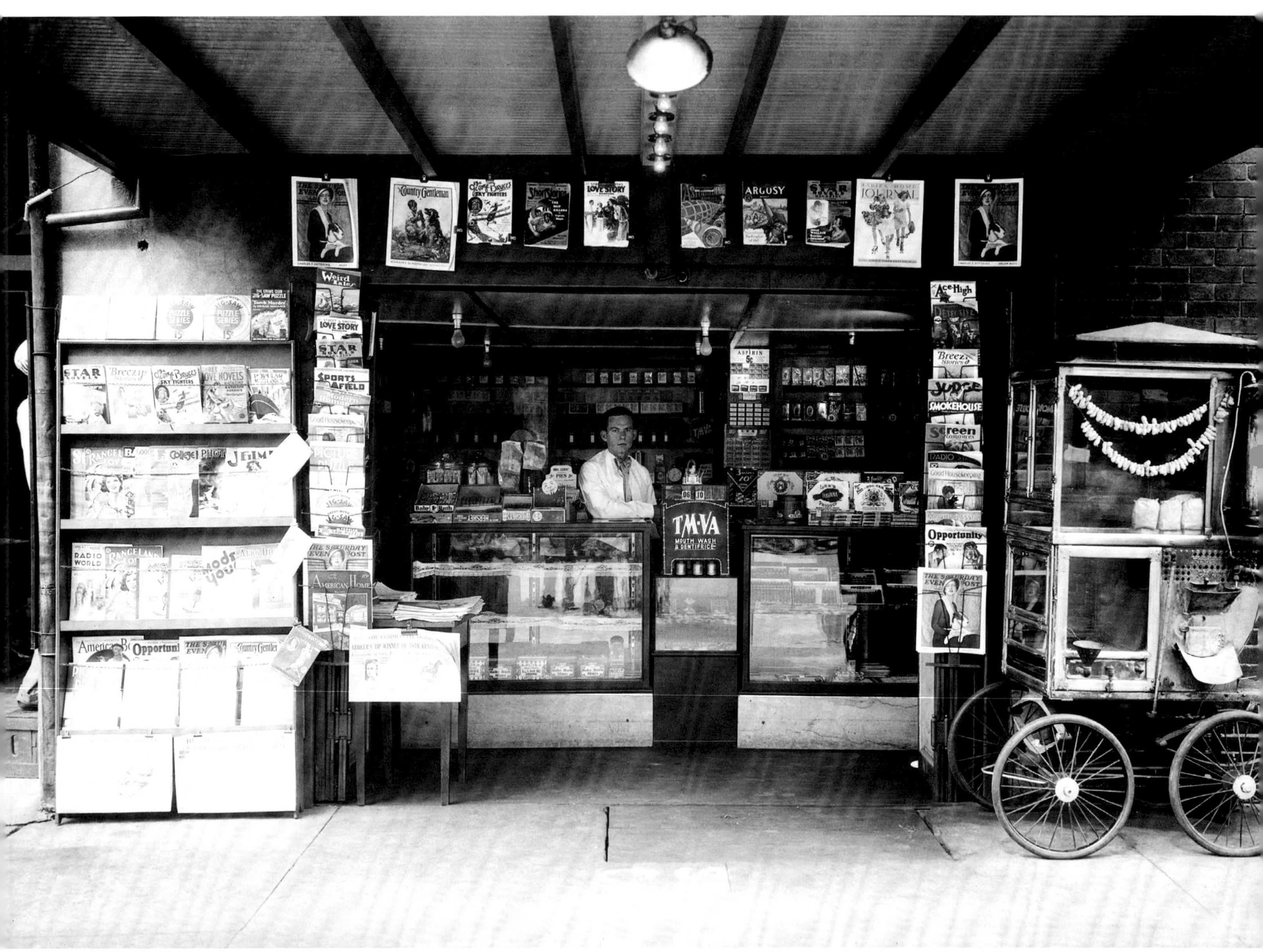

Newsstand, May 1933.

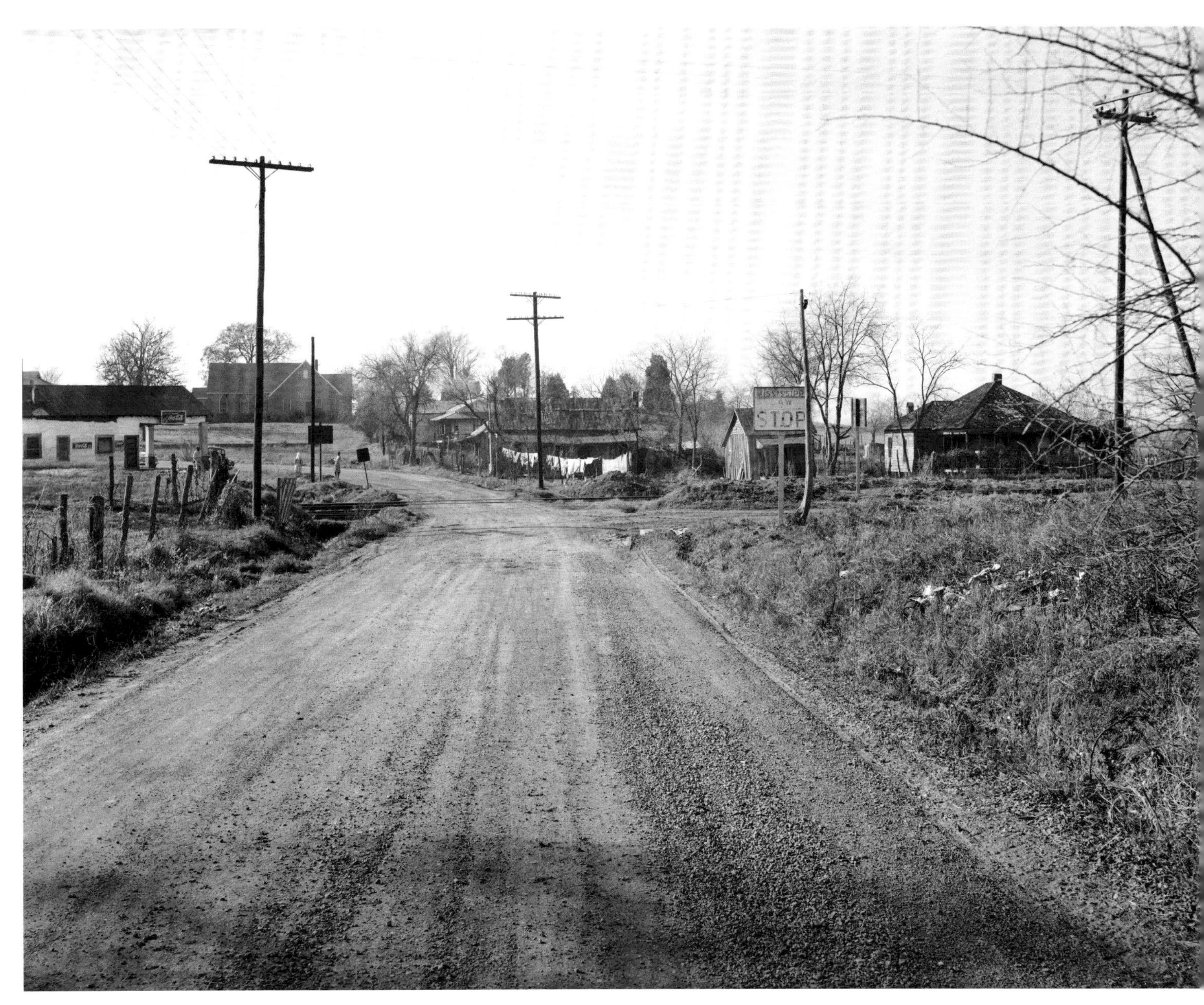

Artesia, west of Columbus in Lowndes County, Mississippi.

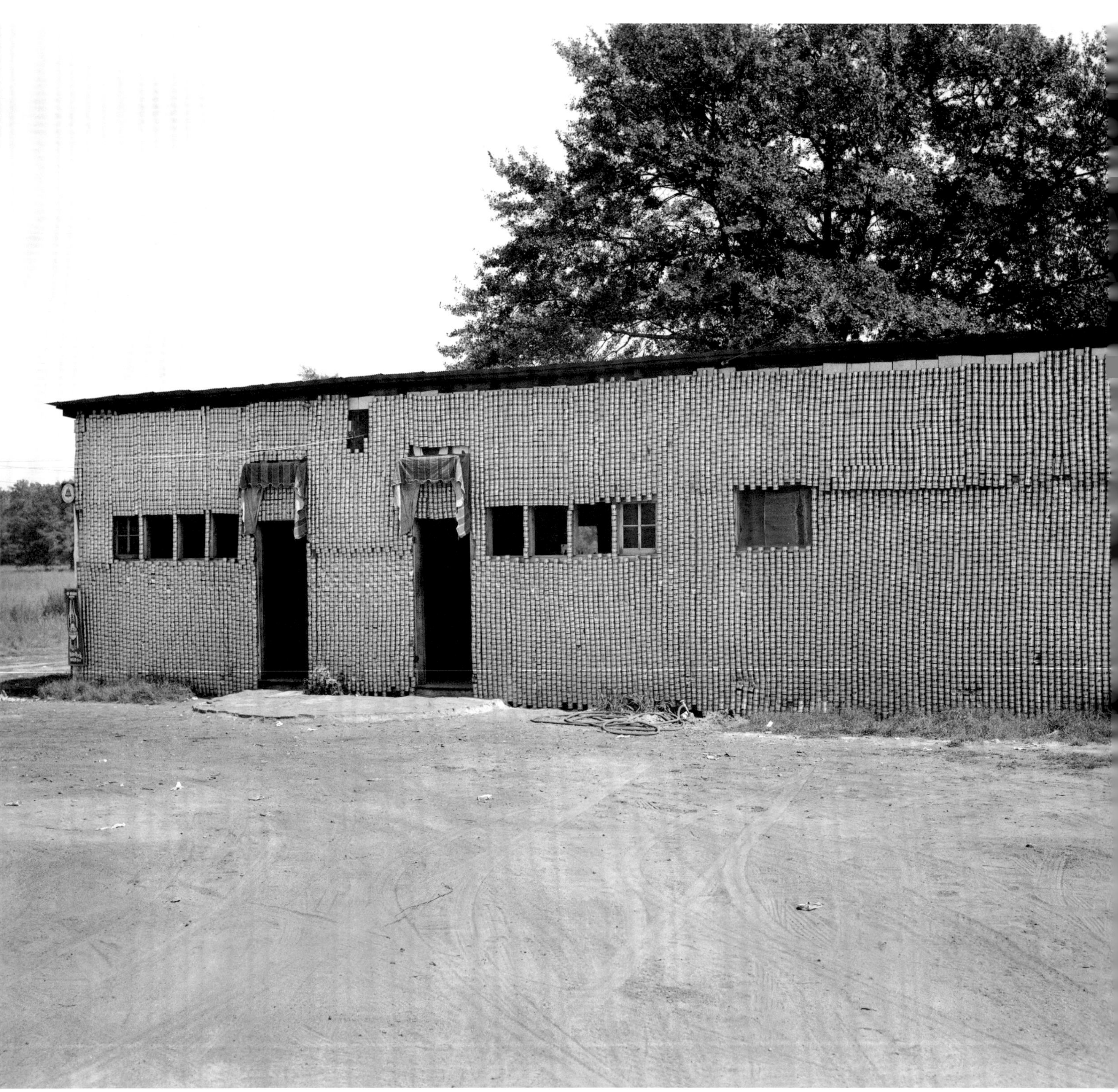

Auction, circa 1920s–30s.

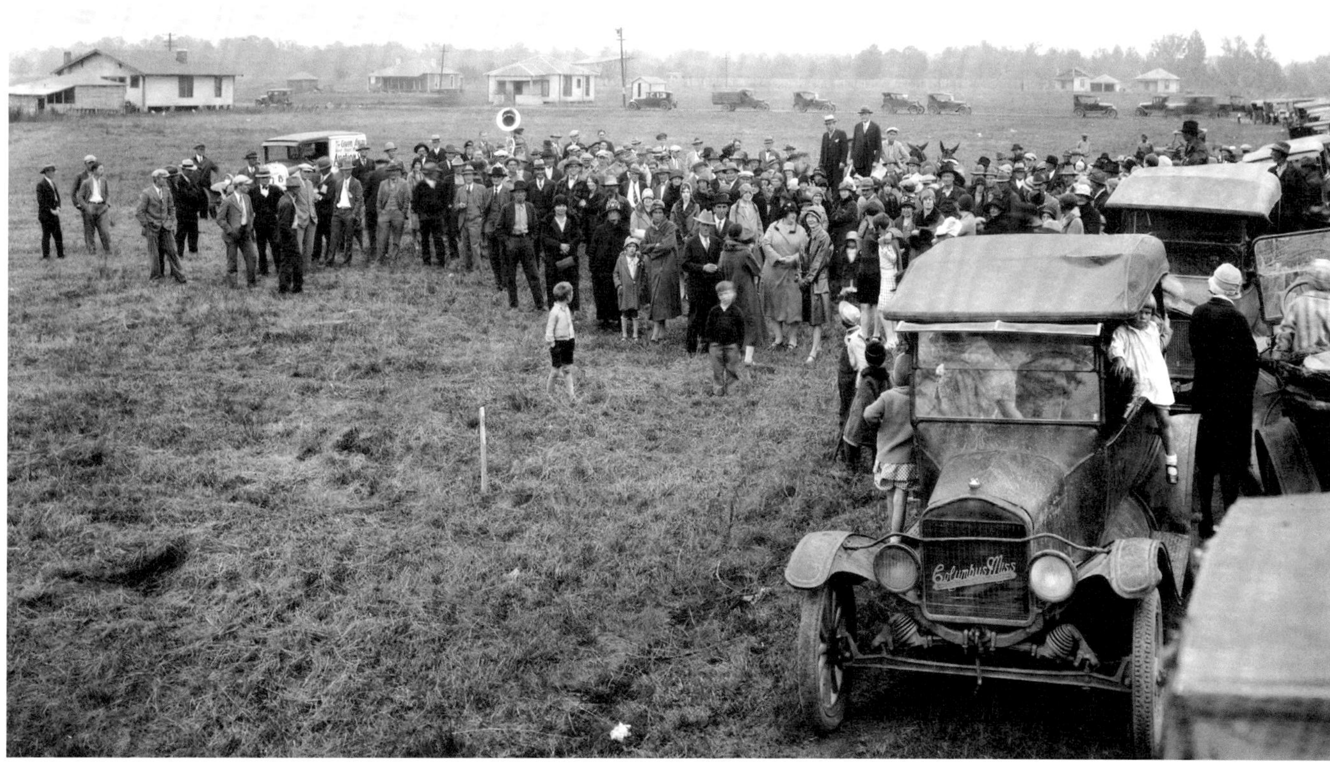

Beer joint with beer can walls on exterior and interior, circa 1930s–40s.

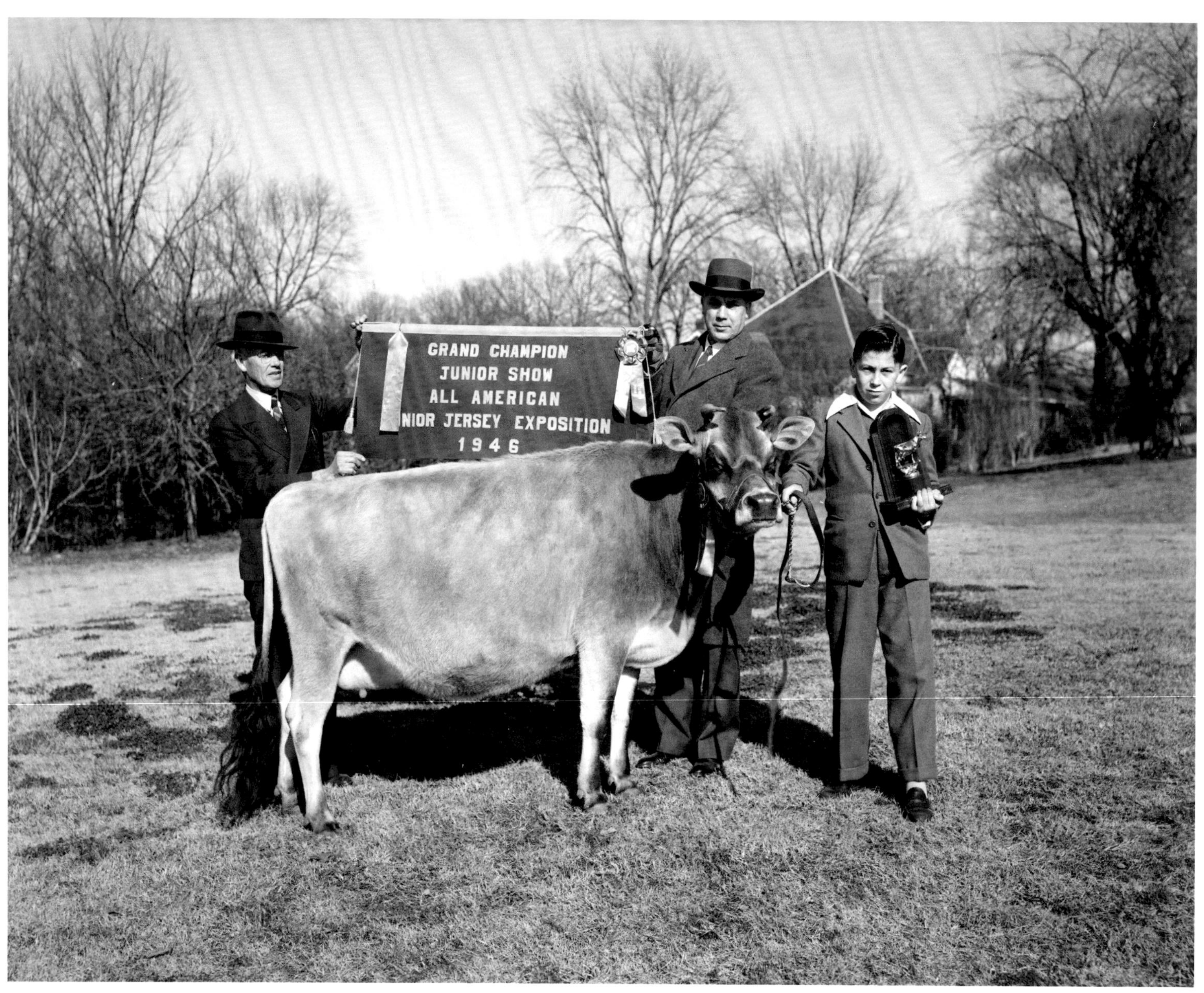
GRAND CHAMPION
JUNIOR SHOW
ALL AMERICAN
NIOR JERSEY EXPOSITION
1946

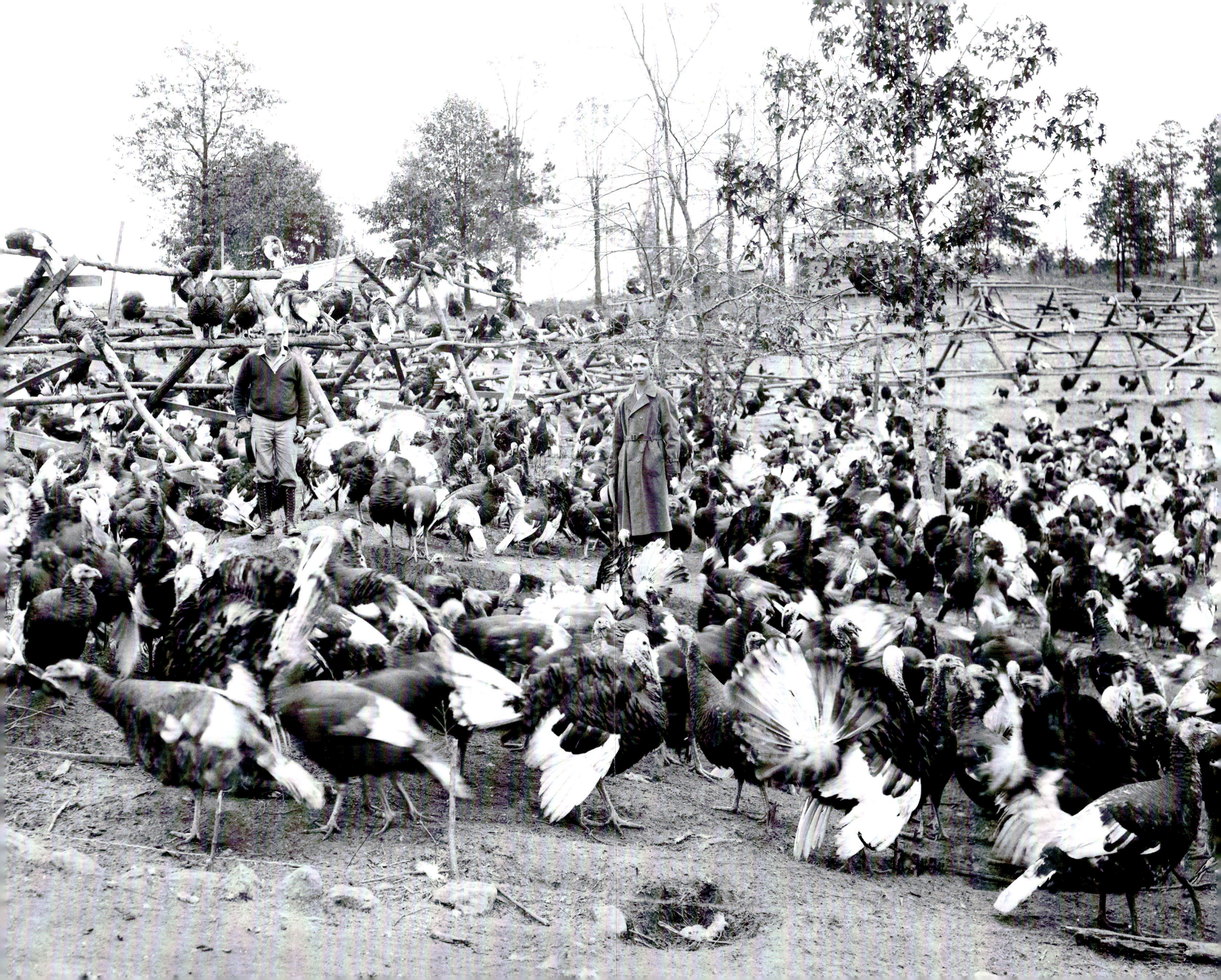

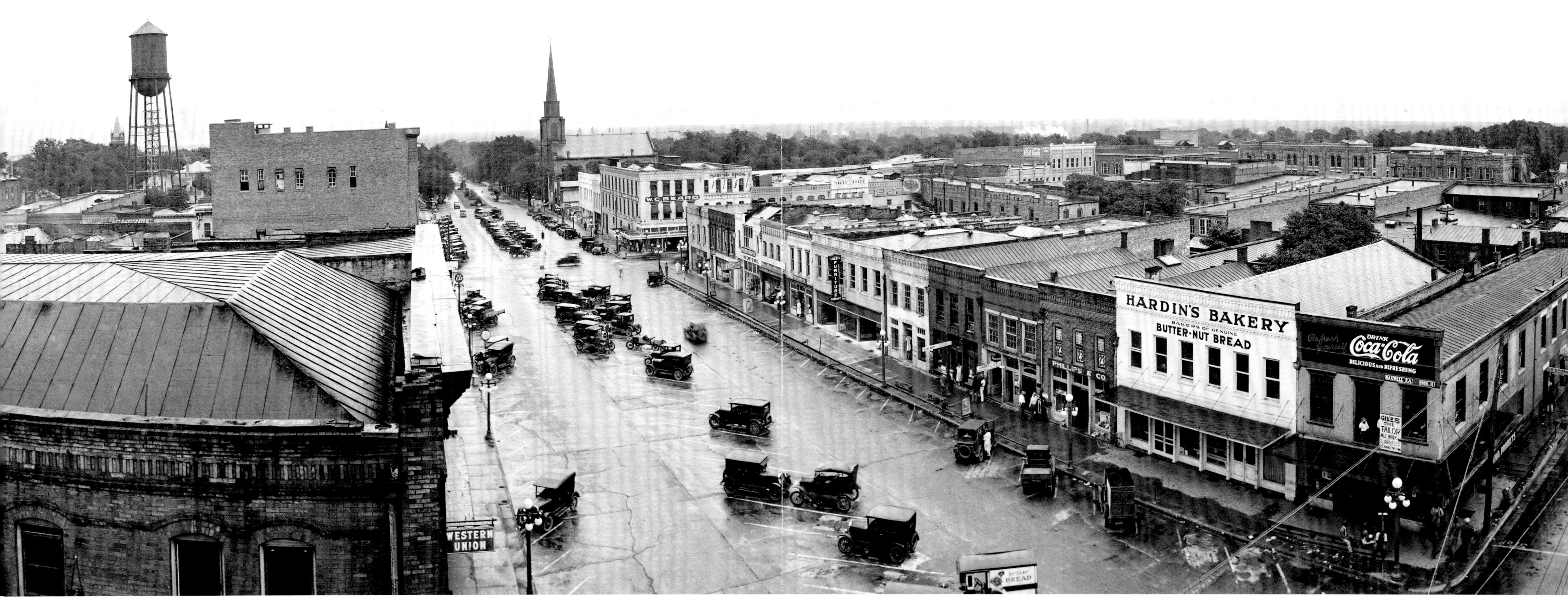
W.C.BEARD
HARDIN'S BAKERY
BAKERS OF GENUINE
BUTTER-NUT BREAD
Refresh Yourself
DRINK Coca-Cola
DELICIOUS AND REFRESHING
MAXWELL P.A.
MISS. 11
GILES THE TAILOR
ALL WORK GUARANTEED
PHILLIPS & CO.
WESTERN UNION
BREAD

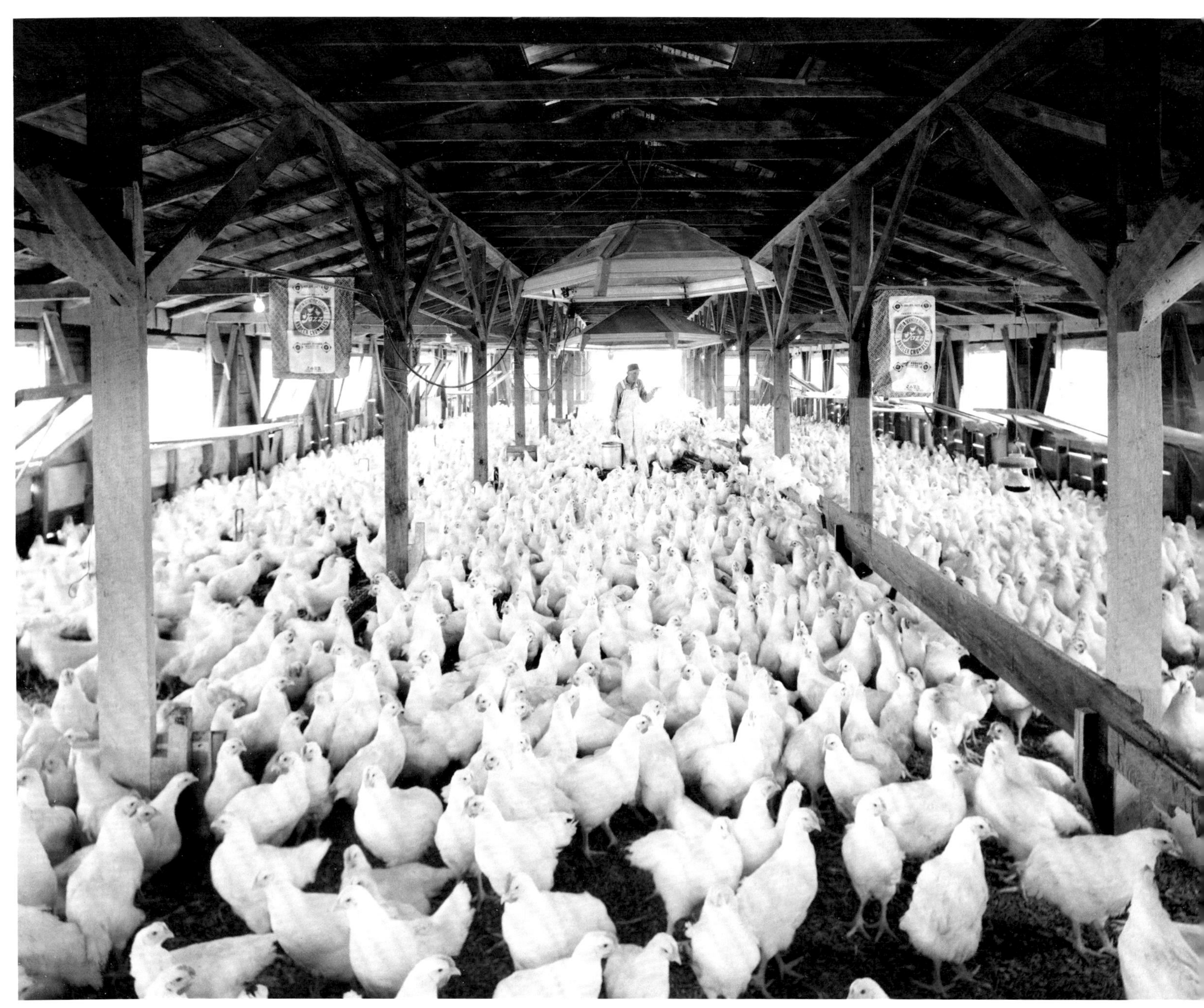

Mr. Gaynes's chickens.

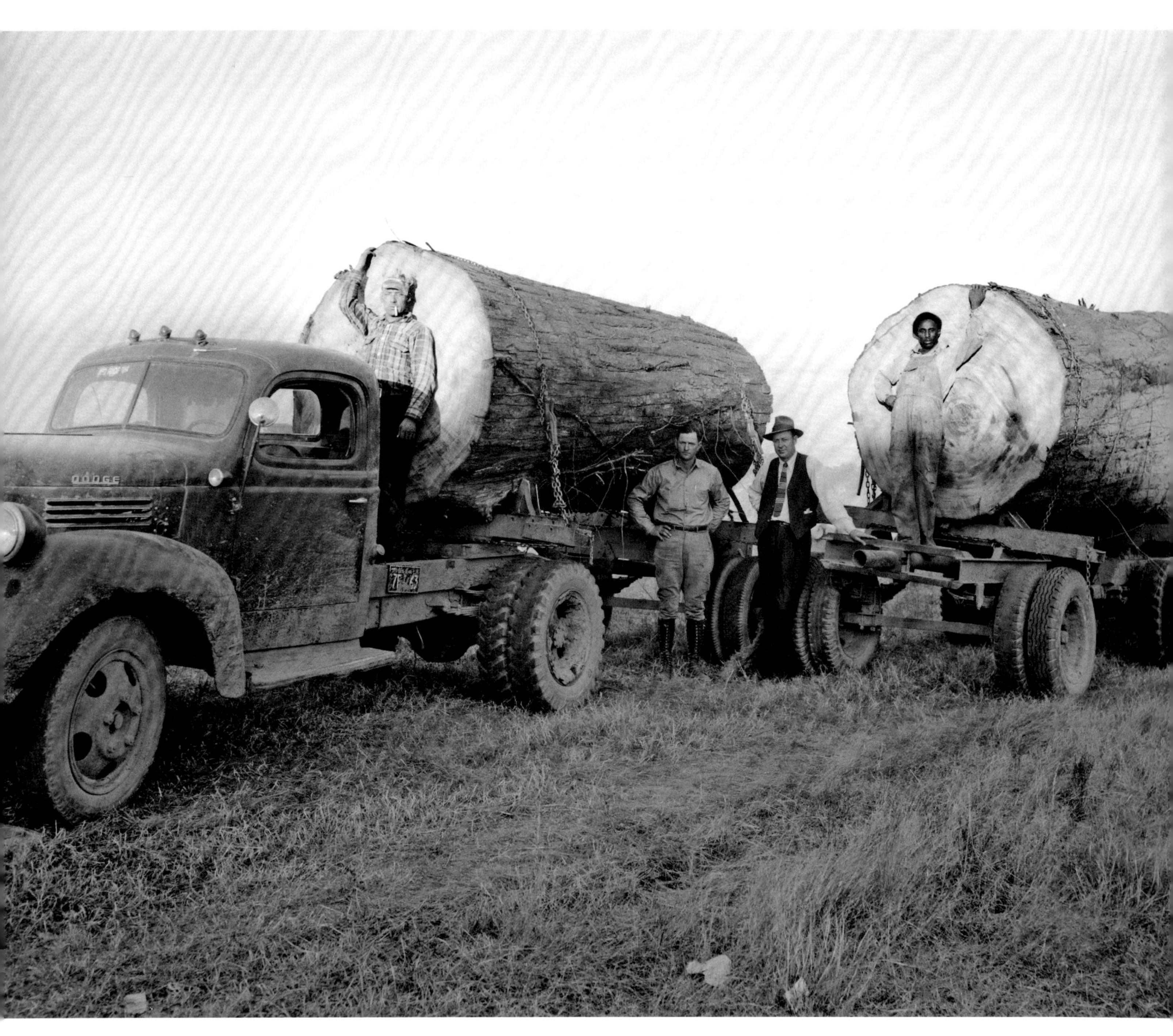

Men with log trucks, from Taylor Machine Works, Louisville, Mississippi.

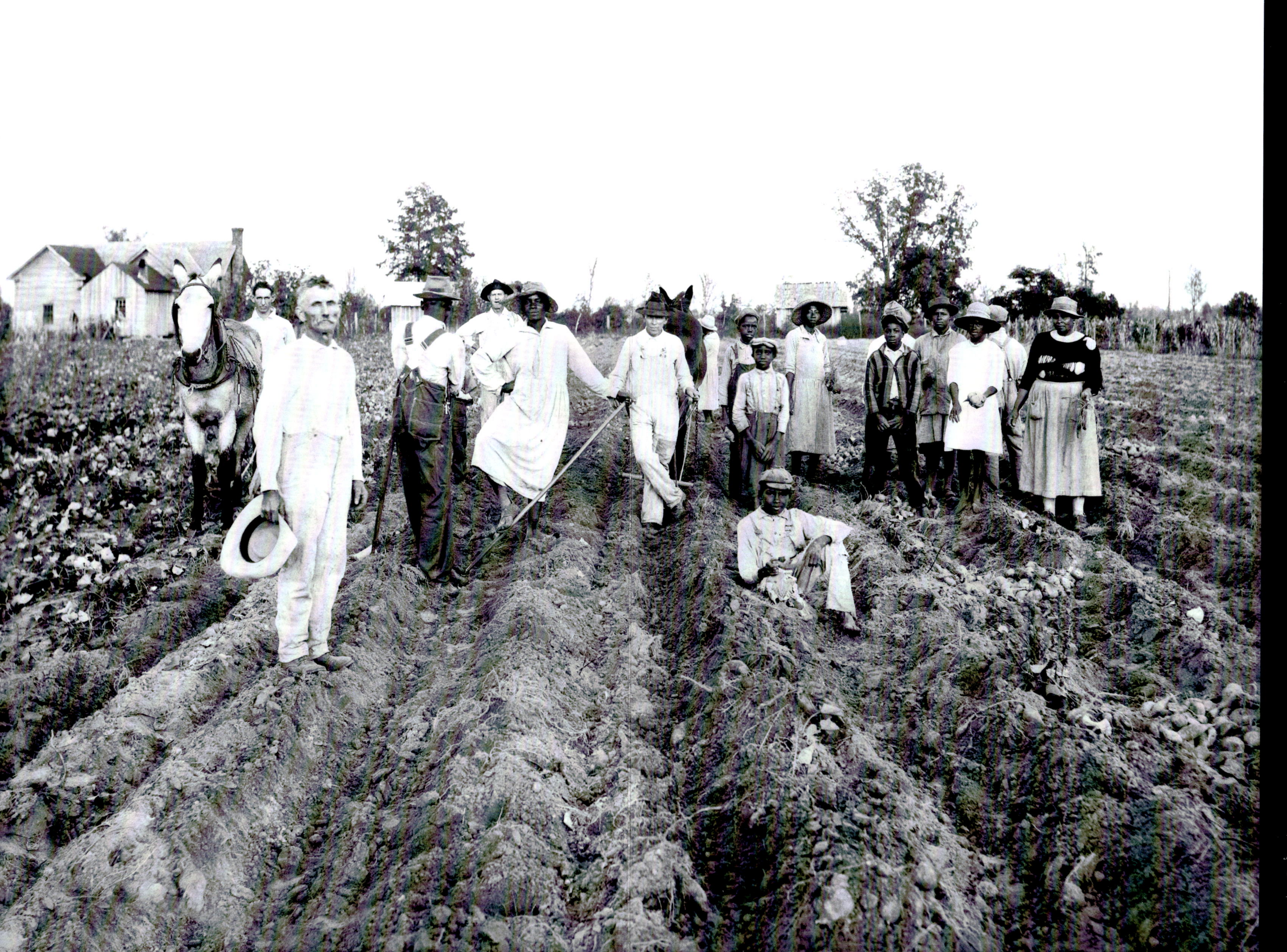

Potato farmers with politician-farmer Johnny Williams (left foreground), *Caledonia, Mississippi, circa 1930s.*

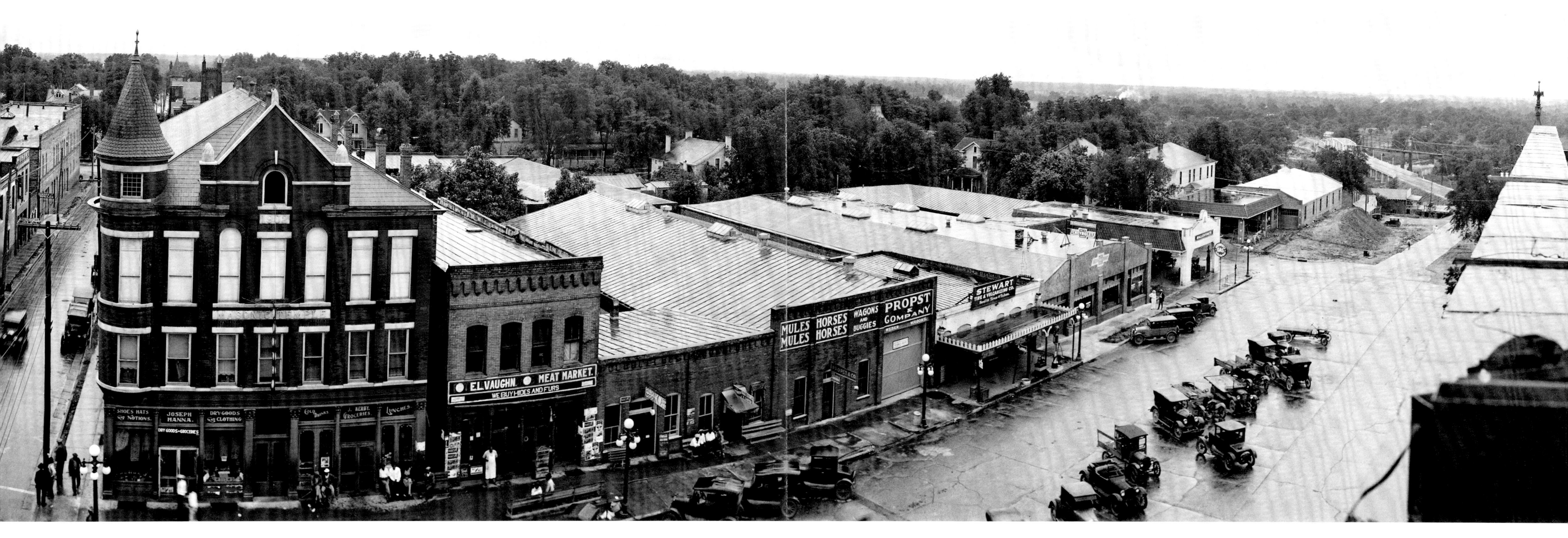

Columbus's Main Street viewed from atop Gilmer Hotel at intersection with Catfish Alley, late 1920s.

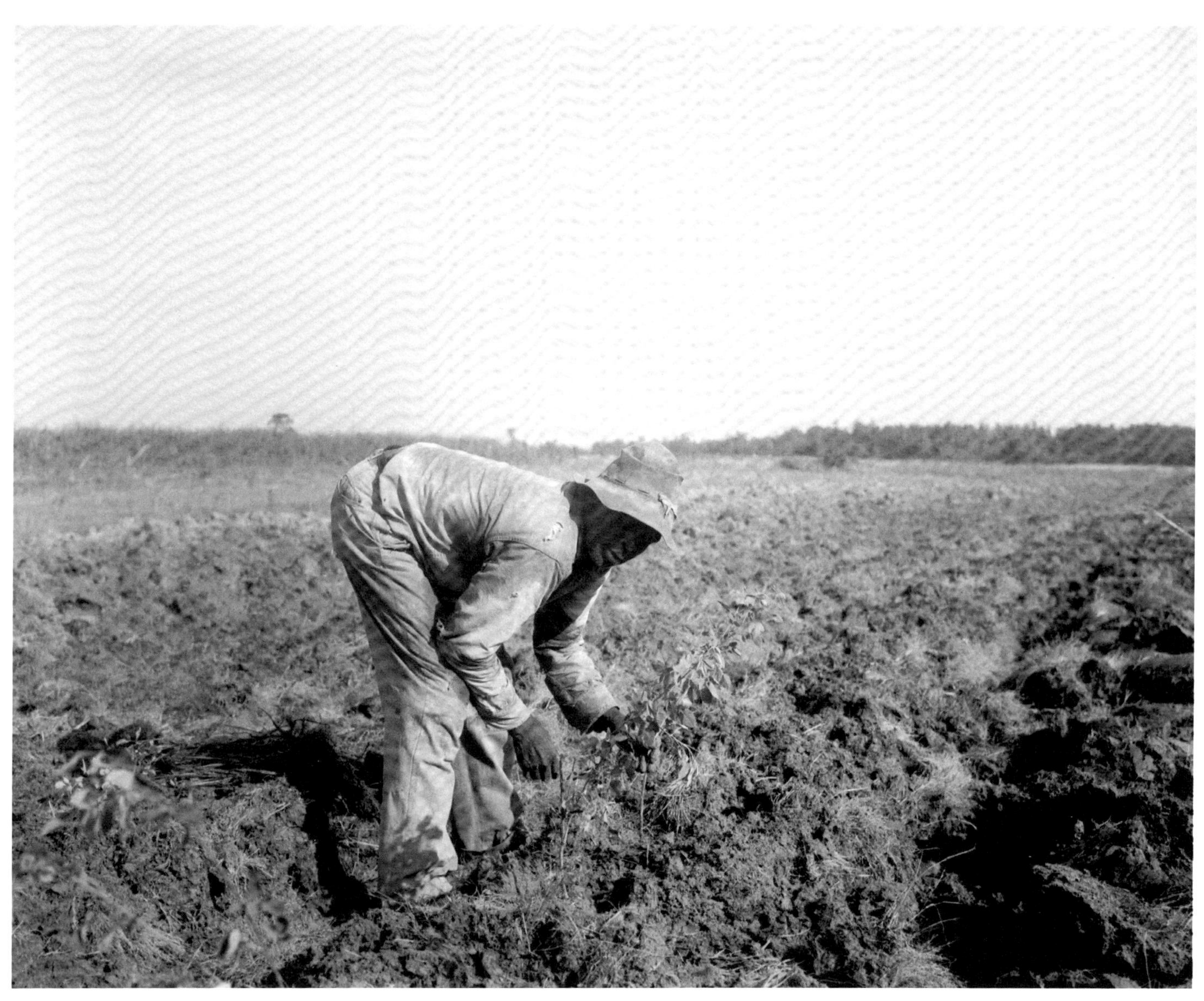

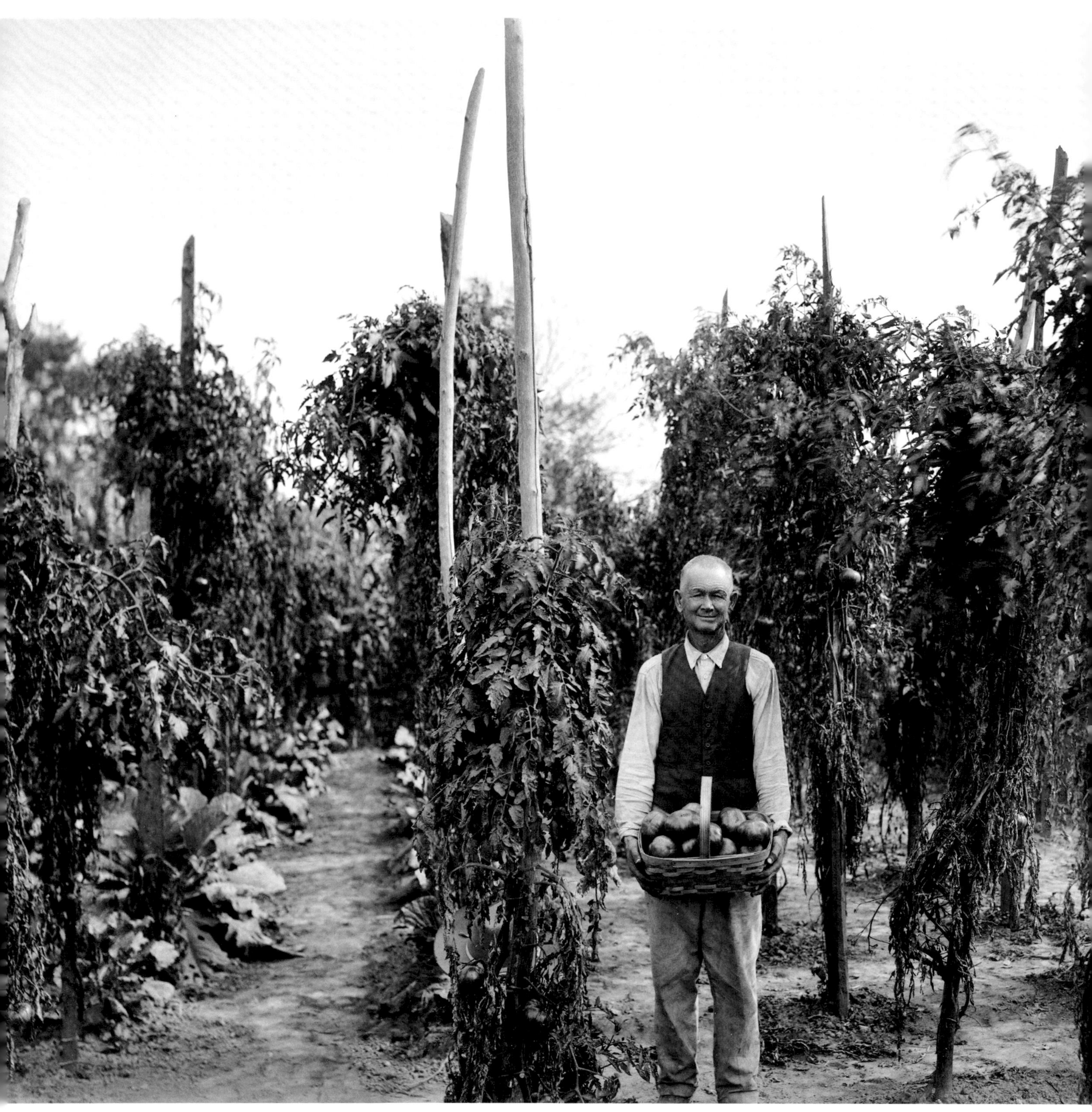

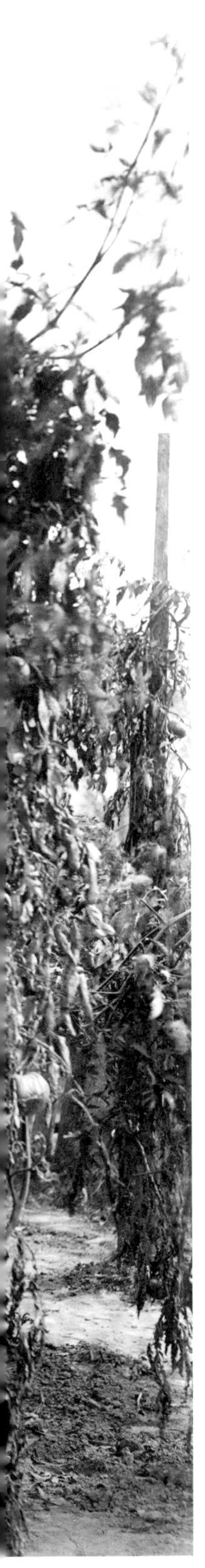

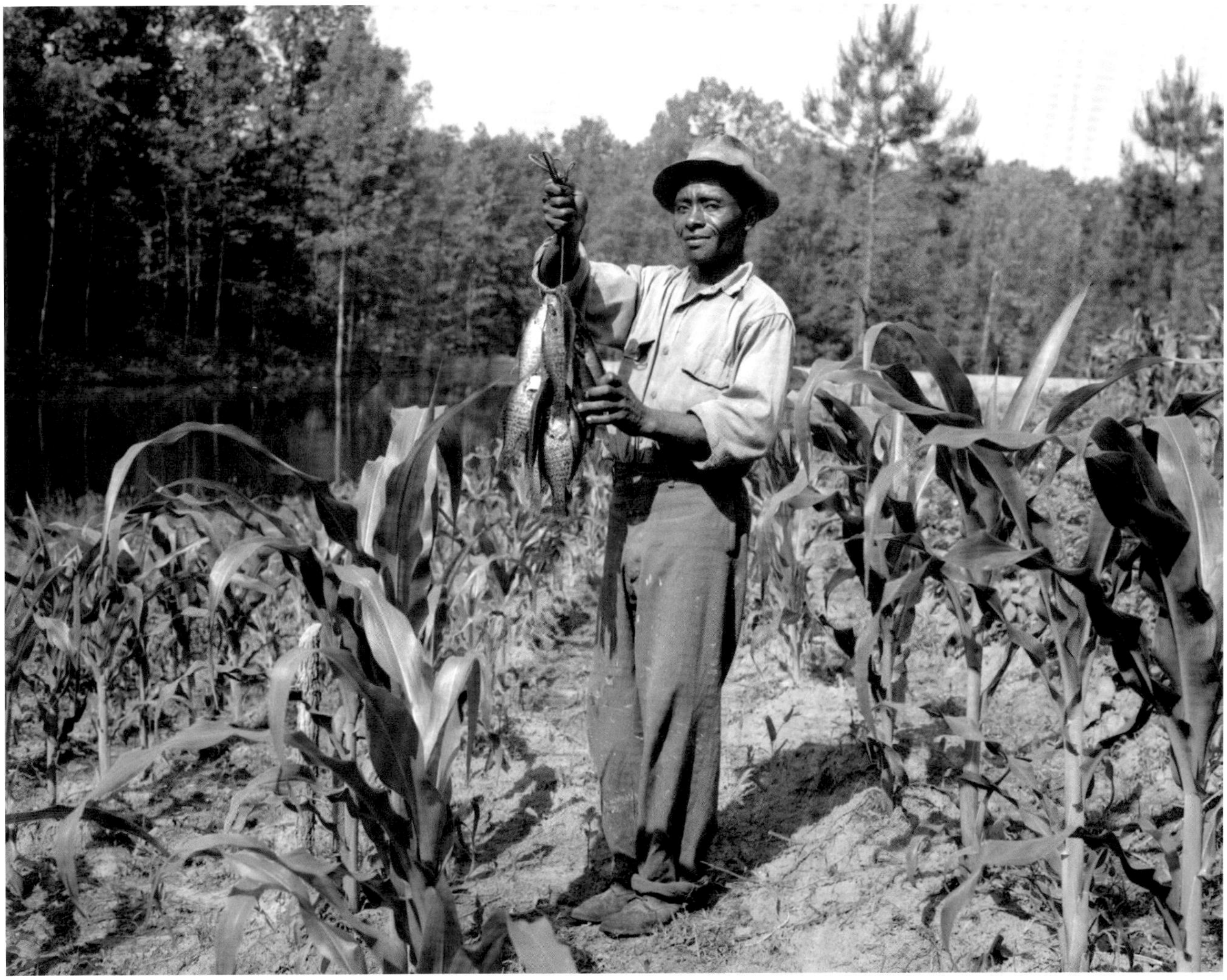

Tomatoes and tomato plants, circa 1920s–30s.

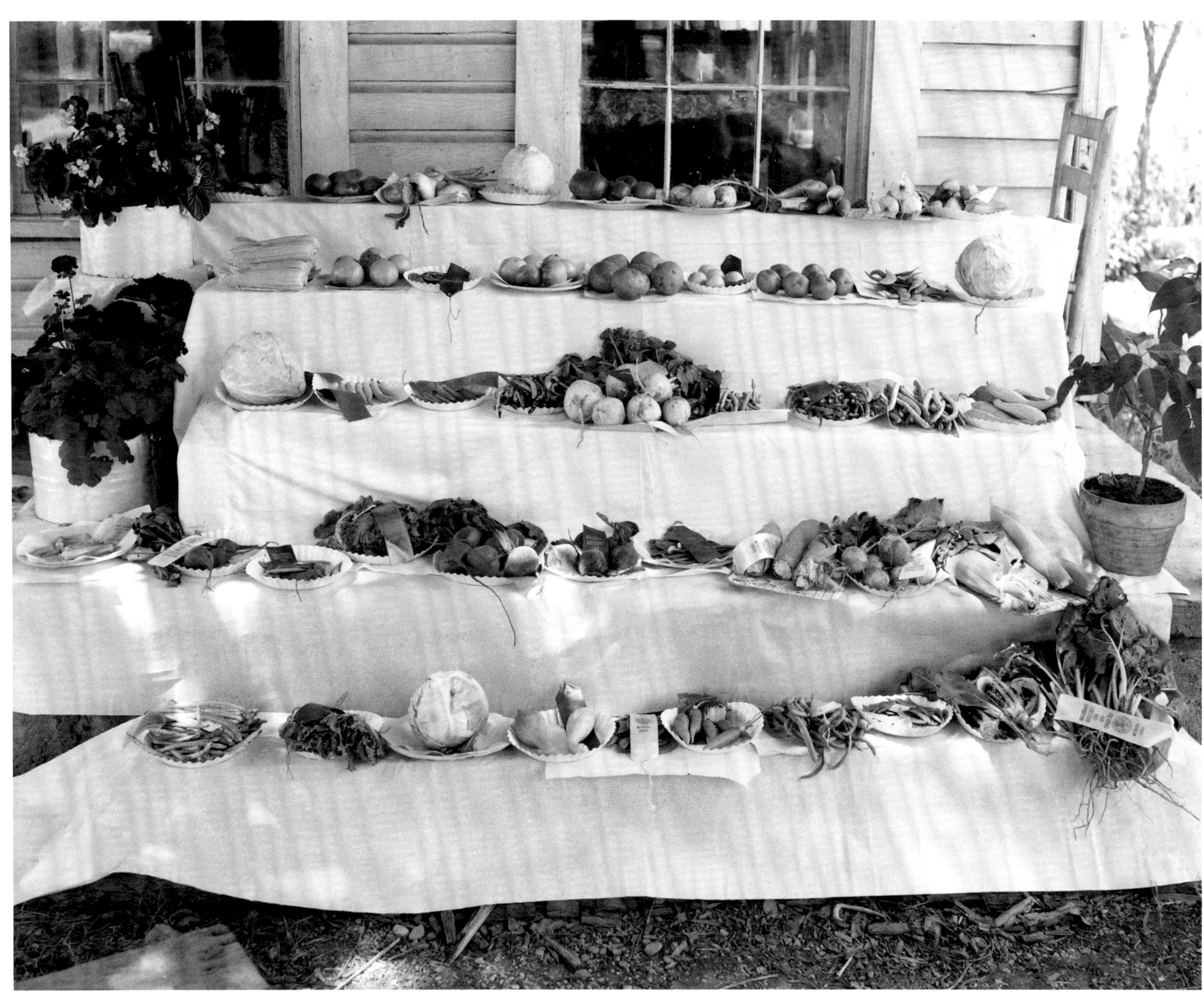

County fair produce exhibit.

WORLD FAMOUS HUNTING DOG TRAINER ER M. SHELLEY, CIRCA 1930

Outside a two-story Craftsman bungalow with deep eaves and abundant windows, set on a wooded hill on the outskirts of Columbus, fifty-two hunting dogs—some of the finest in the nation—are linked. They spread across the lawn in a photograph made from a panoramic negative about three feet wide and eight inches tall. In the center are Er M. Shelley and his wife, Lucille Wall Shelley, dressed in British-made hunting tweeds and riding boots. On the right is a white dog trainer named Albert Baugh. On the left are two dog trainers, Black men whose names are, for now, lost to history.

Known worldwide in hunting dog circles, Er Shelley was a self-taught trainer extraordinaire. From 1921 to 1957, he lived in Columbus. He specialized in bird dogs—pointers and setters—although he also trained foxhounds. People from all over the world sent their dogs for him to train. Sometimes he was training as many as eighty. By the time he moved to Columbus he had achieved acclaim as a hunting dog trainer, field trials handler, and author. One of his famous dogs was the pointer Hard Cash. And he trained Jessie Rodfield's celebrated Count Gladstone. An English setter he trained, Pioneer, won the National Bird Dog Championship. In 1906, at New York's Madison Square Garden, Shelley won the Westminster Kennel Club cup for "Best Exhibit of Field Trial Setters."

Born in Michigan, Shelley considered himself as a conservative hunter, a conservationist. "He went dove hunting, and he went deer and duck hunting. He was a sportsman," his daughter, Virginia Shelley Dornan, said in an interview in 2000. "He would get really upset when he saw these people that would go over their limit." On his first trip to Africa with internationally known sportsman Paul Rainey, their safari killed twenty-seven lions. Many of these became "the Rainey group" after their donation to the American Museum of Natural History. From those same safaris, which occurred from 1909 to 1915, two leopard cubs taken from Africa were donated to New York's Bronx Zoo. Based on his African experiences, Shelley self-published *Hunting Big Game with Dogs in Africa*.

Originally, Shelley had joined up with Rainey in Cotton Plant, Mississippi, near New Albany, where William Faulkner's family lived and hunted. In that countryside Shelley met his bride to be, Lucille Wall. He was forty-five, she twenty-one. After marrying, they first lived at Rainey's lodge, but they soon moved to Columbus after scouting locations in Mississippi and Alabama for a place to live, raise a family, and set up dog training. There Shelley found abundant woodlands, loaded with quail, making it especially suitable for training. Shelley bought his bungalow for the equivalent price of two of his top, nationally rated field trial dogs—$5,000.

As Shelley arrived in Columbus in 1921, G. P. Putnam & Sons published what hunting aficionados now consider a classic, *Bird Dog Training Today and Tomorrow*. Over the years, Pruitt took photographs of Shelley and his dogs for books, magazines, and newspapers. For months at a time, Shelley would go to South Carolina to oversee hunting trips for the president of Standard Oil Company of New York, Herbert Pratt, who had a hunting plantation in Ridgeland, South Carolina. For these hunts, Shelley would ship bird dogs and foxhounds from Columbus. Besides training dogs, Shelley pioneered in an emerging business—dog food manufacturing. He built large ovens in bunker-like buildings so his company, Very Best Dog Food, could distribute food throughout the nation. Shelley would secure leftover food from the local Mississippi State College for Women and mix it with cornmeal. "When they started the ovens up," his daughter, Virginia, said, "it smelled so good you felt like you could eat it yourself."

Shelley died in 1957 at age eighty-five. For decades after, the Pruitt panorama continued to hang in the living room of the Shelley home where Virginia lived. The sweeping scale of the photograph depicts Shelley from his Mississippi base of dog-training operations, the king of all he surveys.

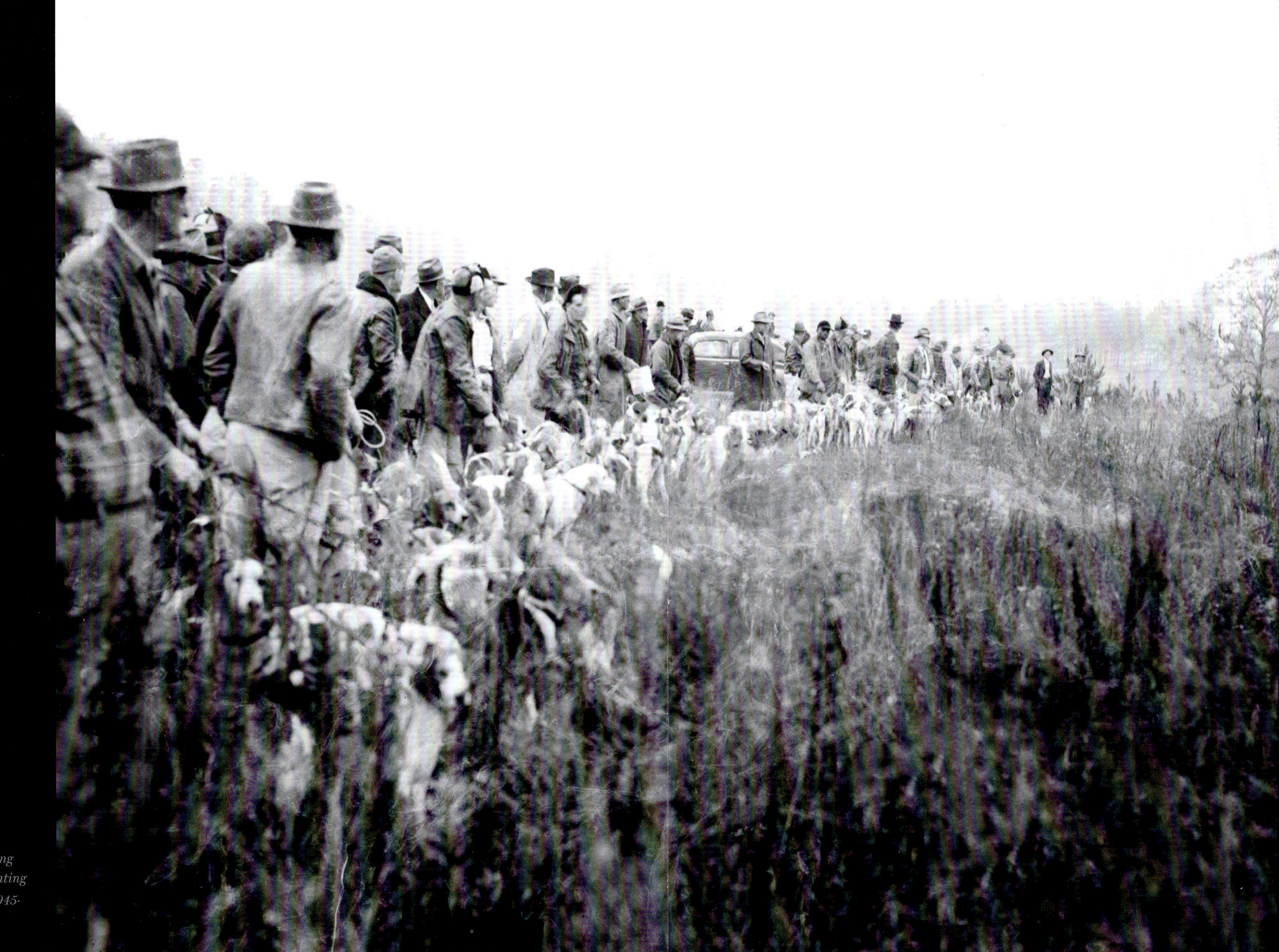

sippi gathering
ewide fox hunting
ation, circa 1945.

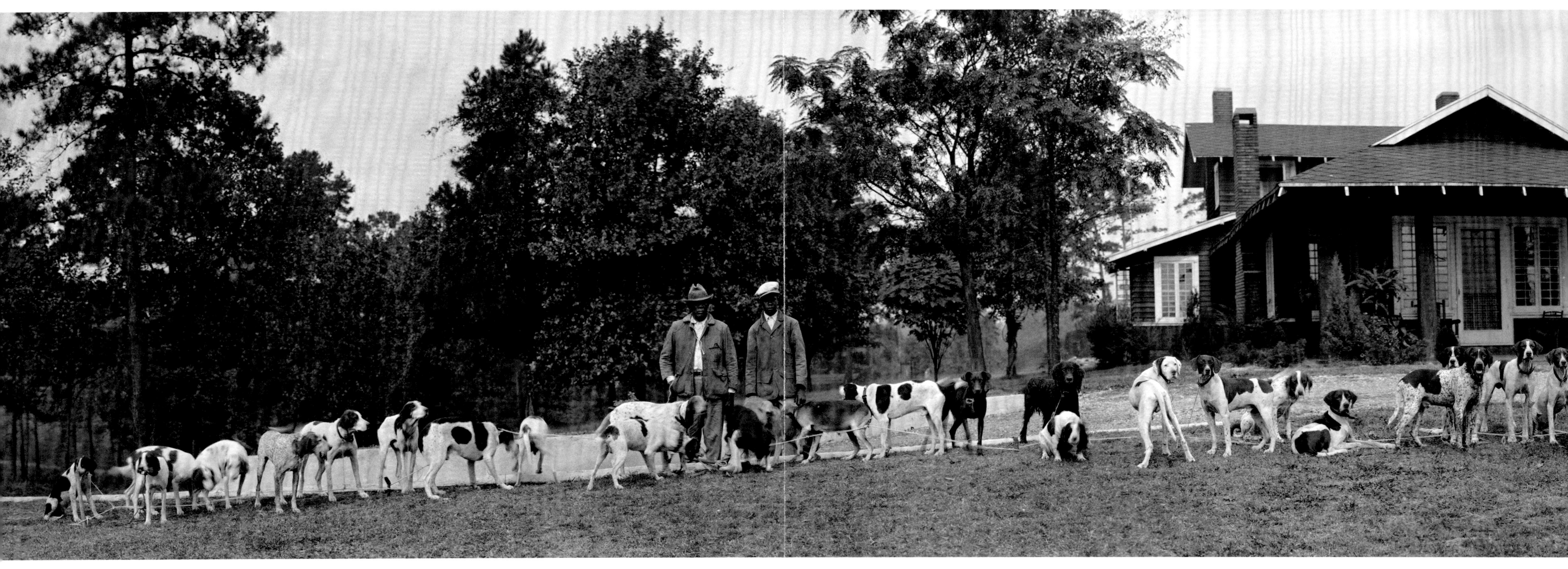

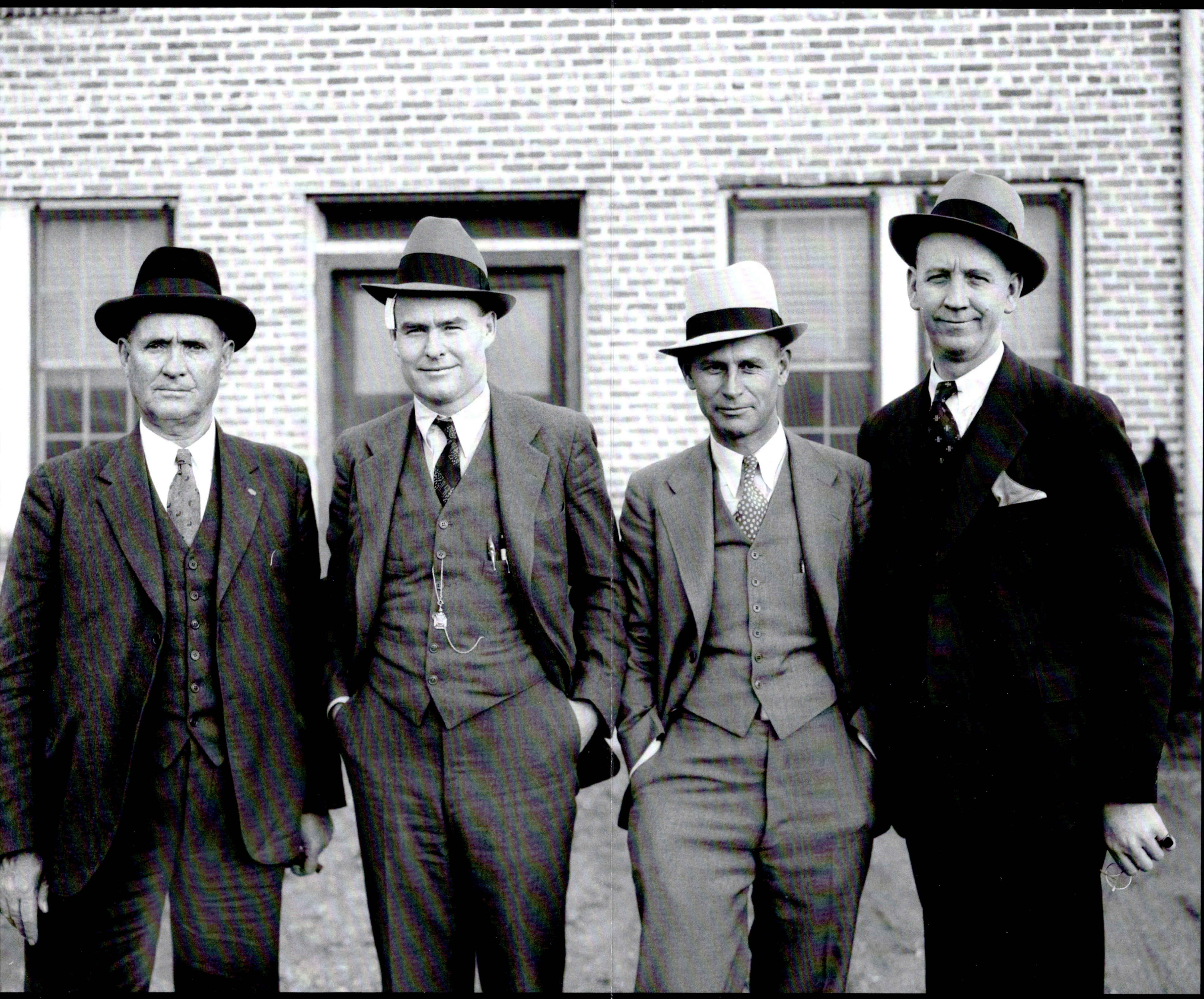

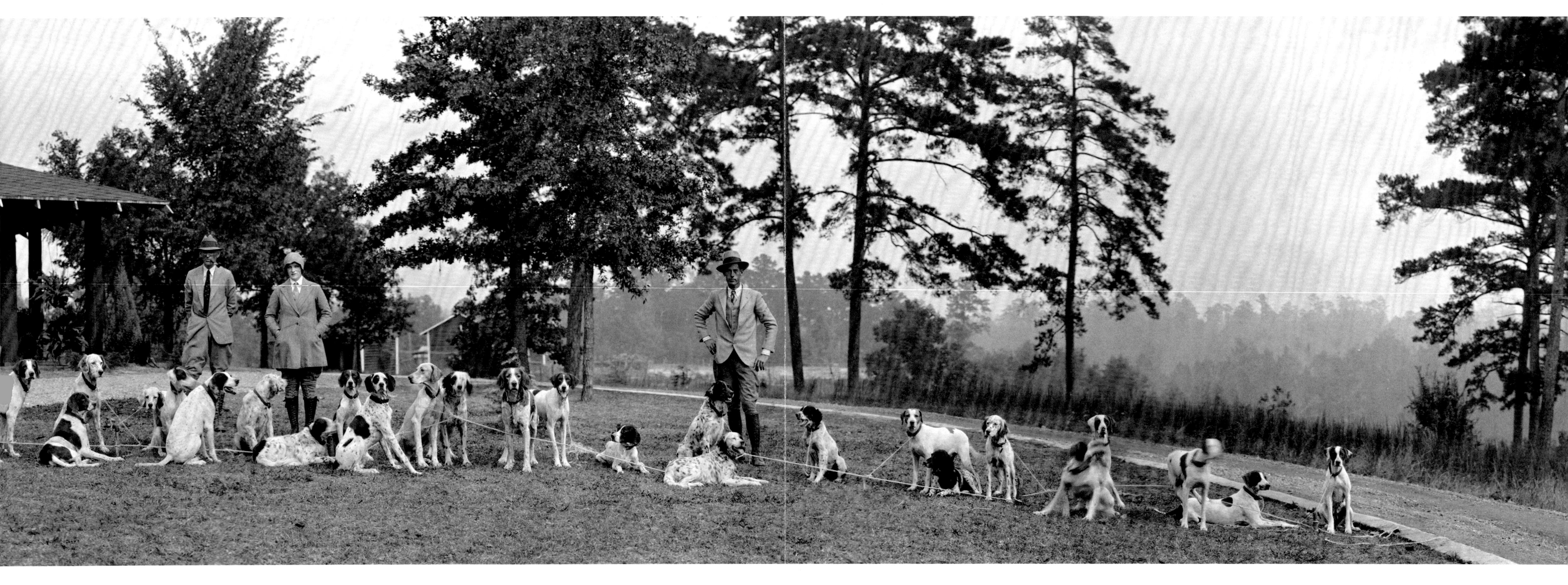

Renowned hunting dog breeder and trainer Er M. Shelley with his wife, Lucille, and three dog trainers, circa 1930.

Newspaper carrier boys, known as "Little Merchants," for the Commercial Dispatch, *outside Main Street office, circa 1928.*

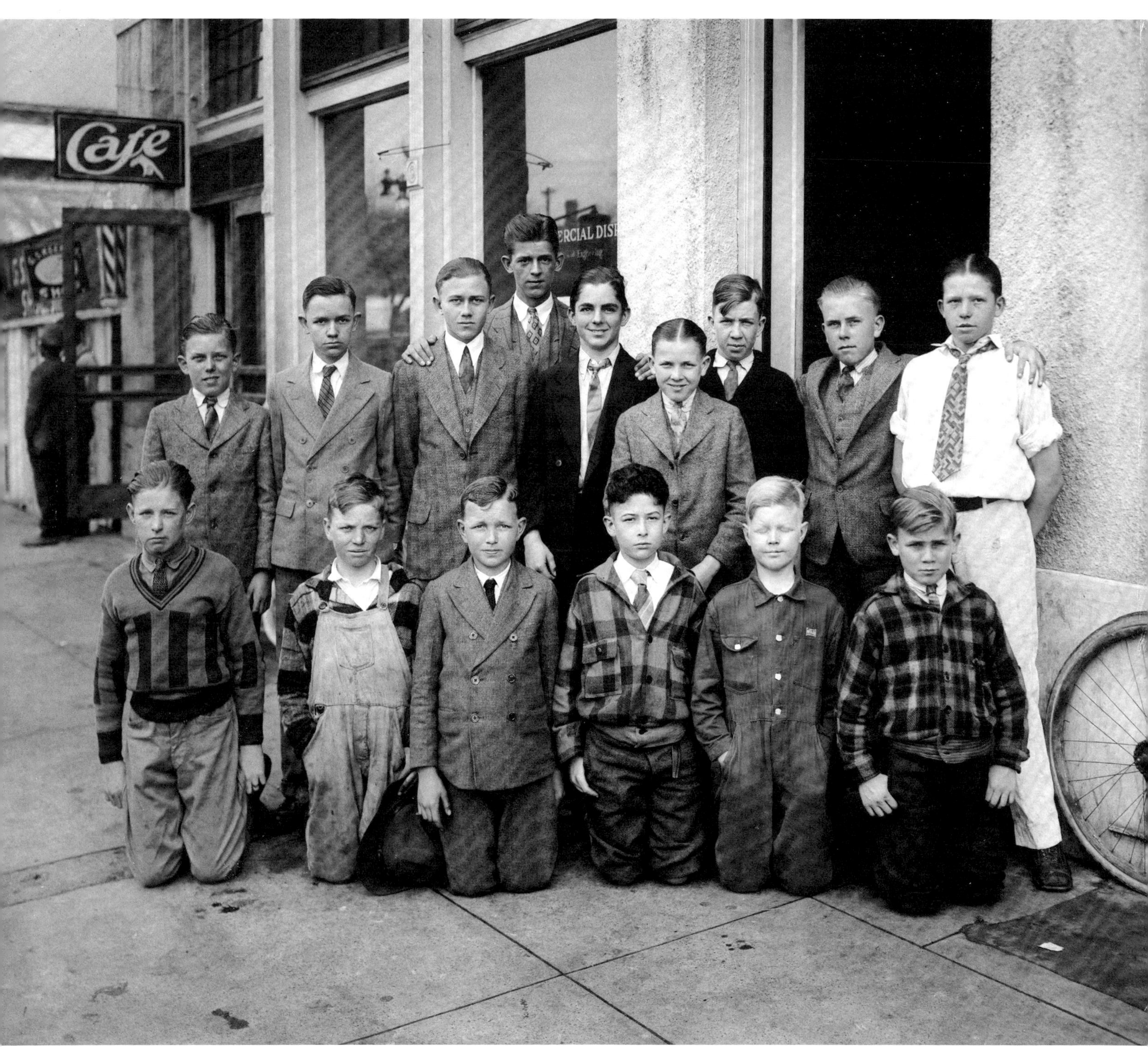

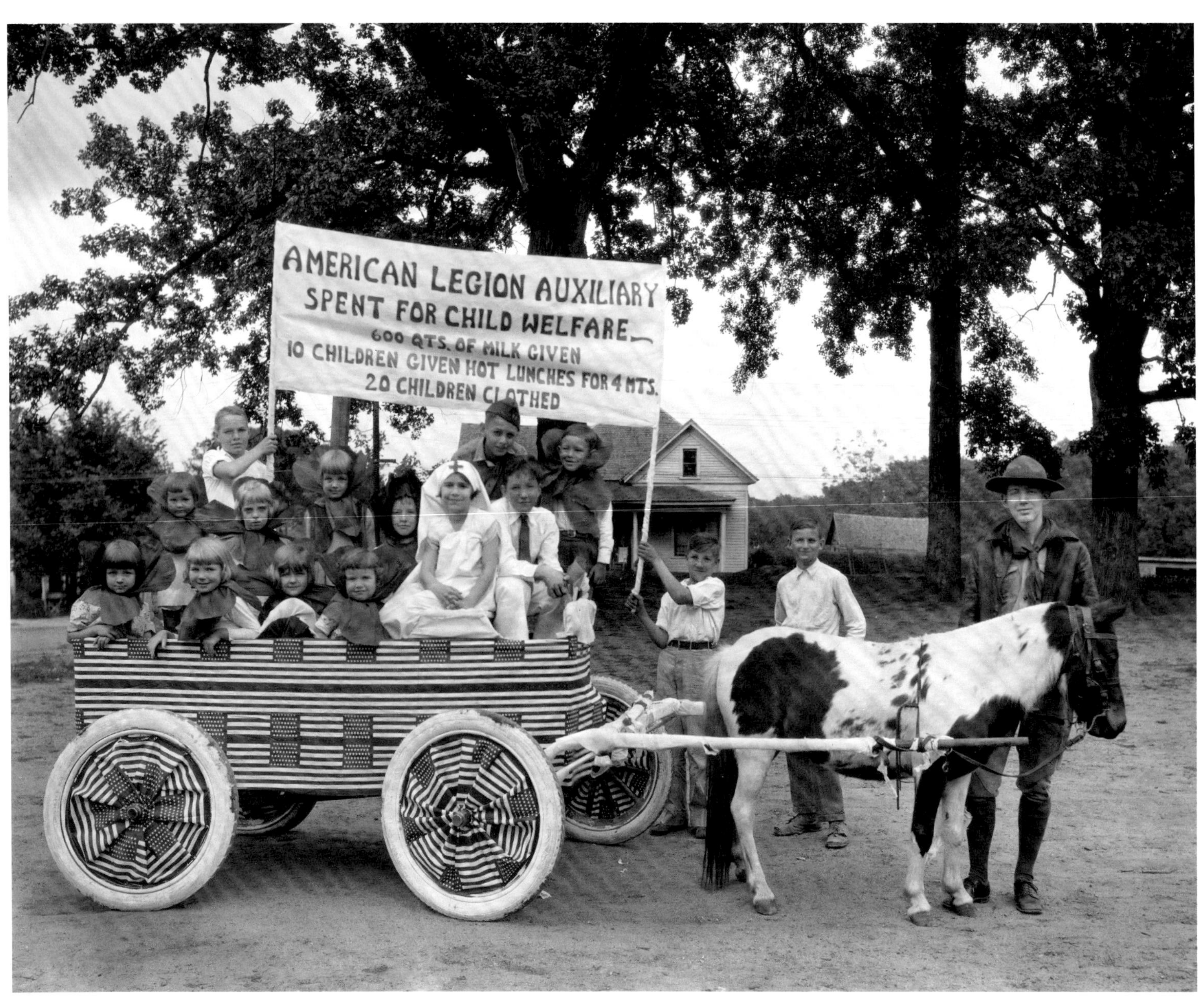
AMERICAN LEGION AUXILIARY
SPENT FOR CHILD WELFARE
600 QTS. OF MILK GIVEN
10 CHILDREN GIVEN HOT LUNCHES FOR 4 MTS.
20 CHILDREN CLOTHED

HAPPY FEED STORE, CIRCA 1925

In a rambling brick building on Main Street, Luther W. Richardson and his wife, Julia Ann Wilson Richardson, operated a dry goods store, grocery, and feed store. At first, they had one store. Prospering in the 1920s, they opened several more, in Columbus and neighboring towns. Richardson's was one of the first local stores to deliver groceries by truck and bicycle. It was a cavernous community gathering place filled with groceries; work and dress clothing for men, women, and children; boots and shoes; supplies for cows, chickens, goats, rabbits, horses, and mules; soft drinks, tobacco, cigarettes, candy, and fishing bait.

In the photograph, the youngest among the nine pictured is Oren Richardson. In 2003, when he was in his eighties and looked at the image, stories emanated from it: an ordinary photograph became extraordinary.

Indicative of the era's race and class strictures, two Black boys stand apart from the whites, holding burlap croaker sacks, apron-like. The photograph likely was part of a publicity campaign for Happy Feed, delivered by train boxcars from its Memphis, Tennessee, headquarters to the Columbus & Greenville Railway station across the street. With his mother, Julia, behind him, Oren is the young white boy, one of his family's six children. In the picture, Richardson's father, Luther, stands on far left.

Prompted by the photograph, Oren spoke of his father's intuitive sales strategy. Two blocks from the store was Mississippi State College for Women. "Two [college] girls came in, and they wanted to look at hose. And [one] liked a pair of hose she thought was really great. And the price on them, I remember, wasn't but a dollar and a half. But she said, 'No. That's not good enough. I want better hose. I want something more expensive.' So my Daddy turns around and pulls out . . . another little box of hose, the same [priced] hose but of a different shade. She said, 'Well, how much are these?' He says, 'These are $3.' [She says:] 'This is what I want.'"

The picture then triggered another story that Richardson had grown up hearing: In the 1920s, Columbus police chief John Morton came to the store looking for two African American men he wanted to arrest. "They didn't work for Daddy . . . they just bought groceries." Before the chief had arrived, the two Black men had run into the store to hide. Luther Richardson knew the men as customers and "good fellows." He knew that they had done nothing worthy of arrest. "Daddy looked at Morton and says, 'They're here. You know they're here. . . . They're in the back of the building.' But, he says, 'You might try to get 'em if you want to. [But] you can't have them.' And so, John Morton decided he wouldn't cross Daddy."

For decades Oren Richardson had kept that Happy Feeds photograph with other Pruitt photographs in a bureau drawer. The visual storehouse reminded him of his past and his family's past, his link to ancestral memories of home. These kinds of family photographs represent what photographic scholar Marianne Hirsch calls "the intersection of private and public history."

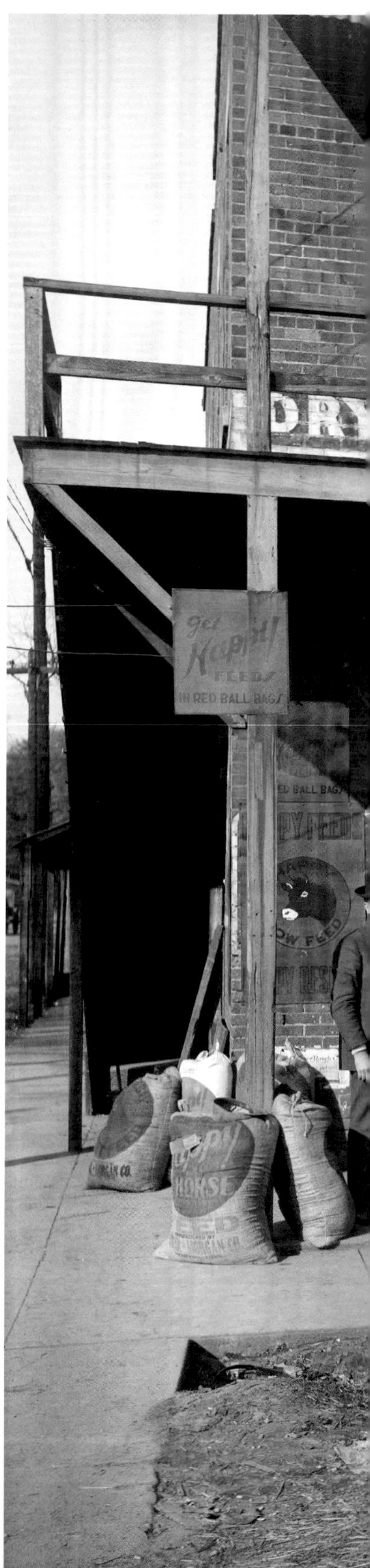

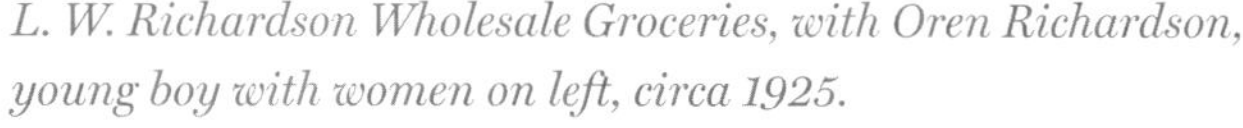
L. W. Richardson Wholesale Groceries, with Oren Richardson, young boy with women on left, circa 1925.

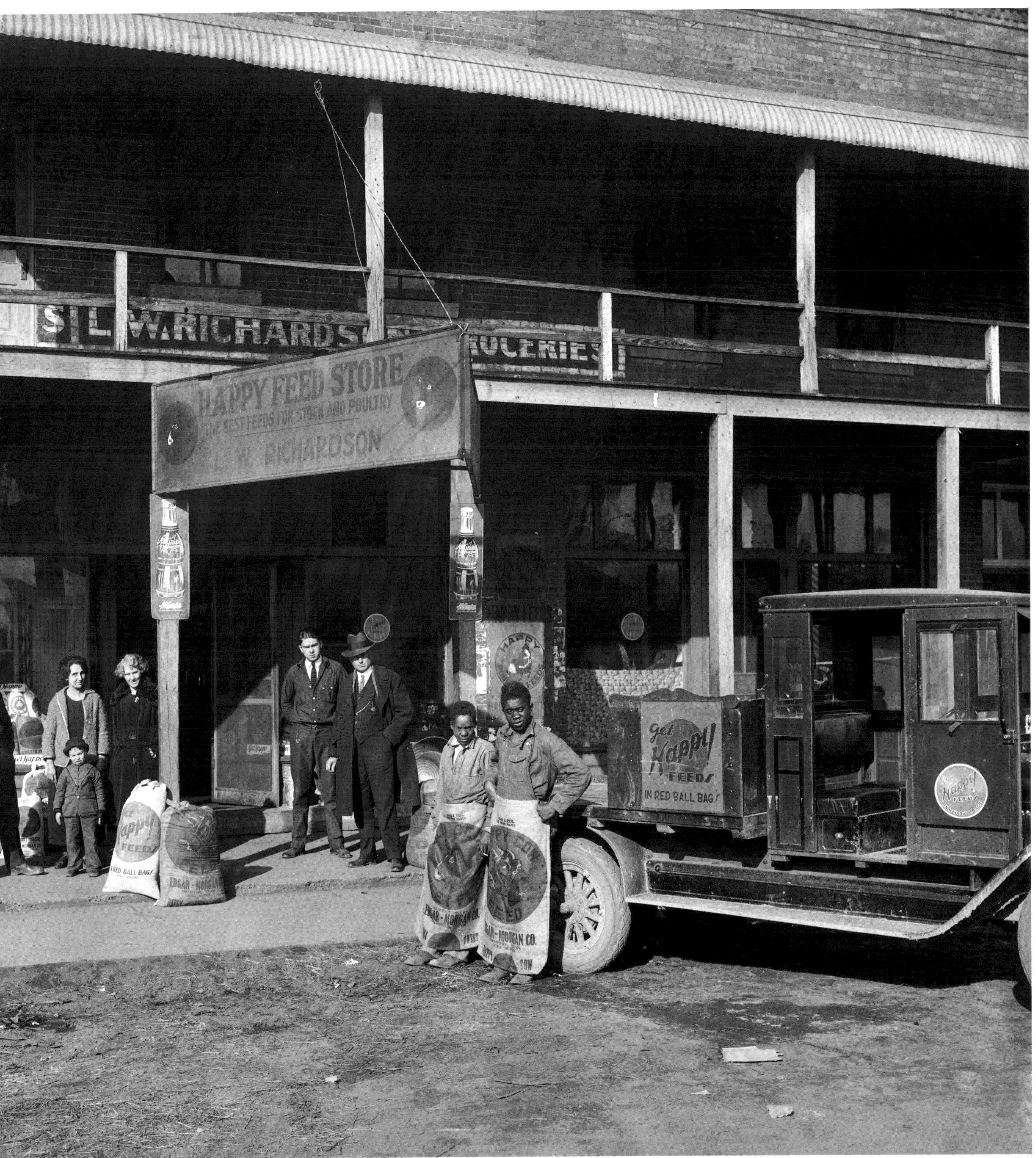
HAPPY FEED STORE
THE BEST FEEDS FOR STOCK AND POULTRY
L. W. RICHARDSON
HAPPY
Get Happy FEEDS
IN RED BALL BAGS
RED BALL BAGS
EDGAR-MORGAN CO.
EDGAR-MORGAN CO.

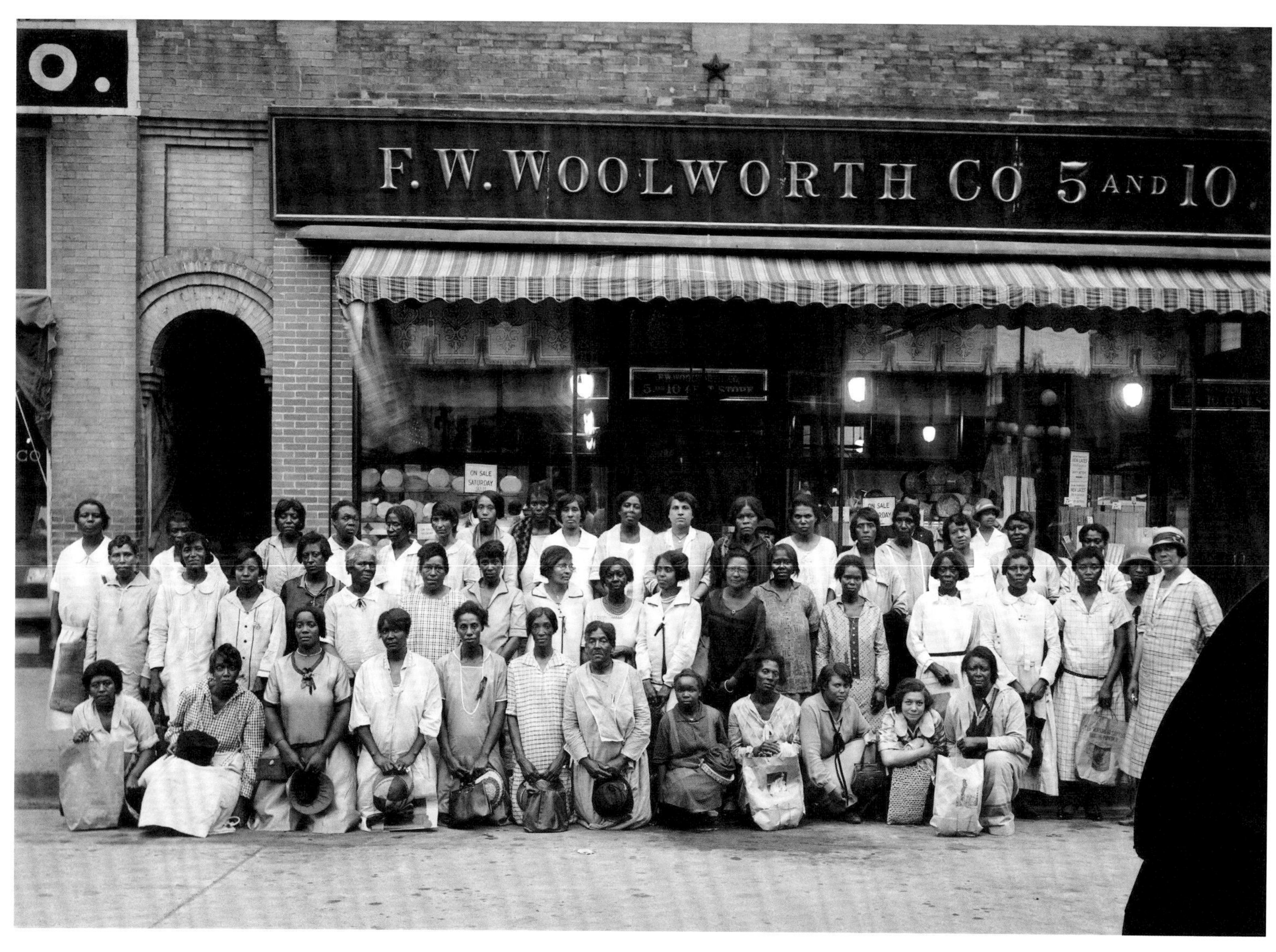

F. W. Woolworth Store, Market Street, circa 1920s.

OSCAR WEST, CIRCA 1930

On a wooden barrel in Pruitt's studio, a young man wears a worn leather jacket. Likely in his late teens, he holds a broom; a tweed cap rests on his knee. He is stoop-shouldered. With confidence and comfort, he looks directly at the camera. His right foot is turned up, revealing his shoe's weathered underside. This Black man is photographed in a white man's studio, the same setting, with the same rug, where white people—the powerful as well as struggling white yeoman farm families—are photographed. This happens in a separate-but-unequal town where Blacks were restricted in where and how they could eat, walk on a sidewalk, drink from a water fountain, shop, see movies, stay overnight in a hotel, or have access to a public restroom.

I found this print among the Pruitt images in 1987. I had no information about the man's identity or the photograph's date. Why Pruitt made the photograph remains a mystery. But in 2000, I discovered the subject's name after showing the photograph to many people in Columbus. Using a once-common term of infantilization, whites and Blacks identified him as "the cleanup boy" for the Brown Buick-Cadillac Company or as the "manservant" for the Floyd Brown family.

I called Mrs. Floyd Brown, Hawley Knox Brown, and she invited me to her Georgian colonial home with its white columns. At over ninety, she had a clear memory. A tiny white woman with a sharp-boned face and immaculately groomed white hair, she lit up when she saw the picture.

"That's Humpy," she declared. He was so named because of an upper back problem, a knot he had his entire life. Then, she spun out a story of Oscar West, his family, his wives and girlfriends. Around the time of this photograph, she employed West to care for her children. He also worked for her husband, Floyd Brown, at the Brown Buick-Cadillac Company. Although she had other Pruitt photographs in her home, Mrs. Brown had never seen this image. "[West] was certainly an honest, good soul. One time he ran across some little children that didn't have any shoes. He ... bought shoes for two little children. No big deals ... just kindness."

With Mrs. Brown's help, I met one of West's nine children, Oscar Lang, an energetic electrician and lover of used Volvos. In his brick ranch-style house, we sat at a table across from one another. As a gift of appreciation, I handed him three prints of his father's picture. Lang had never seen it, and he had no idea why it was made. But he expressed sheer delight to be able to share the picture with his brother and sister. As he looked at his father, he cried.

Then he told one of his favorite stories, how his father inspired one of the Brown children, Floyd Brown Jr., to become an Air Force pilot. A few years after the time of the Pruitt photo, West had taken two wooden milk crates and made an airplane for the then five-year-old Brown. West fashioned a propeller for the crate airplane. Then, spinning it, he said, "All right, now, you're flying.'"

Years later, Brown would become a top-ranking official at the Citadel in Charleston, South Carolina. In the 1960s, on a visit to Columbus, Brown discovered that West was hospitalized. Brown told his mother, "Before I do anything else, I've got to go to the hospital." Brown rushed to see West. "It was a sad occasion for us when he died," Hawley Brown said, "a heart attack in 1964." Some years later, Floyd Brown retired from the Citadel and was living in Charleston. At his home, he hosted Lang, who was living nearby. Brown told Lang, "The reason I'm sitting here now as a retired military colonel, as a flier, is [because of] your Daddy."

The sublimity of the photograph of Oscar West originates from Pruitt's openness and craft, *and* from how West helped to create his own image. The picture compares favorably with ones taken by celebrated as well as lesser-known twentieth-century photographers around the globe. These include Martín Chambi of Peru, Mike Disfarmer of Arkansas, Seydou Keïta of Mali, Doris Ulmann of New York City, Richard Samuel Roberts of South Carolina, and Jno. Trilica of Texas.

(opposite) *Oscar West, circa 1930.*

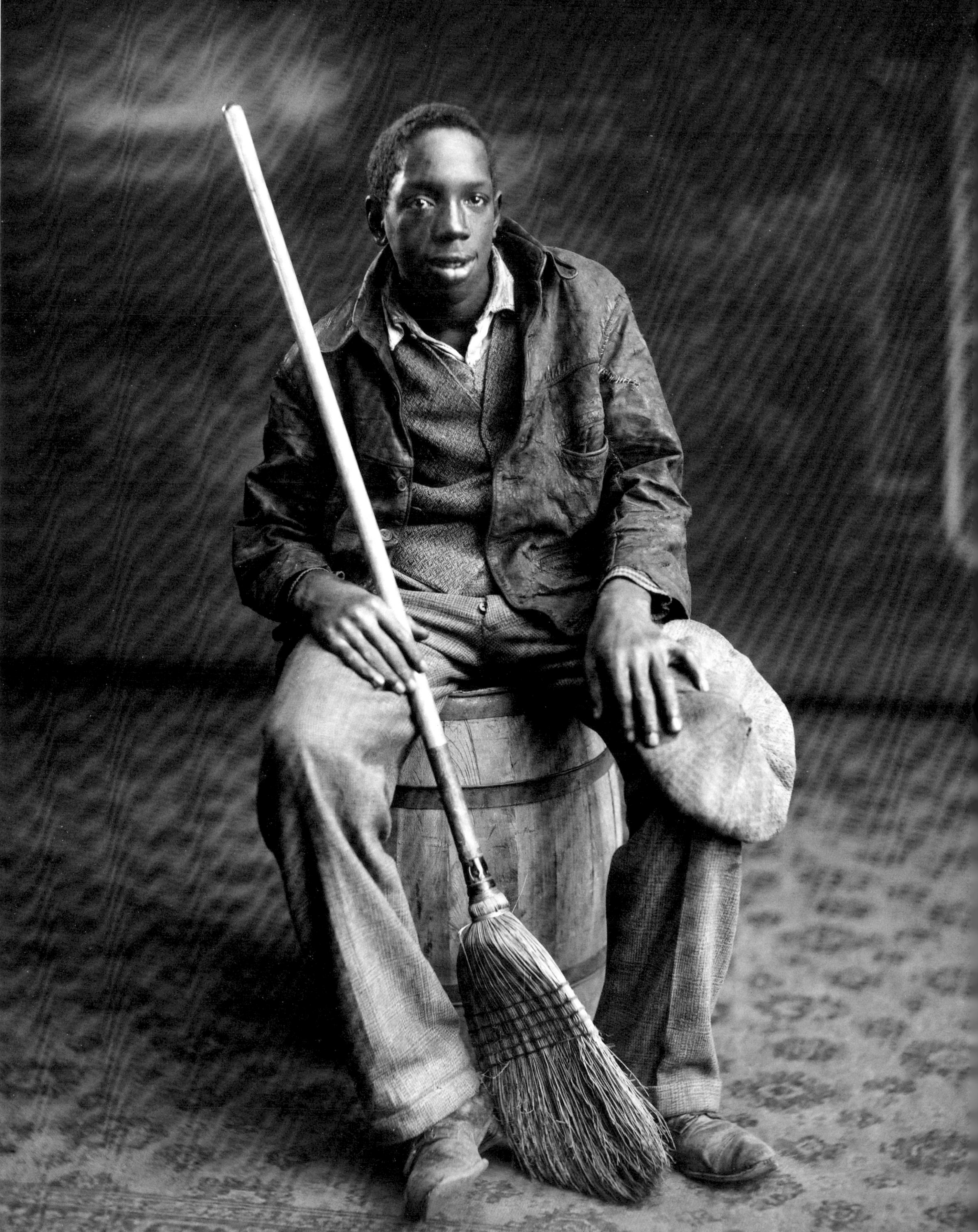

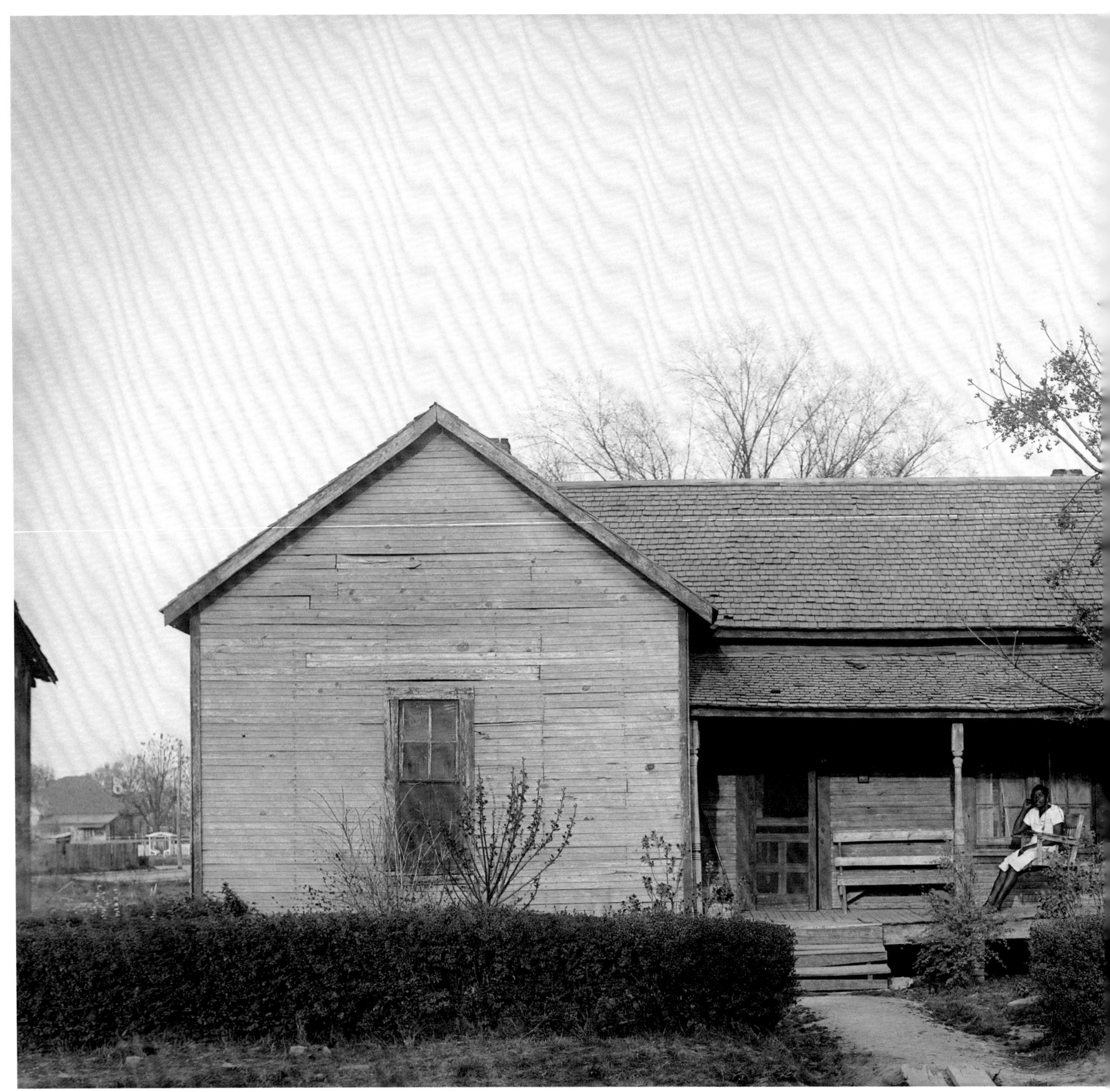

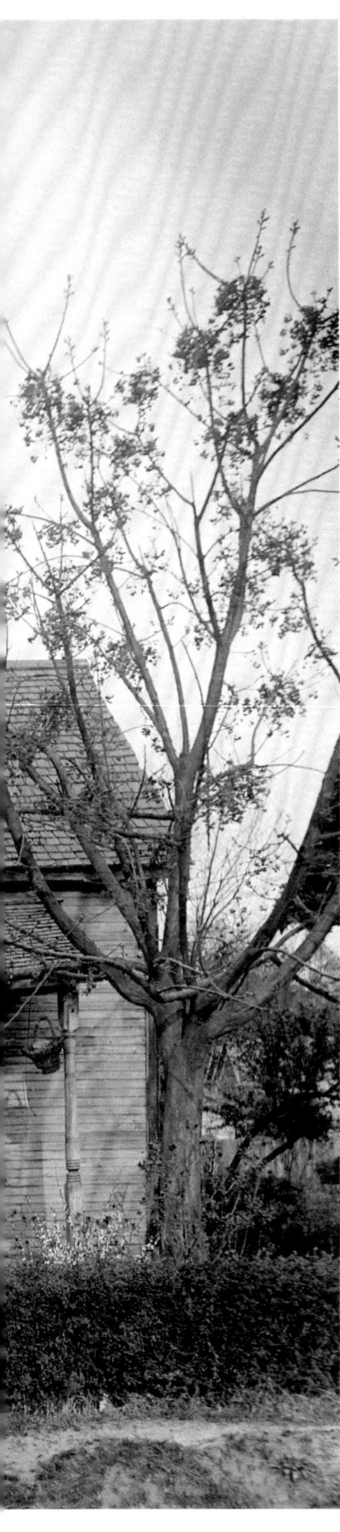

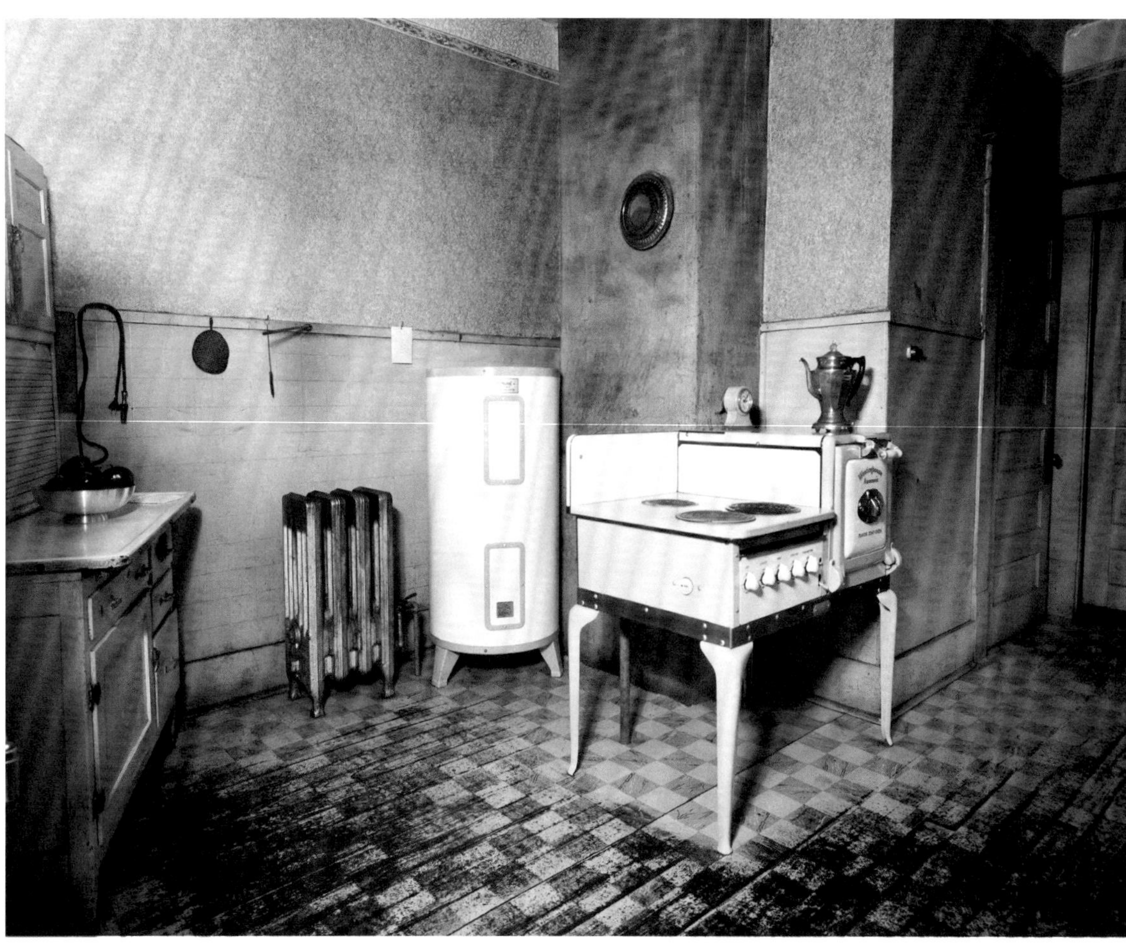

TOUCHED WITH PITY

By the mid-nineteenth century, Columbus was a booming plantation town along the Tombigbee, surrounded by expansive prairie land with black, rich soil ideal for cotton. Steamboats plied the Tombigbee, taking bale upon cotton bale hundreds of miles downriver to Mobile, the Gulf of Mexico, and beyond. During the "Flush Times" between 1830 and 1860, enslaved people from Africa built mansions of brick and wood for white planters. By the 1840s and 1850s, Blacks outnumbered the Anglo-Americans in Columbus and the surrounding area. Then, throughout the Civil War, Columbus found itself in the hurricane's eye of fighting. The closest major battle, Shiloh, was 100 miles north in 1862; thousands of sick and wounded, including Union prisoners, were brought from Shiloh to Columbus to make-shift hospitals and, afterward, from other battles.

In the end, 2,100 Confederate and 40 Union soldiers were buried in Friendship Cemetery by the banks of the Tombigbee. Another 10 Union soldiers, 9 Black and 1 white, were buried in Sandfield, a Black cemetery. According to a 1961 pamphlet of the Columbus chapter of the United Daughters of the Confederacy, four local women, "touched with pity for these dead exiled from home," in 1866 went to Friendship Cemetery to care for the Confederate and Union graves. And "on each wooden marker was placed a chaplet of flowers." This act of commemoration resulted in the creation of one of the nation's earliest

versions of Memorial Day, or "Decoration Day," as the Confederates called it. After reading about the act of kindness by the women in Columbus, New York judge and poet Francis Miles Finch wrote a poem that concludes,

> No more shall the war cry sever,
> Or the winding rivers be red;
> They banished our anger forever
> When they laureled the graves of our dead,
> Under the sod and the dew,
> Waiting the judgement day;
> Love and tears for the Blue,
> Tears and love for the Gray.
>
> ("The Blue and the Gray," *Atlantic Monthly*, September 1867)

Because Columbus was not a site of Civil War fighting, as many as 100 antebellum mansions were preserved, the focus since 1940 of an annual spring Pilgrimage of mansion tours that incorporates textured stories. One story, according to local legend, tells of Jefferson Davis visiting town as president of the Confederacy. One evening, dressed in a nightshirt, Davis addressed a crowd from the balcony of one of the homes. Three decades before, one of those more modest antebellum homes, a two-story brick and wood cottage, had been built by two formerly enslaved Black brothers from South Carolina. Thomas and Isaac Williams had moved to Columbus in 1835. Thomas, a blacksmith, and Isaac, a laborer, pooled their money and, for a premium price, bought two lots one block from Main Street. As the talk of war and secession increased, they apparently feared for their safety, leaving by 1858 and selling their cottage at a loss.

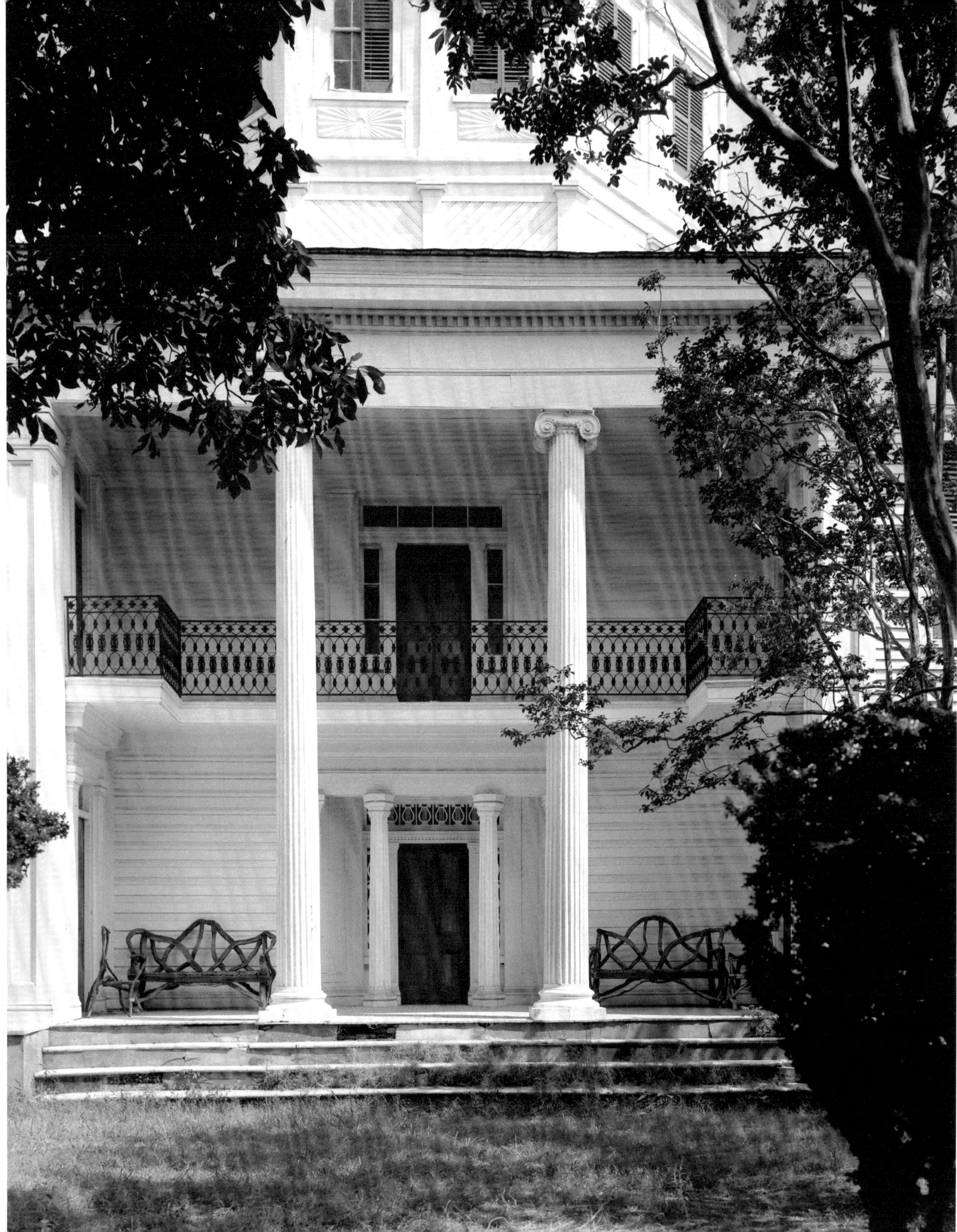

Motorized parade float as part of Decoration Day ceremonies at Friendship Cemetery, circa 1925. In 1866, following the Civil War's end in 1865, flowers were first placed on graves of both Confederate and Union soldiers buried at the cemetery. Focusing especially on the Lost Cause of the Confederacy, the Decoration Day ritual was reenacted annually to commemorate that initial ceremony.

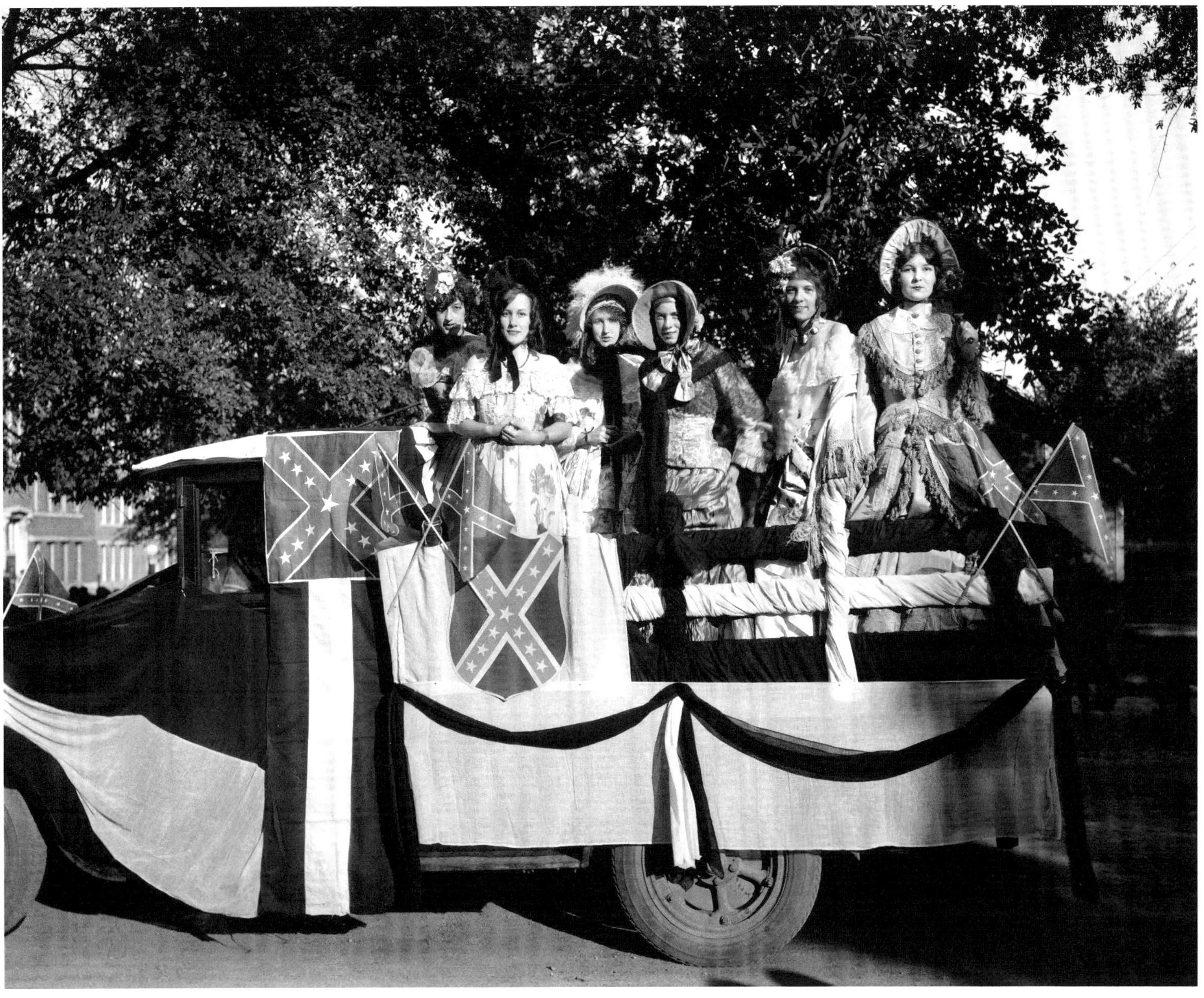

(opposite) *Waverly Plantation, built 1852, on Tombigbee River's western side in Clay County, September 3, 1939.*

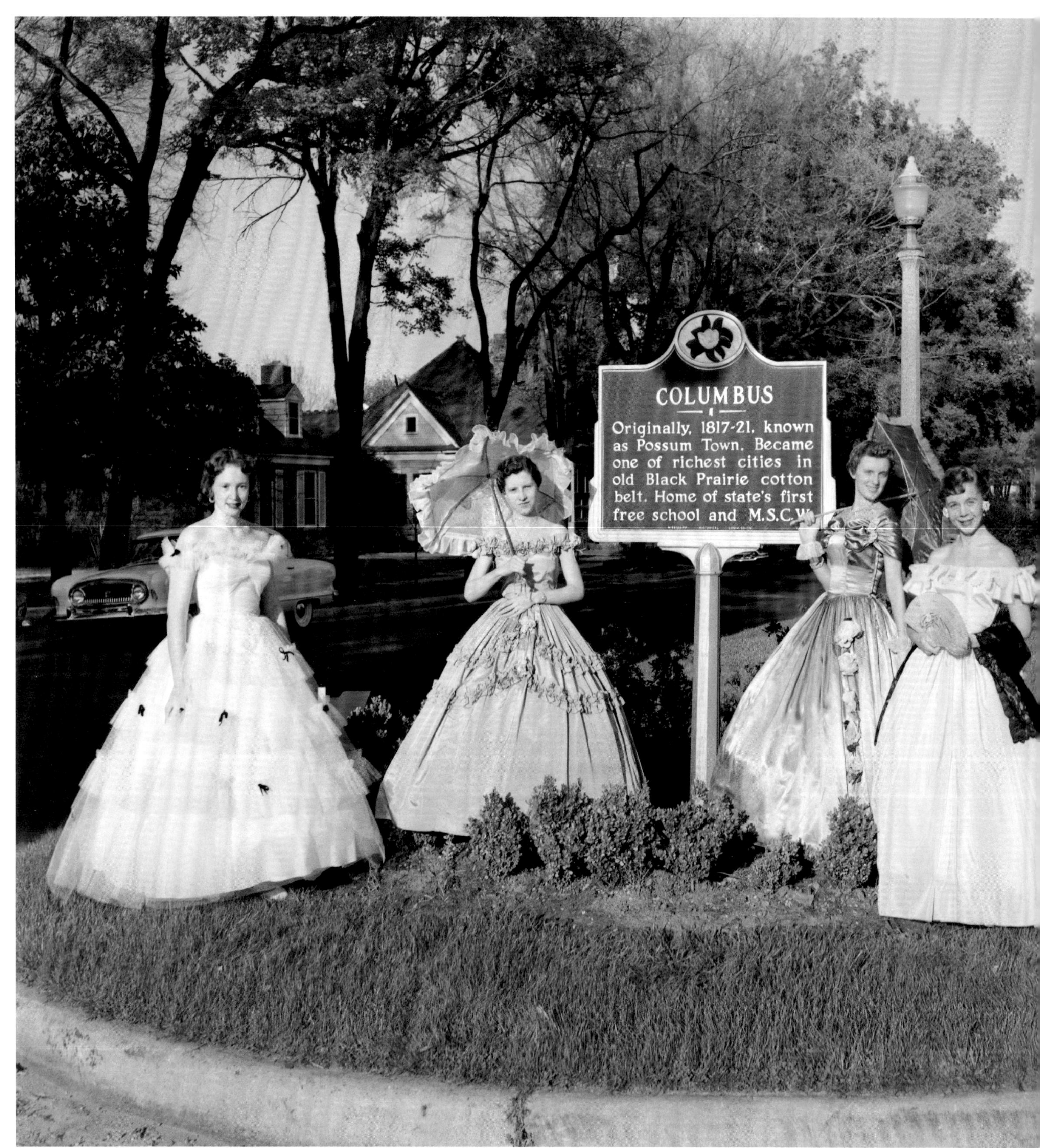
COLUMBUS
Originally, 1817-21, known as Possum Town. Became one of richest cities in old Black Prairie cotton belt. Home of state's first free school and M.S.C.W.

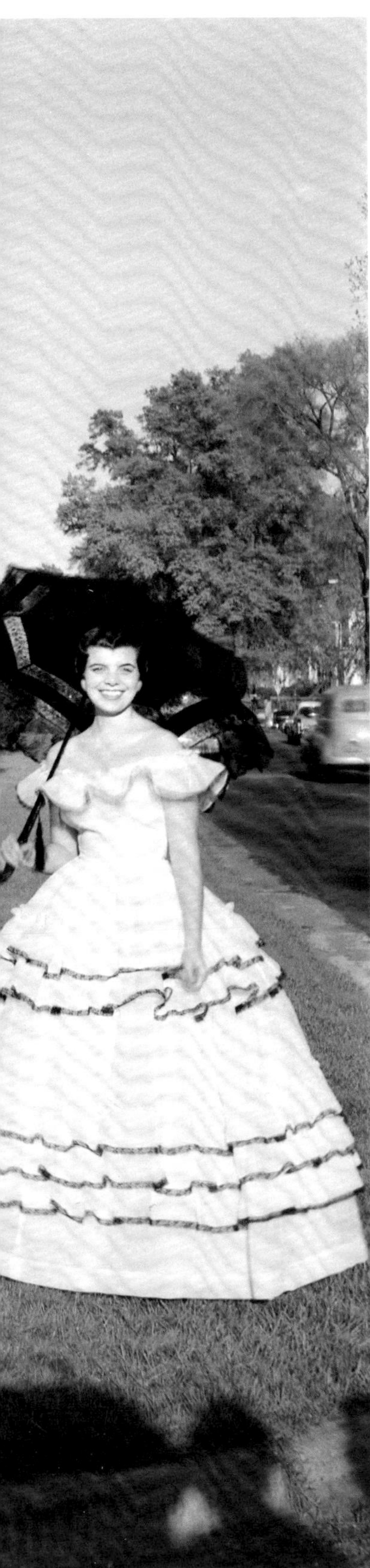

Monument honoring Union and Confederate soldiers who died in the 1864 Battle of Tupelo, circa 1940s.

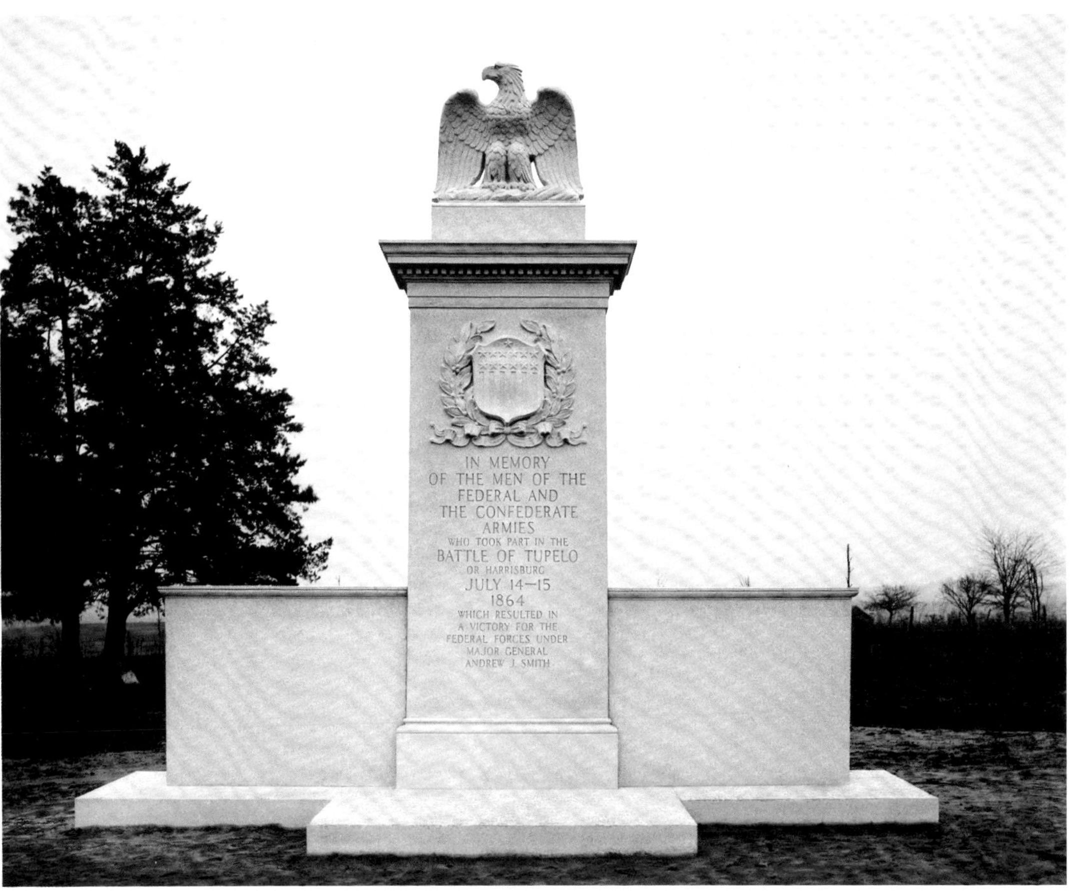

Teenage "hostesses" for annual spring tour of Pilgrimage antebellum homes, circa 1955. From left: *Marjorie Baugh, Emily Fletcher, Paula Harmond, Elizabeth Banks, and Mary Ann Betts. In 1943,* Life *magazine photographer Alfred Eisenstaedt came to town to take pictures of the Pilgrimage's antebellum houses, including Riverview, circa 1847, and Whitehall, circa 1843.*

A CULTURAL CROSSROADS

Tennessee Williams, May 1952

Many a place has its collection of people who achieve celebrity. Pruitt photographed some, though by no means all, of them in northeast Mississippi. During his era, Columbus was a cultural crossroads in terms of who was born, lived, or visited there: folklorist Newbell Niles Puckett (*Folk Beliefs of the Southern Negro*, University of North Carolina Press: 1926), born 1898; sportscaster Walter Lanier “Red” Barber, voice of the Brooklyn Dodgers when Jackie Robinson broke the color line, born 1908; playwright Tennessee Williams, born 1911; world champion boxer Henry Jackson Armstrong, born 1912; and bluesmen Big Joe Williams (“Baby, Please Don’t Go”), born about 1903, and Howlin’ Wolf, born 1910, near West Point. Nearby Aberdeen was home to Bukka White (“Columbus, Mississippi Blues”), born circa 1904, and Albert King, born 1923. Sixty miles away, in Tupelo, Elvis Presley was born in 1935. Author Truman Capote’s parents came to Columbus in 1930 with former heavyweight champion Jack Dempsey.

Edward L. Kuykendall, proprietor of one of the four Columbus movie theaters, was, in the 1930s and 1940s, president of the Motion Picture Theatre Owners of America. In that same era, as a young man, John C. Stennis served as the local district attorney. An advocate for segregation, he would become one of the twentieth century’s most powerful U.S. senators. The first woman to become secretary of the Democratic National Committee, Dorothy McElroy Vredenburgh Bush, lived in Columbus in the 1920s, and in 1938 graduated from Mississippi State College for Women, America’s first public college for women. By 1944 she was appointed to the post that she held through the 1970s, regularly presiding over

Democratic national conventions. By 1950, African American dentist Emmett J. Stringer came to Columbus to set up his practice in Catfish Alley; he was president of Mississippi's NAACP.

In the 1920s, when Charles Henri Ford's father ran the Gilmer Hotel, Ford lived there as a teenager. That's when in 1927 the *New Yorker* magazine published his poem "Interlude." Soon after, he started a magazine that, incredibly, published William Carlos Williams, Ezra Pound, Ford Madox Ford, and Gertrude Stein. Barely twenty-one after publishing his initial volume of *Blues: A Magazine of New Rhythms*, he headed to New York, then Paris. By 1933 he coauthored a homoerotic novel, *The Young and Evil*, banned by the United States, Canada, and England. To this day Ford is considered one of America's original surrealist poets, if not its first. As a college student, Eudora Welty in the 1920s attended Mississippi State College for Women. Later, she corresponded with Ford about their common love of literature. A publisher, filmmaker, artist, and photographer, Ford lived for many years in Manhattan's Dakota apartments. So did his sister Ruth, three years his junior, who also had lived in Columbus and became a Broadway and film star. A friend of Faulkner, whom she met while she studied at the University of Mississippi, she performed in 1959 on Broadway in Faulkner's *Requiem for a Nun*, which she co-authored with him. Faulkner himself stayed at the Gilmer, often visiting Columbus because his stepchildren's grandparents lived there.

Among the most distinguished of Pruitt's subjects, Tennessee Williams, and his maternal grandfather, the Reverend Walter E. Dakin, visited Columbus in May 1952. They had driven from Key West, Florida, in a convertible Jaguar. At the time, Williams was forty-one, his grandfather, ninety-five.

Williams's link to Columbus originated in 1905 when Rev. Dakin and his family, including daughter Edwina, moved there so he could serve as rector of St. Paul's Episcopal Church. The next year in Columbus, Edwina met a traveling businessman, C. C. Williams. Soon they married and left for the Gulf Coast. Within two years Edwina returned to Columbus, where she gave birth to her first child, Rose, in 1909. (Troubled emotionally and eventually subjected to a lobotomy, Rose became the model for Laura in *The Glass Menagerie*. Edwina herself served as the basis for Amanda Wingfield, a character in the same play.) C. C. traveled around the South and developed into a drinker, womanizer, and gambler. On Palm Sunday, March 26, 1911, Edwina gave birth to Thomas Lanier Williams.

Williams would identify Columbus as part of his mother's world. As the photo suggests, Williams was close to his maternal grandfather, a well-read man whose library had served as a refuge for Williams. Not insignificantly, in 1952, Williams and his grandfather had traveled to Columbus on "Eight o' May" weekend. Although President Abraham Lincoln issued the Emancipation Proclamation on January 1, 1863, it was not until federal troops arrived in Columbus on May 8, 1865, after the end of the Civil War, that slavery officially ended there. For decades, Blacks—and eventually some whites—in Columbus celebrated May 8 as Emancipation Day and as a holiday, a day off, for Blacks, domestic workers especially. The celebration included a jubilant parade. In acknowledgment that Black cooks and maids do not work on Eight o' May, the white women of St. Paul's serve lunch on that day to parishioners and community members.

Williams's mother, Edwina, searched for an explanation for what critic Brooks Atkinson called Tennessee's "terrifying knowledge of the secrets of the mind." She recalled when Tom, as she called him, was a two-year-old in Columbus: The sweat of a summer's day weighed down his curls as he dug with a spade in the rectory yard, and she called out to ask him what he was doing. He replied in the plantation dialect he was learning from his Black nurse, Ozzie, "Diggin' to de debbil."

Tom, his mother said, had taken to heart Ozzie's stories of the devil's lair, found deep in the earth. He looked for that lair for the rest of his life. She recalled a scrap of paper on which her son had written, "And in the evenings, when the white moonlight streamed over our bed, before we were asleep, our Negro nurse Ozzie, as warm and black as a moonless Mississippi night, would lean over our bed, telling in a low, rich voice her amazing tales about foxes and bears and rabbits and wolves that behaved like human beings."

On Williams's 1952 visit, the *Commercial Dispatch* column "The Snooper," written by Rachel Shute (who worked for Pruitt retouching photographs) noted, "The literati and illiterati buzzed around excitedly this weekend at having none other than famed playwright Tennessee Williams in their midst." In an elegiac newspaper account, *Commercial Dispatch* reporter Douglas Bateman wrote, "When told of the wealth of material for stories ... which could be conjured from Columbus's colorful characters and the folklore lying idle in the corners of its ante-bellum homes, Mr. Williams laughed gaily and declared: 'I believe I have met some of them already.'"

At the time of this visit, Williams already had won a Pulitzer and the New York Drama Critics Circle award. *The Glass Menagerie* and *A Streetcar Named Desire* had been staged in New York. *Streetcar* had been made into a feature film. Williams later somewhat would pattern Nonno, a character in *The Night of the Iguana*, after Rev. Dakin. "I assure you that the South is the country of my heart as well as my birth," Williams said. "If I were writing about Yankees, I promise you would find every bit as much 'damnation' among them—and not as much charm!"

In 2003, Chebie Gaines Bateman, for decades the head librarian of the Columbus–Lowndes County Public Library, recalled Williams's visit. "I saw a side of Tennessee Williams that I would venture to say was rarely ever seen, and by that, I mean, he was on his best possible behavior. He was not drinking heavily, and he was very modest when people would come up ... everyone wanted to talk to Tennessee ... and hear about his writing and just chat.... [But] he always stepped back and let the Reverend Dakin ... have center stage. The words that describe [Williams's] demeanor toward his grandfather was one of love and tenderness."

Pruitt's pictures of Williams, although not stunning, do what photographs can do: they document. In this case, a famous native son with his grandfather upon their homecoming. "The last I saw of them, I'll never forget, was from the old Gilmer Hotel," Bateman said. "We went outside, and Tennessee and the Reverend Dakin both had on little caps. The top was down [on the Jaguar], and they headed west down River Hill to cross the Tombigbee River Bridge, and that's the last I ever saw of either one of them."

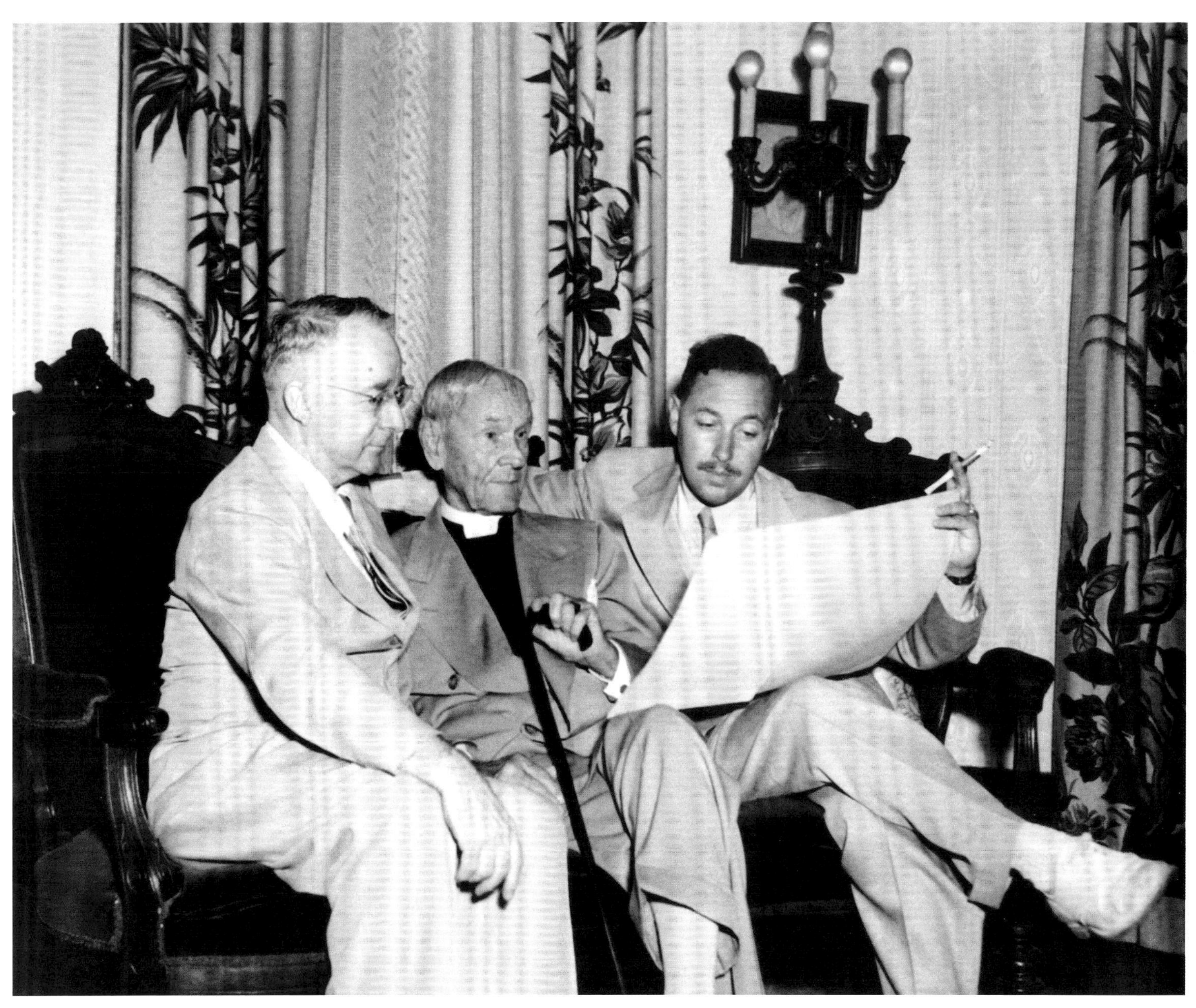

Playwright Tennessee Williams (right) *and his maternal grandfather, Rev. Walter Dakin, during a visit to Columbus, where Williams was born, with Davis Patty* (left) *at Patty's home on Seventh Street South, May 1952. Reverend Dakin had been rector at St. Paul's Episcopal Church. Davis Patty, a banker, was a lay leader of the church.*

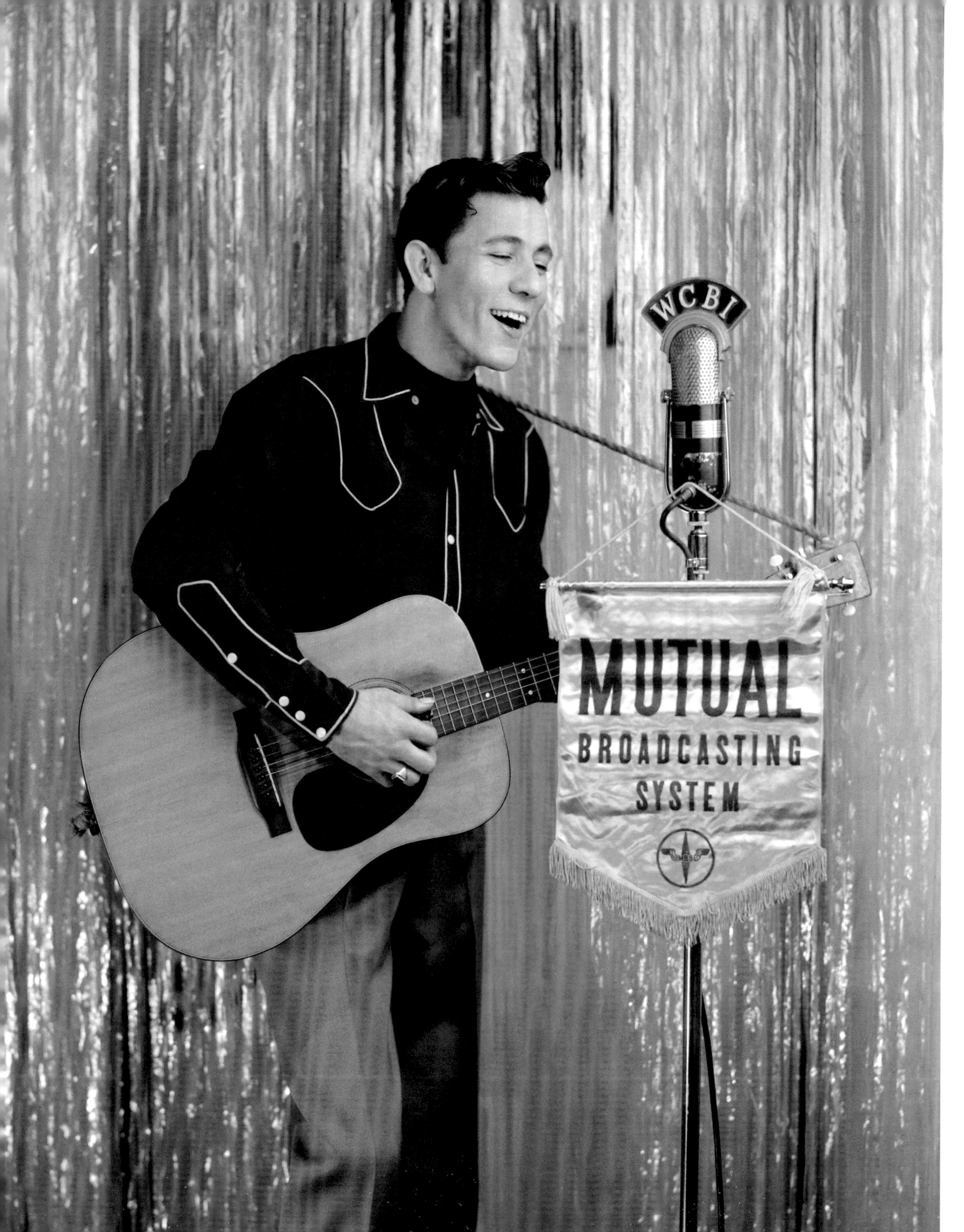
WCBI
MUTUAL
BROADCASTING
SYSTEM

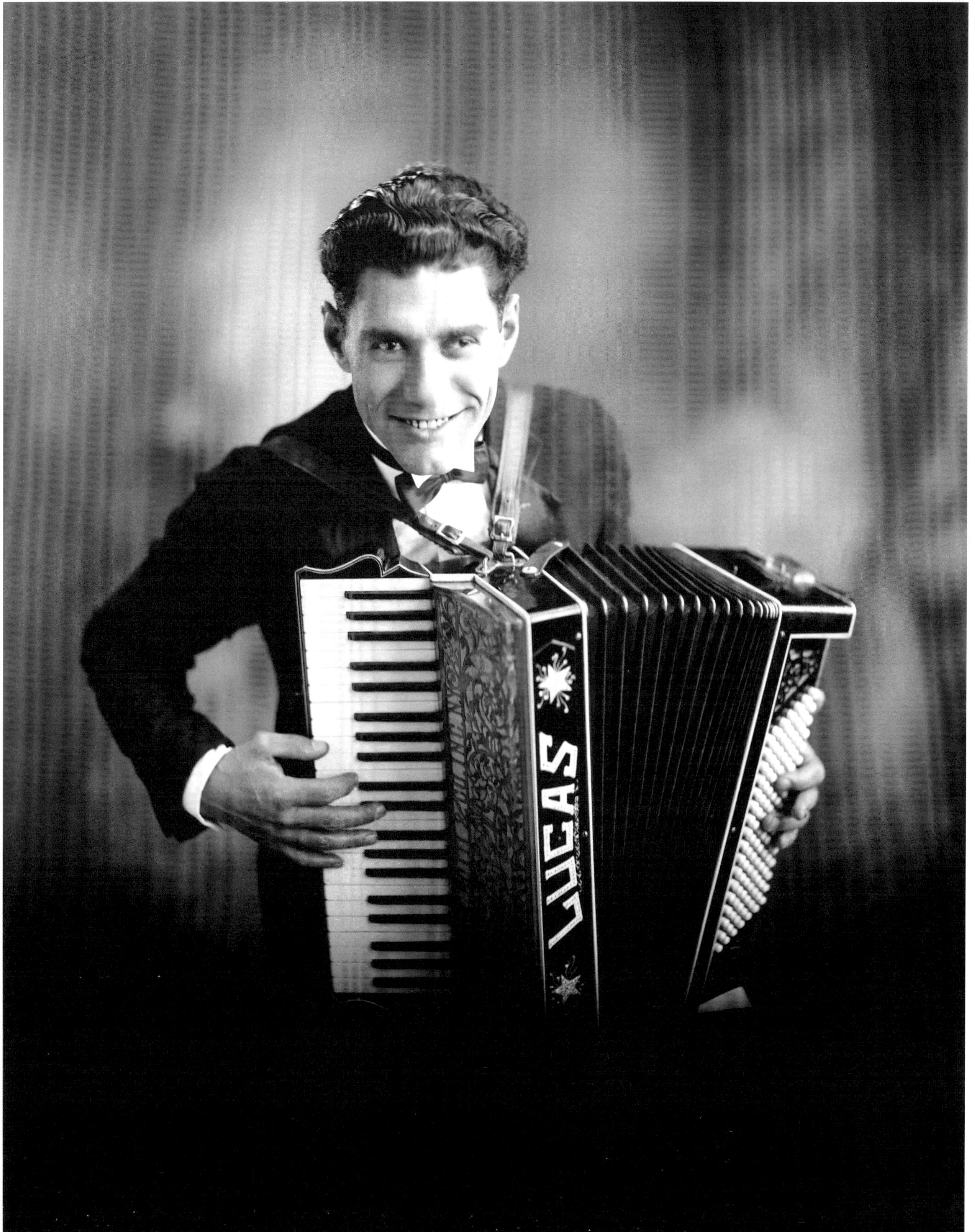
LUCAS

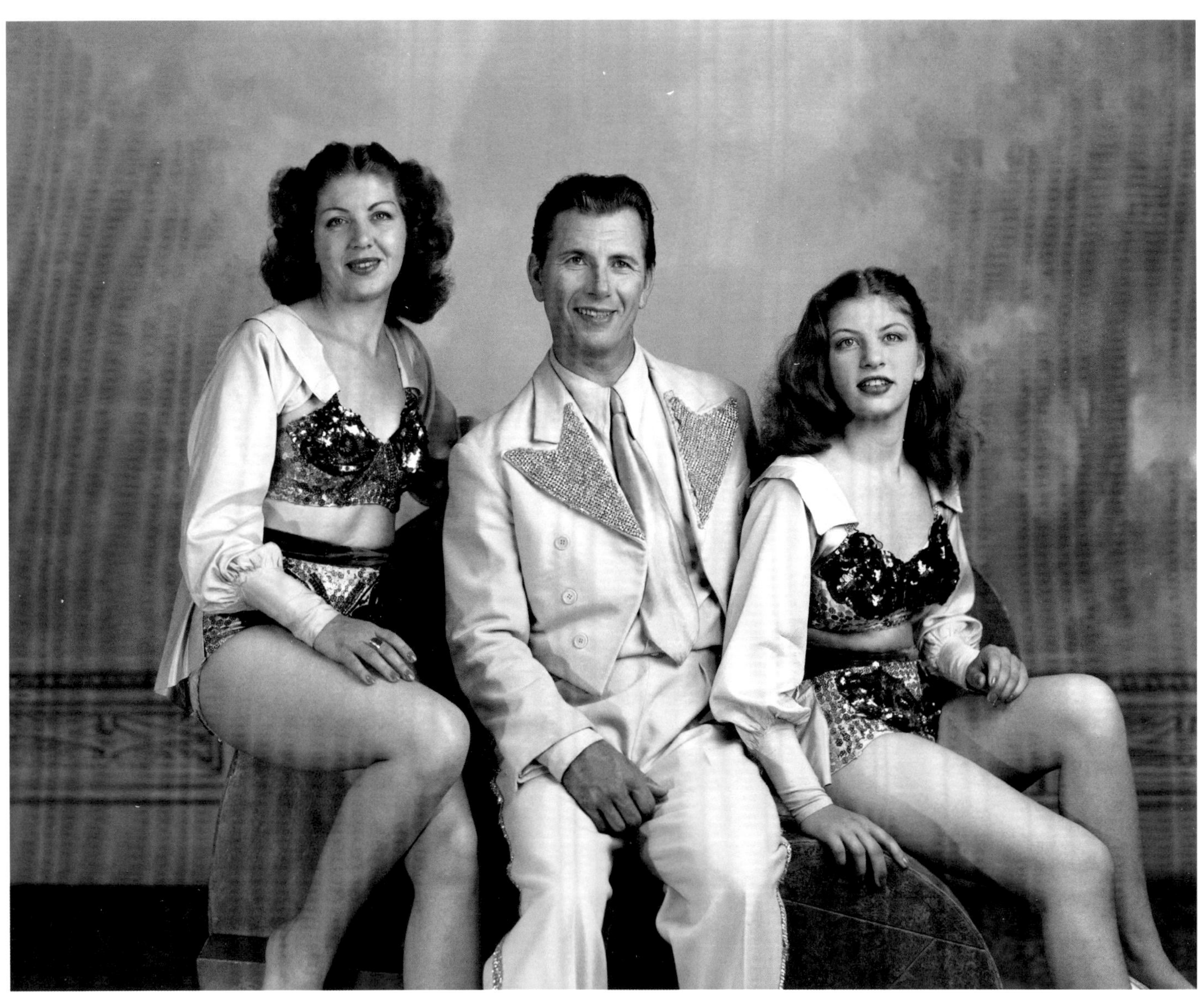

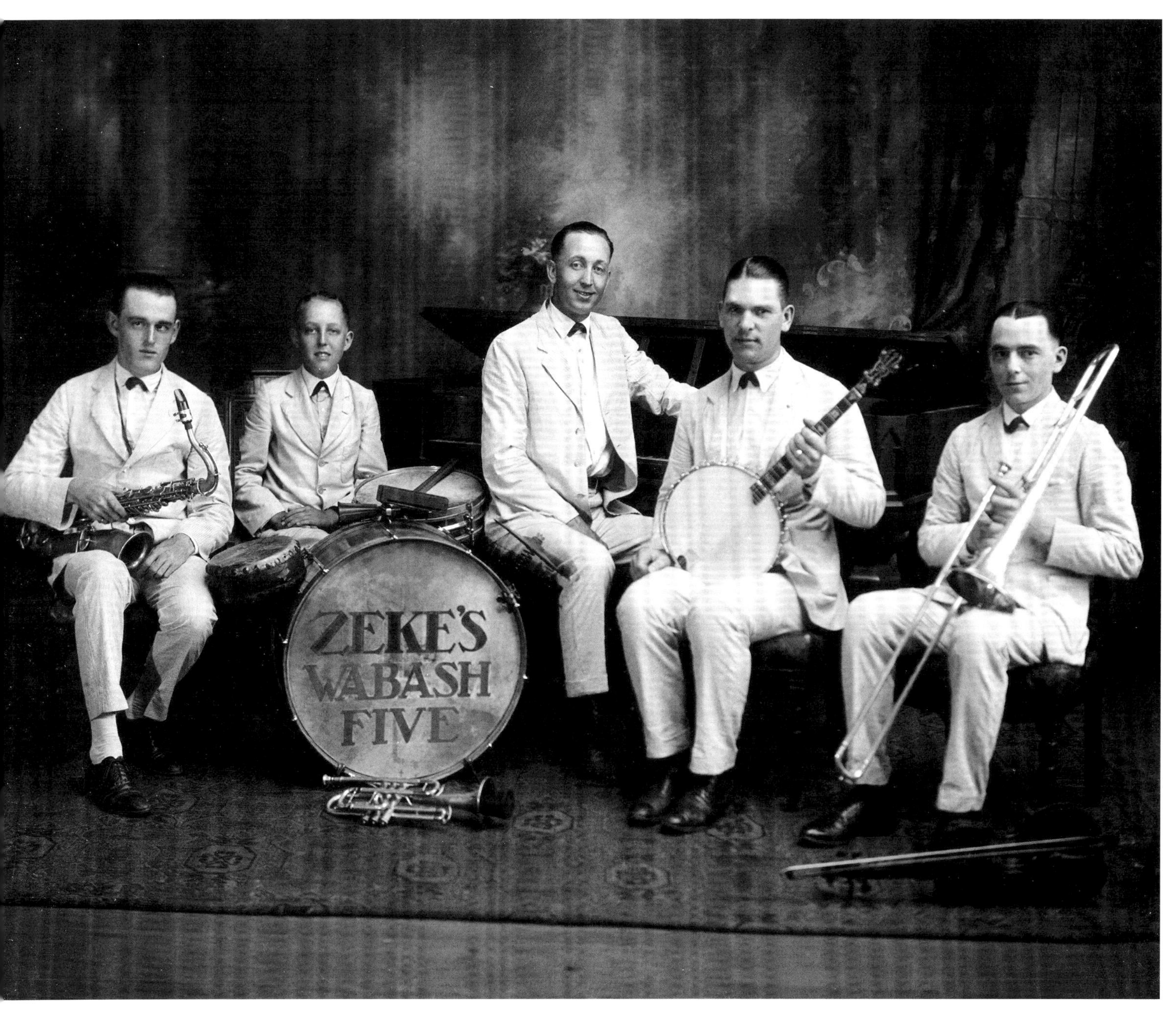
ZEKE'S
WABASH
FIVE

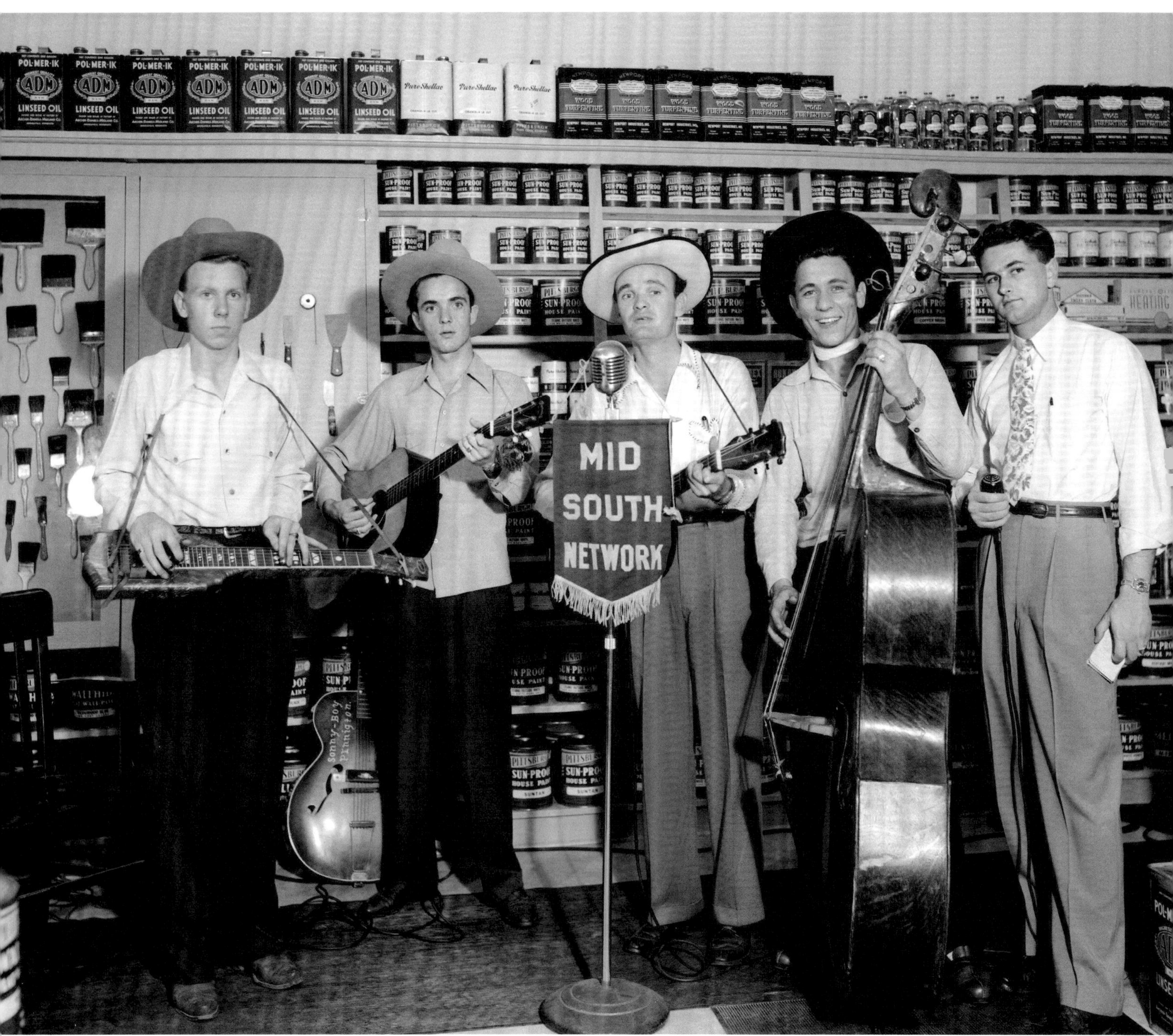
POL-MER-IK
ADM
LINSEED OIL
Pure Shellac
WOOD TURPENTINE
SUN-PROOF
HOUSE PAINT
MID
SOUTH
NETWORK

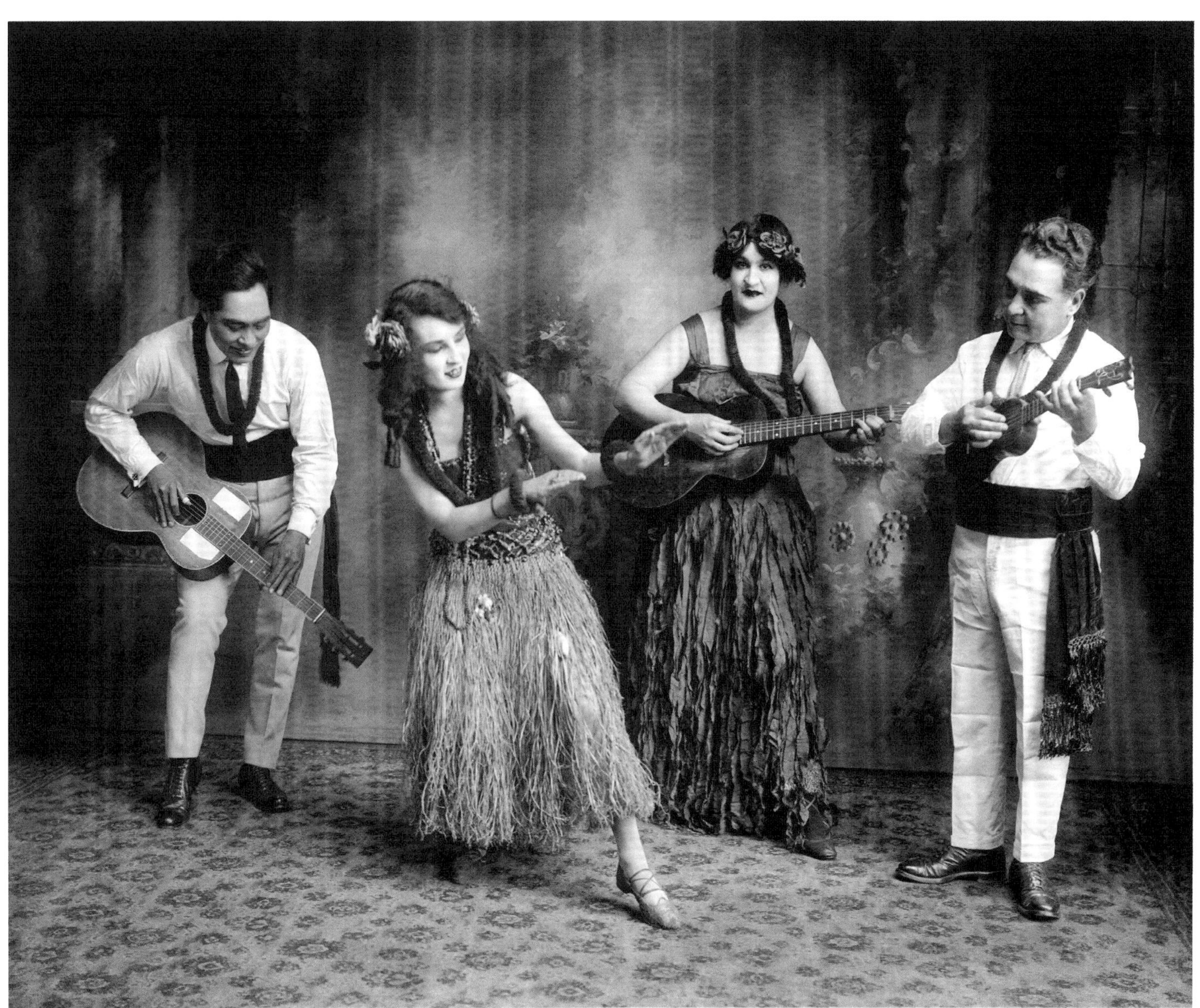

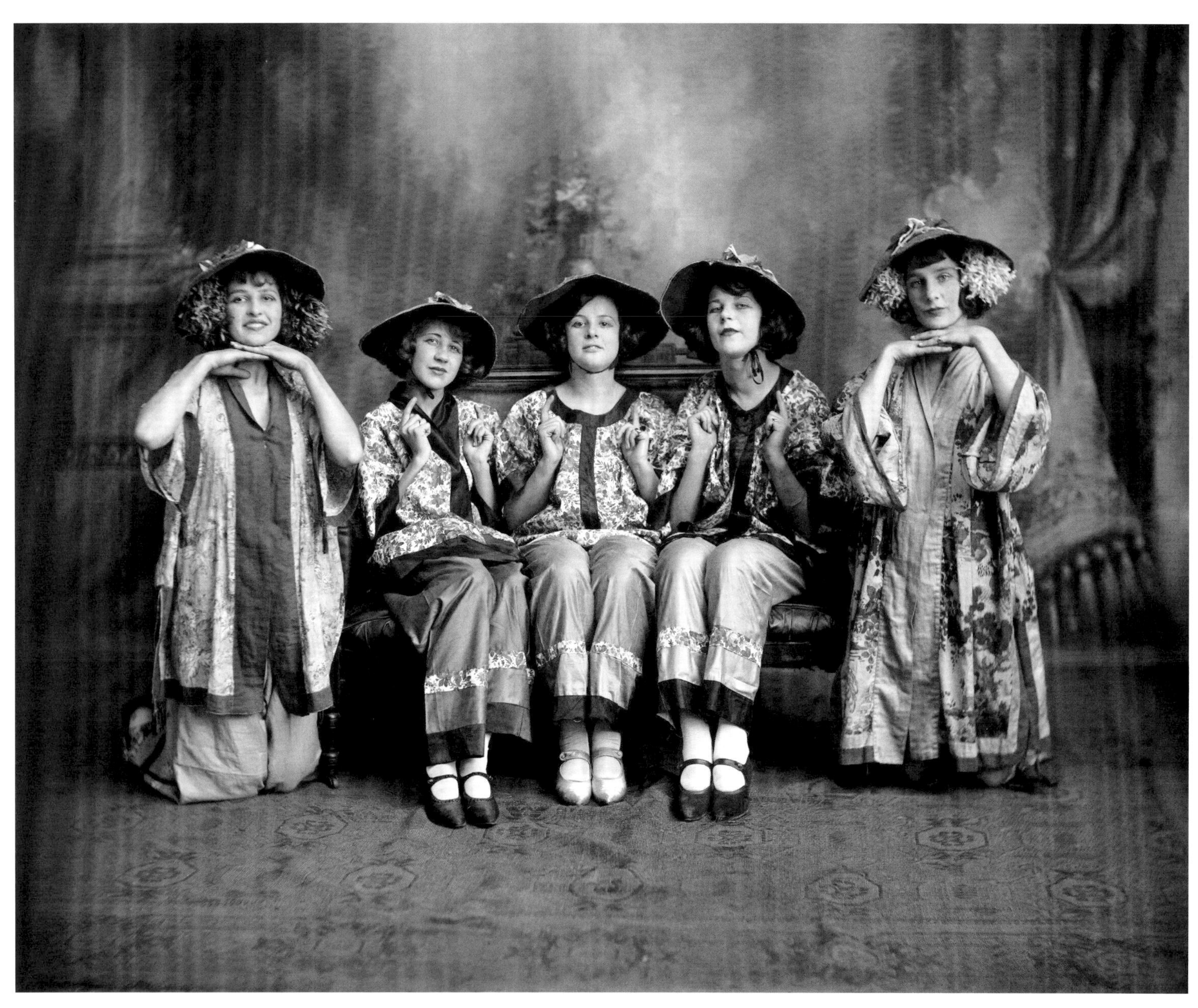

Mississippi State College for Women students.

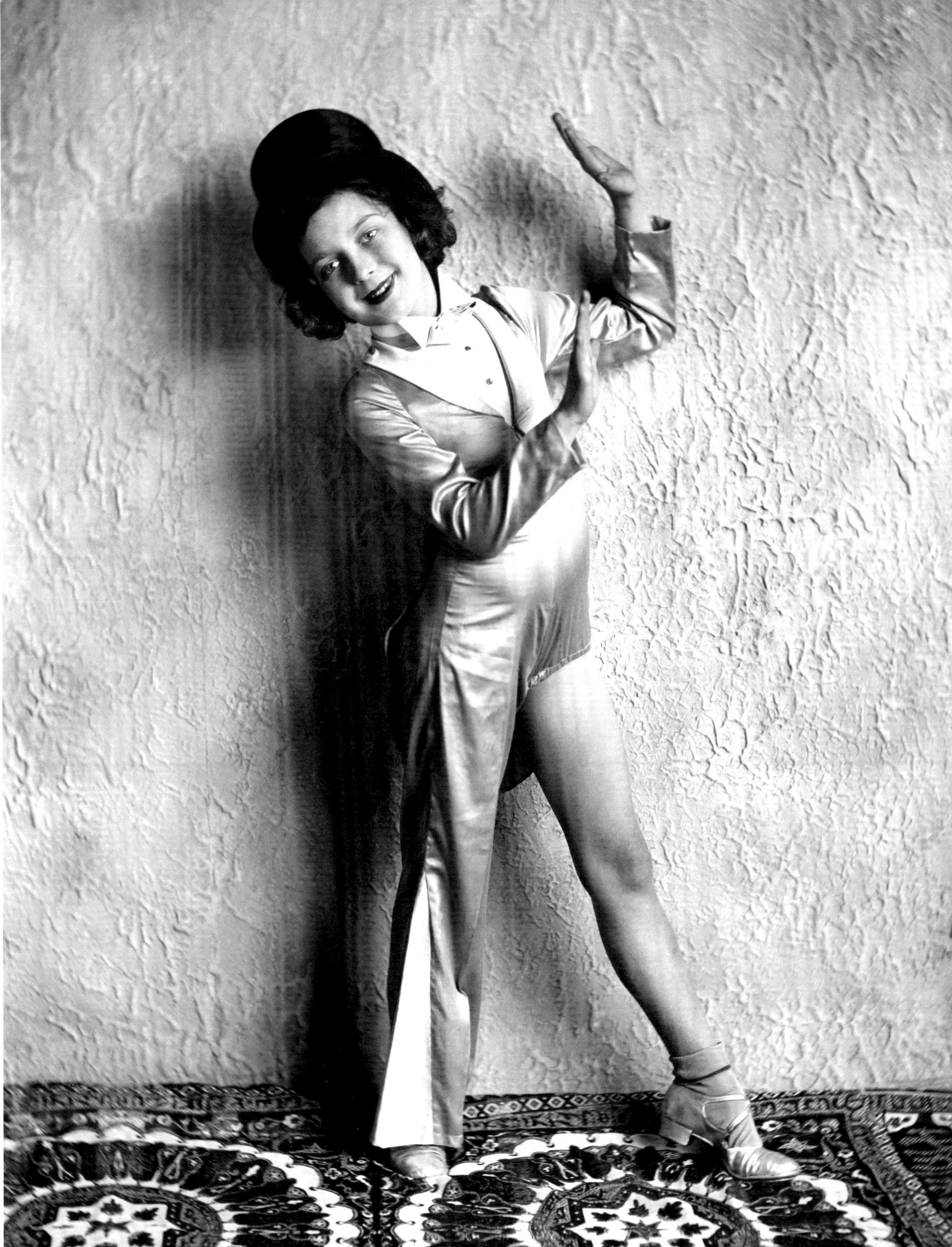

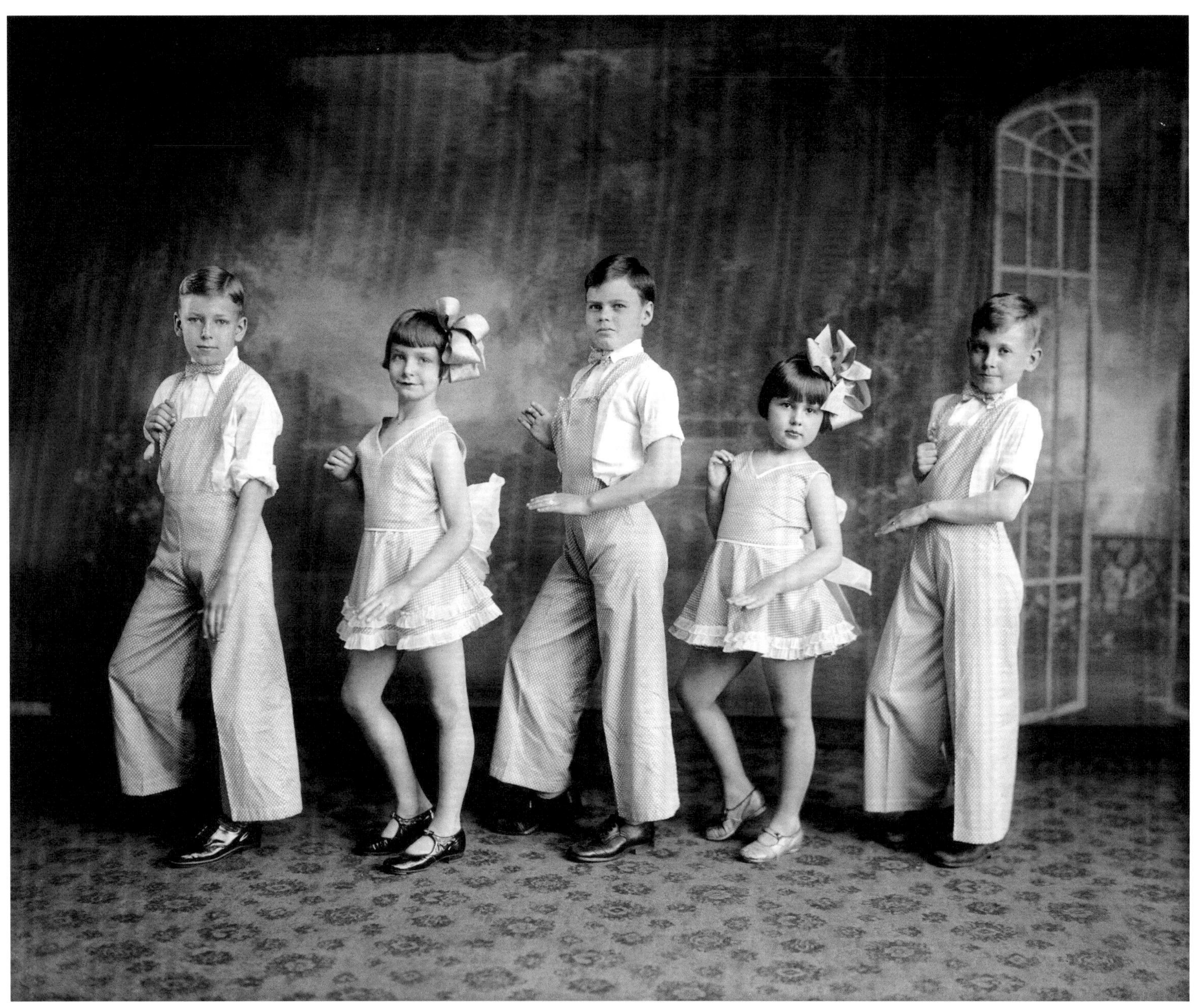

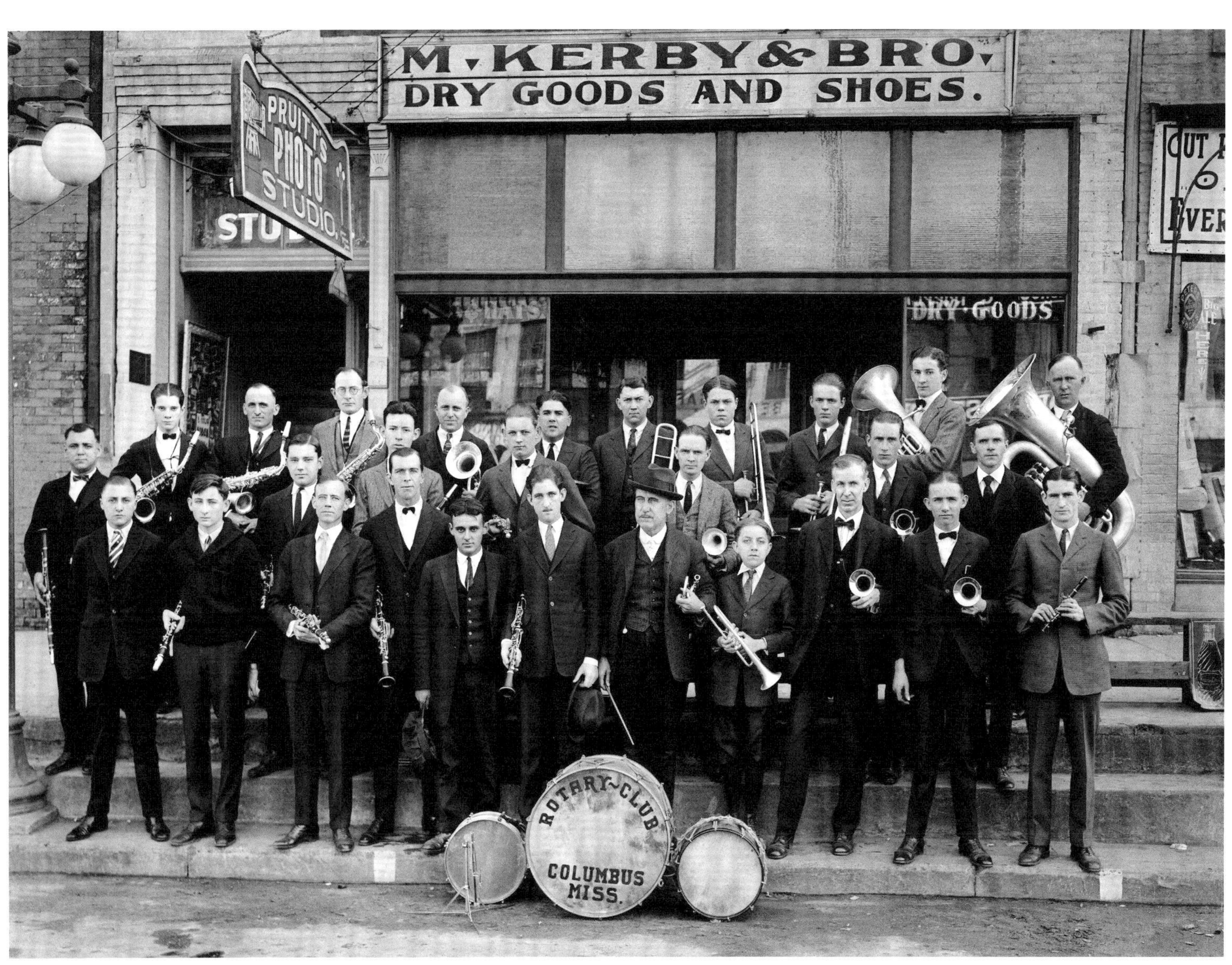

Rotary Club band in front of Pruitt's studio, circa 1920s.

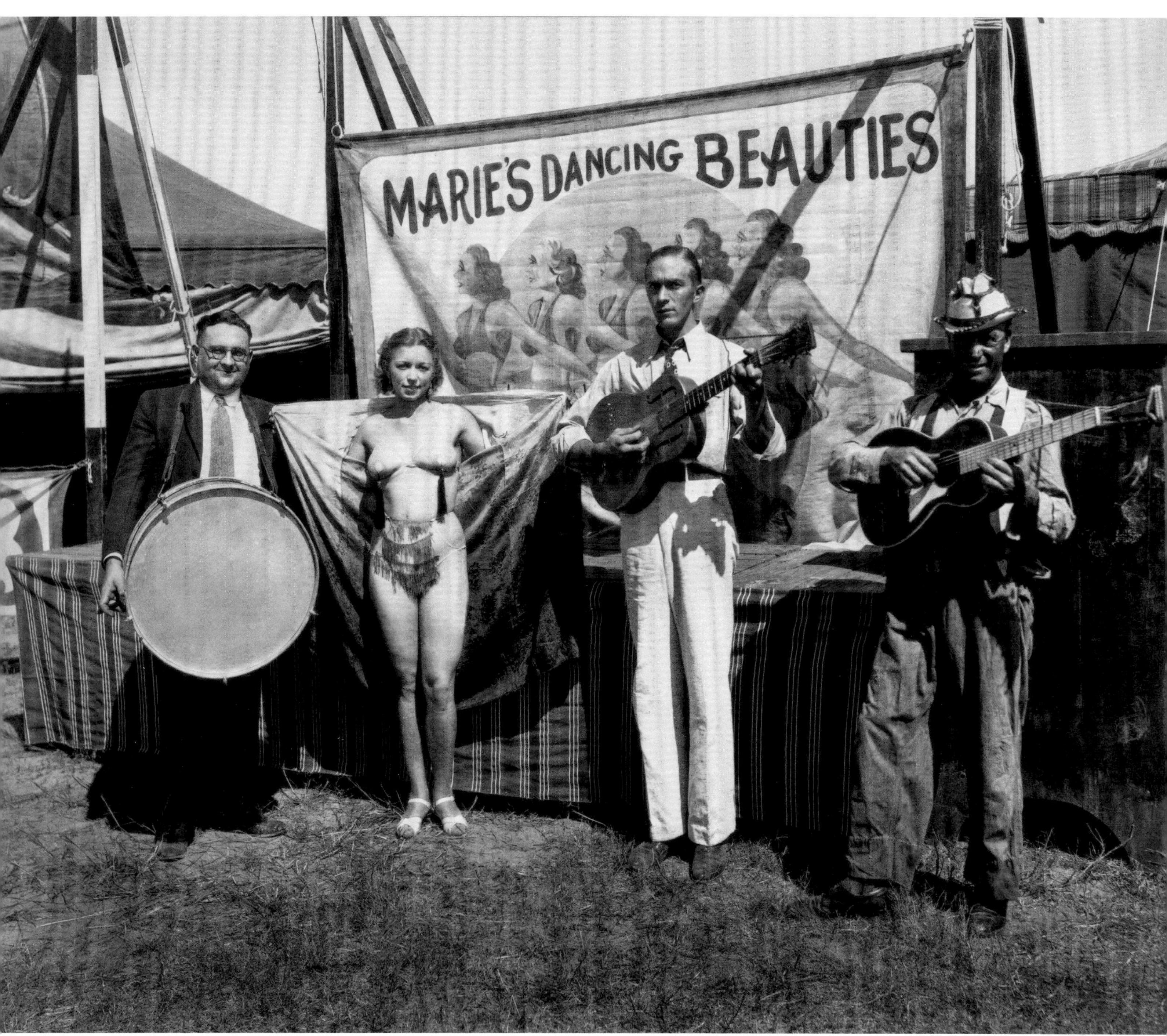
MARIE'S DANCING BEAUTIES

MILLER'S TRAVELLING MUSEUM, WORLD FAIR FREAKS, CIRCA 1930–1935

Twenty-five people appear in this photograph. Regardless of race, ethnicity, gender, disability, or number of tattoos, the people present themselves as exotic "Other." Whether by nature, nurture, or costuming, their bodies are marked, distinguishing them as different. Even the men in suits and hats who run the show seem foreign to Columbus, where cultural, class, racial, gender, and religious boundaries were firmly set: you were white or Black, churchgoer or nonchurchgoer, and so on.

In 1932, around the time this photograph was taken, Tod Browning's *Freaks*, now considered a cult classic, opened in movie theaters. "Can a full-grown woman truly love a midget?" its promotional poster asked. Although the "freak show" was waning with the advent of modernity, it remained a mainstay of world's fairs, carnivals, and midways. Playing on stereotypes, the freak show, with "exotics and ethnics," drew crowds intrigued by scientific and medical advances of the nineteenth and early twentieth centuries. The 1927 Scopes Trial, for example, highlighted debates about social evolution and the biological origins of race.

Through advertisements and news stories, local newspapers, radio stations, and posters, photography played a role in promoting the shows. Scholars such as Robert Bogdan argue that "freak shows" represent a social construction in which entertainment was based on "retailing" of bodies. Although the word *freak* may seem offensive, according to Bogdan, to those in the shows the label was not. "Their main concern," he says, "was to make money." The appeal of the freak show, says scholar Rosemarie Garland

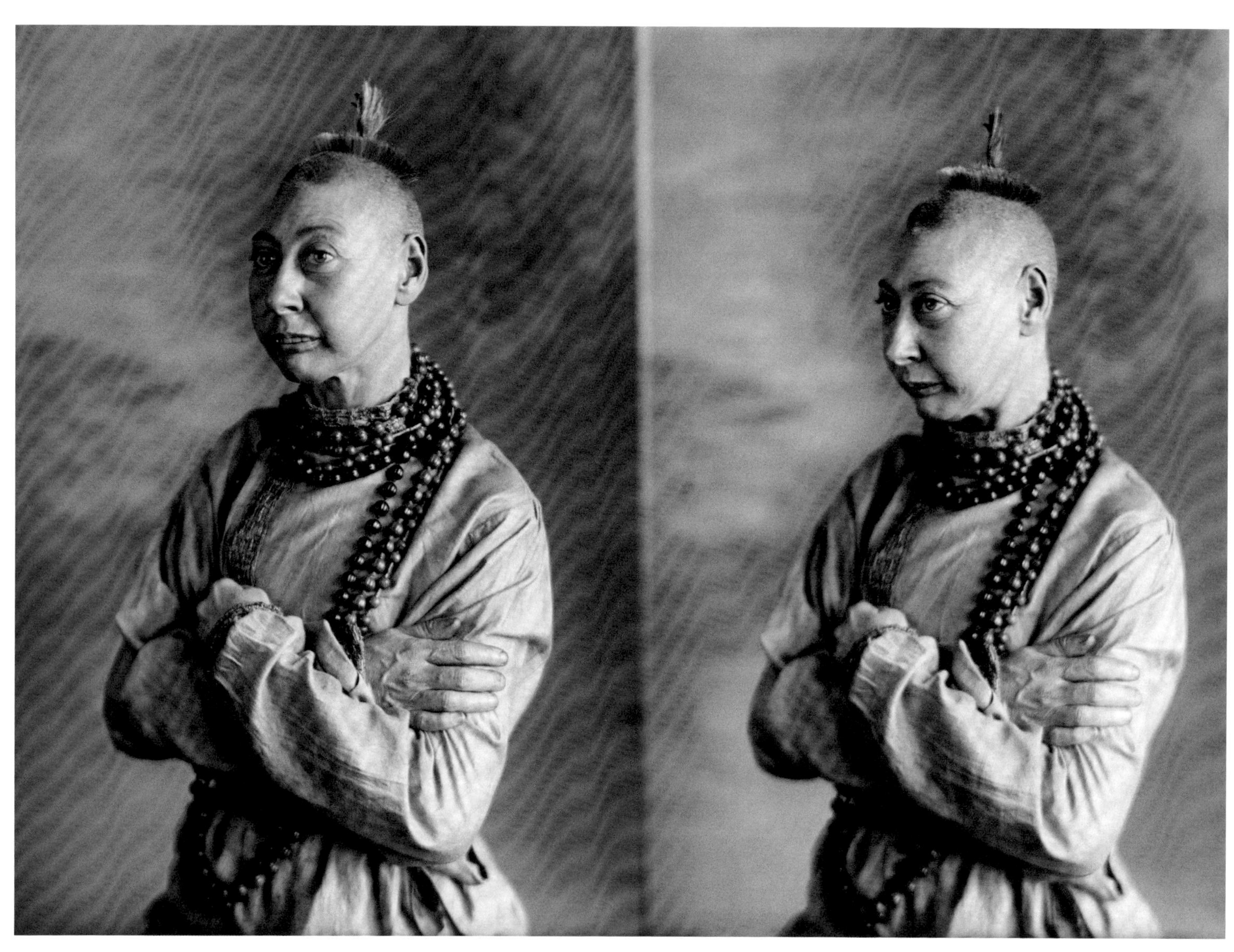

A member of Miller's Travelling Museum.

Thomson, is rooted in how visual difference informs our imaginations about "what we take to be human." The "extraordinary body is fundamental," she argues, "to the narratives by which we make sense of ourselves and our world." Bogdan writes "that every exhibit was a fraud. This is not to say that freaks were without physical, mental or behavioral anomalies. Many had profound differences . . . but, with very few exceptions, every person was misrepresented" to attract an audience and sell tickets. The albino from Australia may have come from Atlanta, or the Wild Man of Borneo may have grown up in Sacramento. The itinerant shows took power and authority from publicity of the "ethnological zoo" popularized by the Chicago World's Columbian Exposition in 1893 and, in 1933 and 1934, the Century of Progress International Exposition, also in Chicago. Photography related directly to promoting the shows.

In their collaborative relationship, studio photographers and freak shows filled a need for Victorian and post-Victorian Americans. The managers and the "freaks" themselves would ask photographers to make their pictures and then use them to promote their show and to sell the postcard-sized photographs to the people who came to the exhibit. Before television and radio, families collected and put into photo albums for display a montage of photographs that might include statesmen, generals, performers, and "freaks"—alongside family members. One of America's most famous nineteenth-century photographers, Mathew Brady, documented freaks exhibited by circus icon P. T. Barnum's American Museum, located across Broadway from Brady's New York studio.

During the Great Depression freak shows rented space in empty buildings. Local photographers would make pictures that the members of a troupe would autograph and sell to patrons. *Billboard* magazine in the 1930s published photographs of freak shows to accompany a weekly column titled "Museums." The stories consisted of accounts written by correspondents from shows as they traveled across America. "Midgets Wanted for World's Fair. Can use any kind of midget whether or not performers. No dwarfs," read a 1933 ad in the Chicago-based *Midget Village News*.

Although it is unclear why Pruitt made the photograph of Miller's, he often photographed carnivals or county fair sideshows. Photographs such as Pruitt's connect with a tradition of the exotic in photography and the currency of freak show images within society.

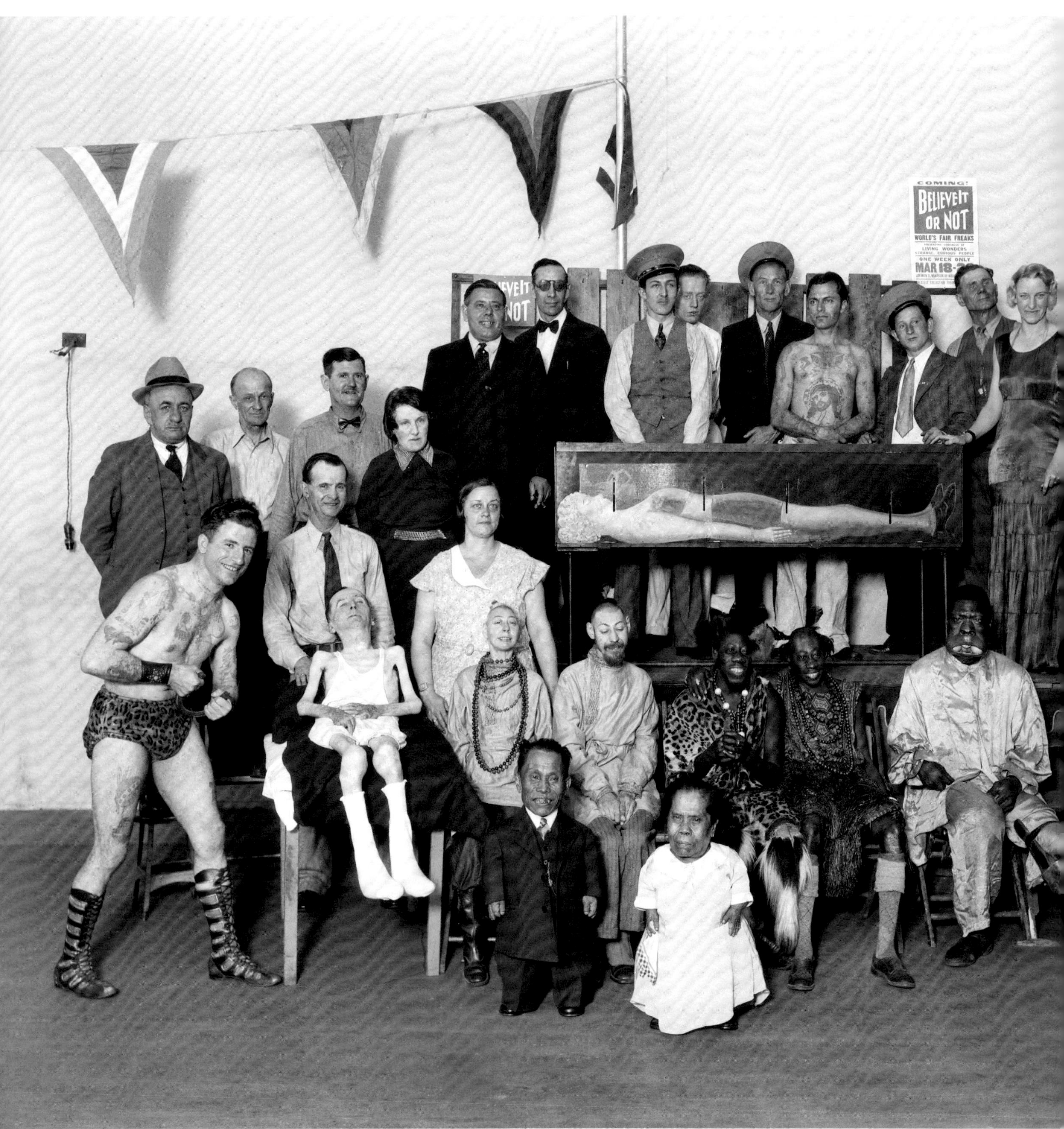
COMING!
BELIEVE IT OR NOT
WORLD'S FAIR FREAKS
LIVING WONDERS
STRANGE, CURIOUS PEOPLE
ONE WEEK ONLY
MAR 18-

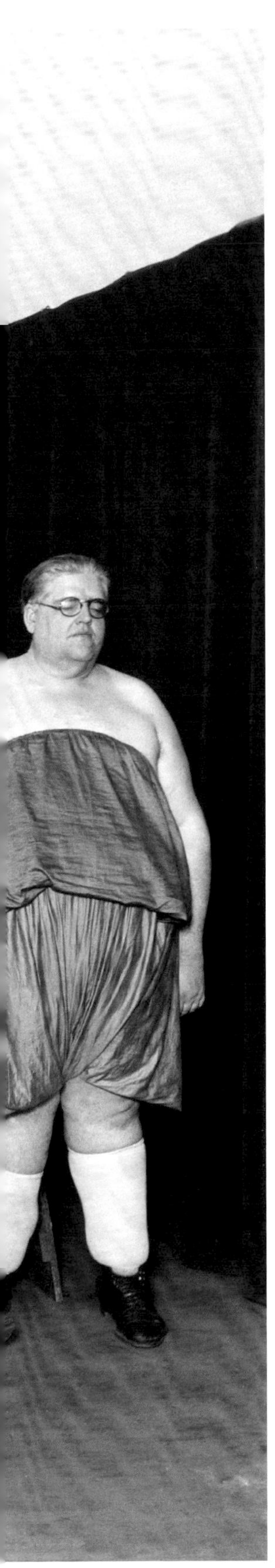

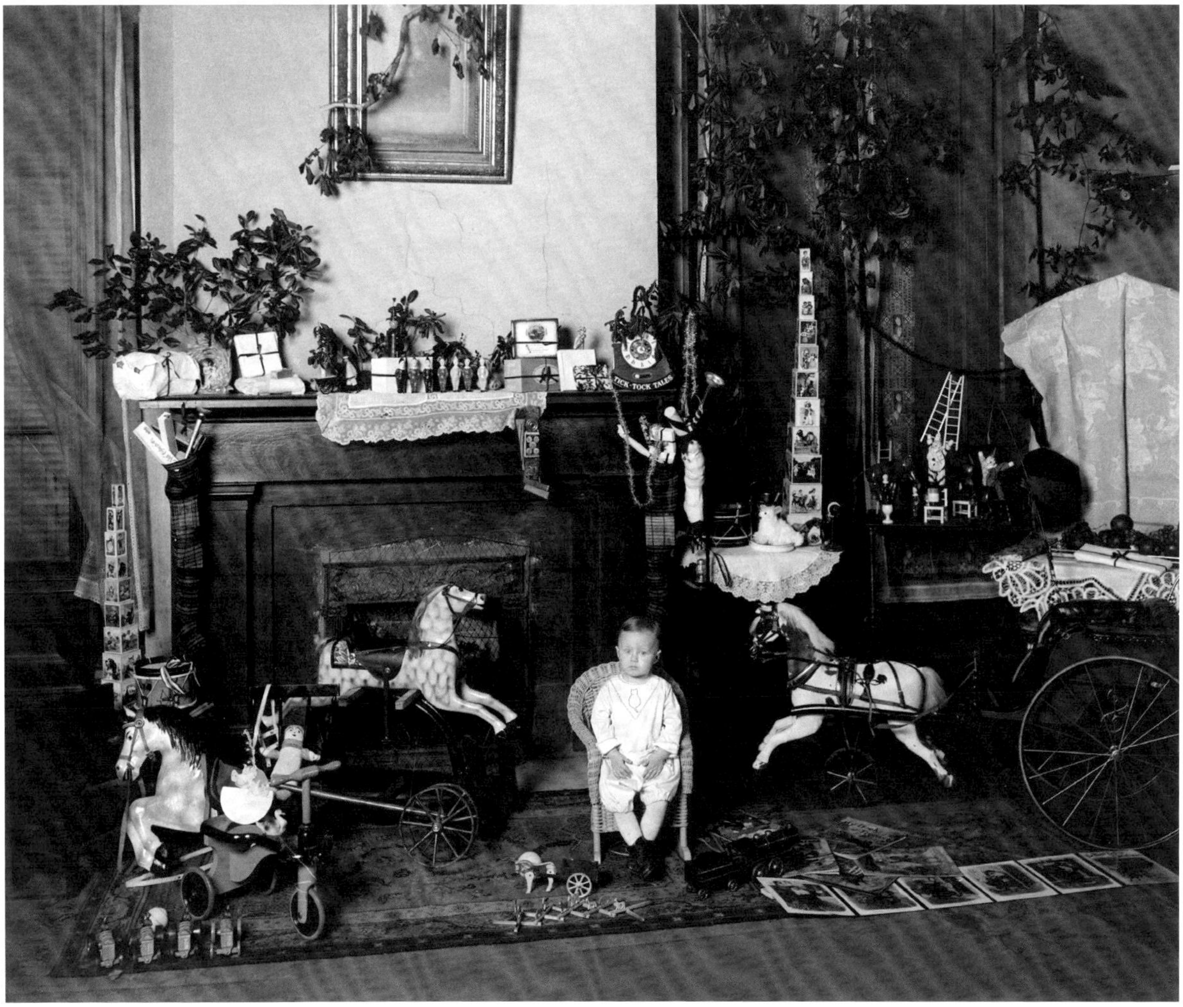

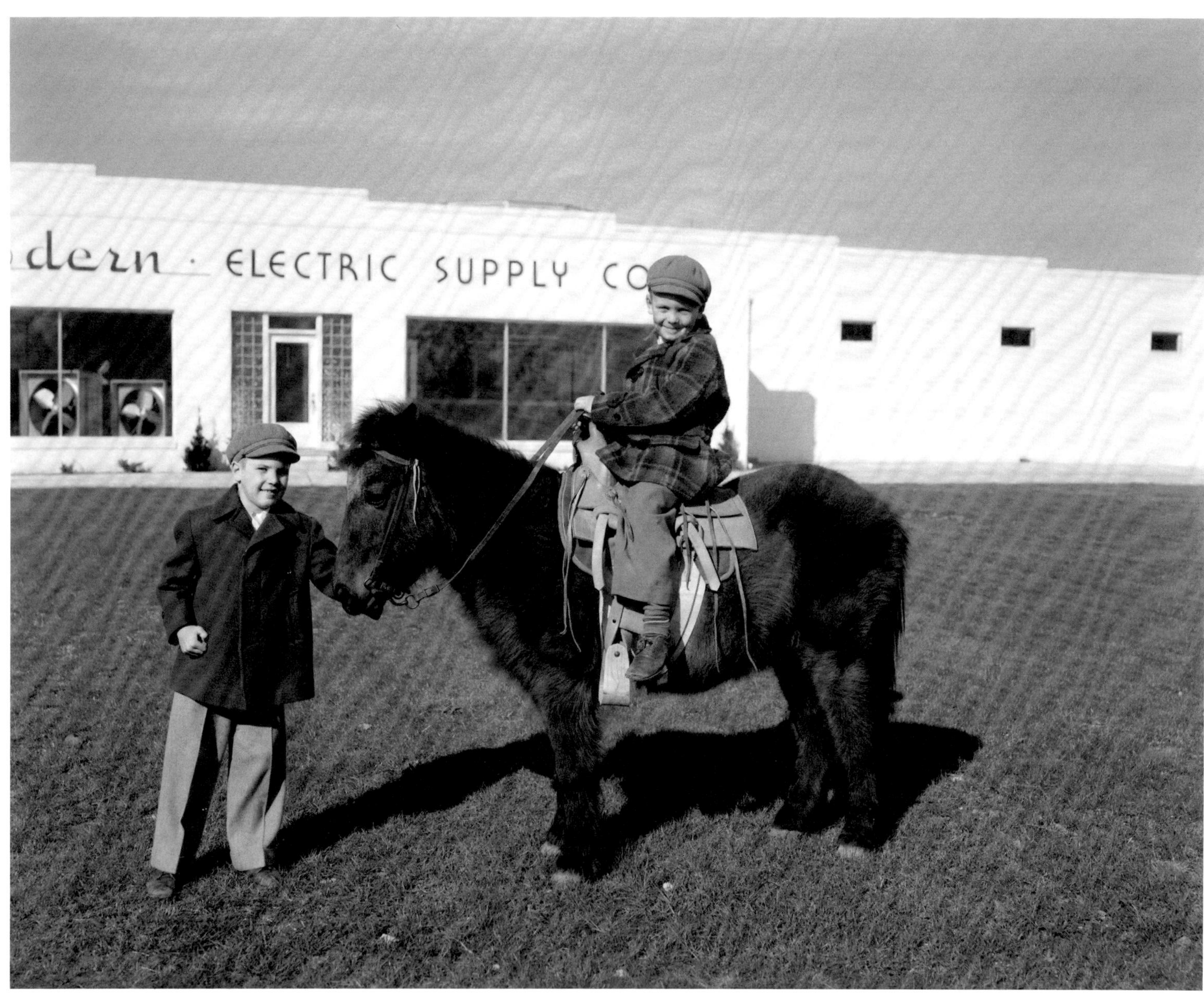
dern · ELECTRIC SUPPLY CO

CAMEL RIDE AT LOCKE'S ZOO, CIRCA 1923

Pruitt photographs offer a visual window into the larger-than-life character of Thomas J. Locke Jr., a wholesale grocer. Locke traveled the nation pursuing his business, political, and civic interests. He also ran an opera house and sold beer, bailing wire, potatoes, sugar, and chicken feed. His name could appear two or three times in one edition of the *Commercial Dispatch*. Sometimes the publicity wasn't positive. Locke killed a colleague in 1927, was tried for murder, then was the defendant in a civil trial. He was acquitted in both. Through Pruitt's images, one can glimpse Locke's life and his friends and family at play, riding on a camel or admiring an abundant string of bass caught at Locke's Lodge, his retreat bungalow.

After he bought the lodge at the southern end of town and adjacent to the Tombigbee, a 1921 news story heralded it as "the handsomest private club house in the state," with facilities that "include electric lights, bath, running water and other necessary club conveniences." In addition, there were terraced grounds, a menagerie he called Locke's Zoo, a boathouse, and a wooden pier that extended to a pavilion in the center of a lake.

In 1922, a Chicago film crew came to the lodge to shoot scenes for a silent movie, *A Pleasant Surprise*. Similar to events in other American towns newly fascinated by movies, locals played roles in the film that then was shown at the Princess Theatre. Pruitt took still photographs for the movie.

Tiger, deer, panthers, black bear, ostrich, elk, and camels at the zoo were the lodge's main attractions. In 1921, a 100-pound turtle "the size of an ordinary washtub," supposedly 100 years old, was captured along the Tombigbee and taken to the zoo. Locke hosted groups for picnics and outings. The editors of the Mississippi Press Association visited. Rotarians from nearby Aberdeen convened a joint meeting with the Columbus Rotary Club to which Locke belonged. Pruitt took a panoramic photograph with a black bear with the posed Rotarians.

Besides being a grocer, Locke was a cattle rancher, a Mississippi highway commissioner, and secretary of the Lowndes County executive committee of the Democratic Party. He was a director of the American Association of Wholesale Grocers and a director of the Mississippi Valley Association, a political and economic development group focused on agriculture, businesses, and manufacturing from Minnesota south to Mississippi. In Columbus, Locke sponsored a recreational baseball team. He was a member of the Mississippi Fair Price Commission, designed to guard against price gouging. He owned the Columbus Opera House, which hosted animal circuses, vaudeville acts, Broadway-style musicals, and Shakespearean dramas. In 1920, Locke joined Prohibition forces. Yet, whether accurate or not, townspeople asserted that Locke sold sugar to moonshiners during Prohibition. And after Prohibition, he capitalized on Lowndes County's approval of beer sales: he became a Budweiser beer distributor.

In Pruitt's photograph of children on a camel, Locke's daughter, Irene, sits in the middle. Hawley Knox Brown, who is not pictured, was a friend of Irene's and often went to the zoo. "It wasn't so tremendous," Brown says. "We all wanted to ride the camels.... This was all we were interested in ... the camels."

A significant detail is the Black man's hand holding the rope for the camel. A whisper of his nose, mouth, tip of his hat, other hand, and pants leg appear. It is unclear why only the "hired hands" were included. Pruitt, however, often worked from a tripod, and perhaps he could not move it easily to take in or leave out the man leading a camel. The shapes of the tiny, barefooted white boy wearing a cap, his body rakishly cocked into the neck of the camel, his hands at the ready on the harness, make the image compelling. So do the legs of the two white girls in calf-high stockings and pointed shoes with double straps. The camel itself presents a striking shape. In the background on the left, you see cages for zoo animals.

Perhaps four years after this photograph was made, on Christmas Eve 1927, significant trouble arrived for Locke. His wife, also named Irene, had requested that they have cherries for Christmas Day. So they made a late-night run to the store of Wallace Stevens, a former city councilman and prominent white retail grocer. She stayed in the car. Locke went inside. For some reason, the two men had an ongoing feud, and that night it erupted in gunfire. Stevens died on the store's floor. Neither Locke nor his wife was injured. Law enforcement officials called Pruitt to photograph the crime scene, including Stevens's body. On the first night after being arrested for the killing, Locke was allowed to stay in the Gilmer Hotel until his own bedroom set could be moved into the county jail. Three days later, he was bailed out of jail.

During the trial, Pruitt served as a prosecution witness. Other witnesses testified that Locke and Stevens had exchanged words too ugly to be repeated in front of women. Two decades ago, when a group of Columbus women looked at photographs of Locke, they nodded as one woman, sotto voce, said the killing was "about a woman." That motive, however, did not arise in news coverage. A jury exonerated Locke. A distant cousin of Locke's, Claudia Locke Rhett, years later told me he was "the nicest man you'd ever want to meet."

Two months after the trial ended, Locke faced a civil trial. Stevens's widow and three daughters sought $300,000 in damages. Again, a jury exonerated Locke. Less than three weeks later, Locke faced questions from federal tax officials, who questioned his claim that his zoo represented an aspect of his wholesale grocery business and thus $9,263 in zoo expenses could be taken as deductions. In that case, Locke lost. A *Commercial Dispatch* news story reported that "even by the remotest stretch of the imagination" the zoo could not be considered vital to the operations of a wholesale grocery business.

Less than a week after the tax hearing, almost one year after the Stevens killing, and just in time for Christmas, a *Commercial Dispatch* front-page story announced that Locke would "play the role of Santa to the poor of the city, and spread sunshine among those not so fortunate." He distributed fruit baskets to those in need for Christmas.

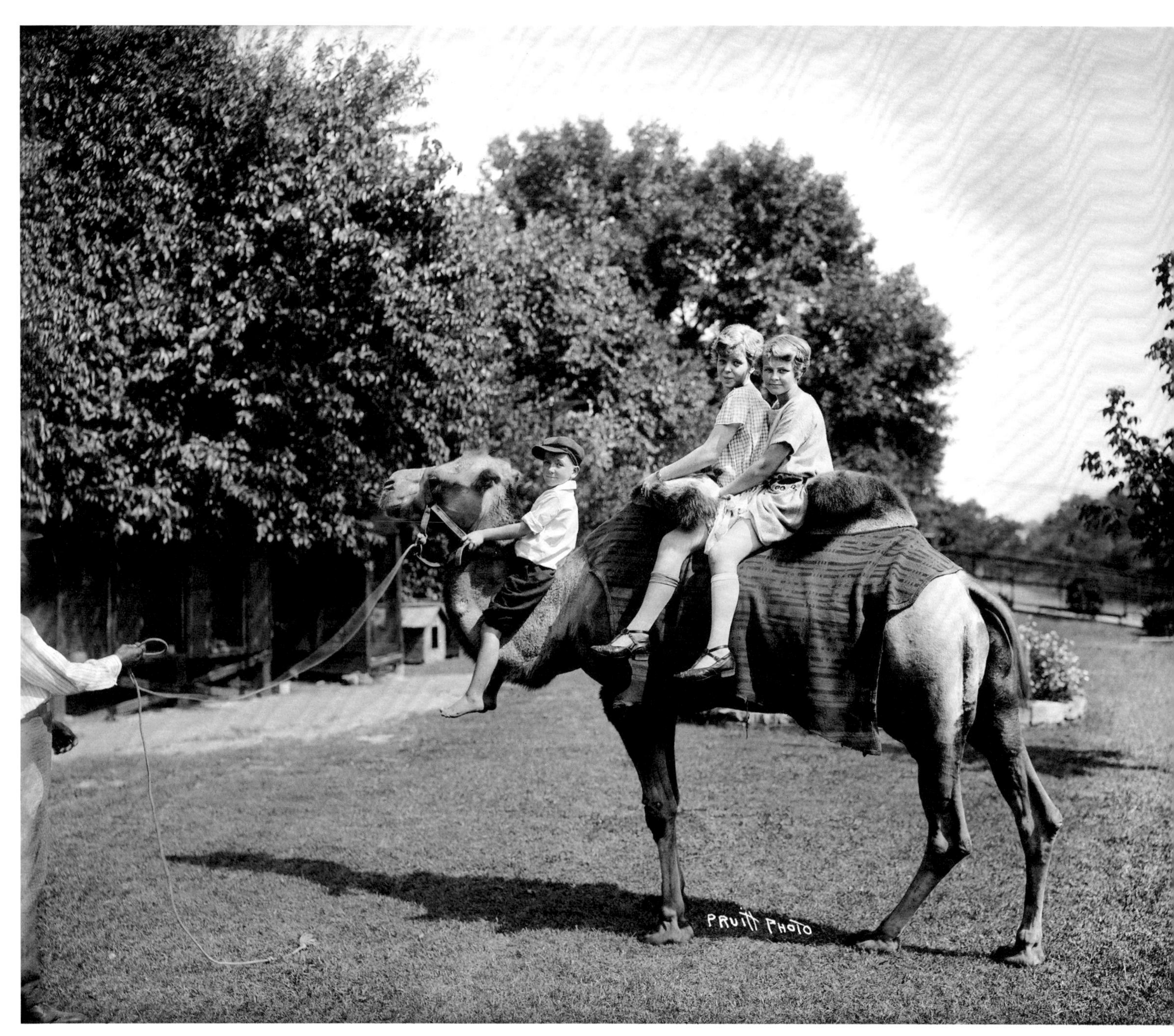

Irene Locke (center), *daughter of Thomas J. Locke Jr., on a camel at Locke's Zoo, circa 1925.*

PRINCESS PICTURE SHOW, 1944

Movies provided a diversion from the Great Depression and World War II in Columbus, and Pruitt photographed expressions of that. There were four principal theaters in the 1930s and 1940s: the Princess, Varsity, Dixie, and Joy. Each included separate seating and separate entrances for African Americans, except for the Joy, which was solely for Blacks and was located not far from the Queen City Hotel that also catered to African Americans. In this era, there was no television, only radio, and no air-conditioning.

Two decades ago, as she looked at Pruitt photographs of movie theaters, Edwina R. Williams recalled when she was a girl in the early 1940s and had a surprise birthday party at the Dixie. "My Daddy took me to the Bell Café because we were getting a Coca-Cola. And that, unknown to me, was the way to get the [other birthday] kids to the Dixie. My Mama made me wear a red velvet dress with a little lace, and I thought: 'Why is my mom making me wear this dress just to go to the café with my Daddy and have a Coca-Cola?' But anyway, it turned out, as my Daddy and I walked into the picture show—I was surprised by all my friends. I was either five or seven. I'm not sure, but I remember what I had on, and it was a fun birthday party. It was *Snow White and the Seven Dwarfs*, and it was in Technicolor."

For Columbus, magical entertainment was linked to commerce. "See Kirma Hypnotize Beautiful Girl on the Stage of Princess Theatre," a 1935 *Commercial Dispatch* advertisement proclaimed. "Kirma the famous hypnotist ... is coming to Columbus to thrill hundreds! Be sure to be on hand to watch him awaken his subject at [the] Princess, after a 24-hour coma." Movie theaters functioned as venues not only for movies but for touring Broadway-style productions, blackface minstrel shows, and wrestling matches.

In 1944 Pruitt photographed a crowd including military personnel and a band from the local Columbus Army Airfield gather outside of the Princess for a movie premiere to generate public interest in buying war bonds. Intriguingly, most of the people pictured are white, save for a Black man and Black woman underneath the sign that says "COLORED BALCONY." A decade earlier in other Pruitt depictions of Black and white crowds outside the Princess, a sign had read "10 cents, Colored Entrance." Edward L. Kuykendall owned the Princess Theatre. His son, also named Ed Kuykendall, said that some white people complained to his father about letting Blacks come to the movies. Kuykendall said his father "didn't care if their skin was Black or white as long as their money was green."

As a child, Jessie Koonce went to movies in Columbus and, as an African American, her strongest memories were of the all-Black Joy Theatre and the Varsity. Koonce, a social worker who was a member of the Columbus Arts Council and the Columbus–Lowndes County Public Library board, in 2003 looked at Pruitt's photographs of theaters and recalled the separate entrances and humiliating second-class treatment: "When you went in the Varsity . . . , you went in the side . . . [by] the bus station. If we had to go to the bathroom, we went to the bus station . . . and if you wanted anything to drink or eat, you got it from . . . the bus station and brought it back in [to the theater]."

Theater owner Kuykendall, who started out in the carnival sideshow business, often relied on Pruitt for photography. But he was far more than the owner of the Princess; he was also one of America's preeminent movie operators. From the early 1930s until the mid-1940s, he was president of the Motion Picture Theatre Owners of America. Based in New York, the organization represented 7,300 theater owners.

Kuykendall's connections gave him inside access to movies, actors, and the latest theater equipment. During the Great Depression, President Franklin D. Roosevelt appointed Kuykendall to the National Recovery Act state board. Owing to his position as president of the Motion Picture Theatre Owners, Kuykendall was in the national spotlight, including during a debate over a motion picture code related to the National Recovery Act. He and lawyer Clarence Darrow, of Scopes Trial fame, had a public disagreement about this. The *Commercial Dispatch* editorialized in 1934, "Darrow may know more about the monkey business and the origin of species than Ed Kuykendall, but when it comes to the picture show business Ed can make a monkey out of Clarence." Kuykendall also drew other celebrity attention. Once, for instance, actor Wallace Beery came with Kuykendall for a visit to Columbus.

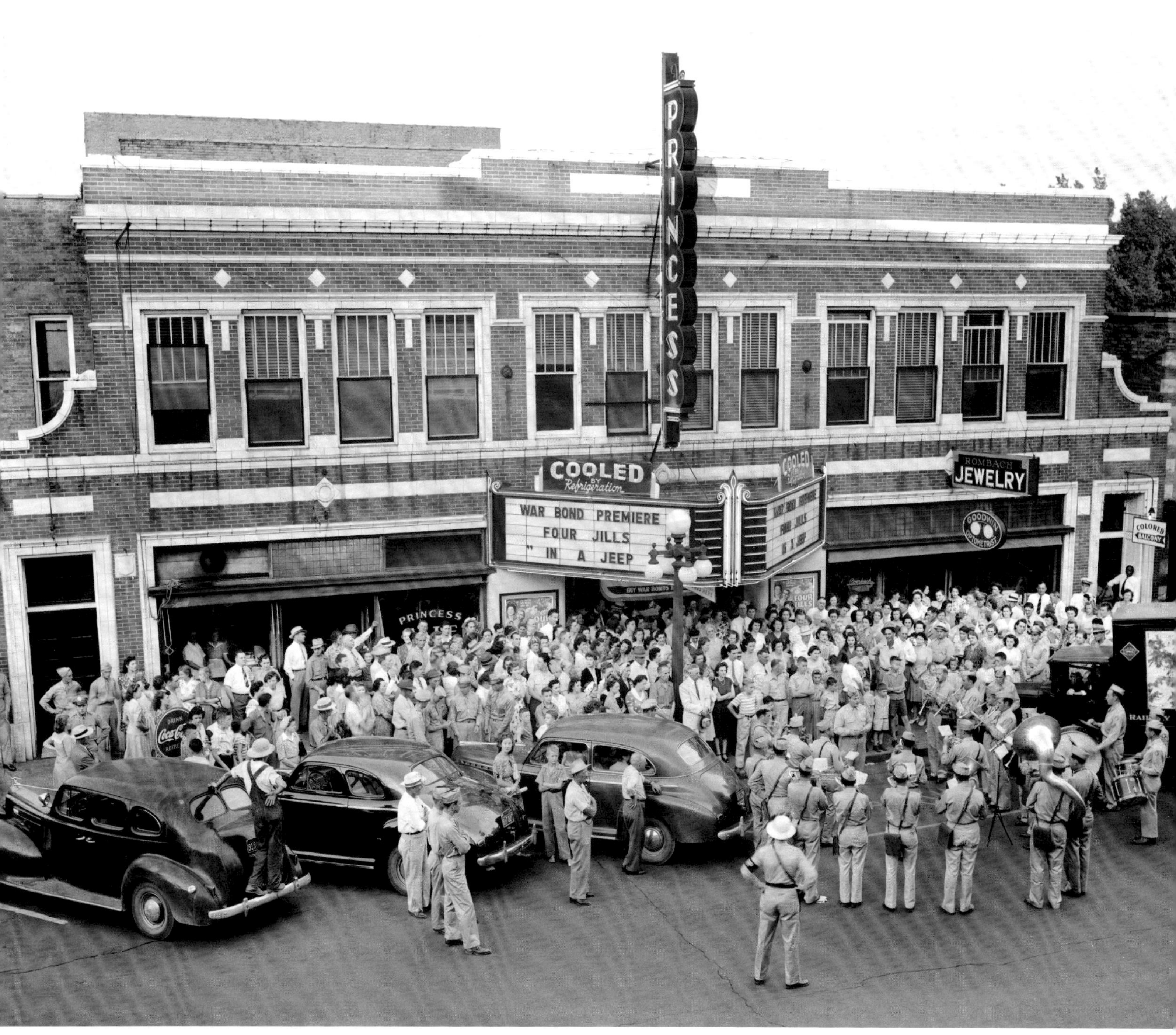

War bond rally during World War II at Princess Theatre, Market Street.

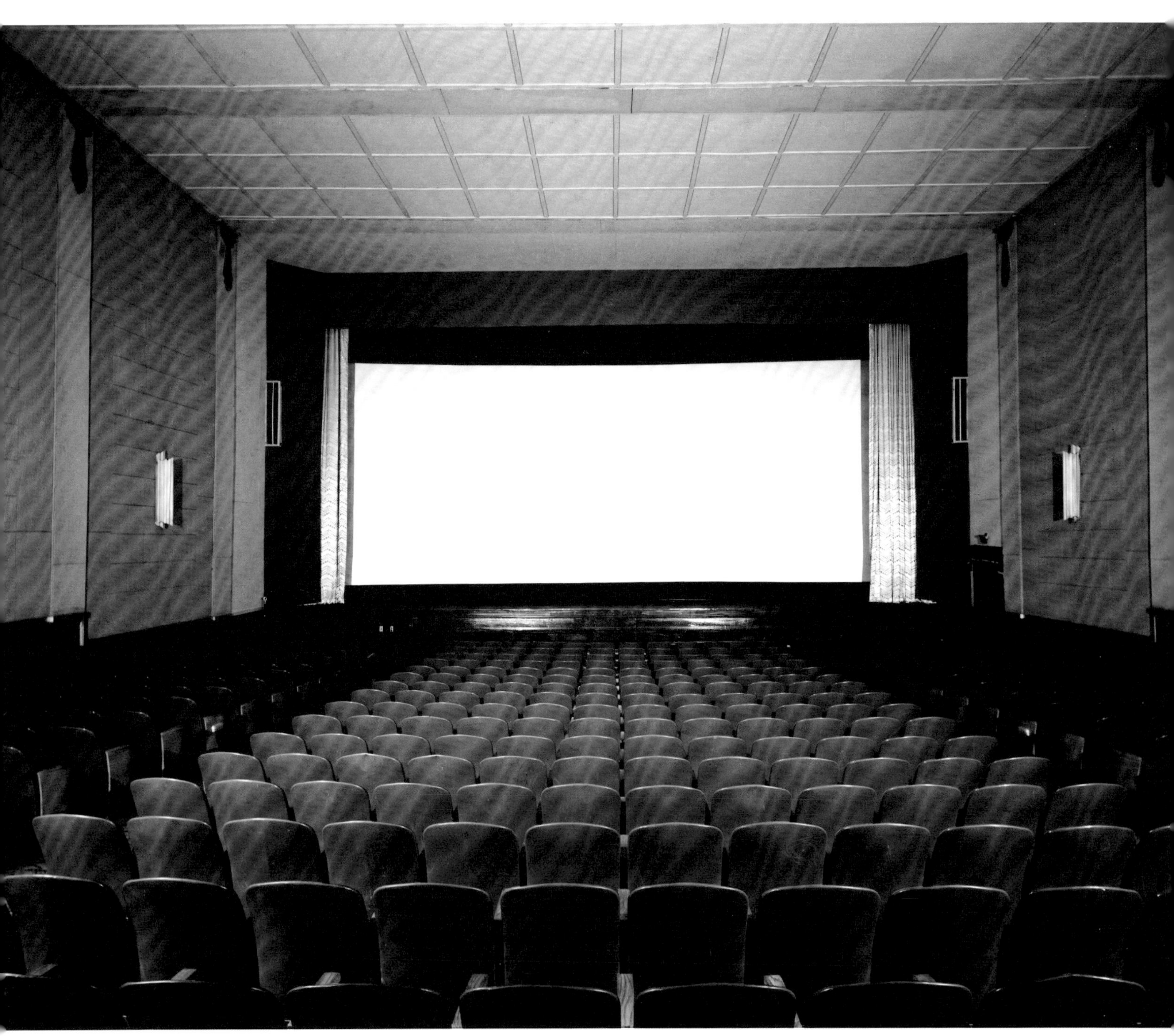

Princess Theatre, Market Street, circa 1930s–40s.

Teenage girls at Luxapalila Creek swimming hole, circa 1925. Hawley Knox (center) *with hand on chin.*

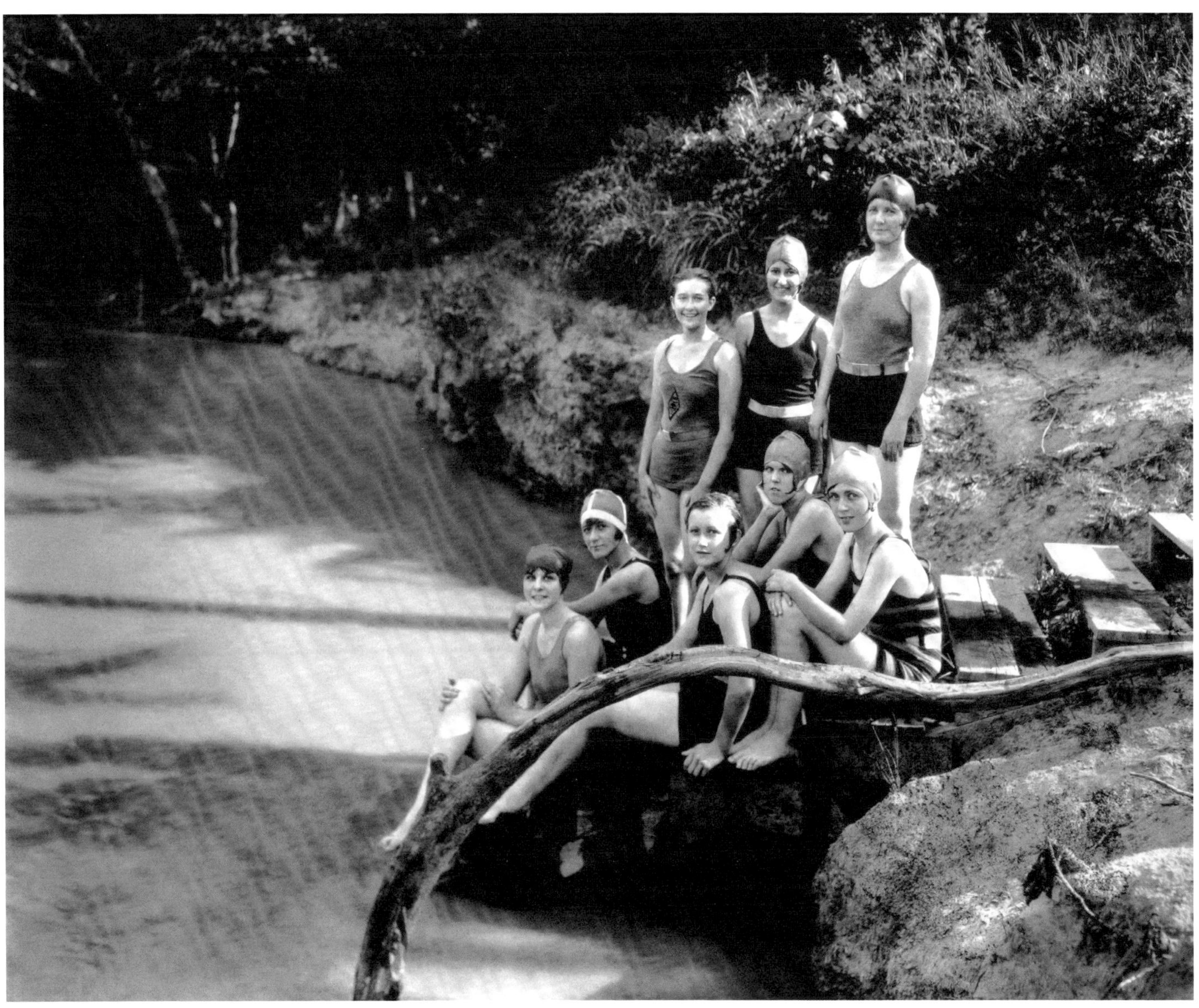

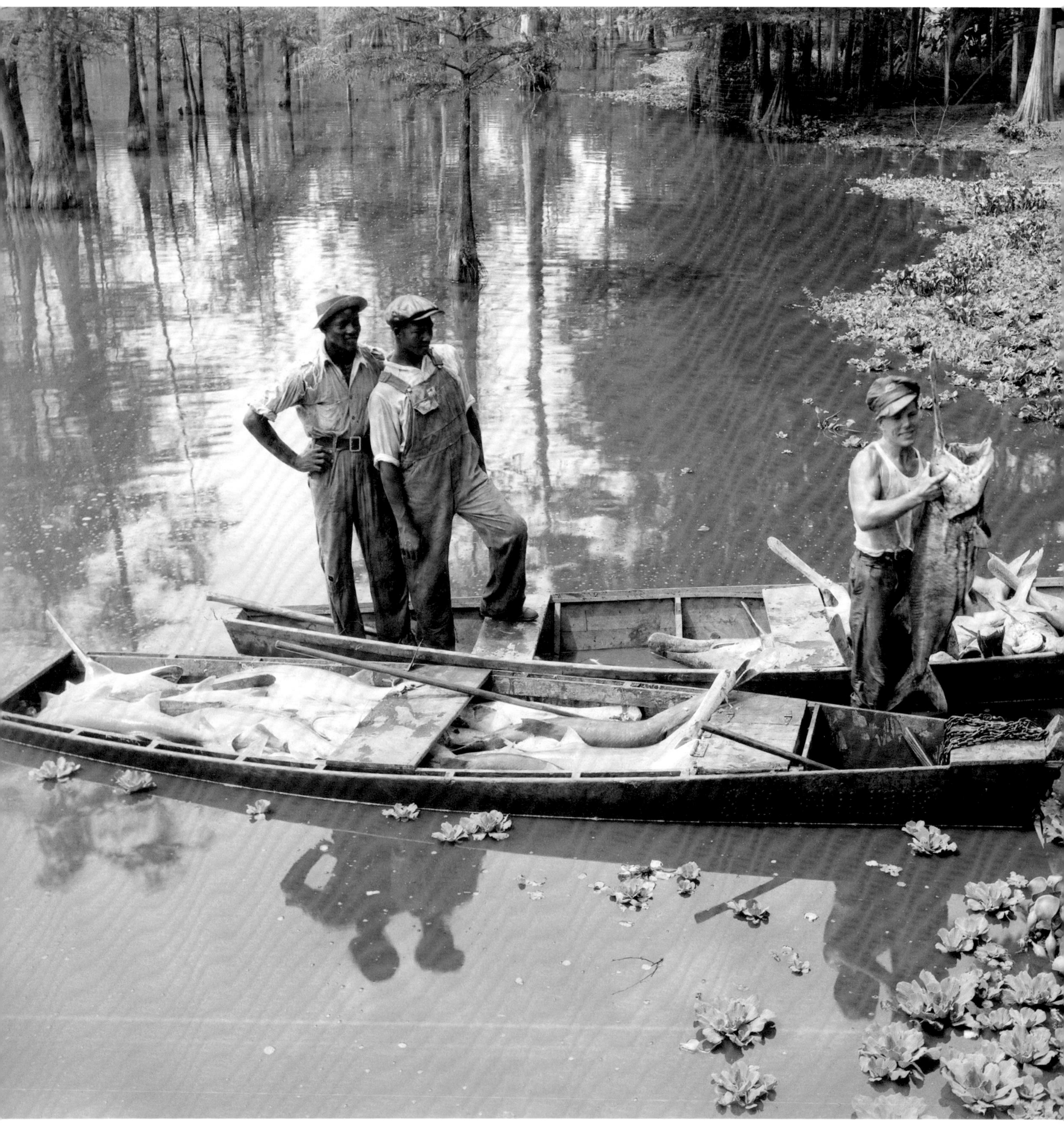

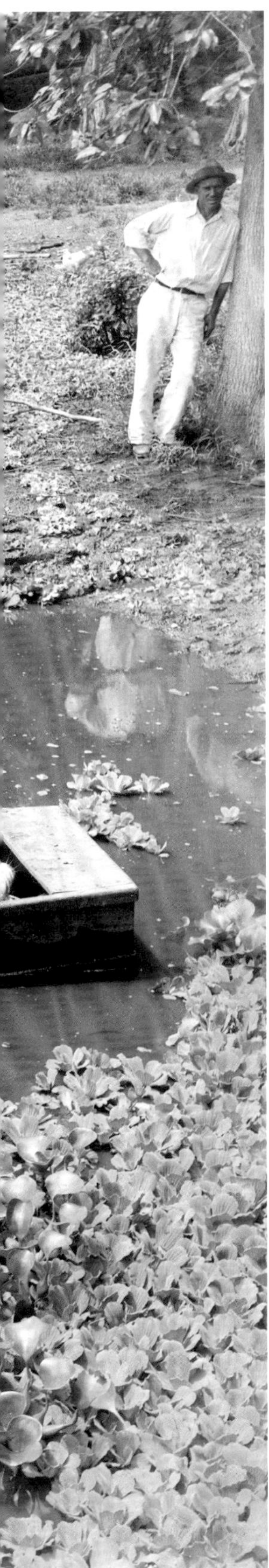

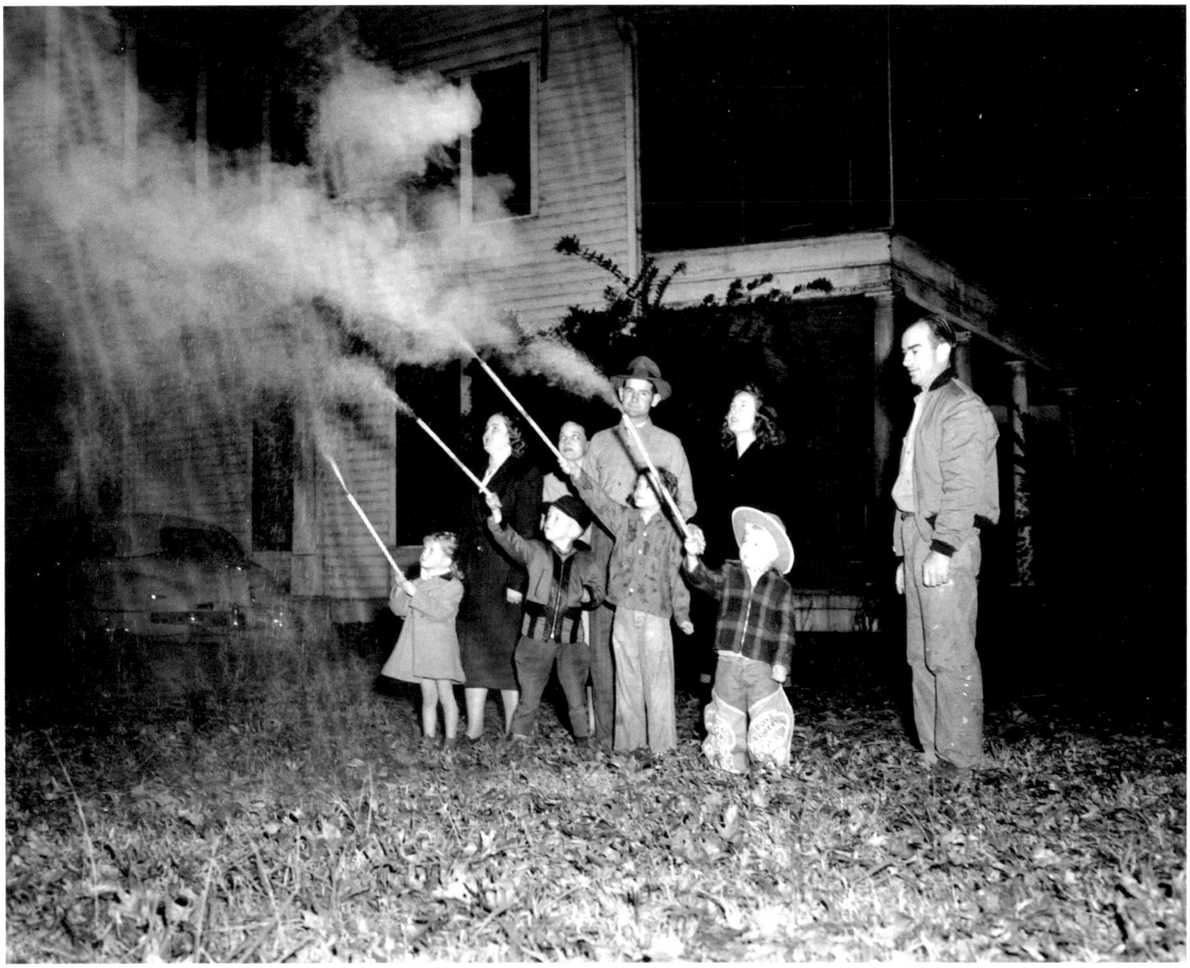

Alligator Lake, circa 1930s. Jim Wilder (center) *holds a spoonbill catfish. William Jimmison is at far left.*

From left: *Hubert Holmes, T. C. Billups, unidentified mechanic, and pilot Jess Windham with two-seater biplane, circa 1920s–30s.*

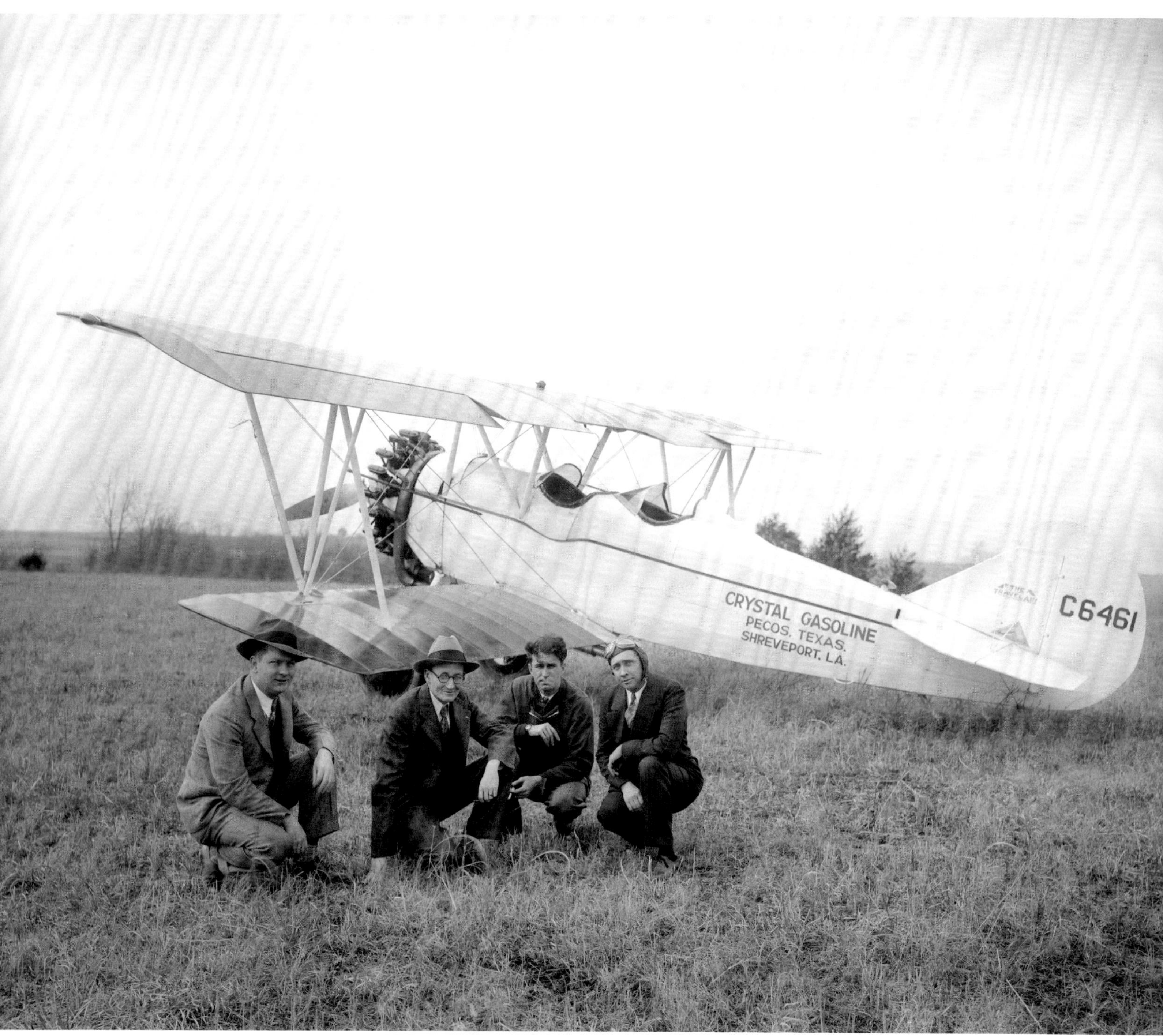

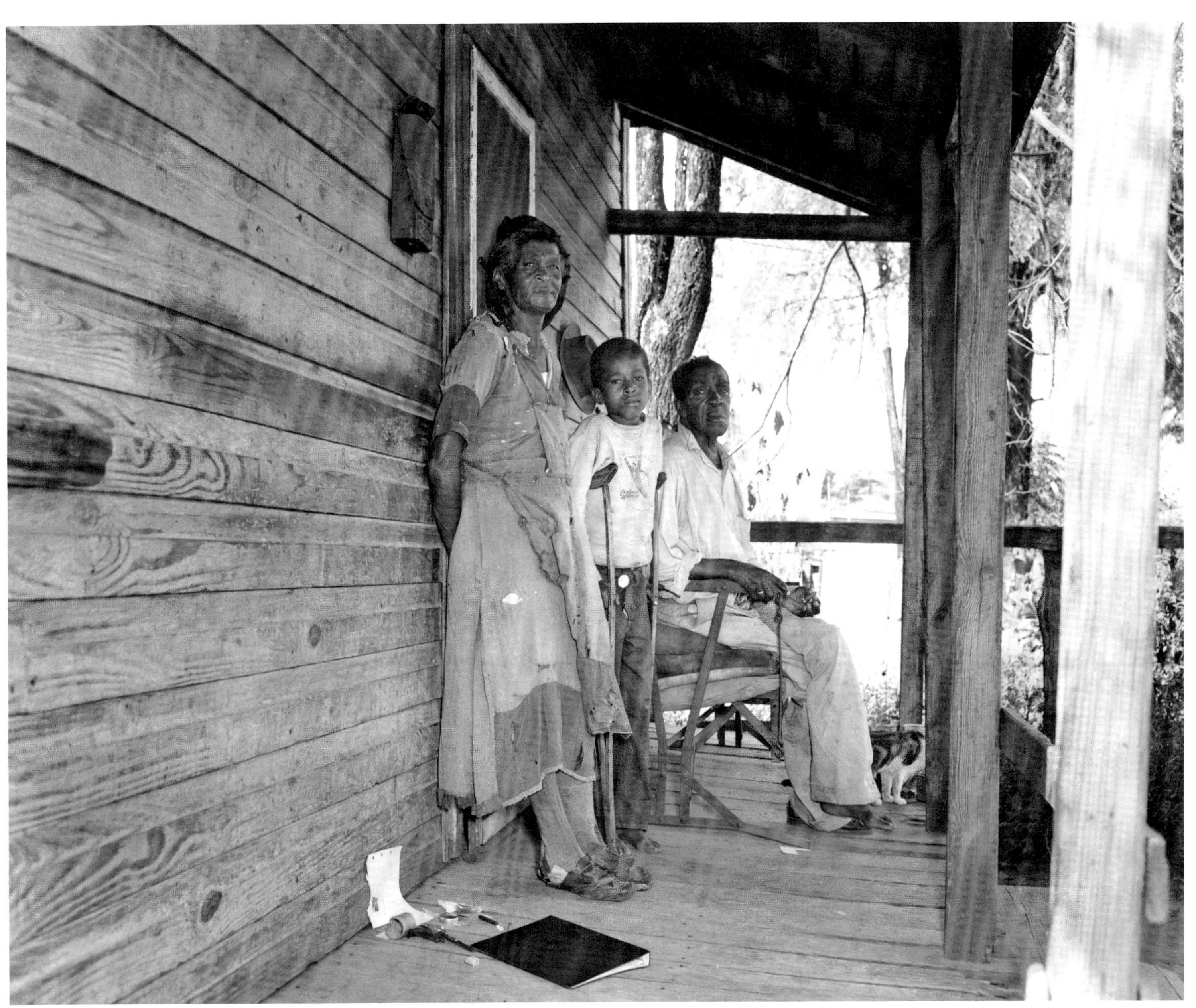

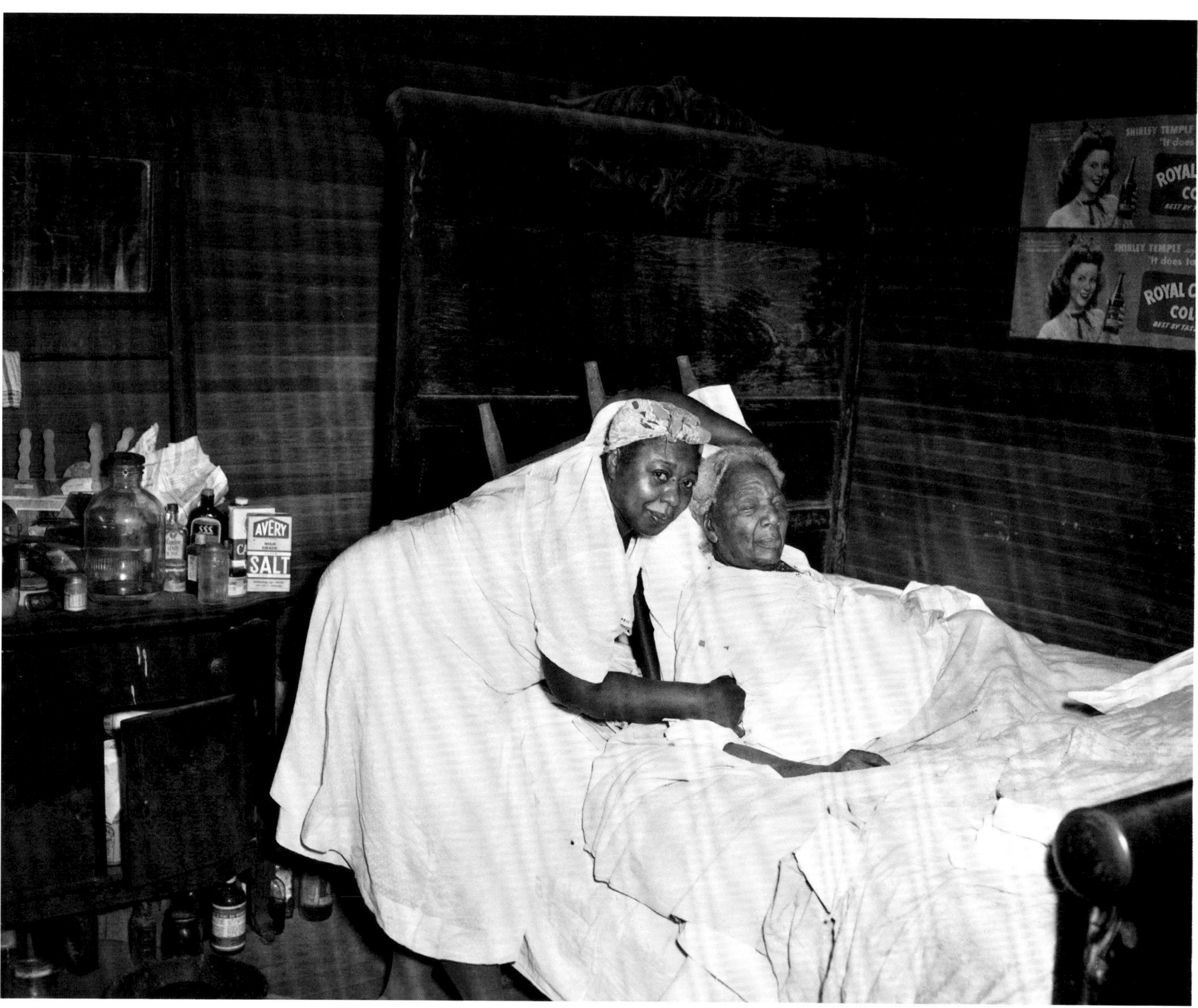
SHIRLEY TEMPLE
ROYAL
SHIRLEY TEMPLE
SSS
AVERY
SALT

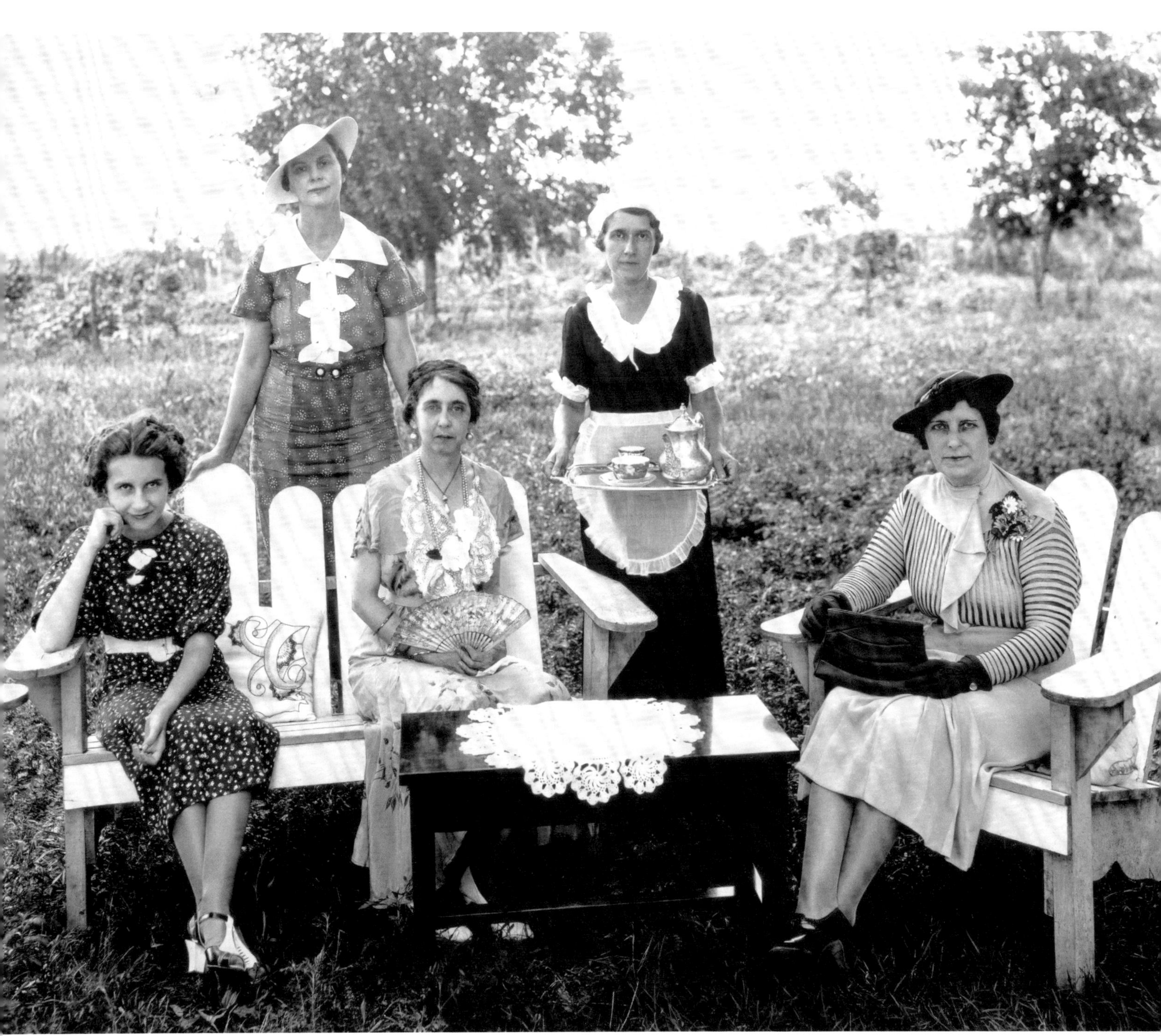

Macon's Dramatic Club.

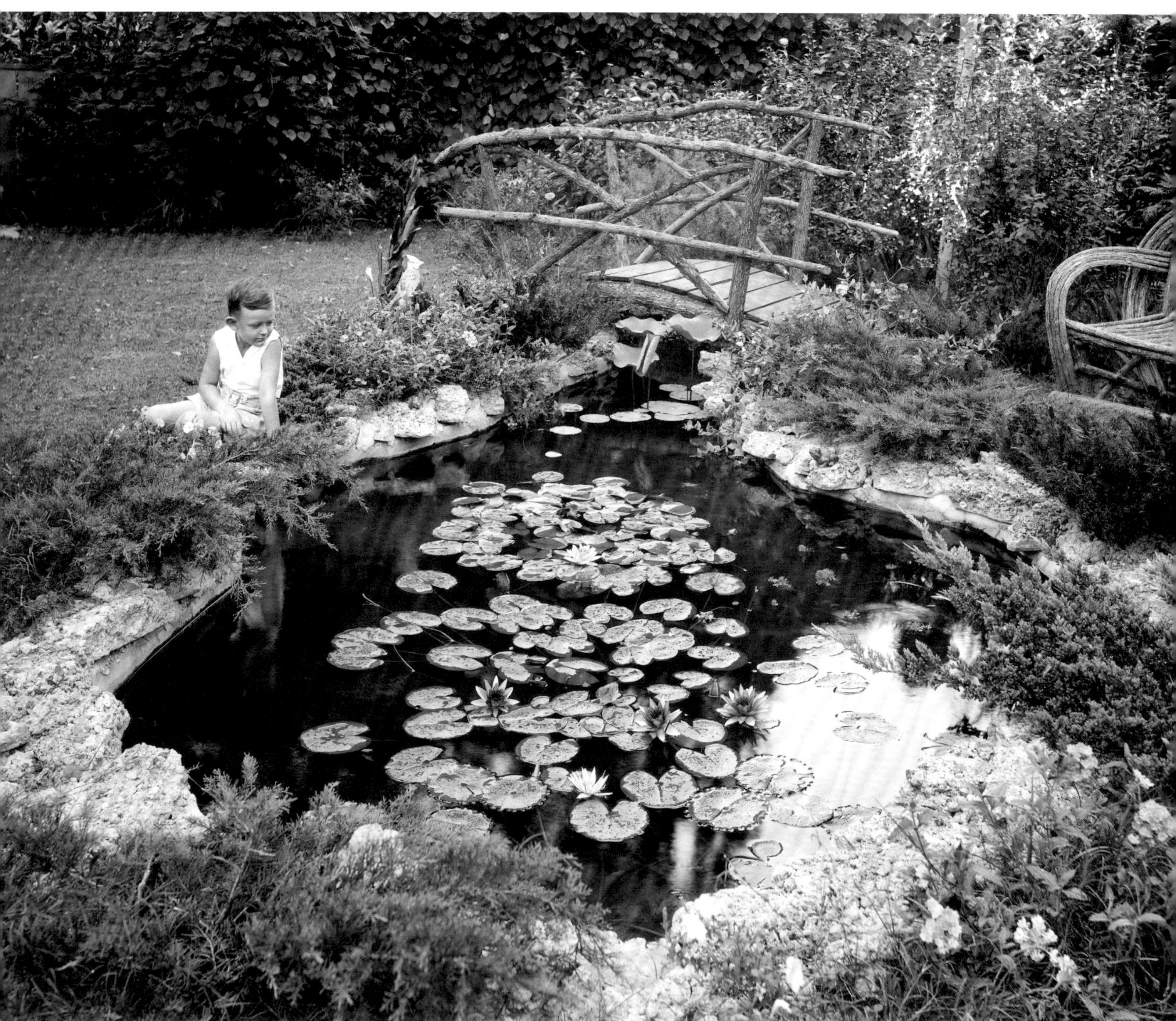

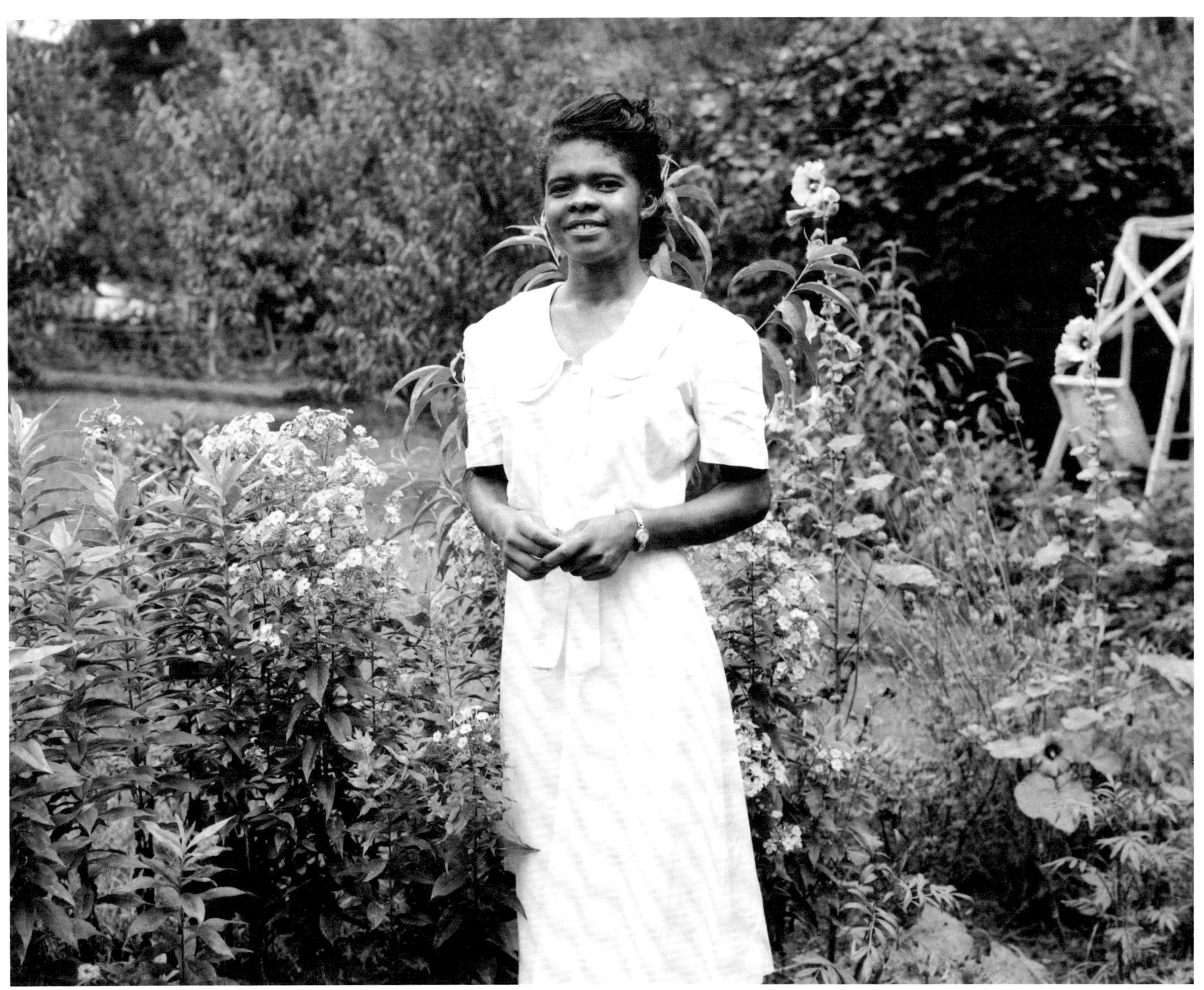

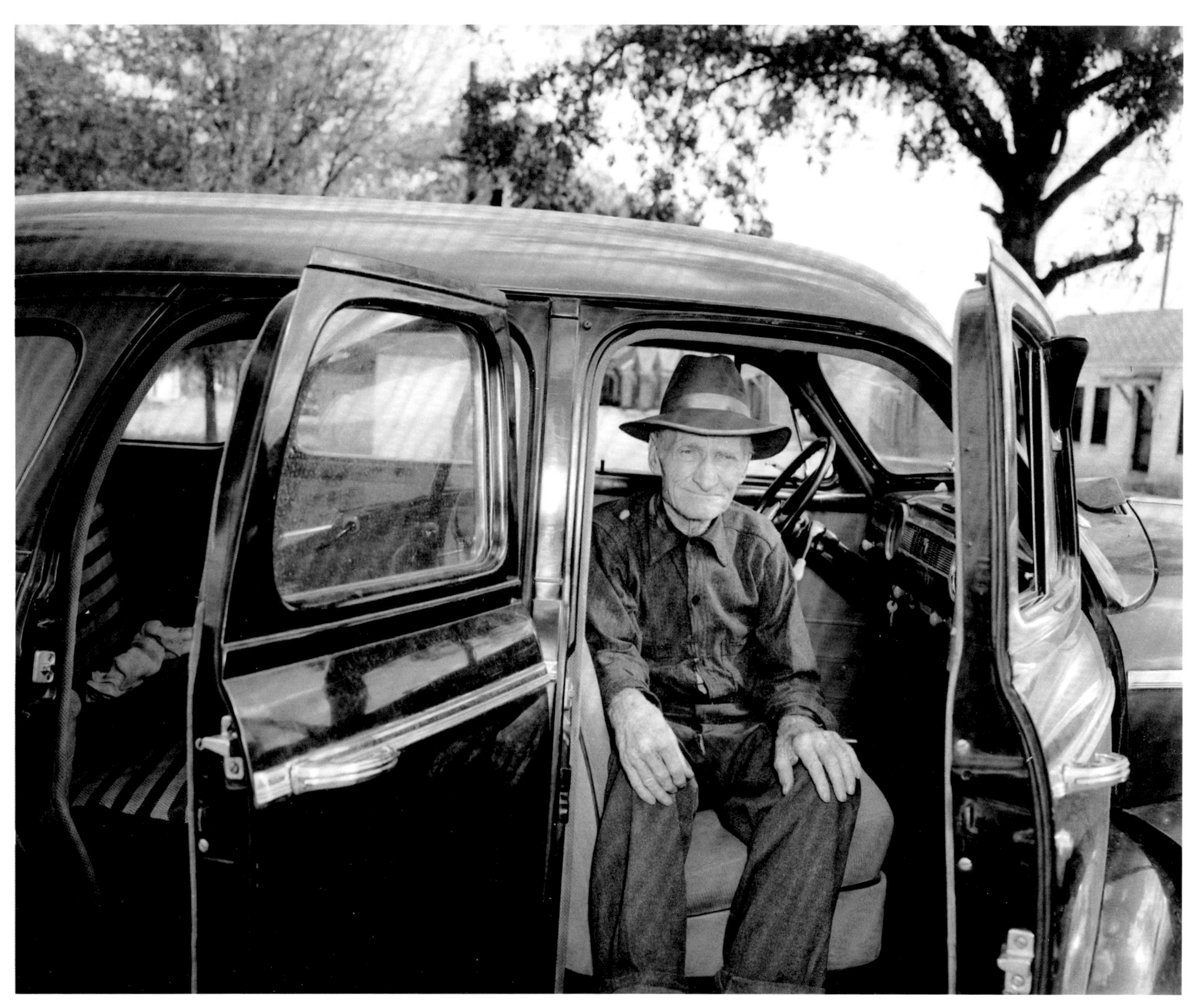

(opposite) *A WCBI-AM radio announcer interviews a Soap Box Derby participant, circa 1950s.*

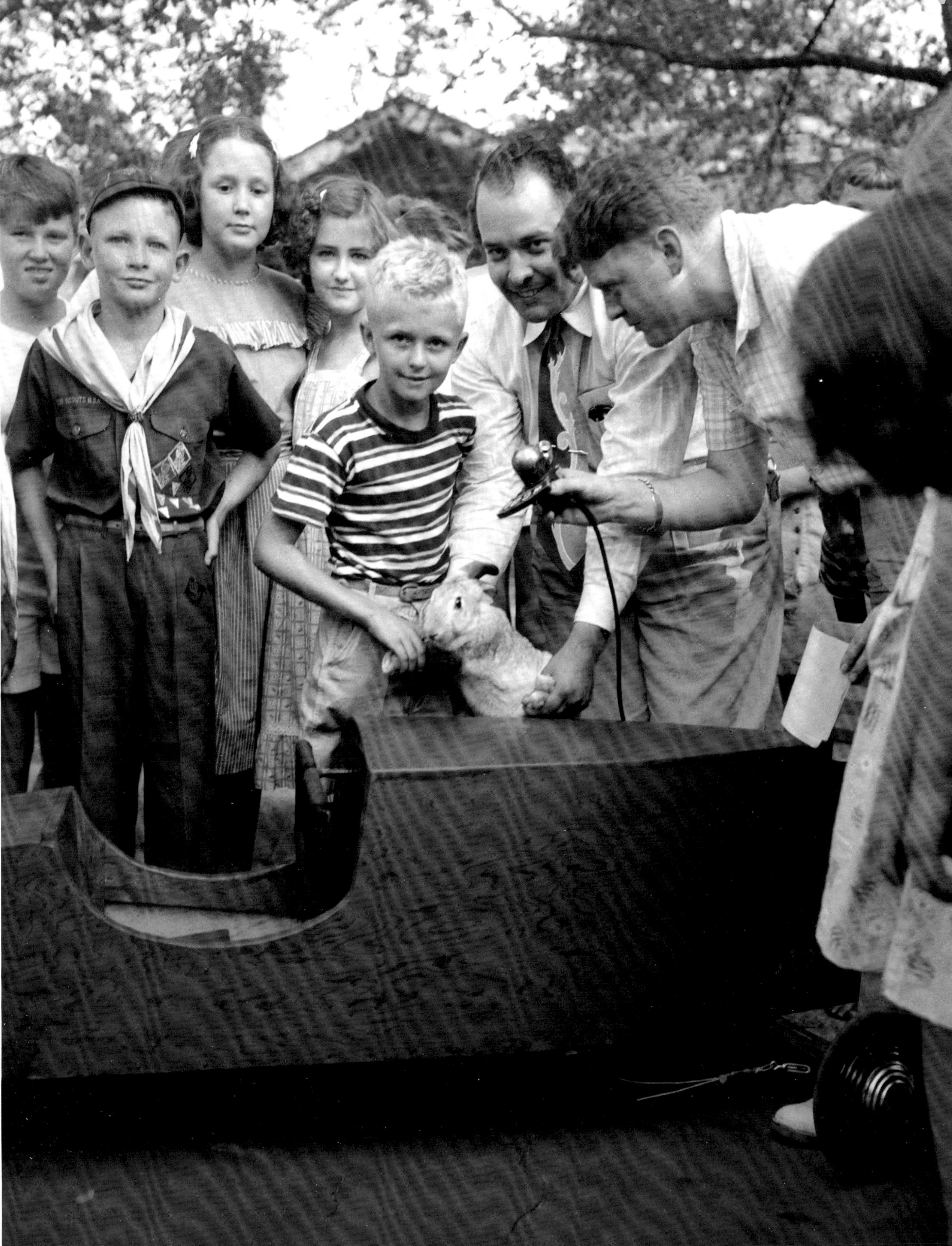

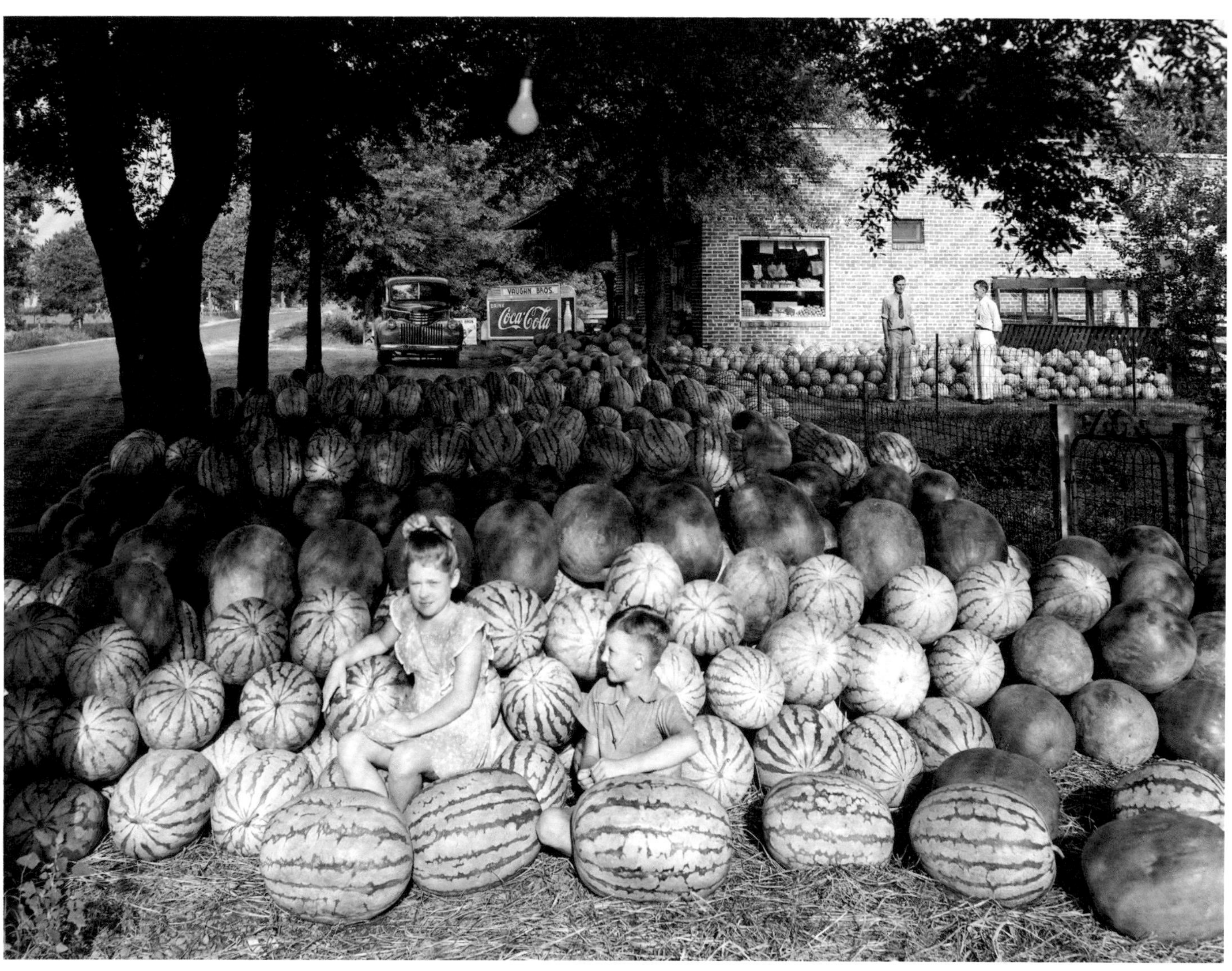
VAUGHN BROS
DRINK
Coca-Cola

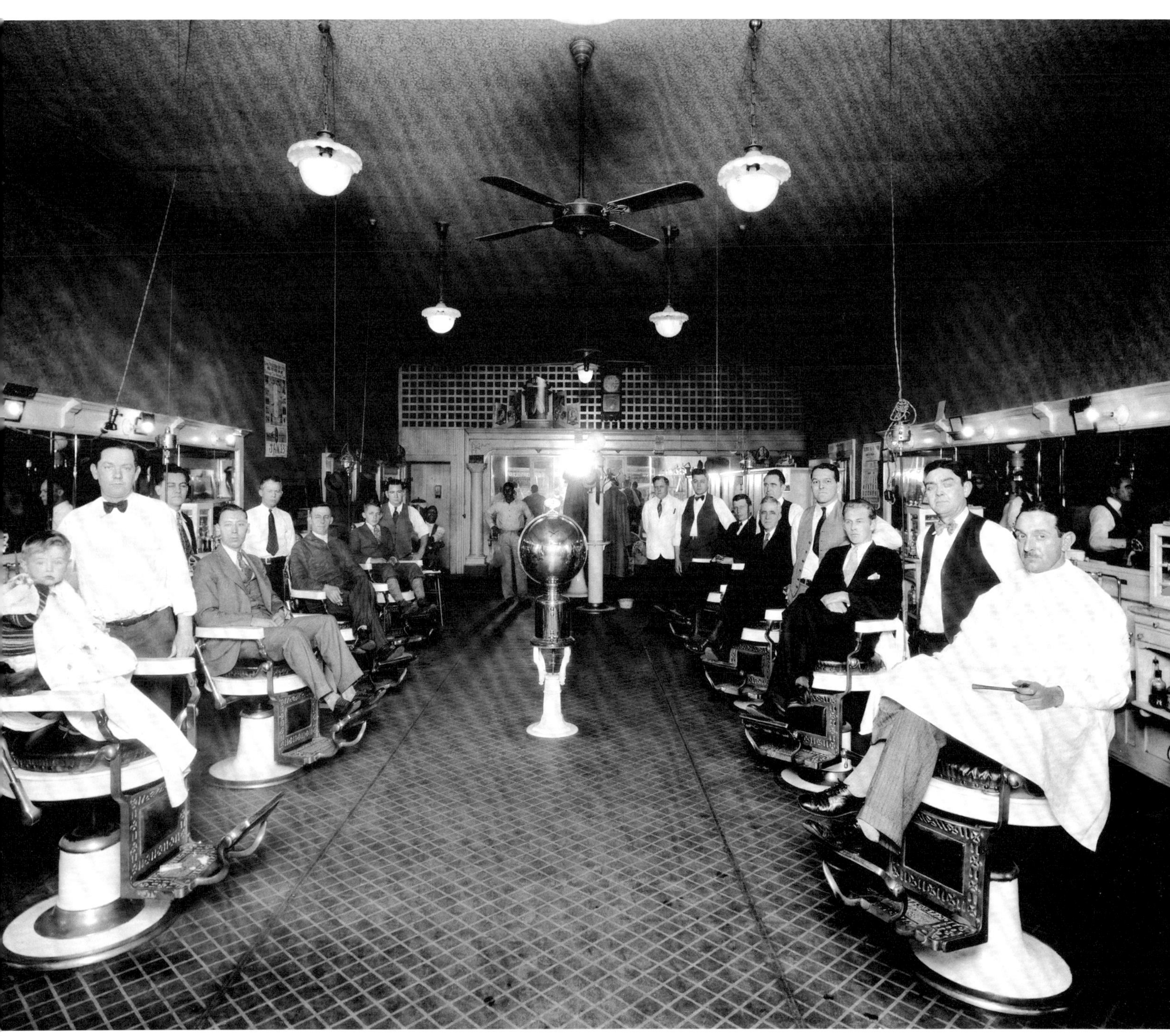

Main Street barbershop, circa 1930s.

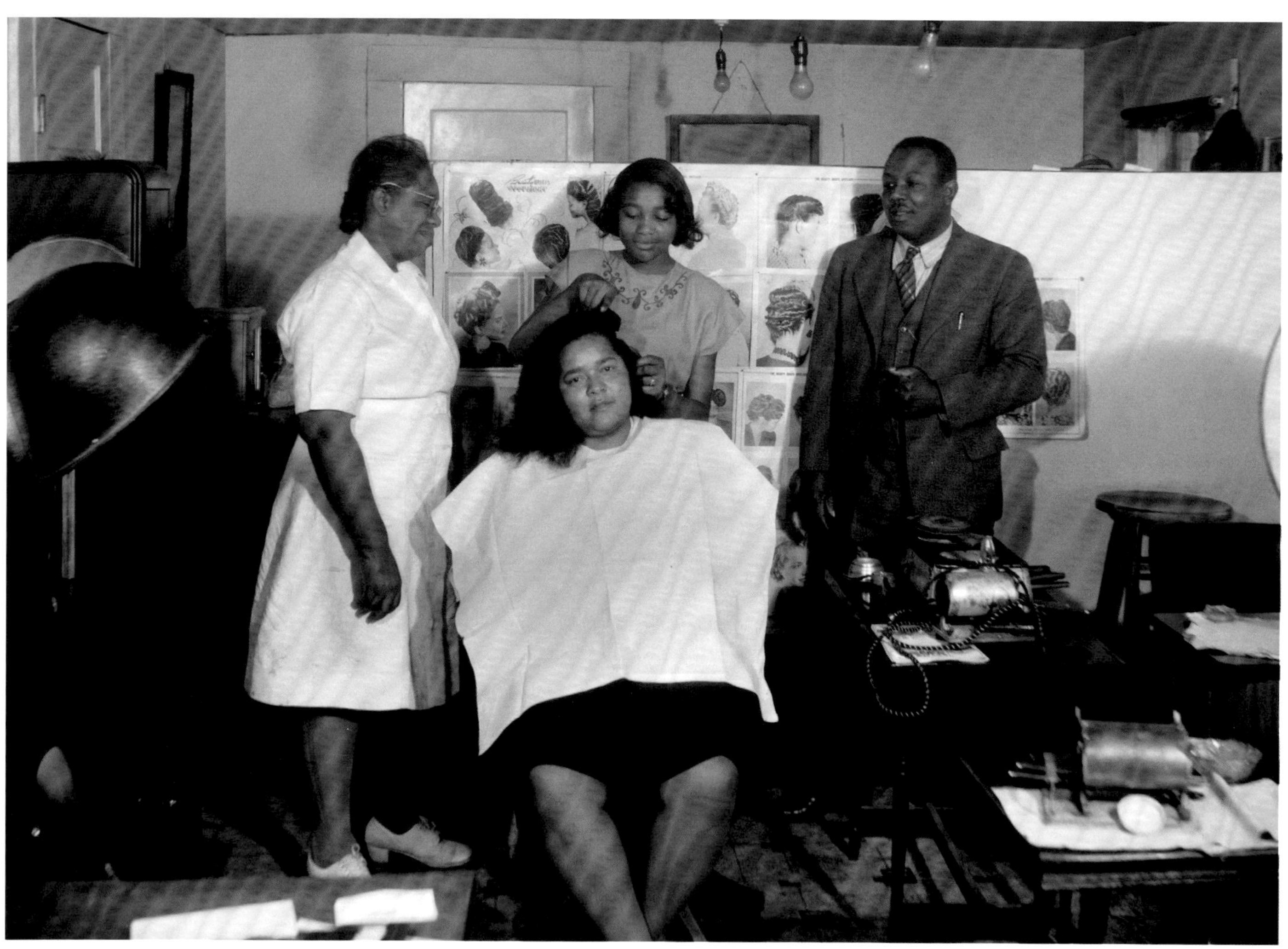

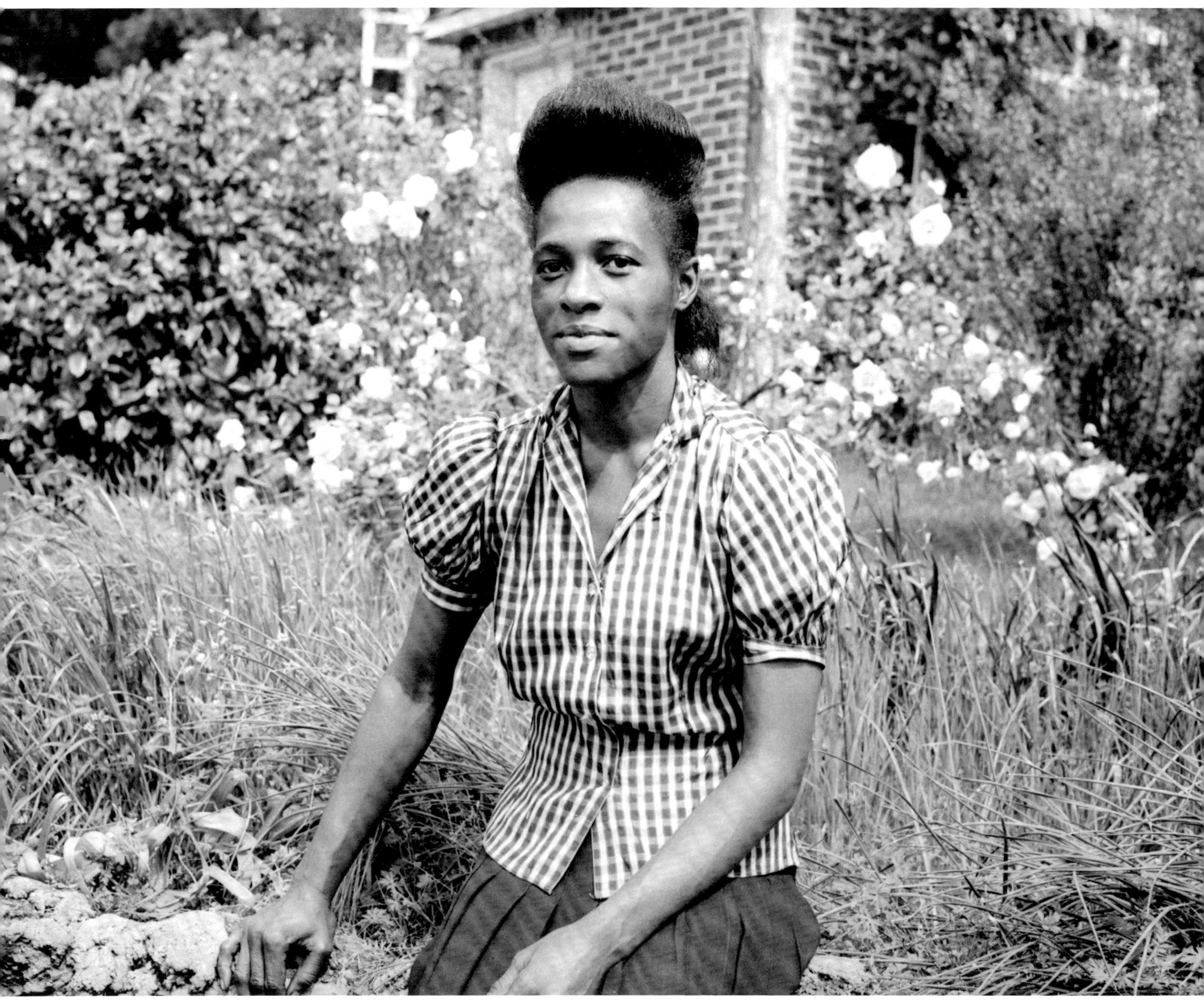

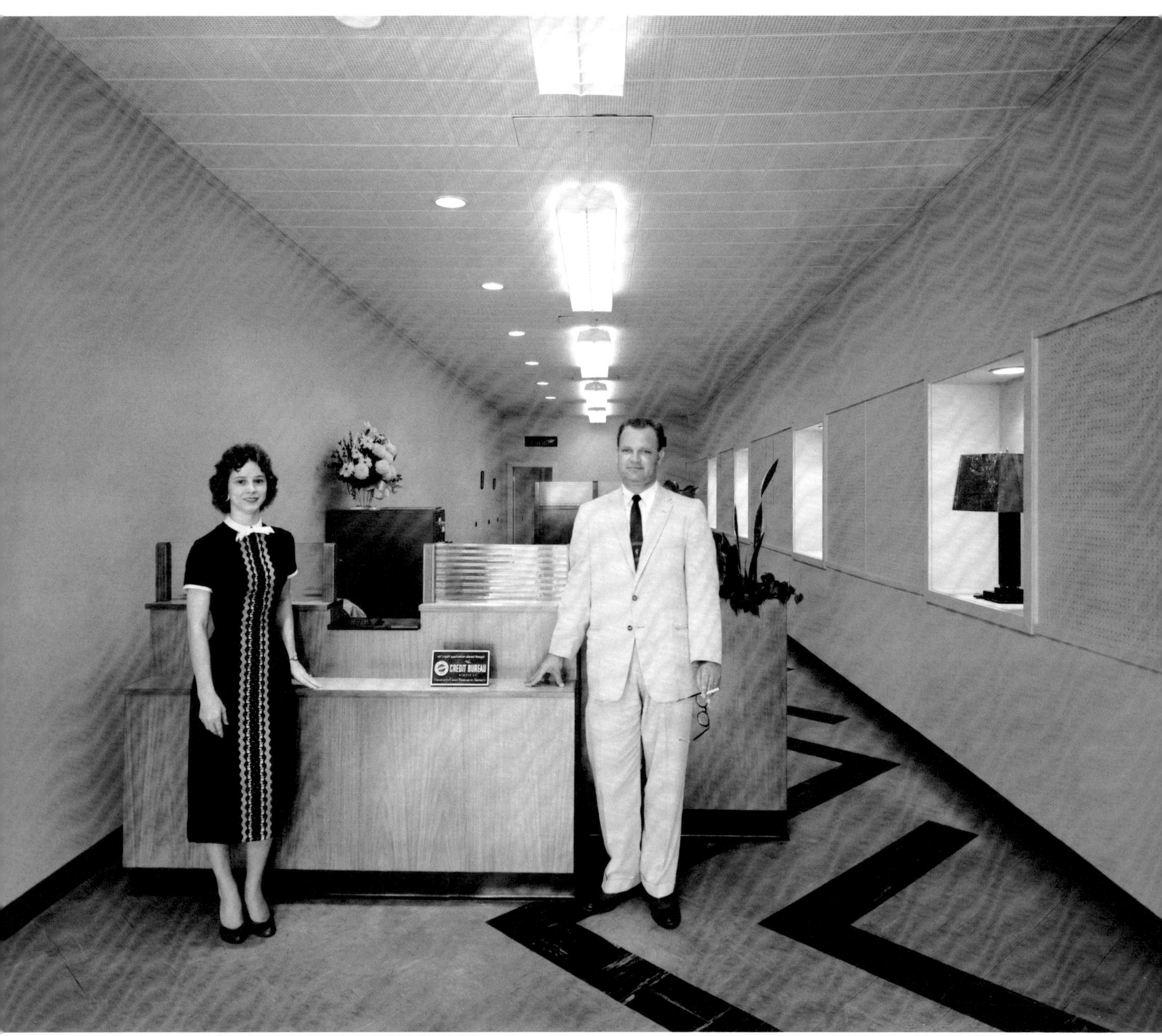
CREDIT BUREAU

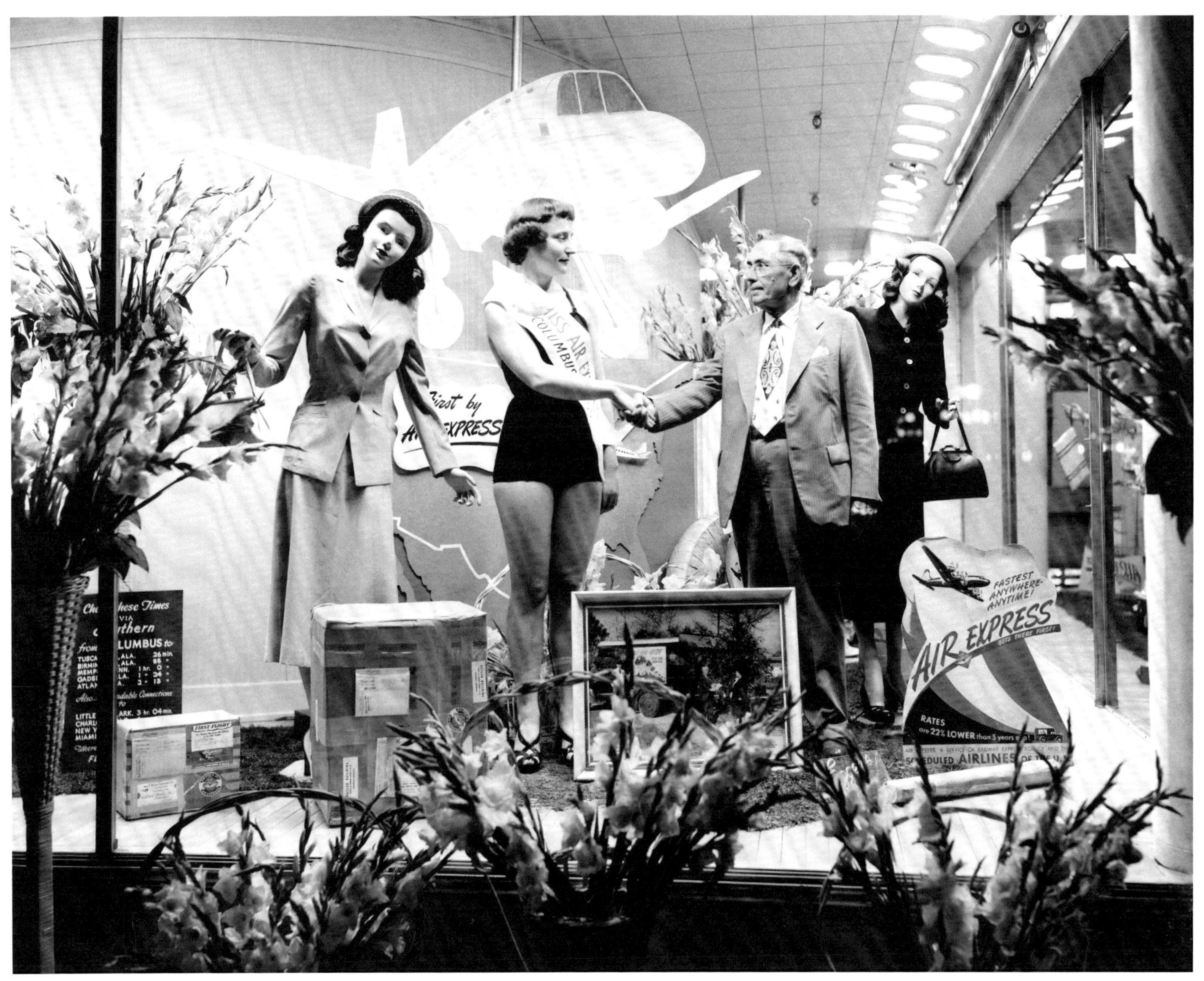
First by
EXPRESS
FASTEST ANYWHERE-ANYTIME!
AIR EXPRESS
GETS THERE FIRST!
RATES
AIRLINES

Egger's Department Store window display.

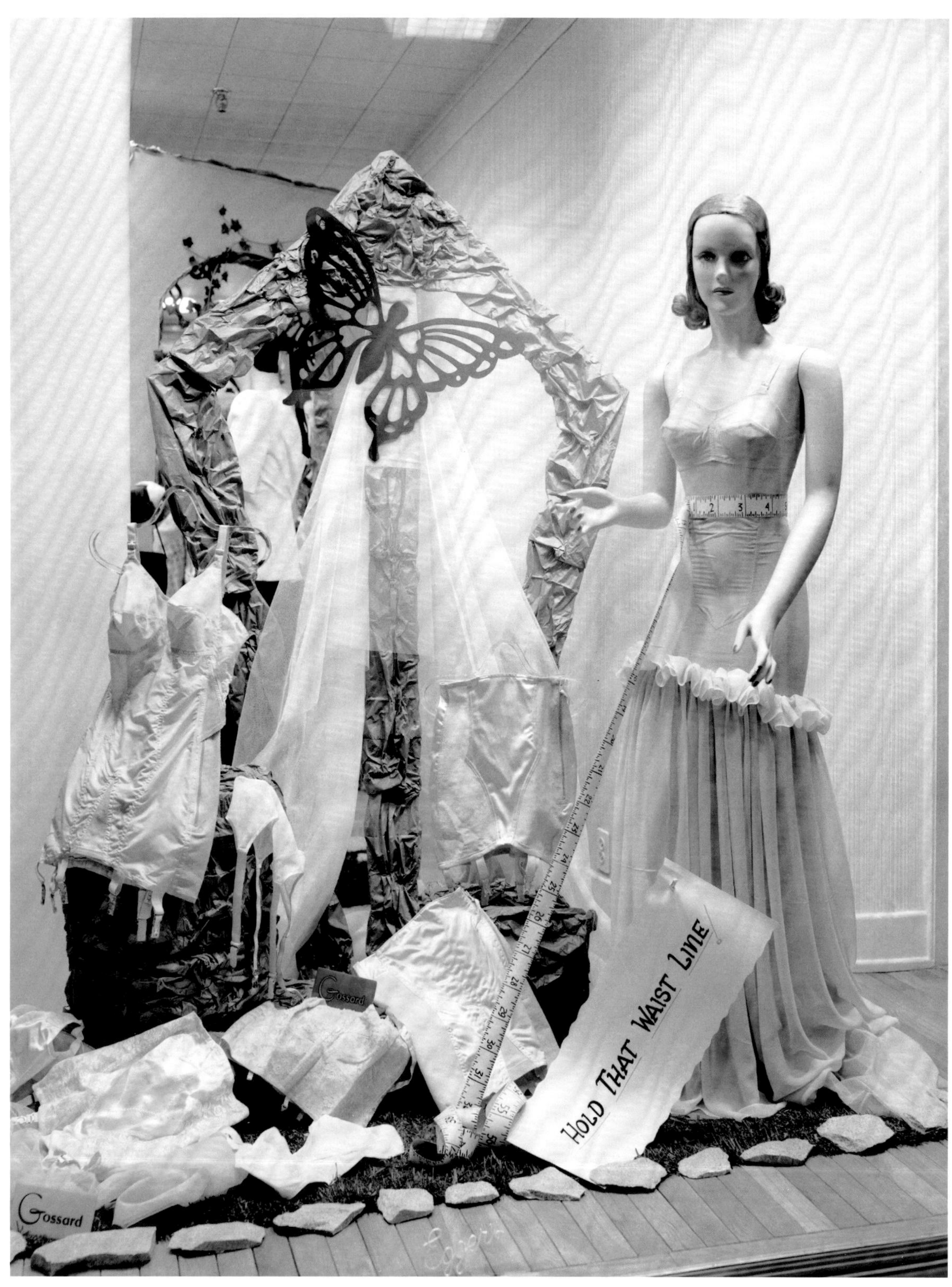

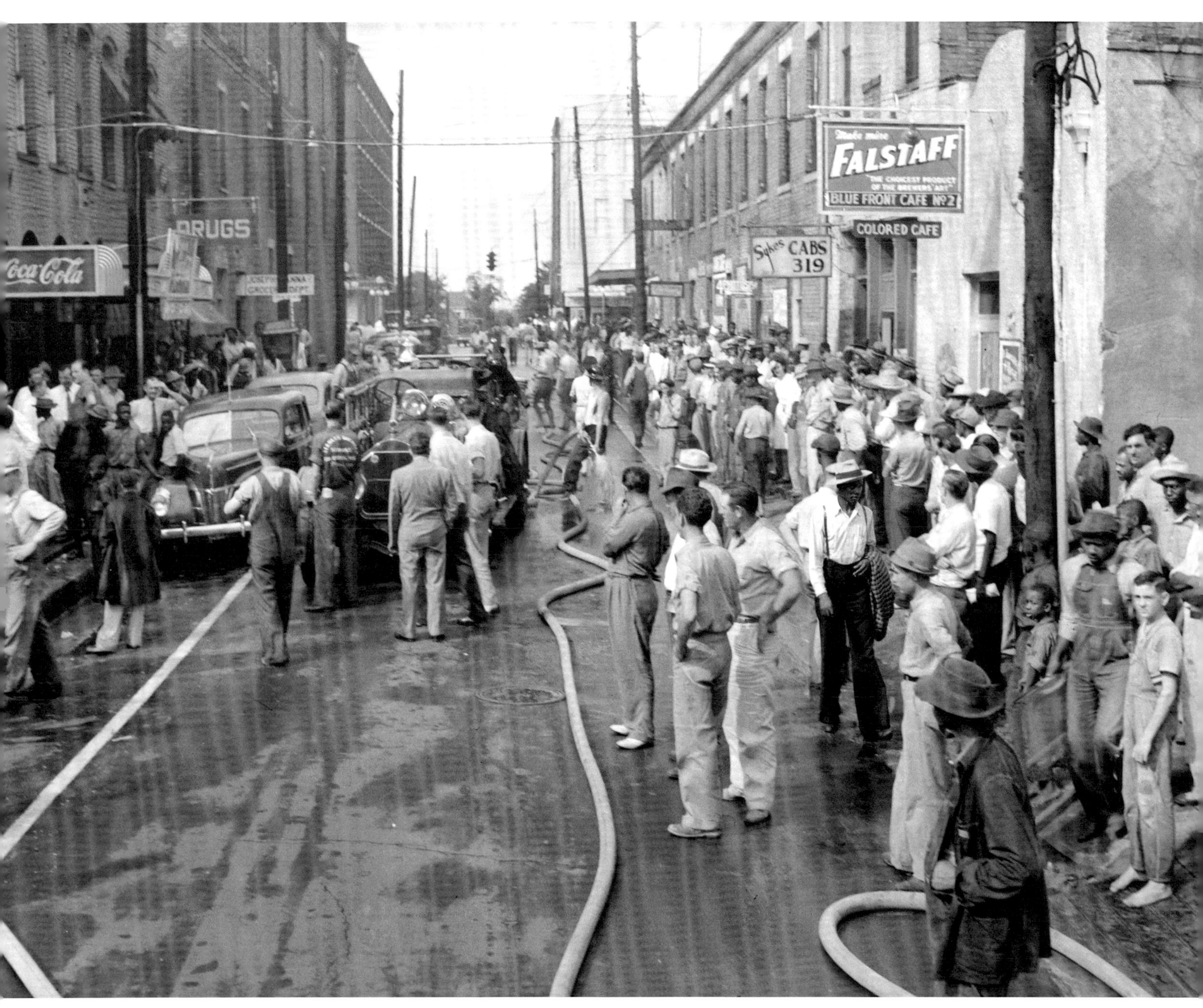

Catfish Alley fire, circa 1940.

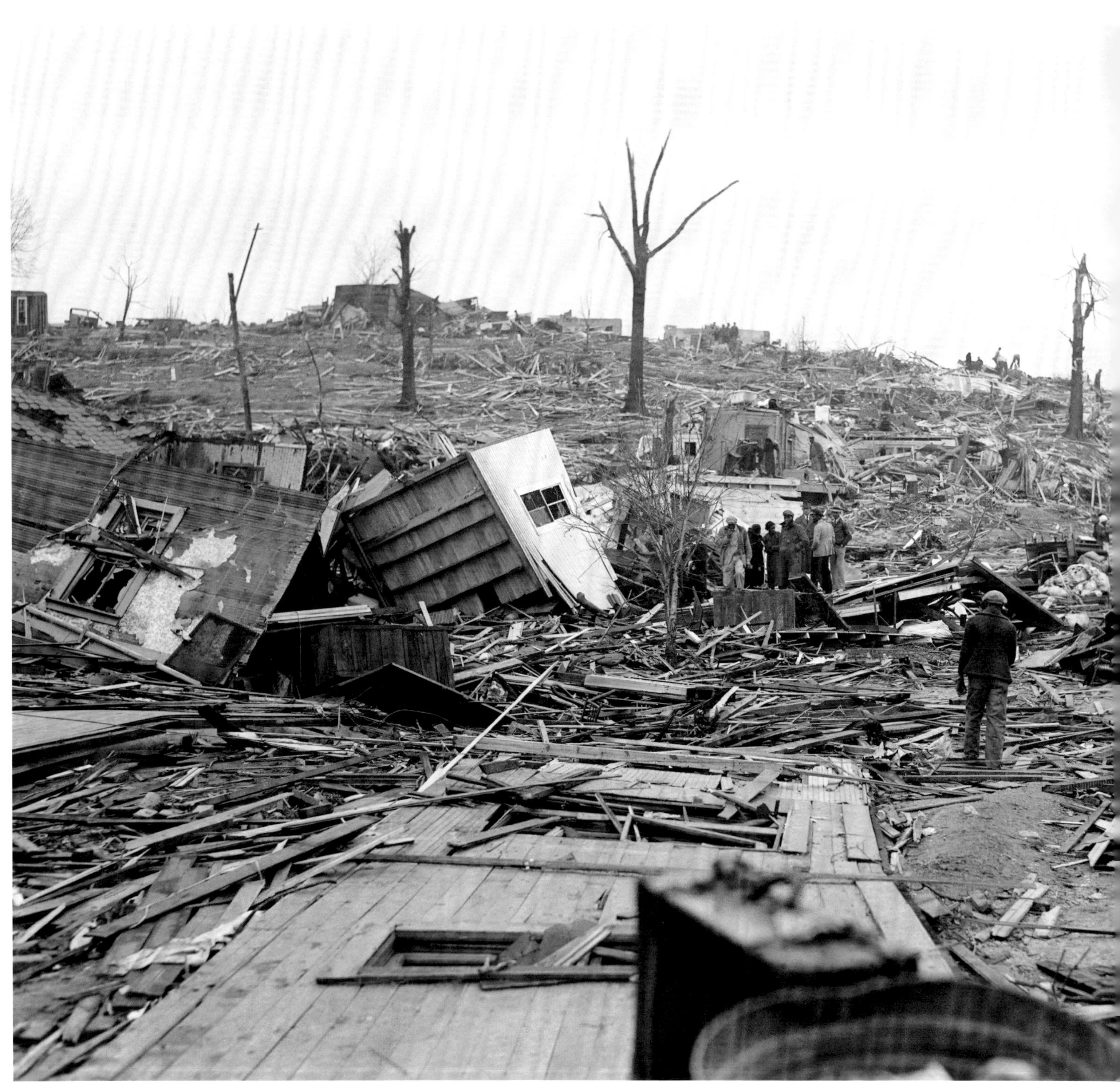

Tombigbee River flood.

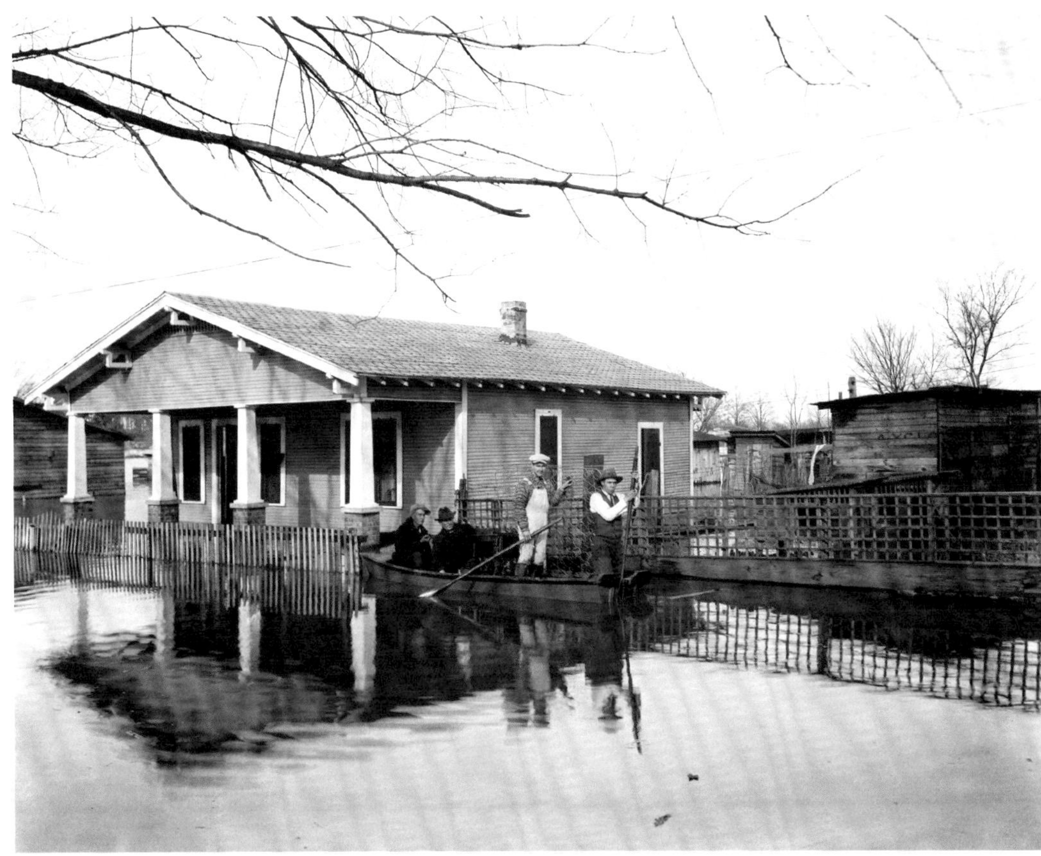

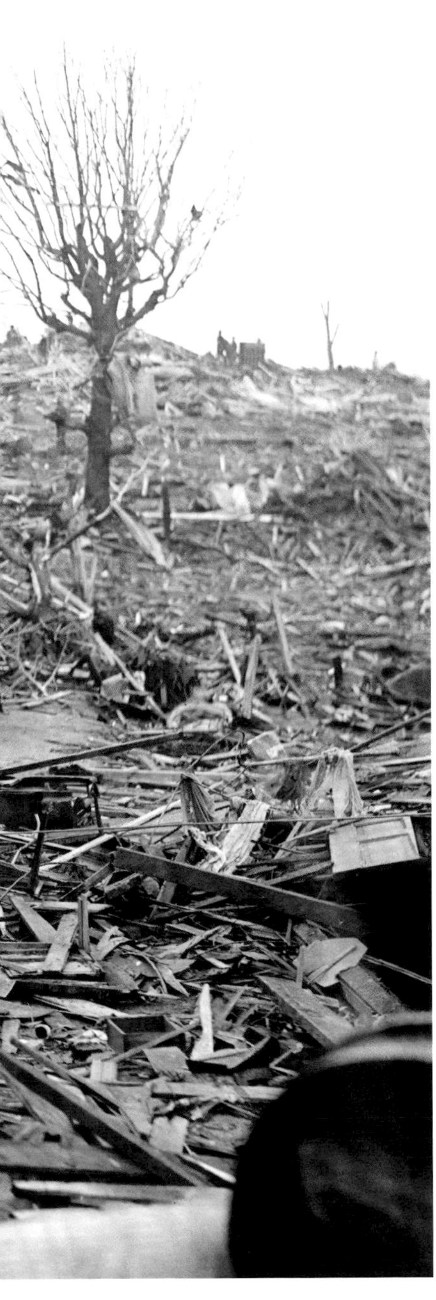

Tornado aftermath, Tupelo, Mississippi, April 4, 1936.

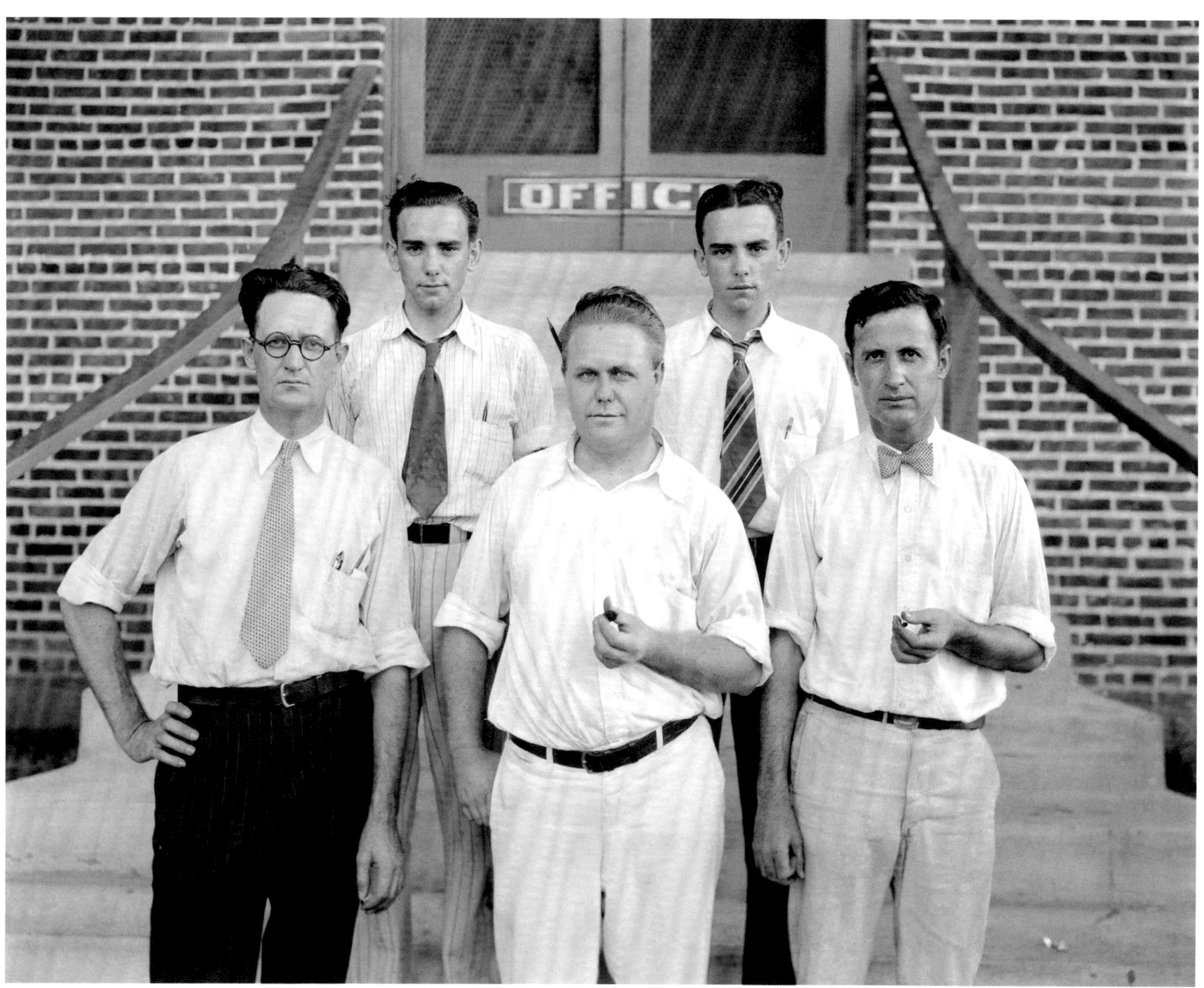
OFFIC

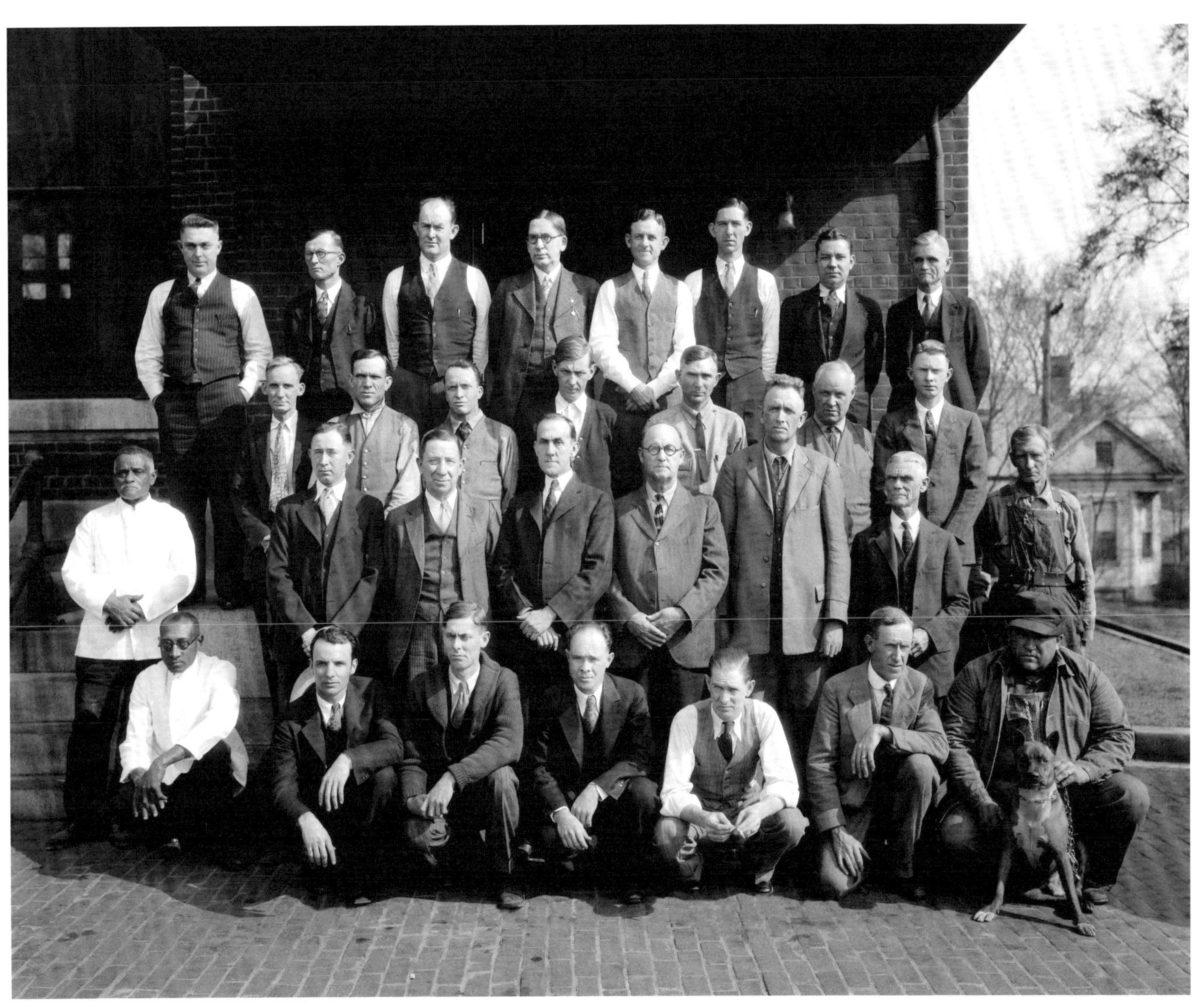

Post office staff, circa 1935.

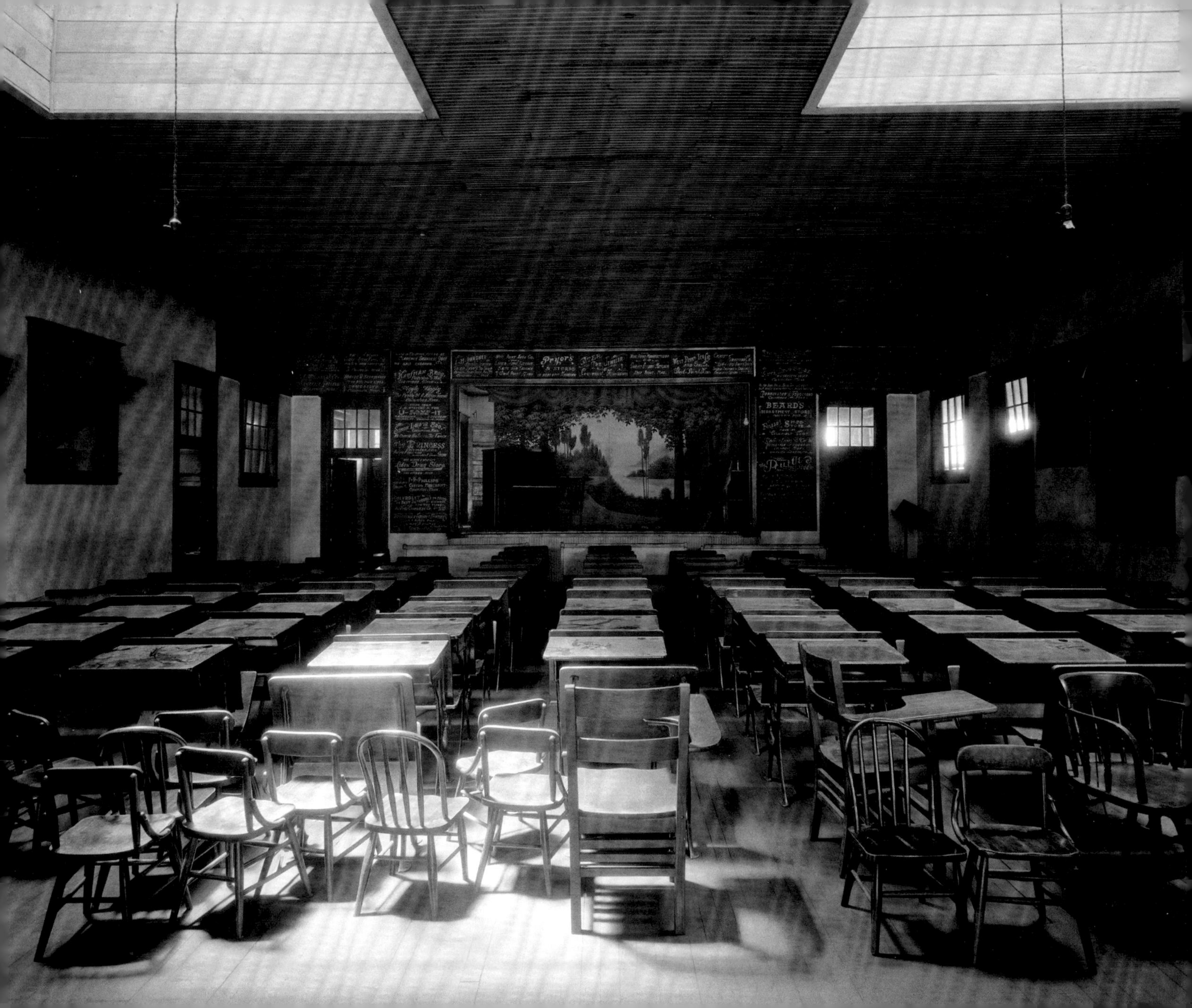
Pryor's
5 STORES
West Point Ice Co.
U-SAVE-IT
The PRINCESS
BEARD'S
DEPARTMENT STORE

Union Academy, circa 1930s–40s. Founded in December 1865 as the first school for freed Blacks in Columbus in a building that originally was a Confederate hospital.

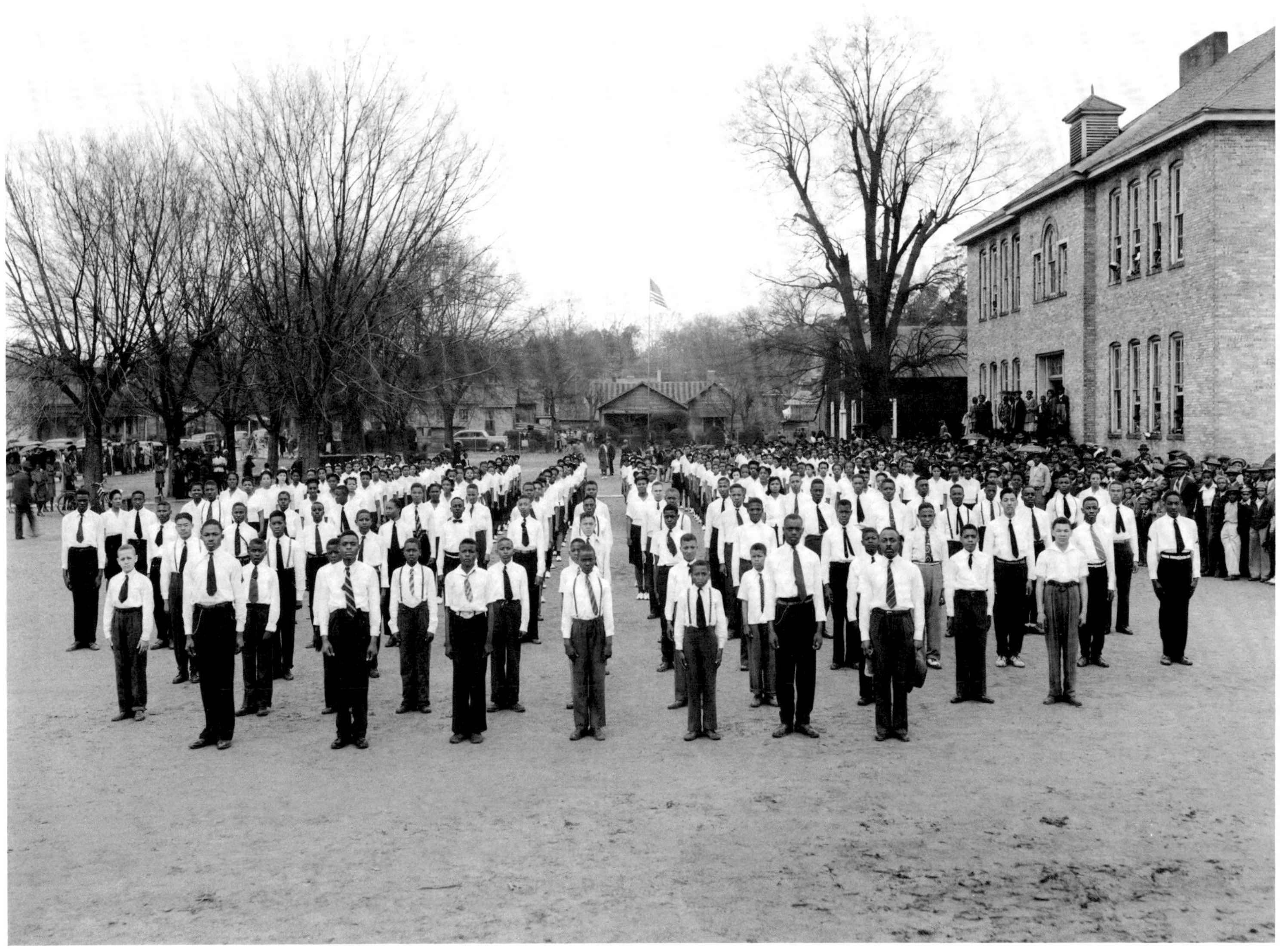

(opposite) *Schoolroom with mural that includes advertisement for Pruitt's studio on lower right.*

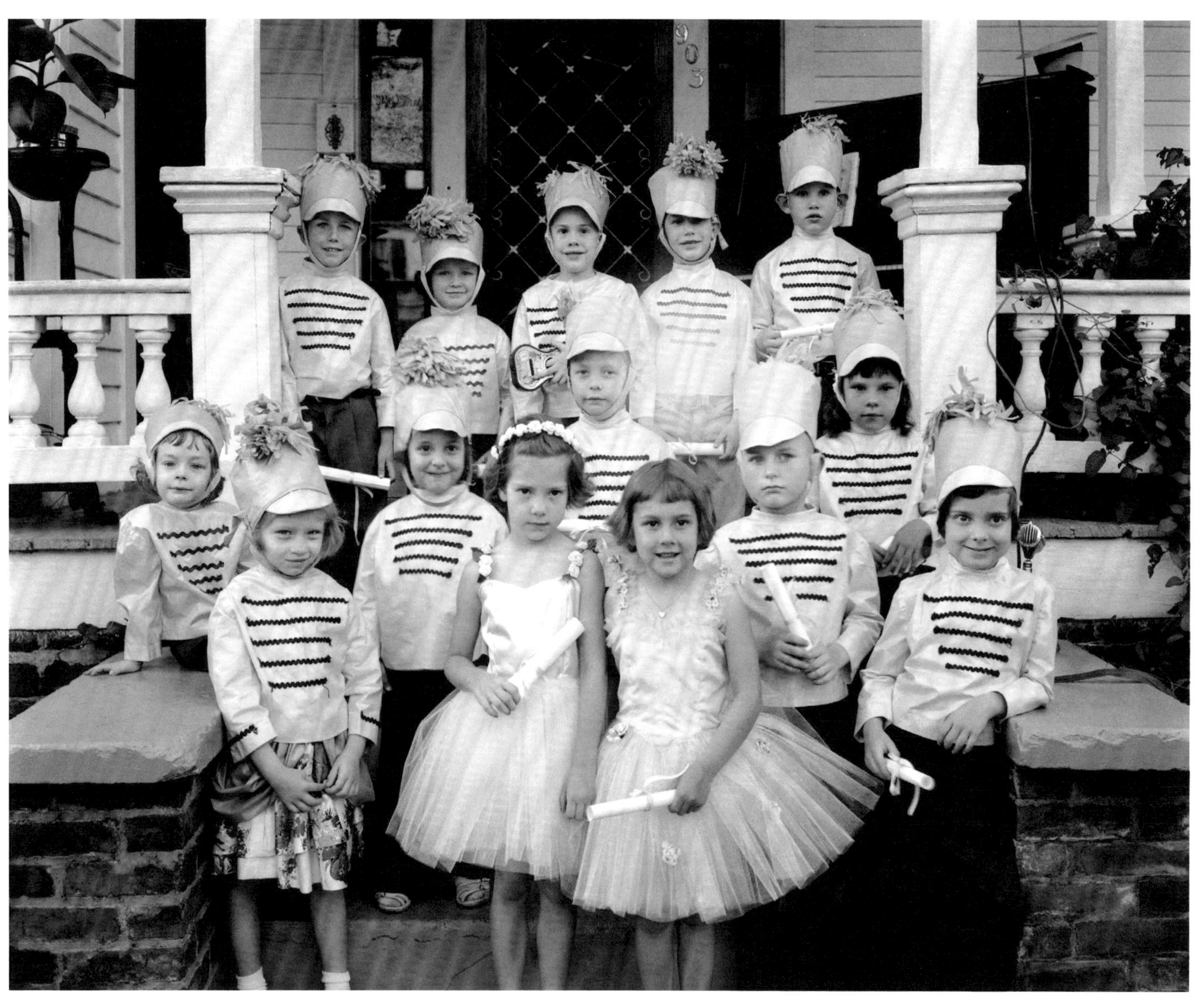

Jack and Jill Kindergarten, circa May Day 1958.
Joy Dill (center) *wears a flowered headband.*

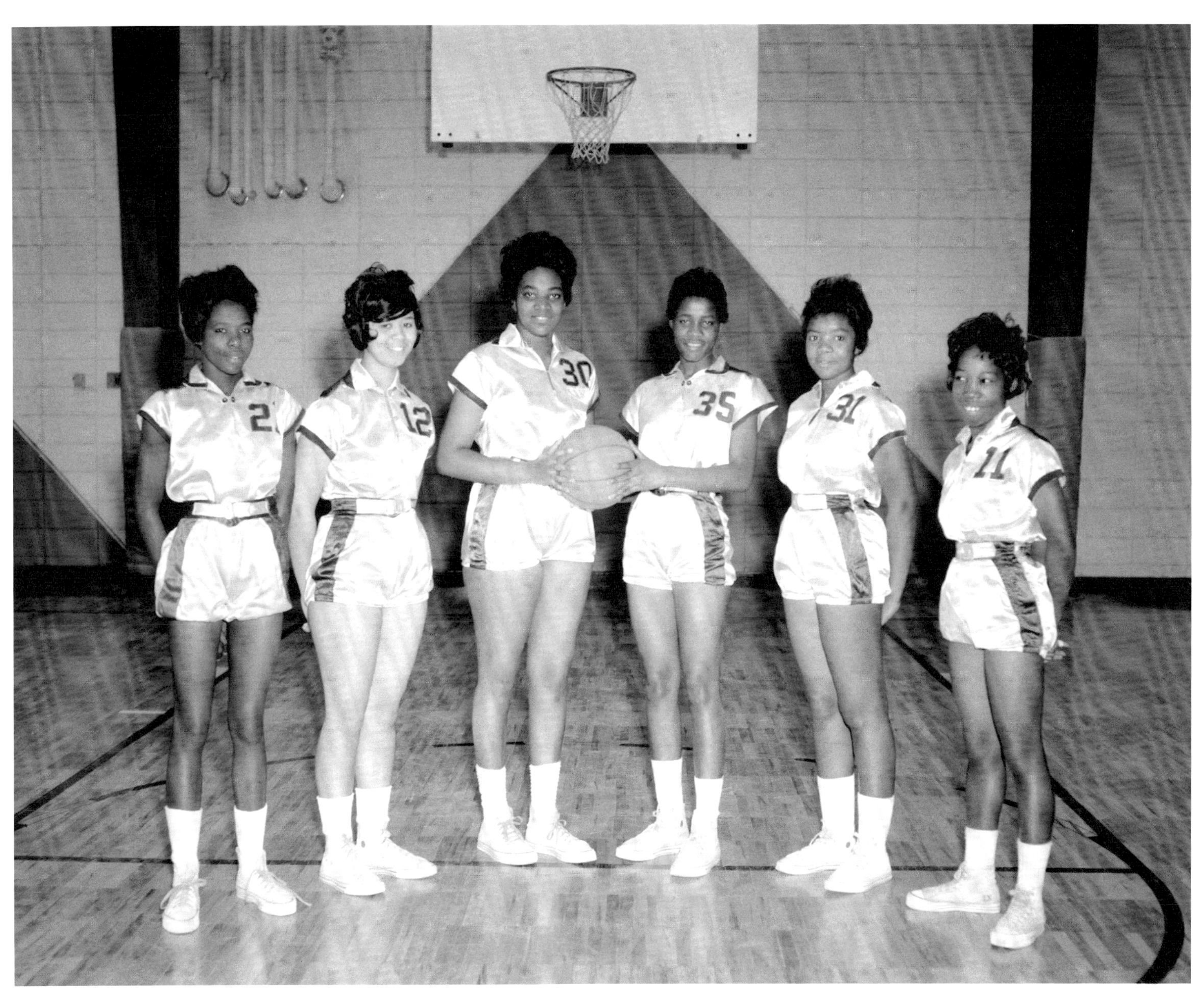

Hunt High School girls basketball team, circa 1950s.

Macon High School girls basketball team, circa 1930s.

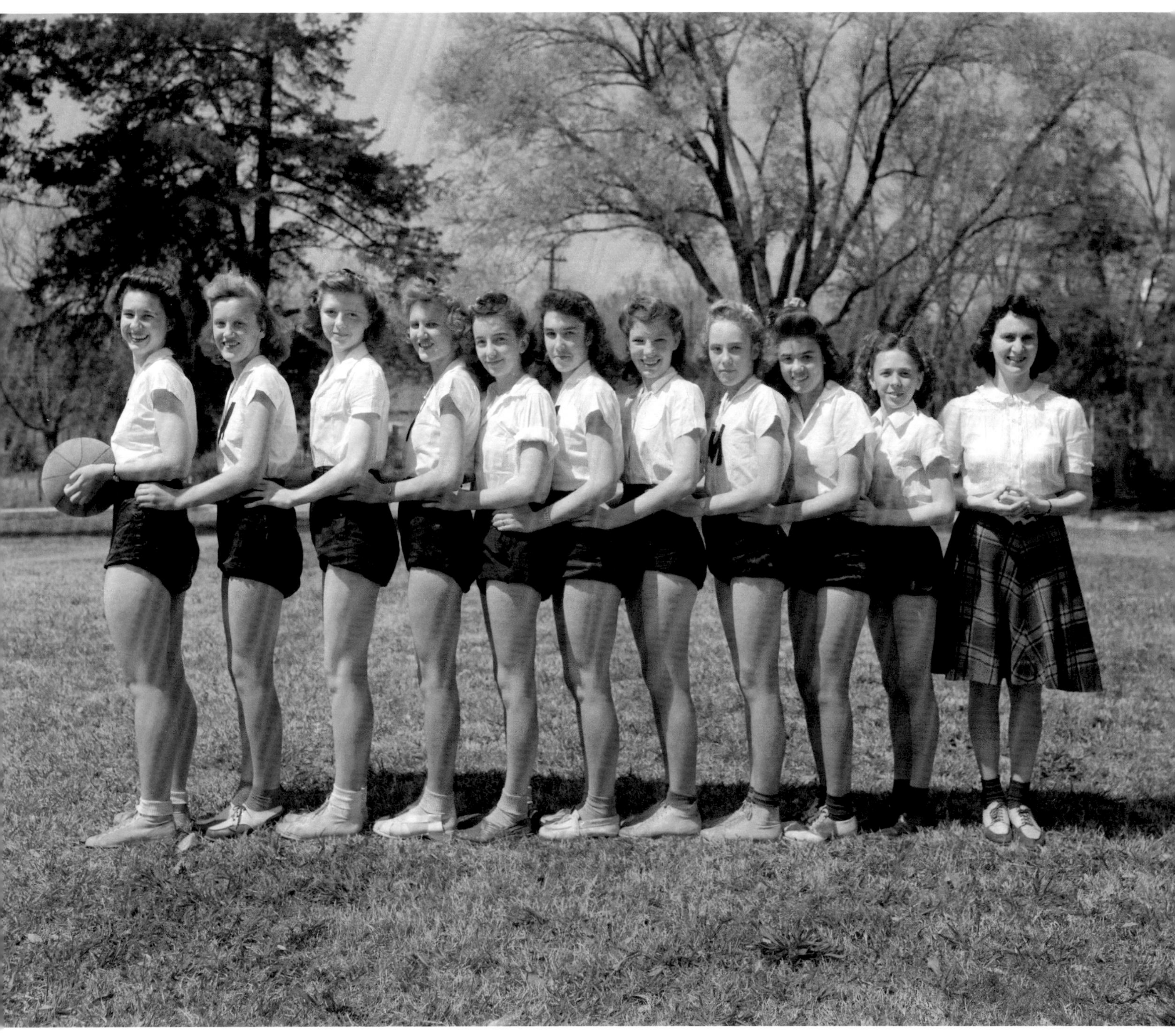

Columbus Redbirds baseball team.

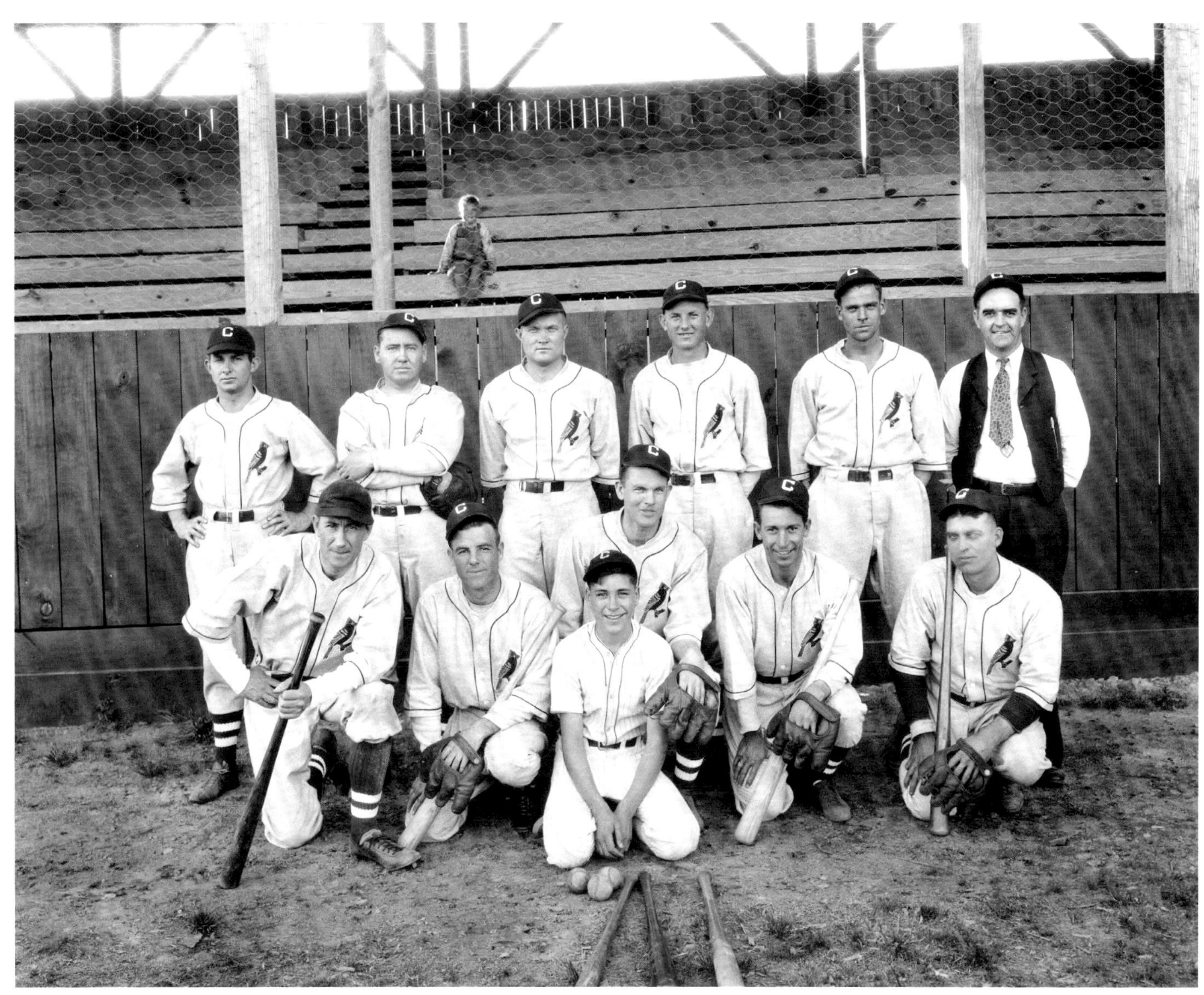

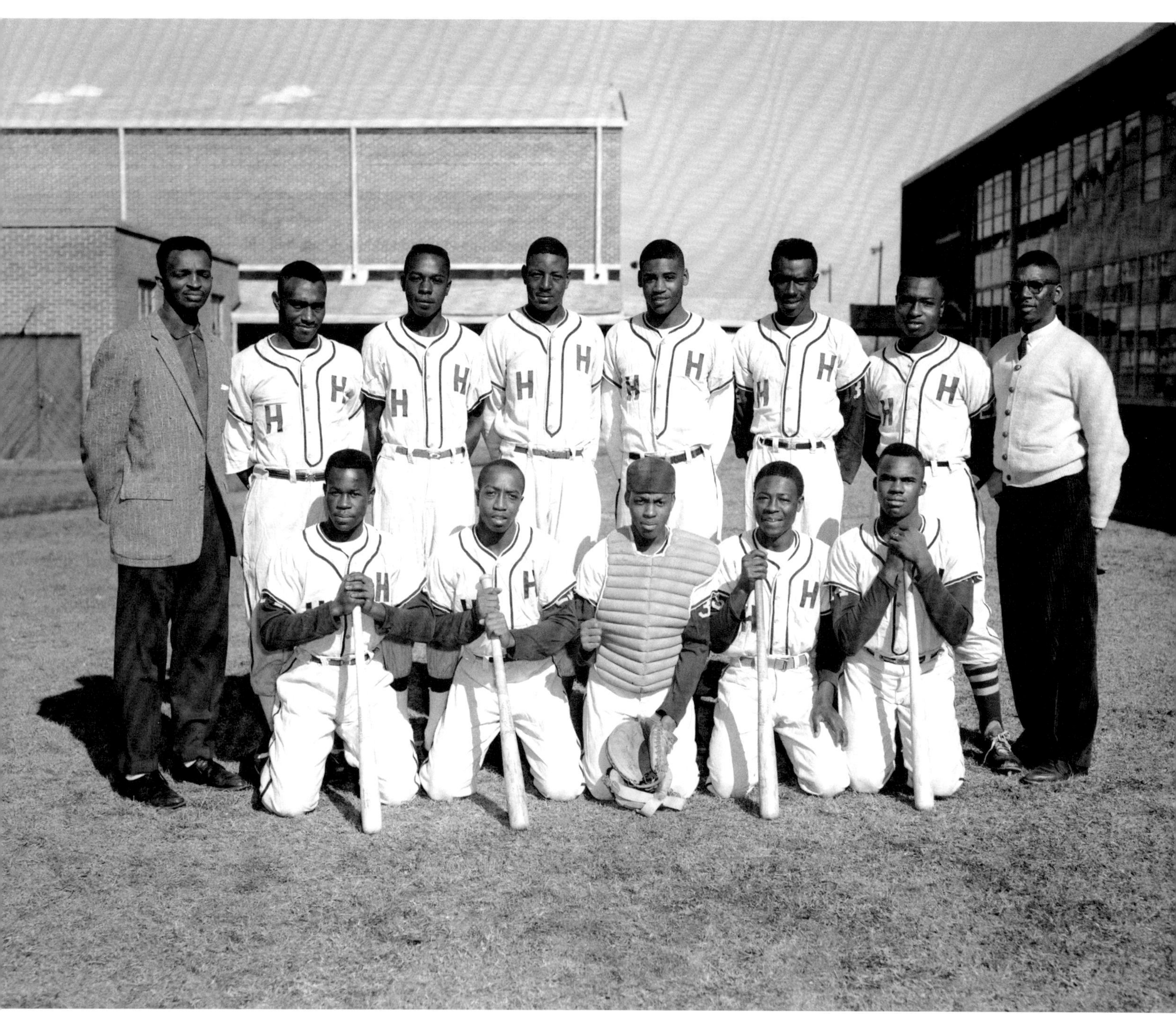

Hunt High School baseball team, circa 1950s.

Hunt High School library.

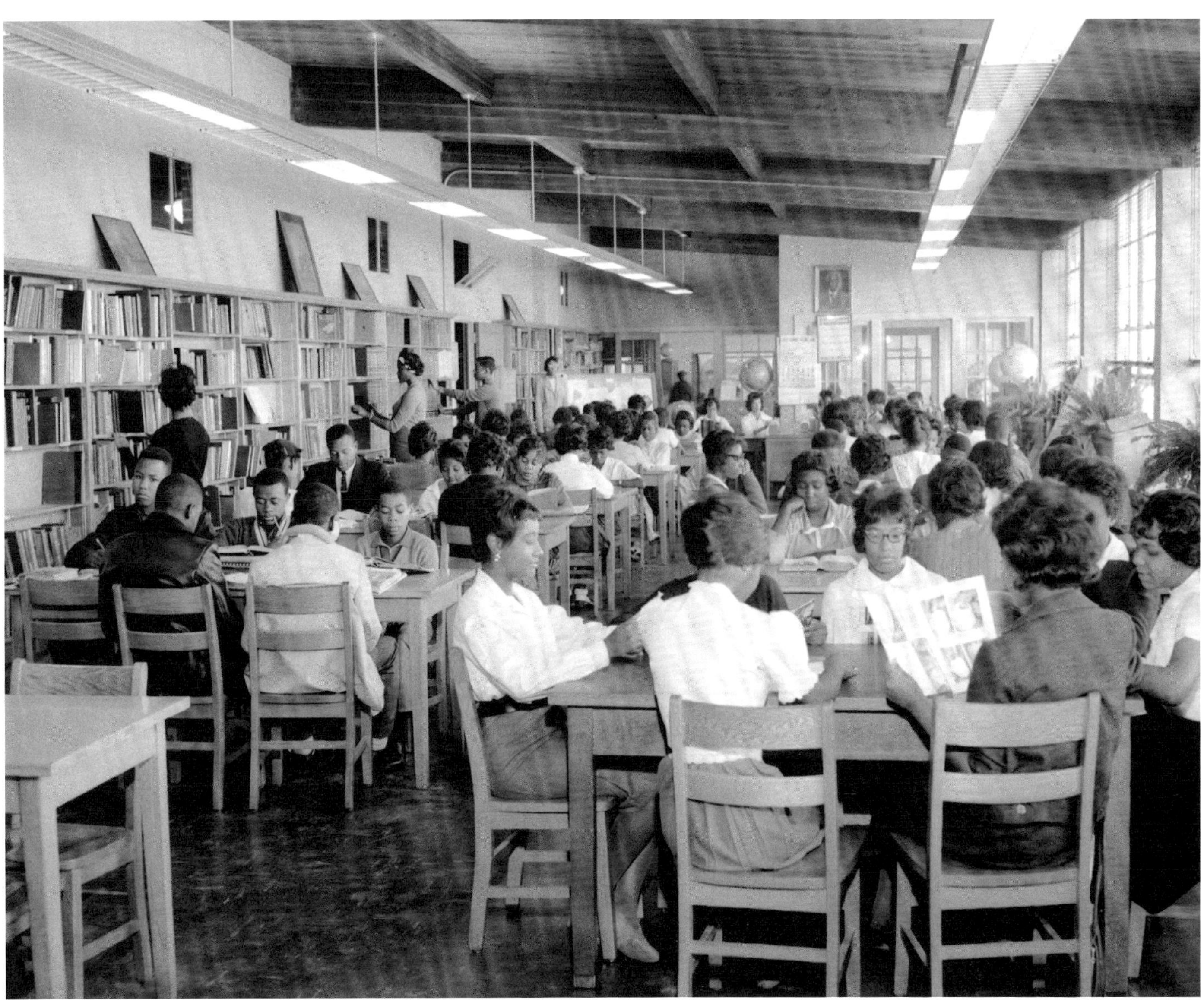

Springtime Zouave exercise demonstrations, Mississippi State College for Women, late 1930s.

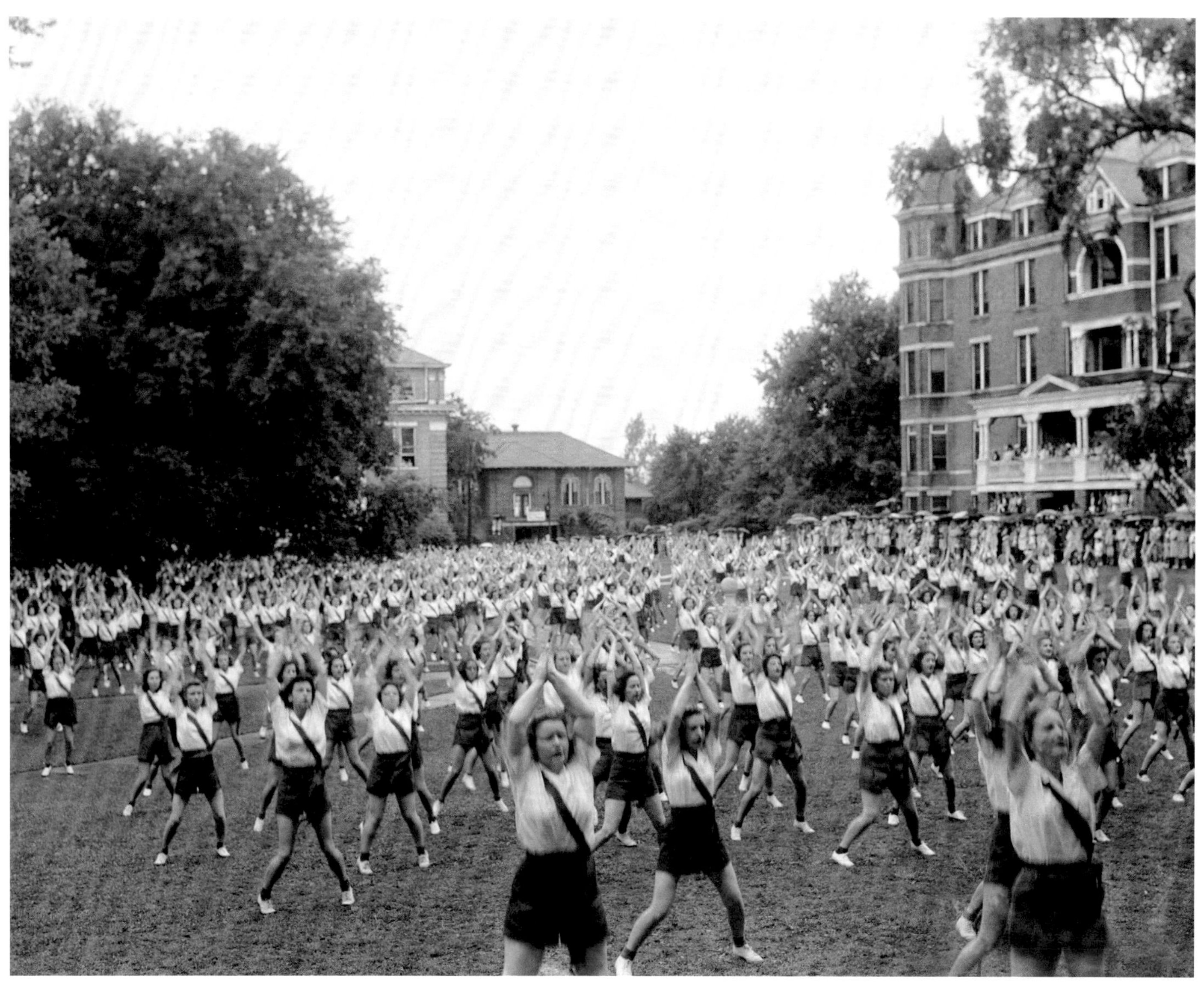

(opposite) *Mississippi State College for Women students dancing "Grecian-style" by pool, circa 1920s.*

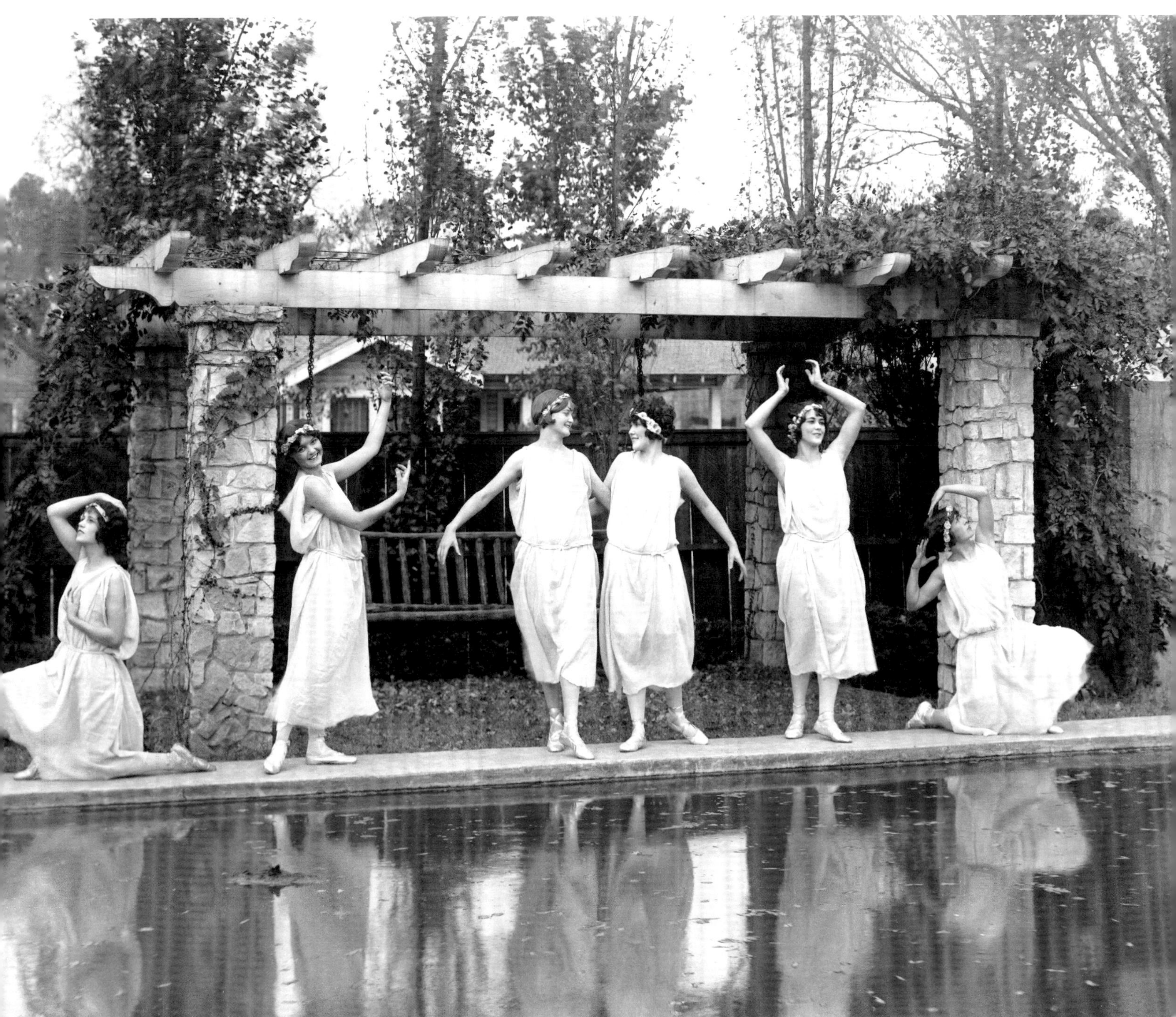

SEVEN BELLHOPS AND GILMER HOTEL MANAGER, CIRCA 1930

Near Pruitt's Main Street studio, the Gilmer Hotel was a central spot for wealthy white power brokers, women's club luncheons, and visiting travelers. The four-story, brick hotel was made from clay hand-dug by Black slaves in 1860. During the Civil War, the hotel was converted into a hospital with hundreds of beds for the sick and wounded, many brought by trains from all over the American South. Over the years, the cast of characters visiting, living, or working at the Gilmer was remarkable. In the late nineteenth century, a Black man named Titus Gilmer (unrelated to the hotel's namesake) operated the barbershop. He had been a Reconstruction-era political figure. A federal Works Progress Administration report in the 1930s described Titus Gilmer as "an expert chess player and a very intelligent negro"—using the lowercase *n*, a marker of disrespect for Blacks.

In the early and mid-twentieth century, Pruitt took pictures there, whether it was speeches by local, regional, and national politicians addressing civic club luncheons or white women eating in the Gardenia Room and making plans for the spring Pilgrimage. Considered elegant for Mississippi, the Gilmer had ample leather armchairs and sofas that filled the spacious, high-ceilinged lobby. A dining room mural depicted Columbus's antebellum homes. Chefs fashioned ice sculptures. Seafood from the Gulf Coast, meats, poultry, and local game distinguished the menu for miles around. President William H. Taft stayed in 1911, heavyweight boxing champion Jack Dempsey in 1930, and the St. Louis Cardinals in 1933. On the occasion of President Franklin D. Roosevelt's fifty-second birthday on January 30, 1934, the Gilmer hosted an elaborate party—one of 6,000 nationwide—to honor the president and raise funds for his charity, the Warm Springs Foundation for Infantile Paralysis. Years later, celebrities Bob Hope and Doris Day dropped by while in town. CBS newsman Walter Cronkite stayed there. The National Fox Hunters Association called the Gilmer its headquarters for its 1947 hunt. On different occasions, actors Clark Gable and Tyrone Power visited the coffee shop. The hotel hosted many a poker game. WCBI radio, for decades the only local station, had its studios there. For some, such as lawyer Charles L. Garnett, known as "Chief" because of his supposed Native American ancestry, and professor Emma Ody Pohl of Mississippi State College for Women, the Gilmer was their permanent residence. Inside the lobby and outside on the sidewalk, people told stories, smoked, and relaxed in chairs while waiting to set off for someplace else.

William Faulkner, an occasional Gilmer visitor, captured the hotel's spirit as a spot that launched adventures. In a semi-autobiographical piece, published in the April 1954 *Holiday* magazine, Faulkner wrote about leaving the Gilmer to get moonshine whiskey at a bootlegger's in the nearby Alabama hills. The car ride on winding gravel roads terrified him. Faulkner's persona concluded, "Lord, You know I haven't worried You in over forty years, and if You'll just get me back to Columbus, I promise to never bother You again."

In Pruitt's photograph, the bellhops' brassy buttons seem to pop from their chests as they deferentially stand by hotel manager J. O. Slaughter, whose family owned and ran the hotel for several decades. Bellhops shuttled luggage from curb to lobby to rooms. They operated the elevator. Late at night, they mopped the black-and-white checkered tile floor. They ferried messages and telegrams, and ran errands for guests around town. There were no white bellhops.

The Gilmer photograph typifies much of Pruitt's work: posed group shots, taken in a straightforward manner. Within the hierarchy of jobs for Black men, to be a Gilmer bellhop was considered quite good. Still, the bellhops served white customers of a hotel in whose fabled dining room the bellhops, their families, friends, and relatives could never eat; nor could they stay in its rooms, even if they could afford the prices. The feeling of the picture is one of racial conservatism. Blacks could be bellhops, but not hotel managers.

That said, the bellhop second from the right is Edward C. Bush, who did become a hotel manager. A decade after this picture was taken, Slaughter helped Bush and his wife, Bessie Will Bush, secure a loan that allowed them to renovate an old hotel in a residential Black neighborhood on Columbus's northside. In 1947, the Bushes reopened the Queen City Hotel, one of the few Mississippi hotels available to Blacks, which was listed in the *Negro Travelers' Green Book*. Black musicians B. B. King, Count Basie, and Marian Anderson and baseball player Jackie Robinson, who broke the color barrier in Major League Baseball, were Queen City guests. In a newspaper interview in 1999, Bessie Bush said, "[Louis] Armstrong or Little Richard would play at the [Queen City] dance hall or [nearby] Union Academy and people would be everywhere—sitting on the grounds, dancing in the street."

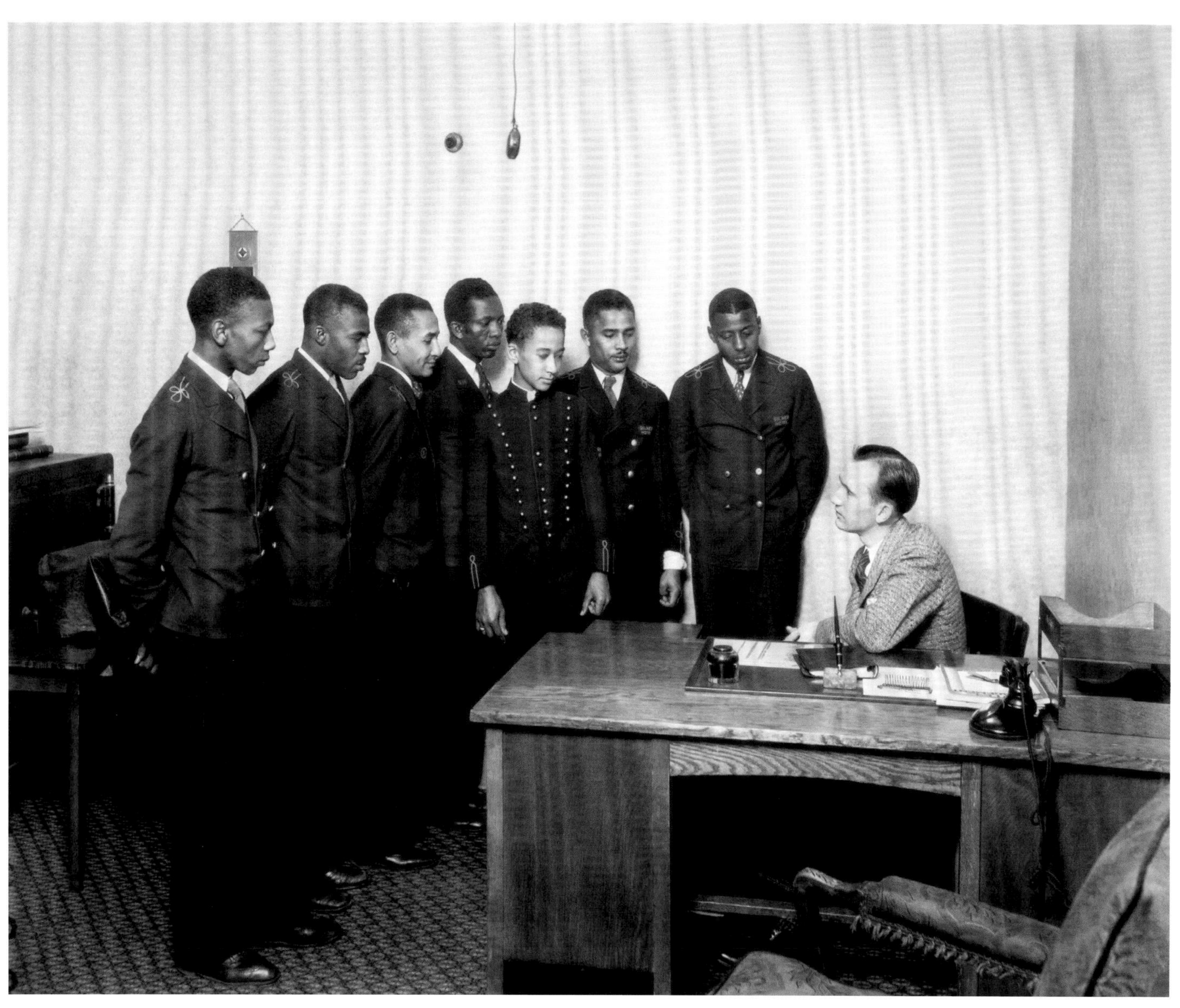

Gilmer Hotel bellhops, circa 1930. Manager J. O. Slaughter is seated. Standing, second from the right, is Ed Bush, prominent Catfish Alley businessman who in the late 1940s renovated and operated the Queen City Hotel with his wife, Bessie Bush.

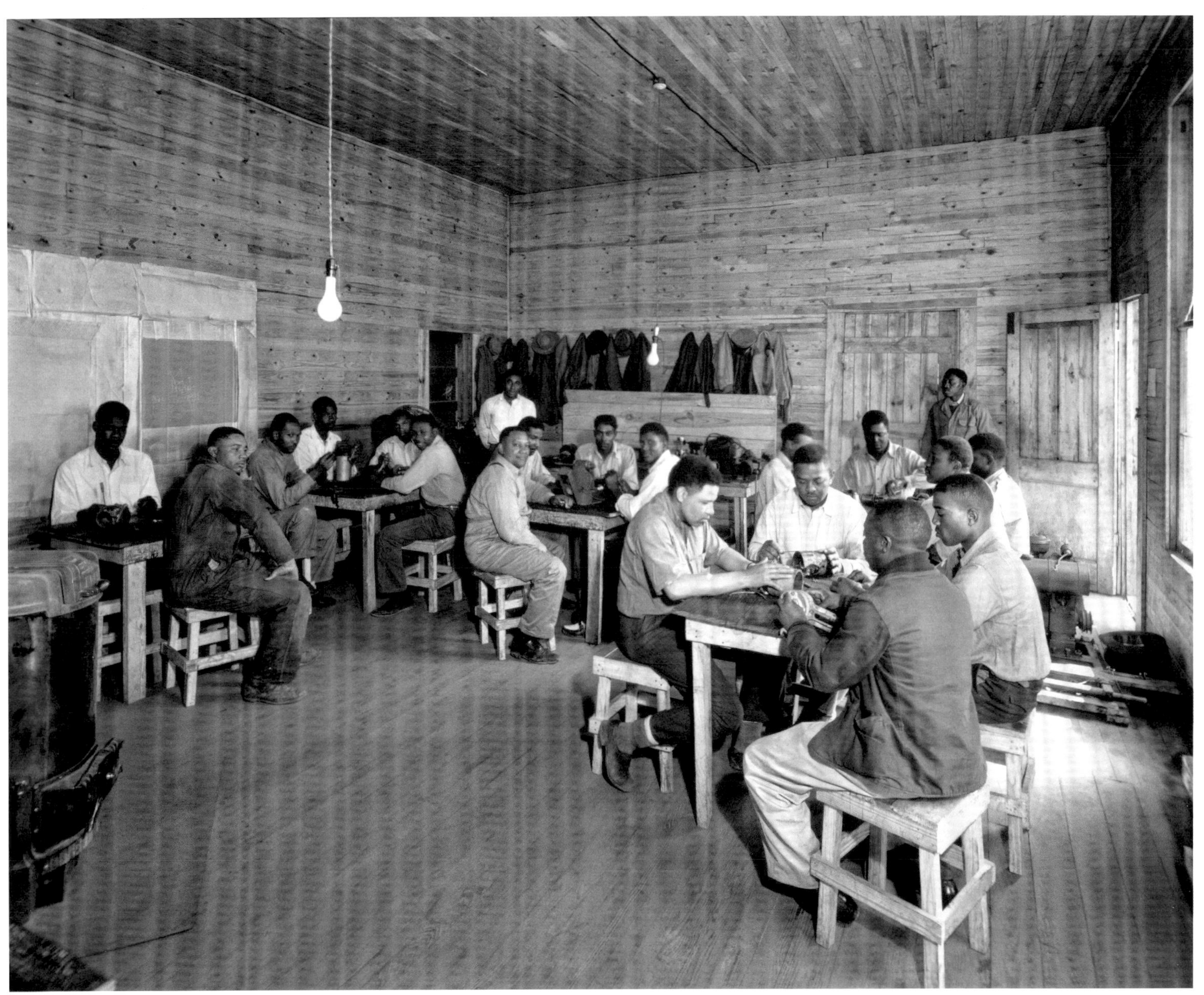

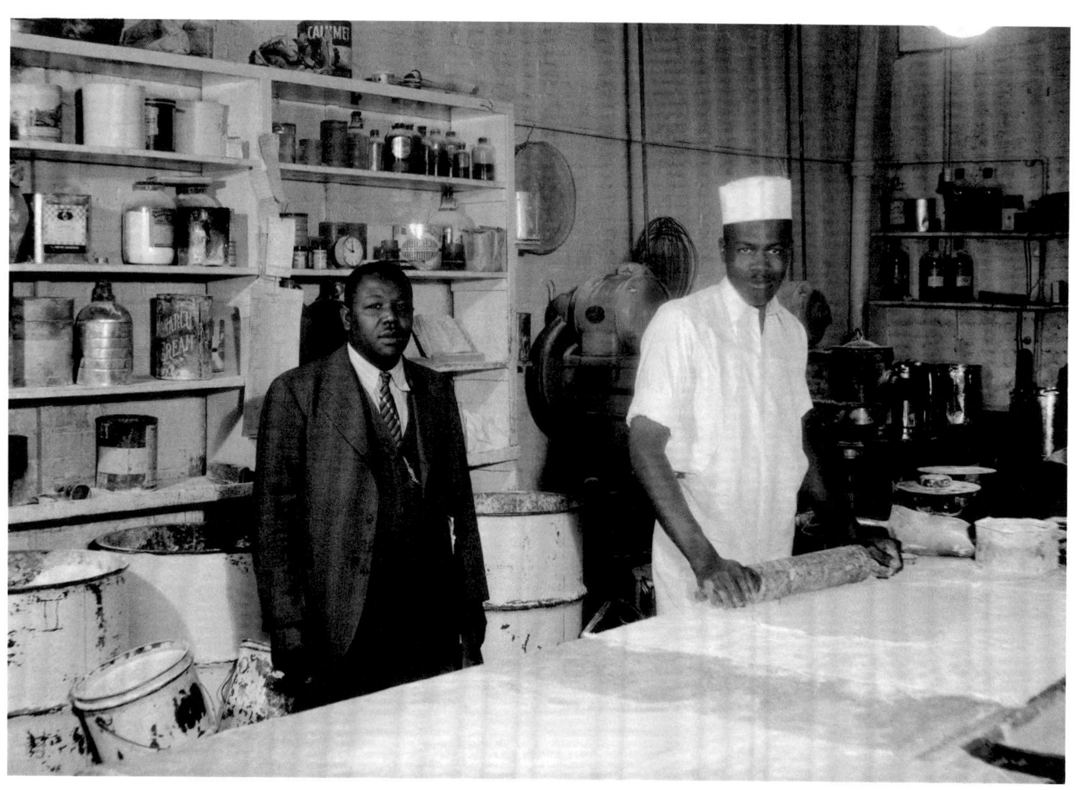

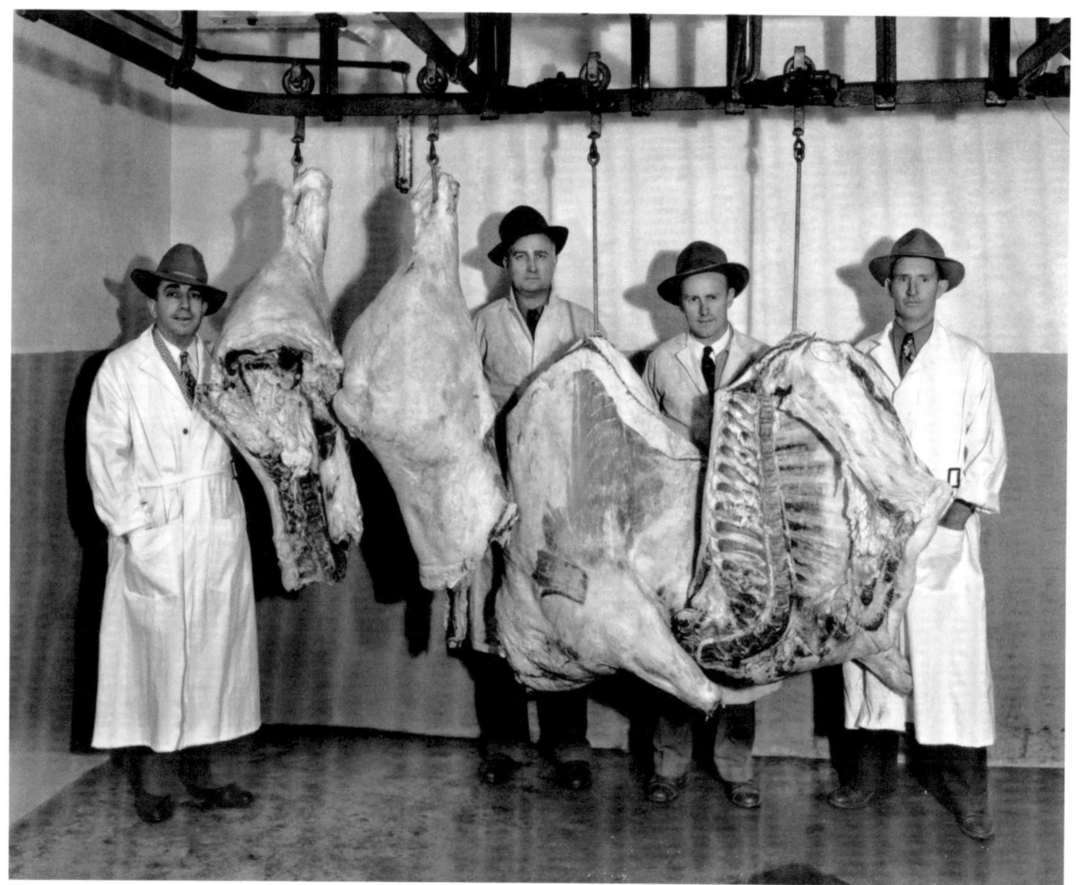

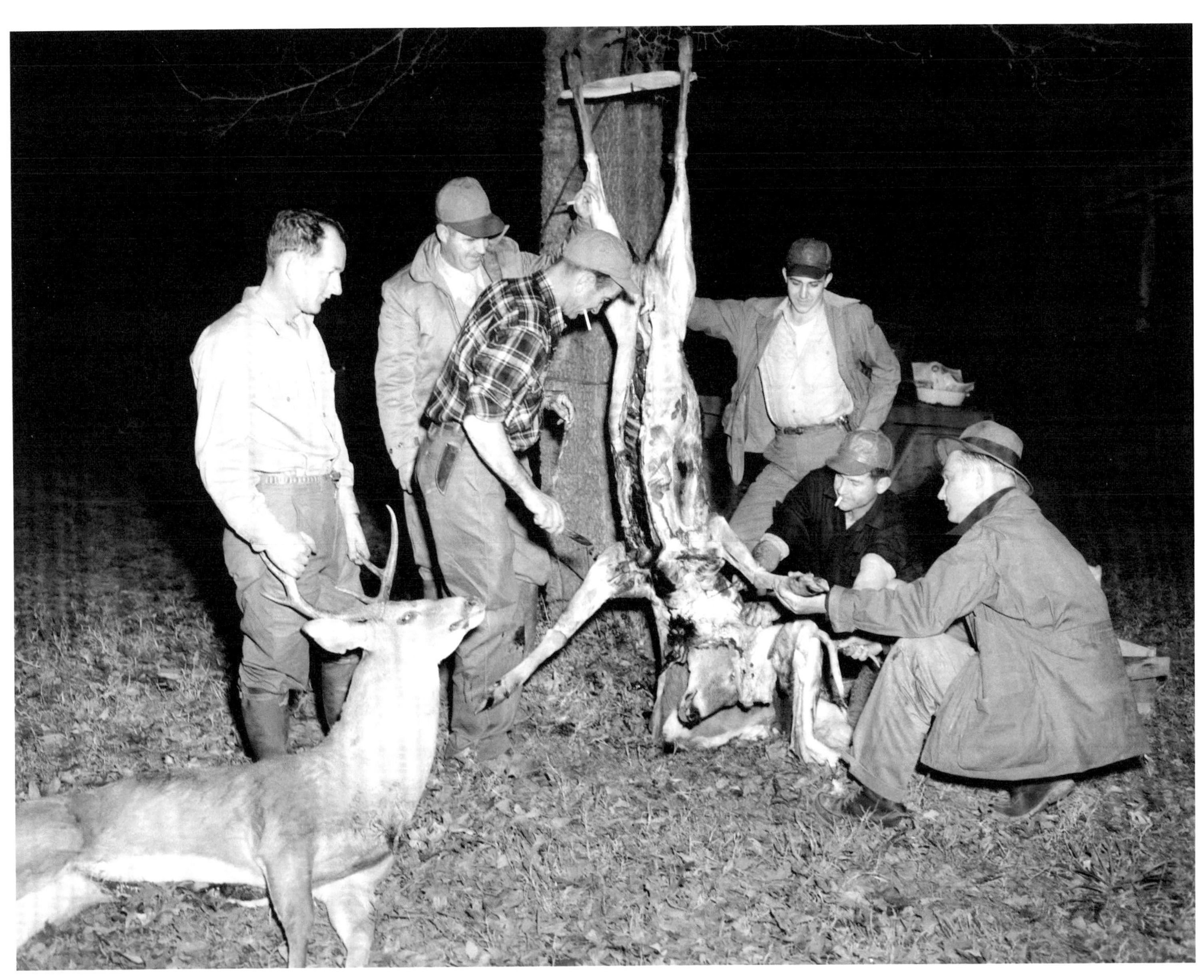

(opposite, bottom) *Columbus Meat Packing Co.*

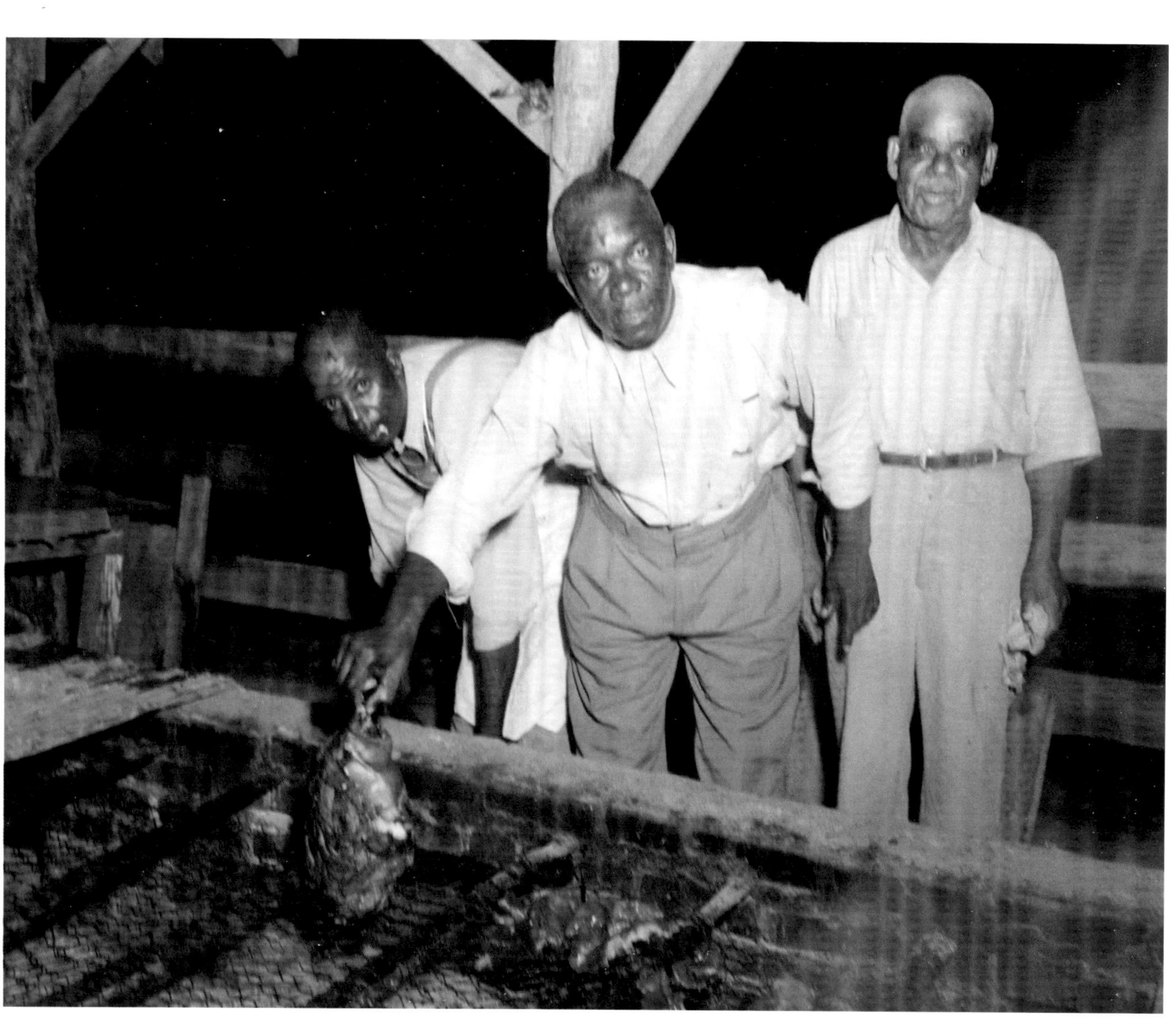

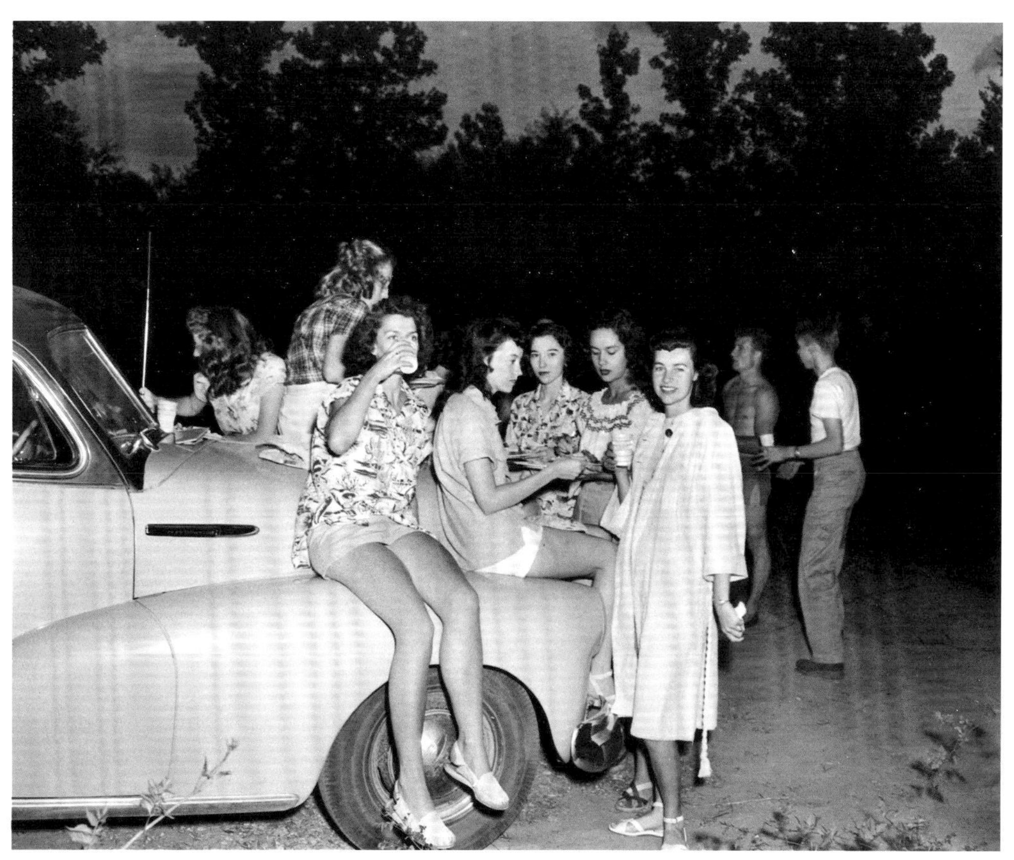

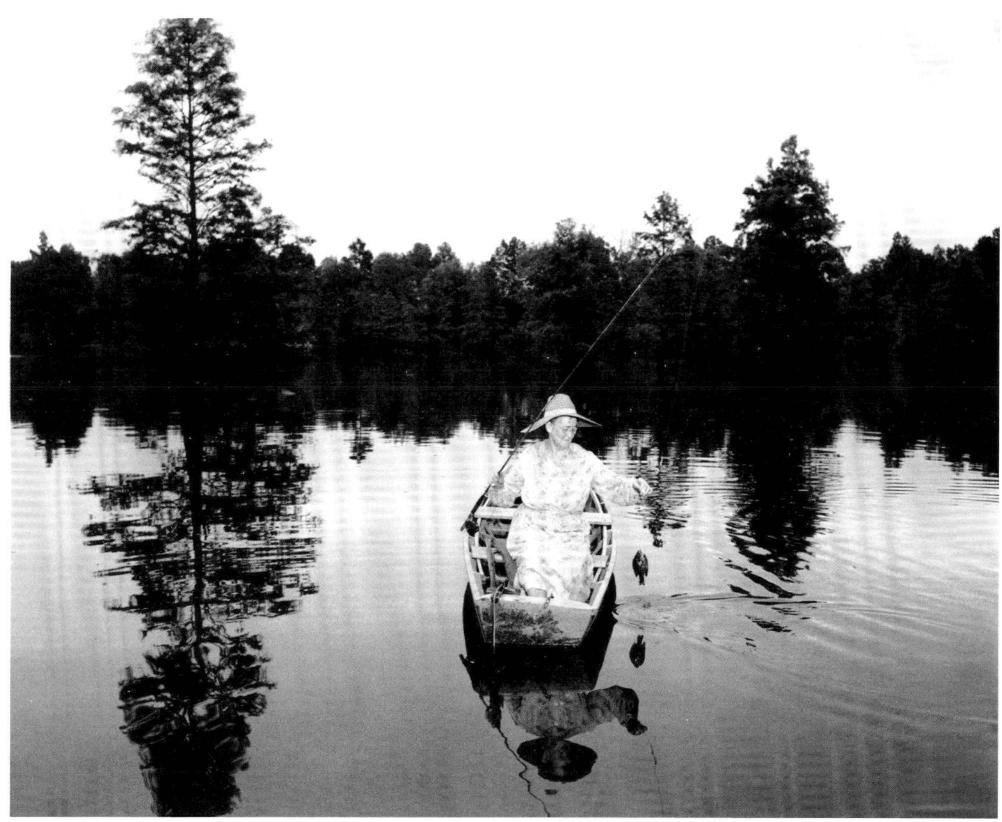

VANISHING TRIBES, 1931

Birney Imes Sr., editor and publisher of the *Commercial Dispatch* in March 1931, wrote an editorial titled "Wanted—A Wooden Indian." He wondered what had happened to the "vanishing tribes" of wooden Indians who stood outside of drug stores and symbolized the Native American connections with tobacco cultivation. The editorial said, "We are advised that wooden Indians are almost extinct."

Wire services sent out the editor's query and eventually newspapers throughout the nation discussed the editorial, mostly in joking ways. Eventually, someone sent Imes "a wooden Indian." Then, for reasons unclear, he posed for a photograph. In a tailored suit, crisp white shirt, and tie and hat in hand, Imes presents himself to Pruitt's camera in the vein of the "Great White Father" tradition of rulers and colonialists negotiating with Indigenous people. The battered statue, likely made not of wood but metal, was a head shorter in stature than the publisher. It exudes defeat.

In wishing Imes success in his campaign, the *Commercial Appeal* of Memphis, Tennessee, responded with its own editorial, saying it hoped Imes "finds enough wooden Indians to start a reservation somewhere in the Columbus vicinity." The Memphis editorialist suggested that Imes might want "to run [the wooden Indian] for public office or use it as an office boy." Imes wrote another editorial that claimed that Columbus had "received the widest national publicity this community has ever received.... Millions of people read stories about the Indians." The editorial referred to an earlier editorial in which Imes raised the question of whether cornbread should be dunked into pot-likker [the soupy juice that results from cooking collard or turnip greens] and then eaten, or rather crumbled into pot-likker. Imes wrote, "If the pot-likker controversy and the search for a wooden Indian didn't do anything more than to divert the public mind from the aftermath of the depression, they do good."

There was another glaring absence, however, from the news coverage: None of the articles mentioned local events involving Native Americans that shaped the nineteenth-century development of Mississippi and beyond. In 1830, 20,000 Choctaw gathered near Columbus, where tribal leaders signed the Treaty of Dancing Rabbit Creek. The treaty, ratified by the U.S. Senate in 1831, required the Choctaw to leave their homes and start westward journeys to Oklahoma on what became known as the Trail of Tears, one of its routes beginning west of Columbus. A few Choctaw were allowed to remain in Mississippi but were subjected to harassment, intimidation, and fraud from land speculators as white settlers flocked to Columbus from Georgia, North Carolina, South Carolina, Tennessee, and Virginia. Additionally, in 1832 the Chickasaw ceded their lands west of the Tombigbee. The fertile Native American territory around Columbus, once belonging to Creek, Chickasaw, and Choctaw, was auctioned off with bids starting at $2 an acre. Hardly a lodging room could be found because of the rush of speculators. The remaining Native Americans sought refuge in an isolated area in Neshoba County, outside of Philadelphia. A century later, in 1945, the federal government formally recognized the Mississippi Band of Choctaw Indians who had settled there.

To this day, Native American names identify both the state itself and many of its geographic features, including local waterways such as the Tombigbee ("Box Maker" or "Little Box") and the Luxapalila ("Floating Turtle" or "Turtle Crawls There"). Columbus and Lowndes County are rich in Indigenous history. Among the famous Choctaw from Columbus was Peter Pitchlynn, of Native American and European ancestry. After the Treaty of Dancing Rabbit Creek, he moved to Oklahoma with the Choctaw and eventually became their principal spokesman in Washington, D.C. His father, John Pitchlynn, had been appointed by President George Washington as an interpreter for the Choctaw and settled near Columbus in the early nineteenth century. He married a Choctaw woman, and they farmed a large tract west of Columbus near the Tombigbee.

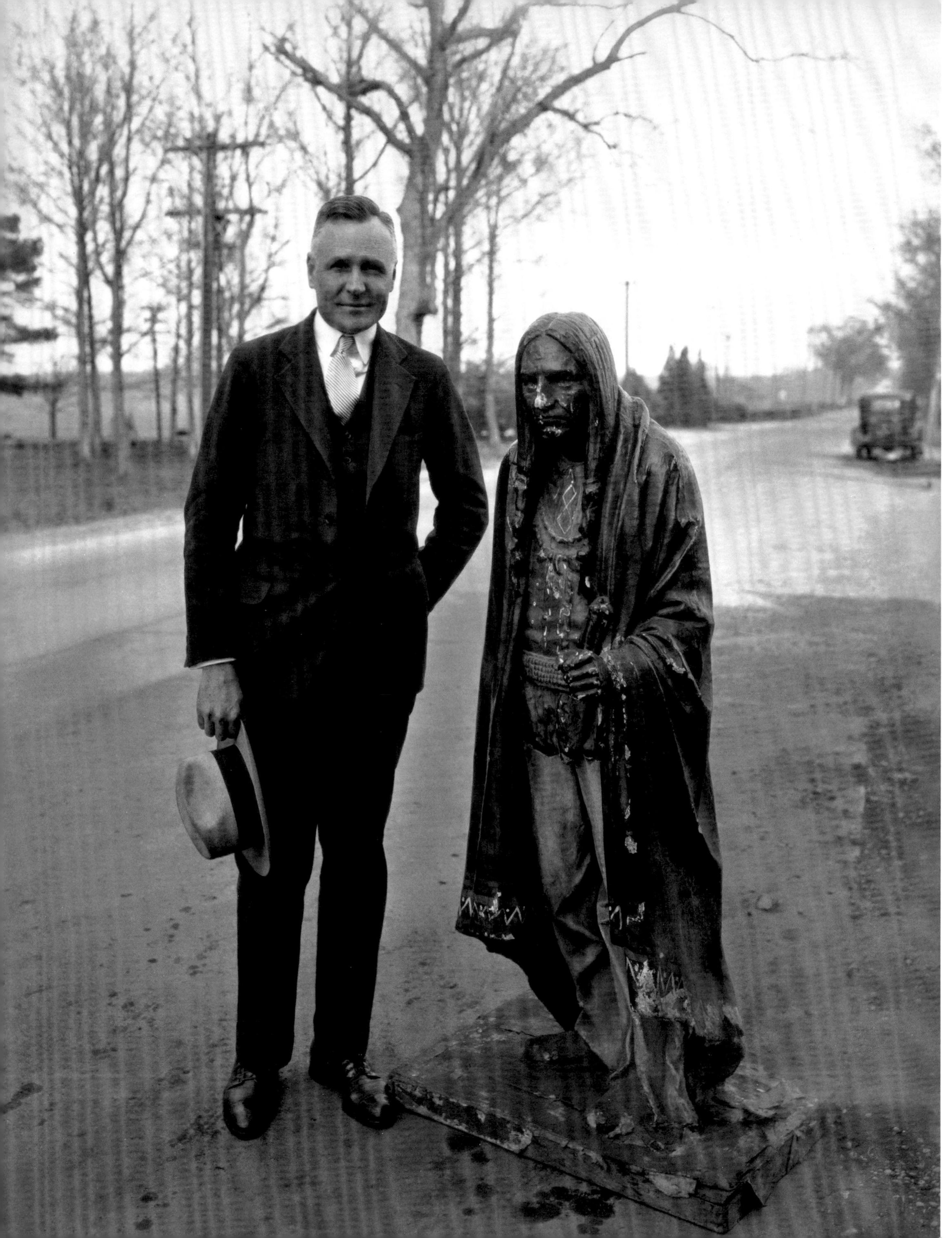

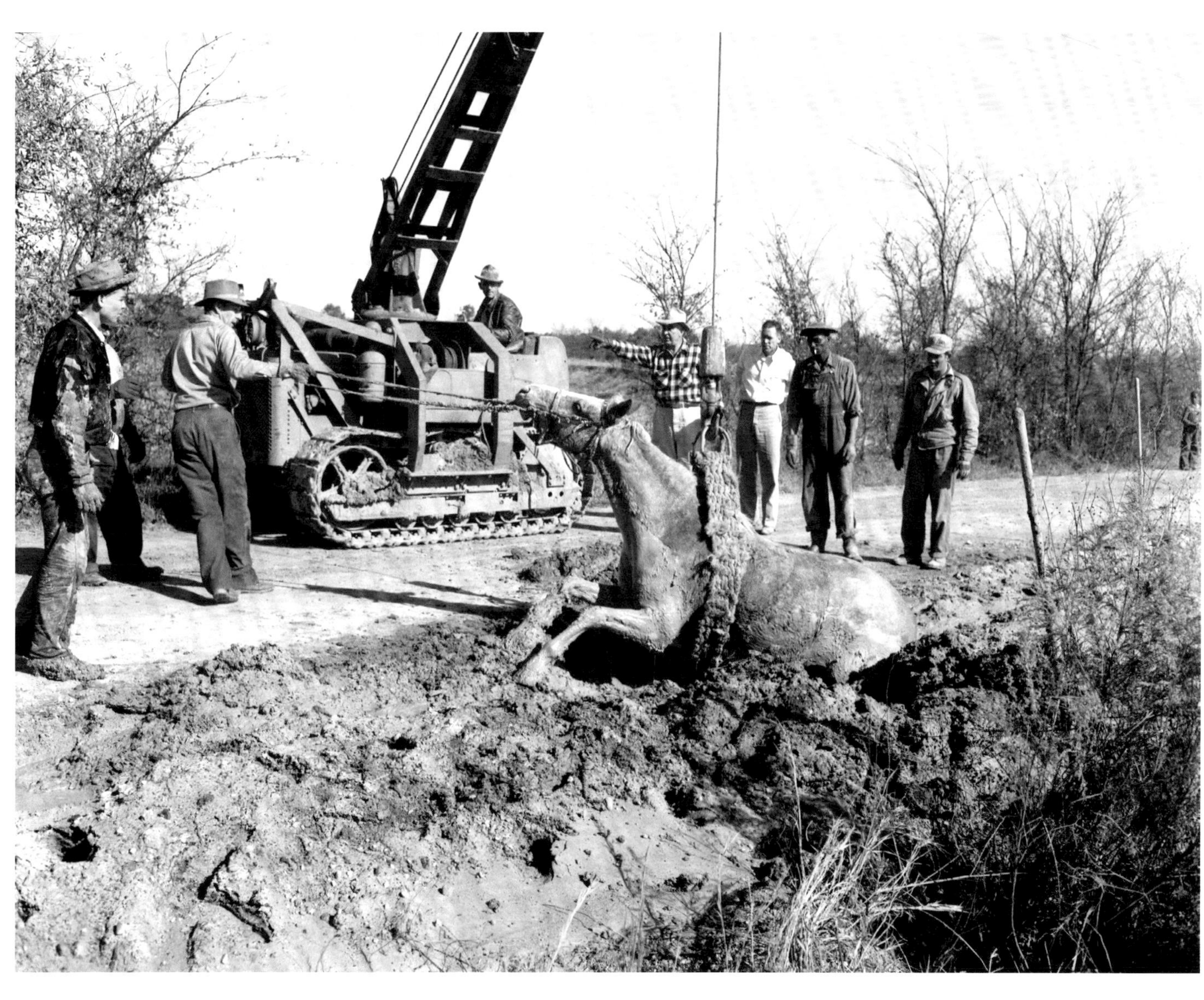

(opposite) *Birney Imes Sr., editor and publisher of the* Commercial Dispatch, *with statue representing a Native American, 1931.*

Ed "Sonny" Edmondson, circa 1950.

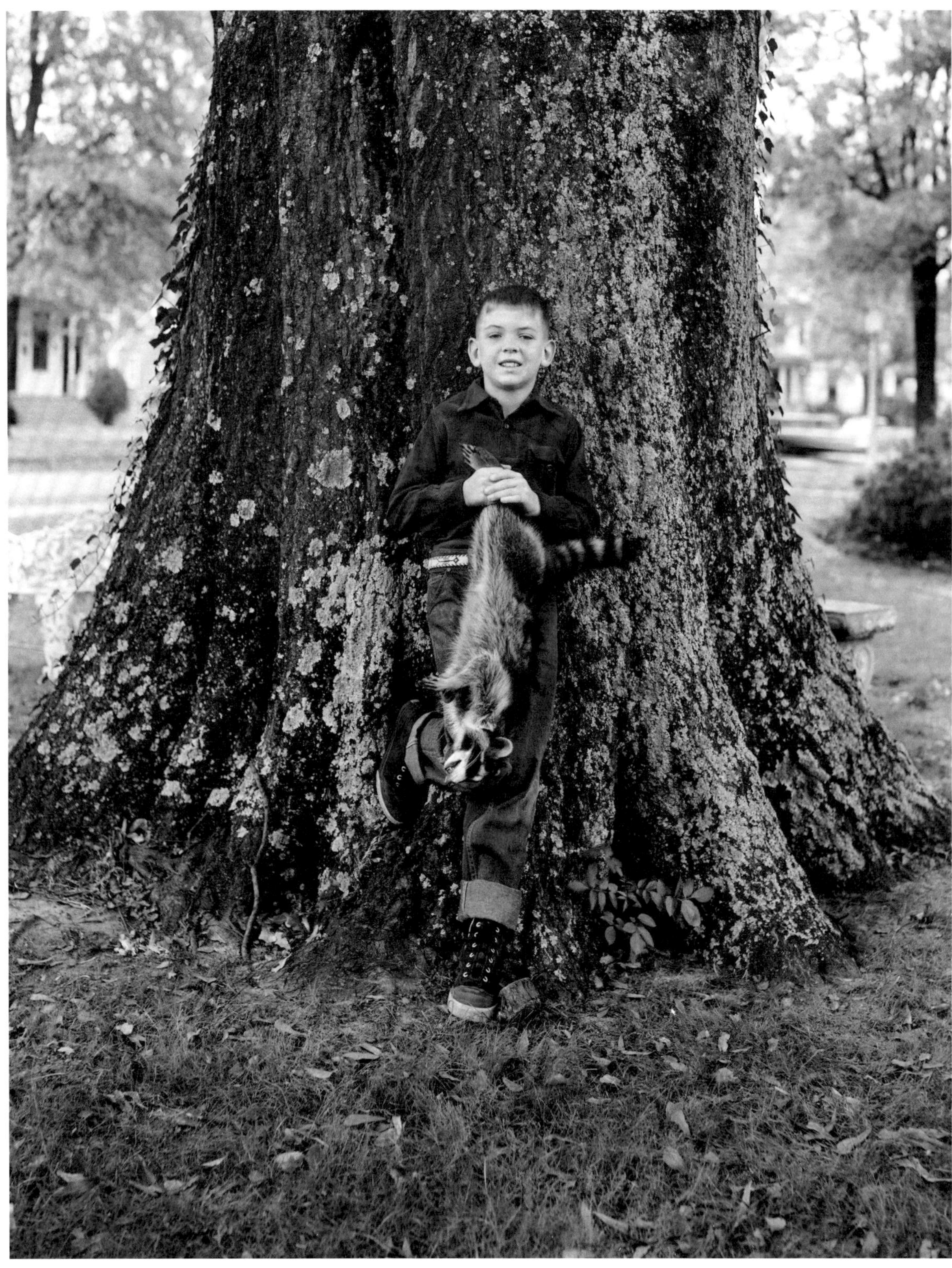

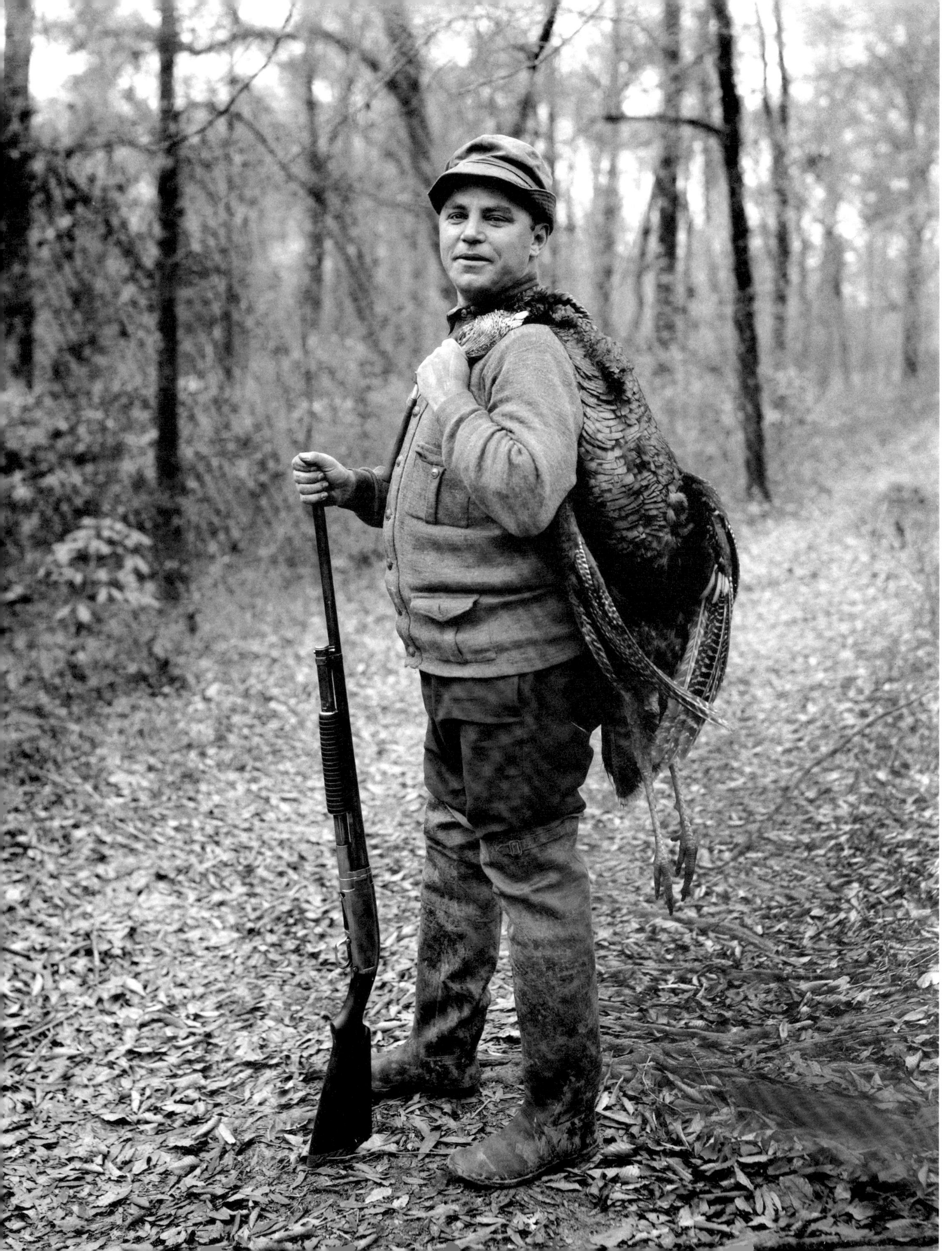

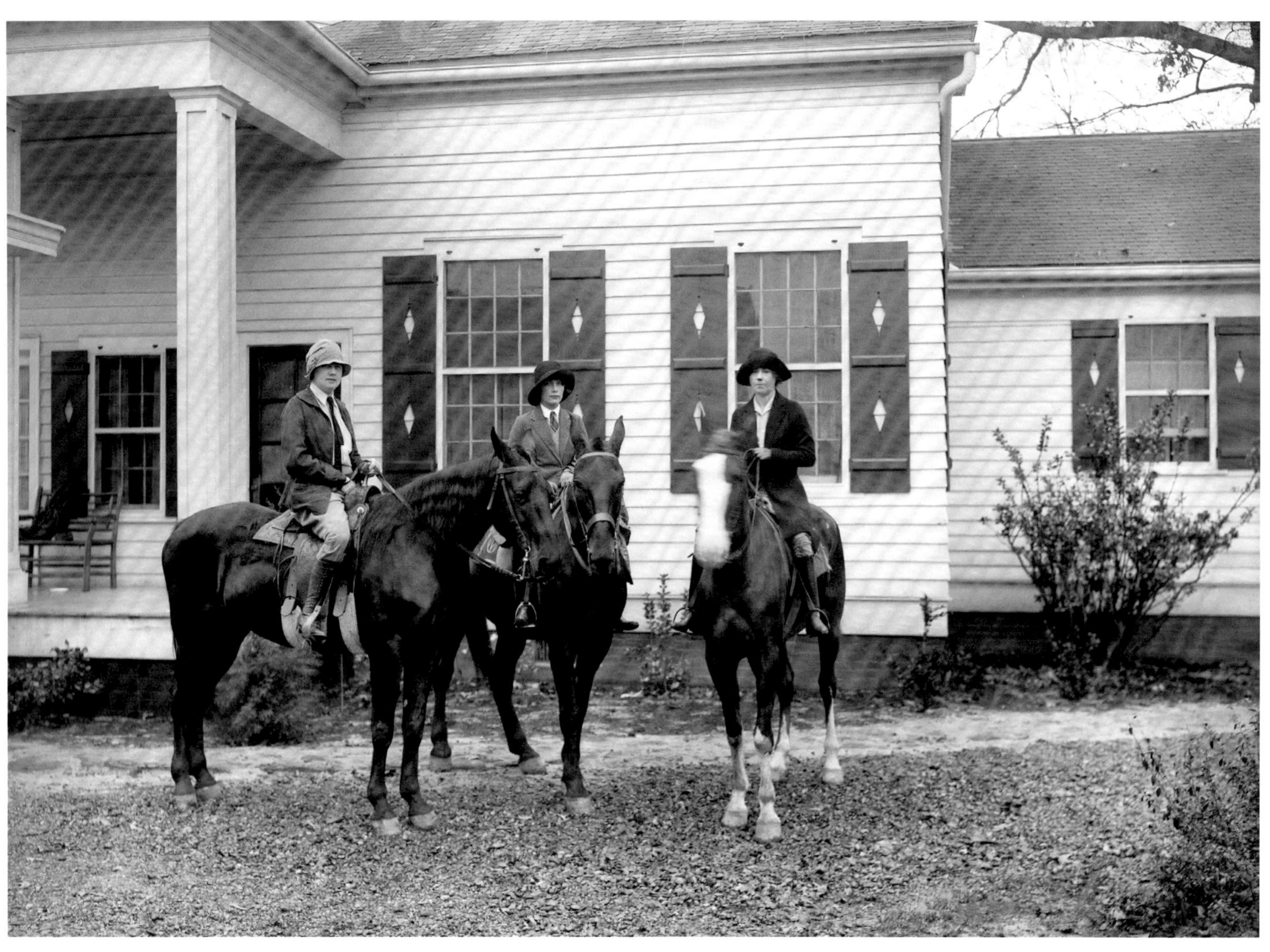

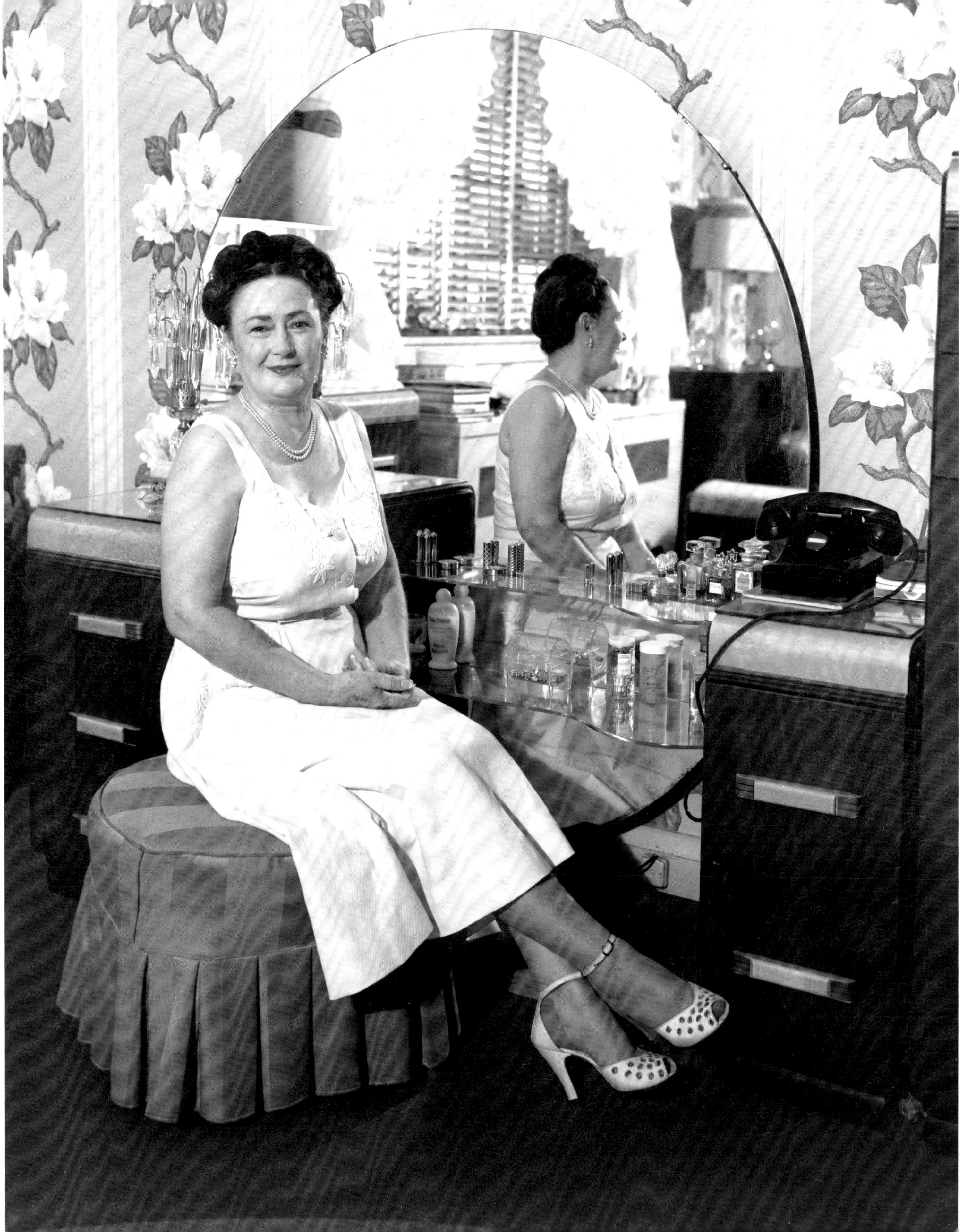

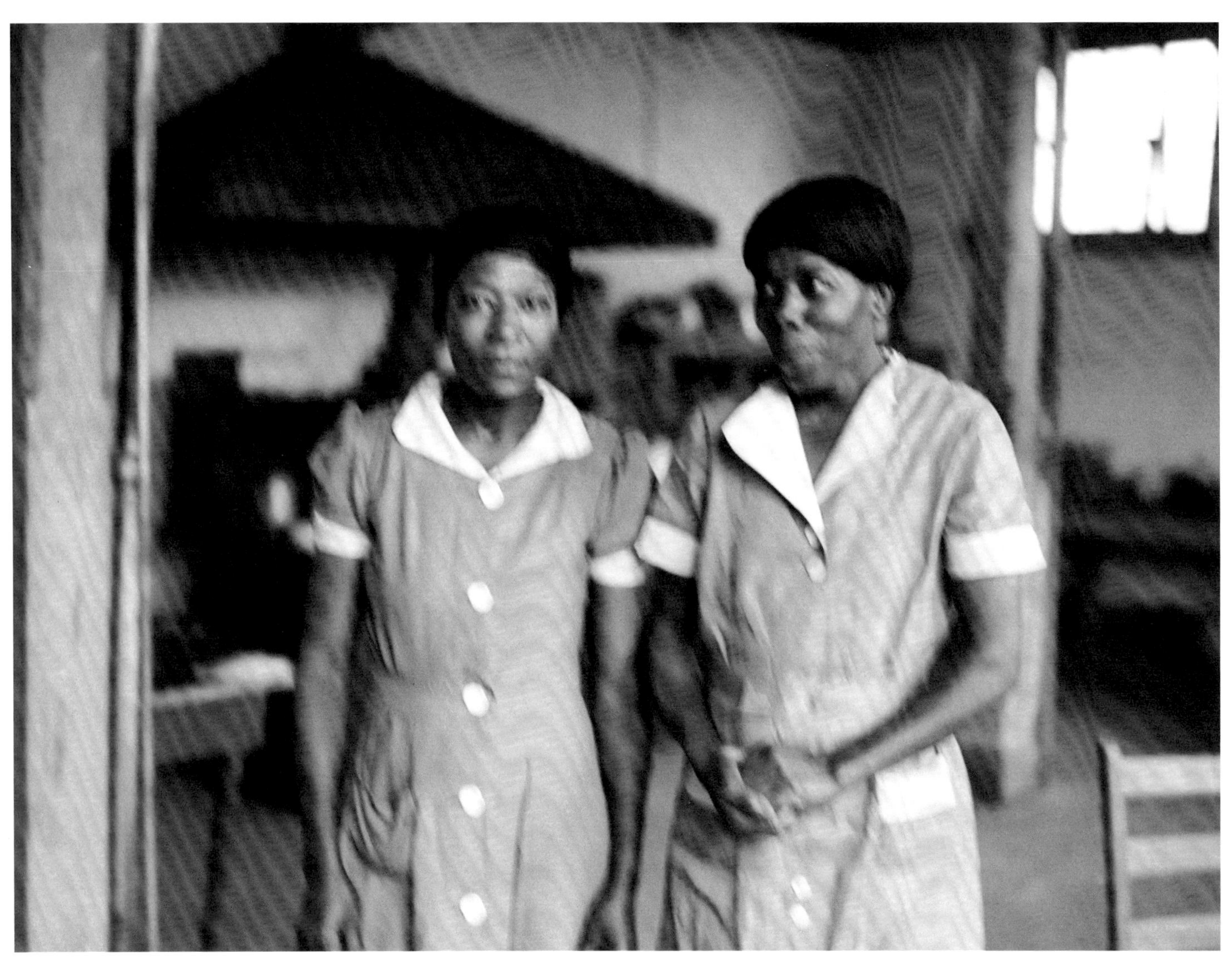

(opposite) *Blind man with cane and tin cup whistles on southwest corner of Main and Market Streets, soliciting donations, circa 1950s.*

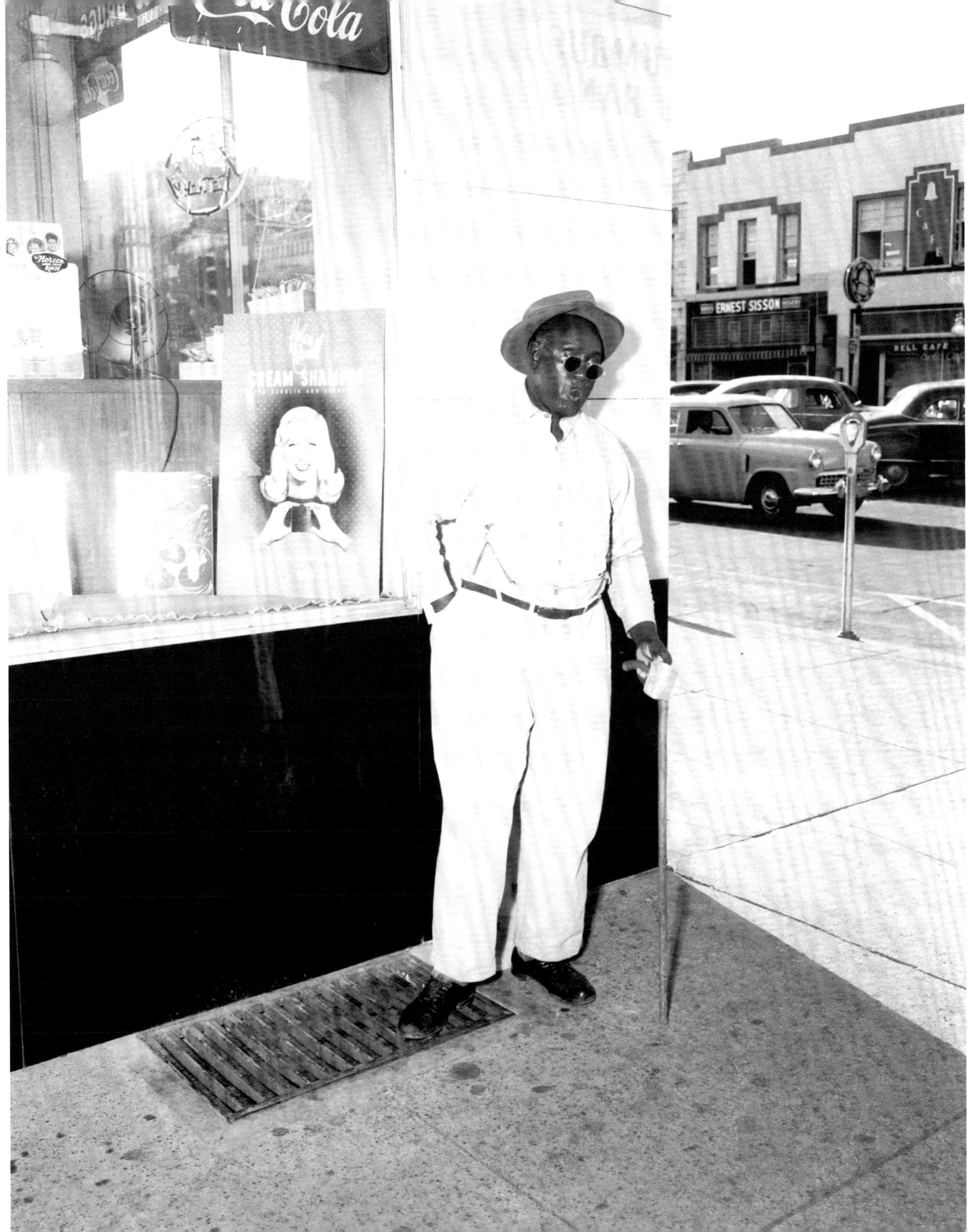
Cola
CREAM
ERNEST SISSON
CAFE
BELL CAFE

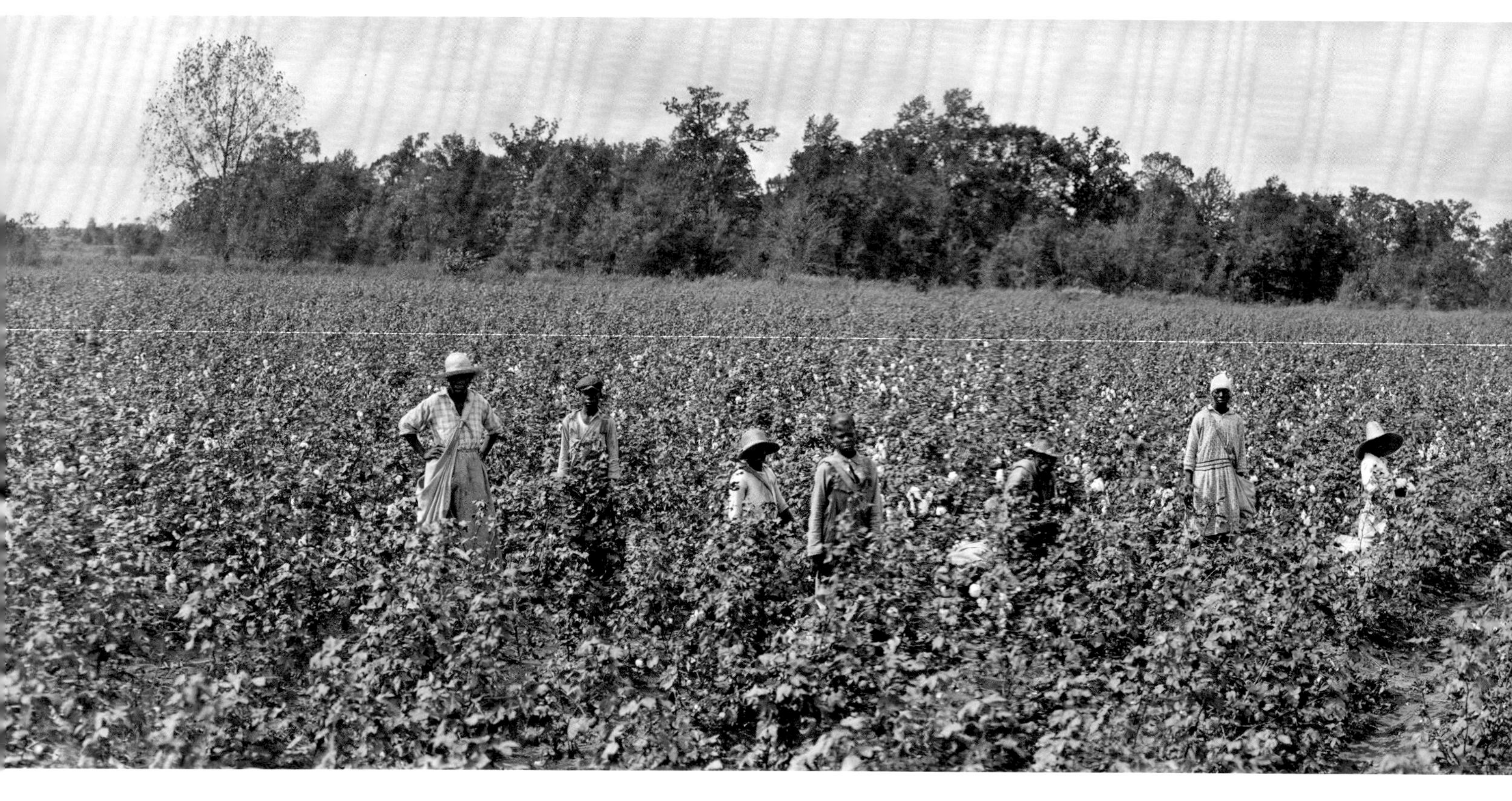

Picking cotton, likely in Black Belt Prairie of southwest Lowndes County of Artesia, Crawford, or Trinity, circa 1920s–30s.

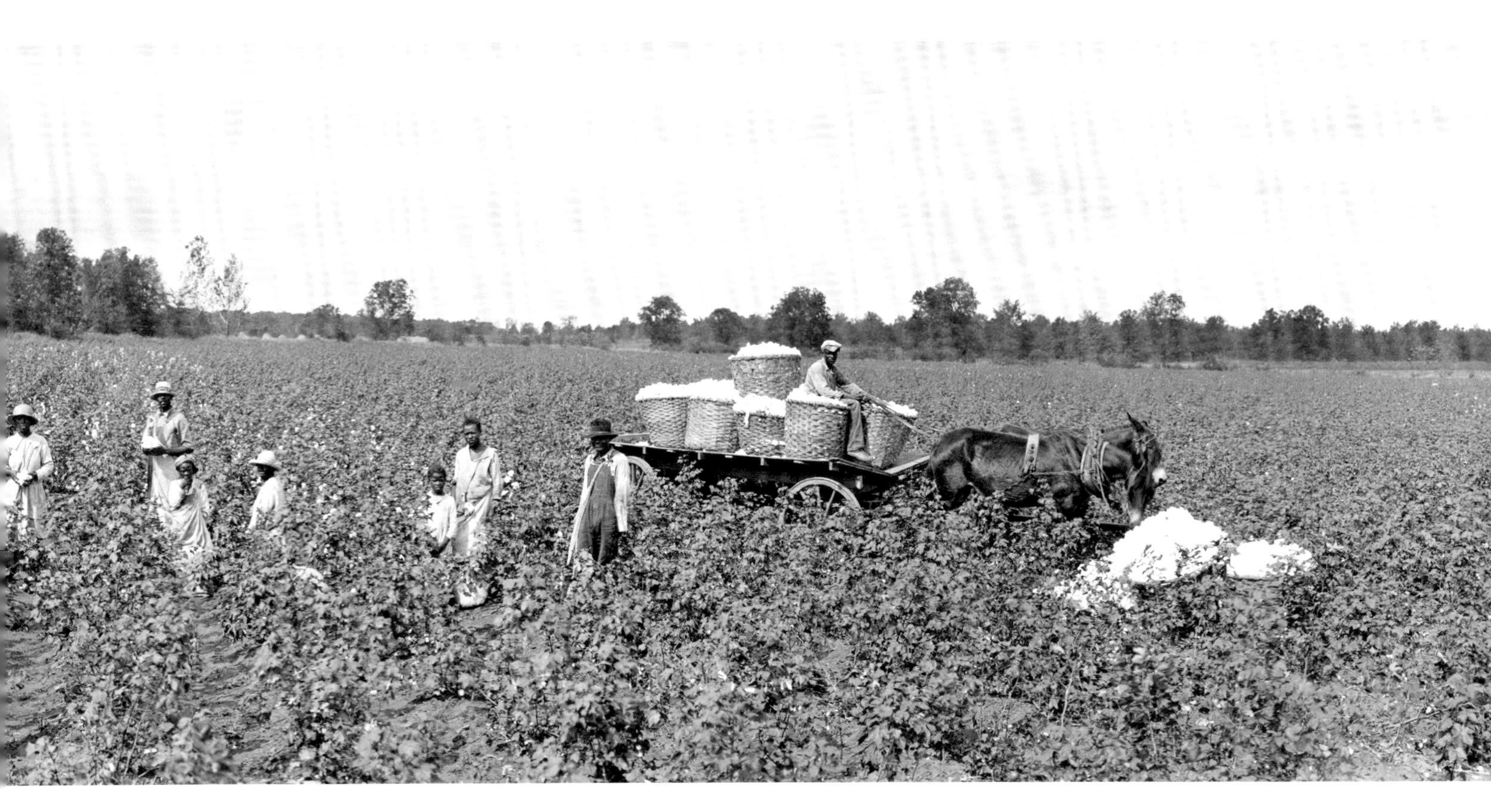

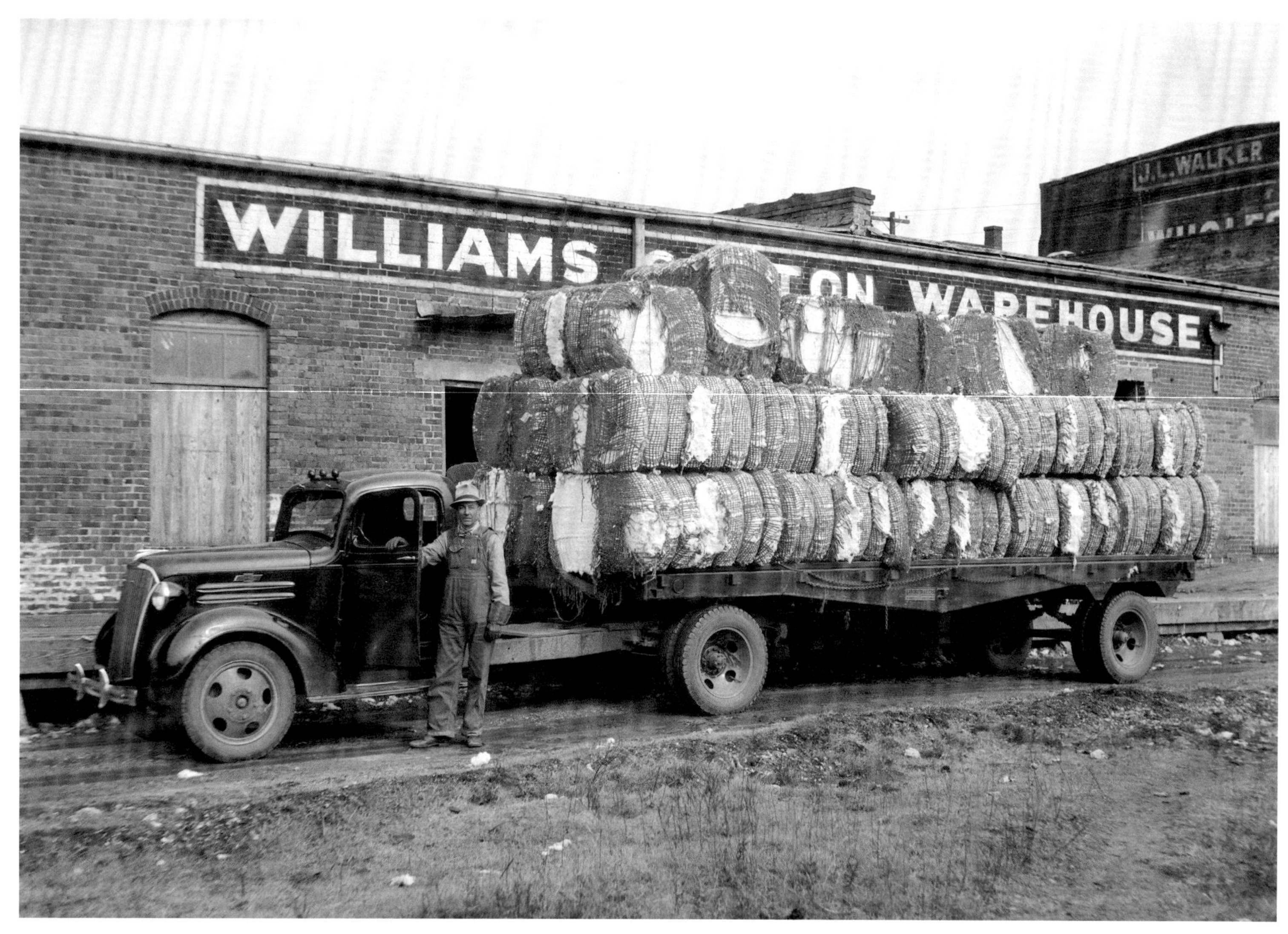

Cotton bales at Williams Cotton Warehouse, circa 1930s. By 1860, Lowndes County produced 50,000 bales of cotton and 1 million bushels of corn annually. For at least another century, agriculture played a key role in northeast Mississippi.

MINSTREL SHOW, CIRCA 1920S

I wish I was in de lann ob cotton

Ole time dar am not forgotten

—"Dixie's Land: A Southern Plantation Negro-Song" by Daniel Decatur Emmett, first performed in New York City by Bryant's Minstrels, April 4, 1859

Seventeen white youngsters, adorned in blackface, pose as a troupe of cotton pickers. This photograph contains a narrative, though a limited one. Cotton bolls spill from a handmade woven basket. The galvanized tub evokes those in which poor Blacks and whites scrubbed and washed clothes for their own families and those of their employers.

The scene conjures the biting comment made by Black writer Zora Neale Hurston: "Everyone seems to think that the Negro is easily imitated when nothing is further from the truth. Without exception I wonder why the blackface comedians are blackface; it is a puzzle—good comedians, but darn poor n——." In the early twentieth century, minstrel shows performed at local movie theaters and set up tents for performances on the southside of Columbus, where the Confederate Army once had a weapons arsenal. Pruitt's negatives reveal that throughout his career he photographed whites blackened for minstrel shows and community plays.

In 1828, a century before this minstrel photograph was taken, a white man, Thomas "Daddy" Rice, first stepped onto a Kentucky stage with burnt cork applied onto his face. Rice, like Dan Emmett of "Dixie" fame, popularized minstrelsy. Rice would dance, sing, and "wheel about, turnabout, do jis so; an' ebery time I wheel about, I jump Jim Crow." Minstrelsy, in fact, had its roots in "the white backlash against abolitionism," scholar Jan Nederveen Pieterse writes. "In minstrelsy there was room for criticism of the 'excesses and abuses' of slavery, but not slavery per se.... Their main content came from the myth of the benevolent plantation." The minstrel show spread throughout the land, at first the domain of whites, then eventually Blacks, who also would blacken their faces for pay. By the 1890s the minstrel show began to produce "coon songs." These featured exaggerated characters such as Zip Coon, an unreliable and thieving fellow.

Mississippi and the South had no monopoly on minstrelsy. Blackface flourished on northern stages more than southern ones, and minstrels entertained presidents, including Abraham Lincoln. New York City drew the biggest crowds for minstrels in the nineteenth century. Scholar Eric Lott writes in *Love and Theft*, "The minstrel show has been ubiquitous, common coin; it has been so central to the lives of North Americans that we are hardly aware of its extraordinary influence."

With the advent of movies, some critics argue, blackface reached its zenith: first with the embodiment of the "brute beast Negro rapist," a white man in blackface, in D. W. Griffith's *The Birth of a Nation* in 1915. Then arrived an even more confusing concept: a blackface Jew, Al Jolson, in the *Jazz Singer* in 1927. In that same era, white performers Freeman F. Gosden, known on stage and radio as "Amos," and Charles J. Correll, who was "Andy," entertained audiences around the country in blackface (and blackvoice). *Billboard* magazine featured a weekly column titled "Minstrelsy." Blackface performers often lived and worked in cities of the North and Midwest. Nederveen Pieterse writes, "One clue to the lasting popularity of the minstrel show is no doubt the principle of role reversal: in blackface whites can play their black alter egos." Examples abound of minstrelsy's lingering legacy into the late twentieth and early twenty-first centuries. Filmmaker Spike Lee documented this painfully in *Bamboozled*. With a searing persistence of cultural love and cultural theft, the Pruitt image depicts the entertainment practice that scholar Susan Gubar calls "blackface lynching."

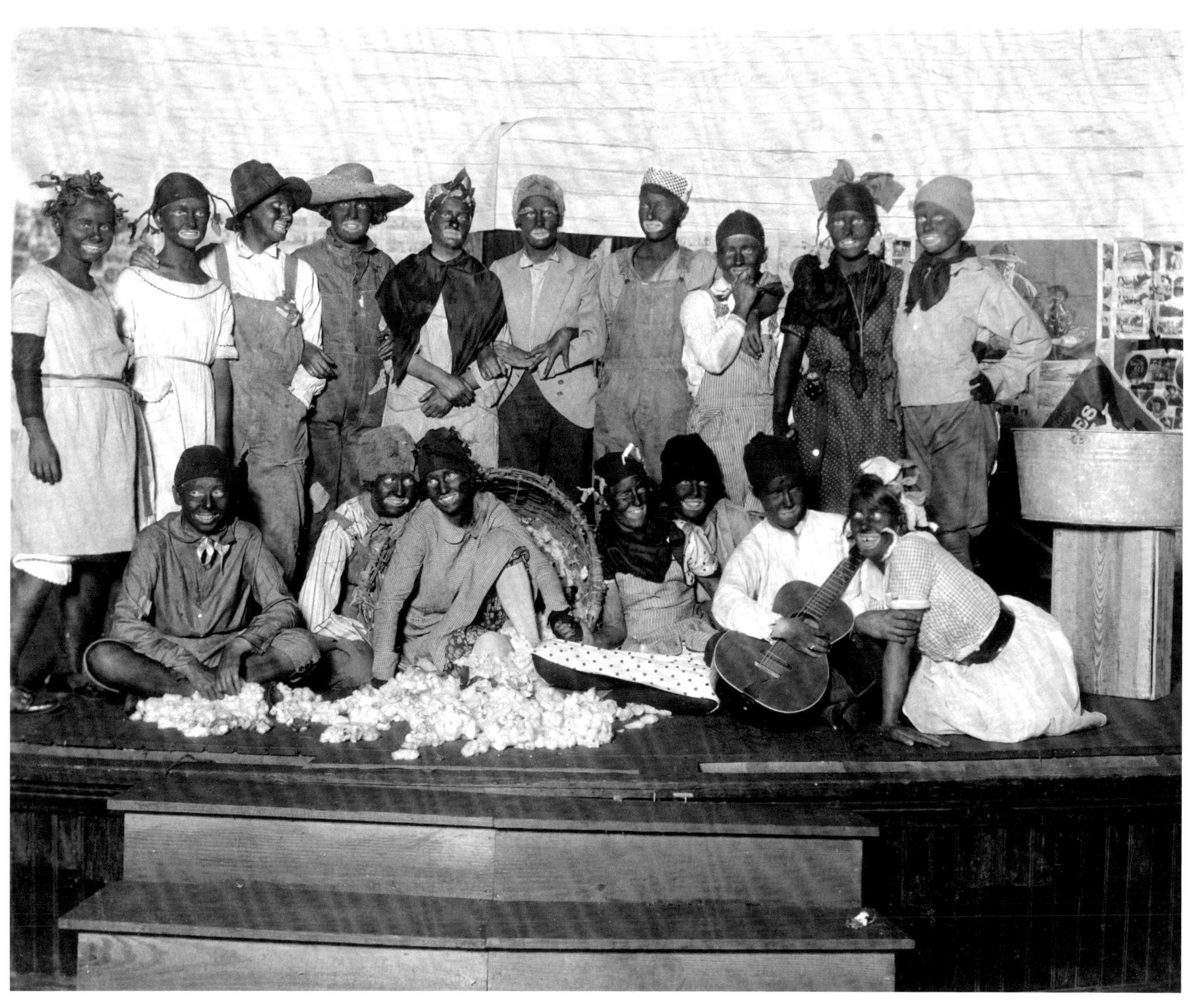

White school children as minstrels in blackface, circa 1920s.

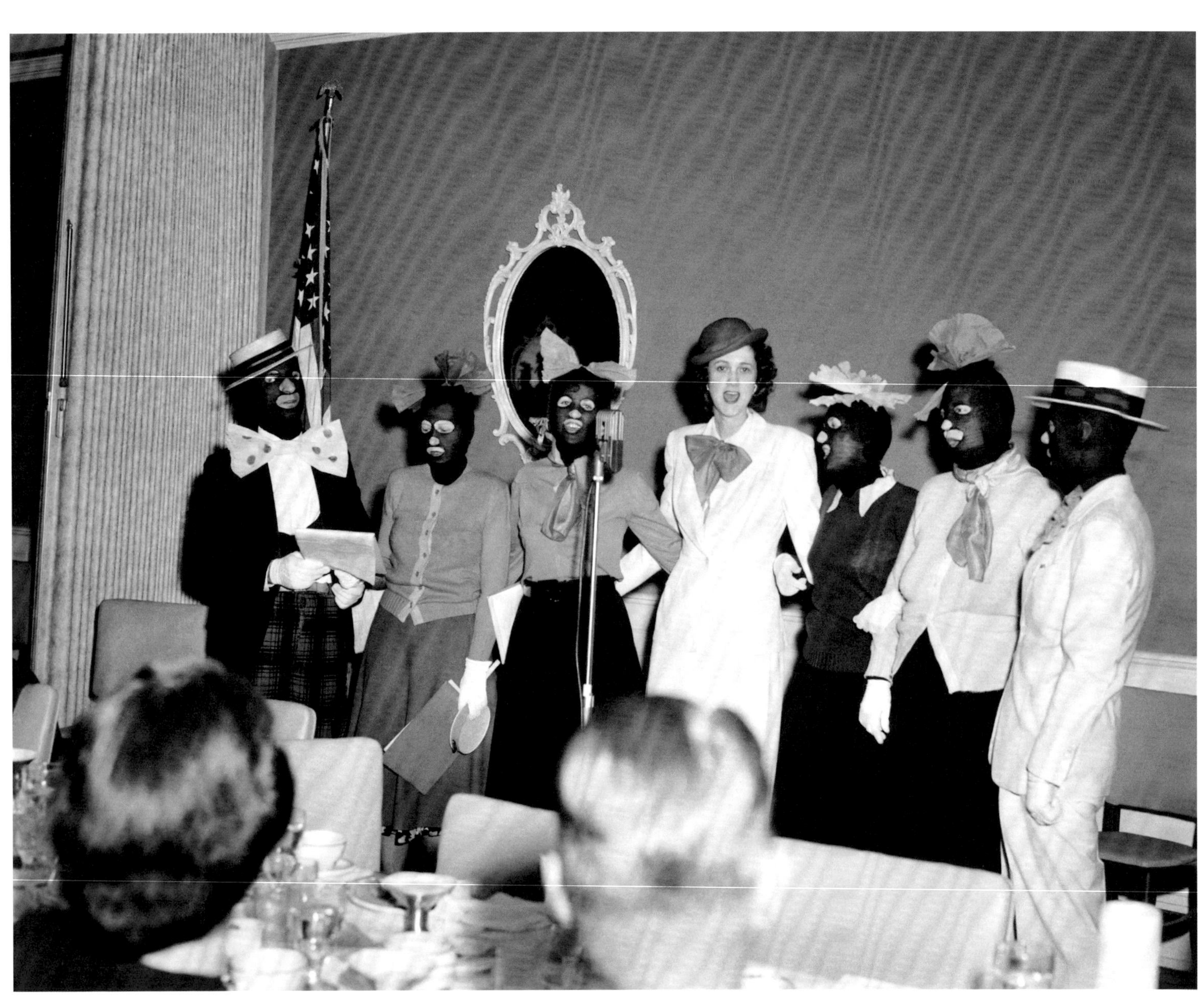

Kiwanis Club blackface minstrel show at Gilmer Hotel, circa 1940s–50s.

A RACIAL CRUCIBLE

Both of us, the white boys and the black boys, began to play our traditional racial roles as though we had been born to them, as though it was in our blood, as though we were being guided by instinct. All the frightful descriptions we had heard about each other, all the violent expressions of hate and hostility that had seeped into us from our surroundings, came now to the surface to guide our actions....

Our battles were real and bloody; we threw rocks, cinders, coal, sticks, pieces of iron, and broken bottles, and while we threw them, we longed for even deadlier weapons.

—Mississippi novelist Richard Wright, Black Boy, *1945*

In the 1930s, the Columbus Chamber of Commerce published a promotional brochure titled "Columbus, the Friendly City." The group proclaimed, "We have few major crimes in the county and 95 percent of the petty offenses are committed by our colored population."

In Mississippi and around the world, racial and ethnic identification has been used to justify segregation, fear, misunderstanding, hatred, and violence.

Two examples come from the American South at the turn of the twentieth century. Rebecca Latimer Felton, a Methodist lay leader, advocated lynching Blacks in an 1897 speech on Tybee Island, Georgia: "If it takes a lynching to protect women's dearest possession ... then I say lynch a thousand a week." In 1904, Mississippi governor James K. Vardaman, known as the Great White Chief, said, "If it is necessary, every Negro in the state will be lynched; it will be done to maintain white supremacy."

Some may say it is unfair to conflate lynching with legal executions. But scholars such as historian David Oshinsky assert that merely shades of difference existed between the two in the American South. Juries were composed only of white men registered to vote. Legal restrictions made it nearly impossible for Blacks to register and thus serve on juries. In 1940, less than one-half of 1 percent of Blacks in Mississippi were registered to vote. During Reconstruction, 56 percent of the registered voters had been Black and 46 percent, white.

Theodore Bilbo, when he was a U.S. senator for Mississippi in 1946, declared his Ku Klux Klan membership. He told journalists that a Mississippi law forbade Blacks to vote in white Democratic primaries, saying, "The best time to keep a n— away from a white primary in Mississippi was to see him the night before." In that spirit, some years before, in 1922, the Klan road on horseback along Main Street in front of Pruitt's studio, and he documented that.

In 1933 and 1934, Pruitt photographed two of Mississippi's last executions by rope hanging outside the Lowndes County Courthouse; Black men were convicted of killing white people. The district attorney in both cases was John C. Stennis, who would serve as U.S. senator for more than four decades (1947–89) and become a prominent Democrat in the battles over integration.

EXECUTION OF JAMES KEATON, MAY 1934

Early on Friday, May 25, 1934, Pruitt draped his camera's black cloth over his head to photograph the people on the gallows before him. Shortly after 2 a.m., Pruitt made the image of six white law enforcement officials surrounding James Keaton, a Black man. Their pose creates a *tableau vivant*, a living picture, at death's moment. An all-white, all-male jury convicted him of killing white service station owner Fred Hayslett. At the time, Mississippi allowed, in essence, local-option execution; each county, not the state, could undertake executions. Keaton wears bib overalls and an open-collared, long-sleeve shirt. Leather straps wrap around his feet, knees, and chest. His hands are bound behind his back. The thick rope noose is loose around his neck and attached to gallows. Sheriff Harry West, on the right, smiles. Onlookers watch from the open courthouse window behind; others lurk beneath the scaffold.

Absent from the photograph is District Attorney Stennis. Also not pictured are the many Blacks, including preachers, who were present. On the courthouse lawn for hours before the execution, they had sung spirituals through the night. At age twenty-two, Keaton gazes straight into the camera. His look is not easy to read. He seems to smile or perhaps smirk. Before the cowl was pulled over his head, he said, "Goodbye, everybody."

Minutes later, underneath the gallows, Pruitt documented a stereotypical execution spectacle: nineteen white men cram under the scaffold to be photographed with the body, suspended by a rope through the gallows trap door. A city policeman and deputy sheriff offer dutiful looks. Another man looks astonished. Others smile.

Two months before, Keaton had been arrested for shooting Hayslett, who had gone "to get a drink" with three friends late one Sunday night after his station had closed. The white men had surprised Keaton, who was inside and once had worked there. A shooting occurred; Keaton fled and later was found hiding under the porch of his house. By mid-April, an all-male, all-white jury found him guilty. In the Lowndes County Courthouse's criminal case file, few records of the case remain. Pruitt photographs are not among them. One document, however, reveals the tenor of the times. Keaton's defense lawyers submitted to the judge an instruction for the jury. It read:

> Gentlemen of the Jury:
> The Court instructs you that Mulattoes, negroes, Malays, whites, millionaires, paupers, princes, and kings, in the courts of Mississippi, are on precisely the same and exactly equal footing. All must be tried on facts, and not on abuse. Only impartial trials can pass the Red Sea of this court without drowning. Trials are to vindicate innocence or ascertain guilt.

The judge refused to give the jury this instruction, a message calling for a color-blind approach for Black defendants during Jim Crow. Three decades earlier, using similar language, the Mississippi Supreme Court had reversed the murder conviction of a Black man. In doing so, the court cited racial prejudice by the prosecutor. In the *Michigan Law Review* in 2000, Michael J. Klarman wrote that the Mississippi Supreme Court repeated in 1921 the argument that, as Klarman phrased it, "the humblest human being, be he white or black, red or yellow, is entitled to a fair and impartial trial on the sole issue of guilt or innocence under the law and evidence of the case." Klarman added, however, that "everyone knew that Blacks could not serve on southern juries, that Black lawyers could not command a fair hearing in southern courts, that Black witnesses were treated as less credible than whites, that the death penalty never was imposed for the rape of Black women."

In Keaton's case, Stennis, according to the *Commercial Dispatch*, urged the jury to convict Keaton and to "help advance civilization by removing this cancer" from the face of the earth. At the trial's conclusion, the newspaper applauded the rapidity of the indictment, trial, conviction, and sentencing—all of which occurred "within a week's time." In spite of this pace, the newspaper's editorial concluded that "the defendant was not denied any of his constitutional rights" and that Keaton would "expiate his crime on the gallows."

In 1934, when Fred Hayslett was killed, his son Charles Hayslett was twenty-one. The death in the family exacerbated what the Great Depression had wrought. As the oldest of three boys, Charles was charged with providing for his mother and two brothers. In a 2002 interview, after Charles had retired as a manufacturer's sales representative working and living throughout the South, the trauma and loss still shone on his face and resonated in his voice. When offered an opportunity to look at a photograph of James Keaton on the gallows, Hayslett declined.

Even in her nineties, Sarah Lusk, a white woman who ran a dry cleaning business on Market Street, vividly recalled Keaton and his trial and execution, saying she did not believe he committed murder. The night before he was hanged, she visited him in jail. "He didn't do it. I know he didn't," Lusk said in a 1994 interview. She knew who was responsible for Hayslett's death, she said, but did not want to disclose their names.

No matter who was responsible for Fred Hayslett's death, the Pruitt photographs document how one town meted out its version of justice during Jim Crow.

A LYNCHING IN THE HEAT OF SUMMER, 1935

In July 1935, the phone rang at Pruitt's home. It was Sheriff West's office. Come quickly, Pruitt was told; there's been a double lynching. With that, Pruitt, who kept his camera equipment at the ready in his car, sped on paved roads and then gravel ones. Eight miles south of town, in a churchyard, he found lynched from an oak tree the bodies of young "Negro farmers," as described by Associated Press accounts published around the nation, including in the *New York Times*. Pruitt took pictures of the bodies of Bert Moore and Dooley Morton.

They had been accused of harassing a white woman, Mrs. Rass Wooten. Two weeks earlier, newspaper accounts reported, Moore and Morton allegedly came to Wooten's house and told her they were going to attack her. An automobile coming to the house had frightened them away. Her husband was out of town, attending to his Arkansas lumber business. After the incident, a guard was posted at the home. Later—about four days before the lynching—one of the Black men returned, allegedly scuffled with the guard, seized the guard's gun, and fired one stray shot. Wooten became involved in the fight, throwing a lit kerosene lantern at the Black man. It exploded. He fled.

By Sunday morning, July 14, law enforcement officials had arrested Moore and Morton. Later, on a day when the temperature reached 97 degrees, Deputy Sheriff Parker Harris surreptitiously took them from jail in Columbus, planning to take them to Aberdeen, twenty-five miles north of Columbus.

By the time Harris had driven the prisoners four miles north of Columbus, a mob of thirty-five men in a motorcade of six automobiles overtook his car. They seized Moore and Morton and drove them south of Columbus to the Zion African Methodist Episcopal Baptist Church, not far from the Wooten home. "Each was made to stand on top of an automobile with his hands tied behind him and a noose fastened around his neck," the Associated Press reported, based on a *Commercial Dispatch* account. "The ropes were knotted to the tree limbs and at a given signal the cars were driven out and the bodies swung downward."

News stories painted a gruesome picture, saying "hundreds visited the spot of the execution." Parker George, at the time in his late twenties, said, "Everybody went down there." At 5:30 p.m., many hours later, the bodies were cut down. A wire service account noted, "Columbus and Lowndes County were in a high state of excitement during the double lynching, but when the mob had dispersed they quieted down." The *Commercial Dispatch* editorial page offered no comment about the lynching, and Pruitt's photographs did not accompany two local news stories about it. The young men were among 20 documented lynchings in Lowndes County and among the more than 576 lynchings from 1877 to 1950 in Mississippi, the most of any state in the nation. The official death certificate listed Morton's age as seventeen. The state of Mississippi's Vital Records department, in 2007, reported that it had no death certificate for Moore.

Pruitt's photographs, nonetheless, provide visual evidence. The bodies of Moore and Morton hanging lifelessly and barefooted, side-by-side; their clothes tattered, their necks wrenched by thick ropes. One image depicts their bodies and a white man, wearing a straw boater hat and kneeling with back to the camera, gathering their pantlegs into a grasp, apparently to keep the bodies steady for the photograph.

Some fifty years after this, Pruitt's daughter Irene said in an interview that her father reported having seen a butterfly alight on the tongues of the men after they were hanged. A white man told me the same story—that he saw the butterflies. Neither he nor others spoke of the spiritual significance of butterflies, which for some Christians symbolize the risen Lord and in some cultures represent the soul, living or dead, and also can represent resilience or resistance. Nor did local people reference the connections scholars draw between the crucifixion of Jesus Christ and the lynching tree and how these relate to the Klan lynch mobs with fiery crosses invading the sacred space of Black churchyards.

Despite a 1908 federal law against mailing lynching images, the Pruitt photograph became a postcard. Likewise, ACME Newspictures distributed the photograph nationally in July 1935. The *Chicago Defender*, a Black-owned newspaper, published the image under the headline "White Civilization." The caption read in part: "We know you don't like to see gruesome pictures like this—neither do we like showing them to you. But as long as our white citizens insist upon ... taking such pictures as these to sell as souvenirs of their barbarity, it is our duty to present them to you." Decades later, as a way to urge Blacks to register to vote during the civil rights era, the image became a voting rights poster emblazoned at the bottom with white letters that spelled MISSISSIPPI. The state headquarters for the Student Nonviolent Coordinating Committee, the Freedom House in Jackson, displayed the poster in the mid-1960s. The use of the Pruitt picture by civil rights workers troubled the Mississippi Sovereignty Commission—a state agency created in the 1950s that used undercover agents and spies to thwart federal efforts at racial integration. In 1964, five months after the murder of three civil rights workers in Neshoba County, commission director Erle Johnston Jr. wrote *Commercial Dispatch* publisher Birney Imes Jr. asking for information about Pruitt's lynching photograph. Johnston was upset. Besides being used by civil rights workers and by Mississippi political activists at the 1964 Democratic National Convention, the lynching image was published in *Afro World*, *Jet*, and *Man's World* and in liberal political brochures in the North. This publicity was done, in Johnston's mind, "to besmirch the image of Mississippi." Since then, the photograph has been used in documentaries and television programing about the American South, including in a 2016 documentary about writer James Baldwin, *I Am Not Your Negro*, and in a 2021 CNN special focused on singer Marvin Gaye's anthem "What's Going On."

In Montgomery, Alabama, there is now a lynching memorial. The Equal Justice Initiative, led by Bryan Stevenson, created in 2018 the National Memorial to Peace and Justice, 800 rusted steel columns hanging from a massive, open-air structure. Each column is labeled with the name of a county in the United States where Blacks were lynched. On the columns are listed the names of those known to have been lynched. The Lowndes County column records, among others, the names of Bert Moore and Dooley Morton. No one was ever charged with their murder.

SEARCH FOR A COLD-EYED WITNESS

Roy Stryker, as director of the 1930s federal Farm Security Administration photographers, urged his cohort to document the Great Depression's ravages. Historian William Stott quoted Stryker as believing that photographs should convey "not only what a place or thing or person *looks* like, but it must also tell the audience what it would *feel* like to be an actual witness to the scene."

Pruitt's pictures transmit what Mississippi felt like, in the spirit of what writer Henry James called "solidity of specification." The lynching photographs serve as cold-eyed witnesses. In my search for people connected to Pruitt, I met in 1994 with Emmett J. Stringer, a dentist. At the time he was seventy-five, living in a ranch-style house on Highway 69, not far from where the Moore and Morton lynching took place.

In the 1950s, Stringer served as president of the Mississippi chapter of the National Association for Advancement of Colored People. His visible NAACP leadership made him a target for Klan harassment—and assassination plots. NAACP colleagues already had been killed under mysterious circumstances. The dentist lost his ability to borrow money from Columbus banks. His wife, Flora, who had a master's degree from Columbia University, was fired from her teaching job. He was audited by the Internal Revenue Service. His automobile liability insurance was canceled. The Stringers moved into an interior bedroom in case their home was bombed. He kept weapons there and carried a revolver. He received threatening phone calls. At night, the same cars would pass his house, again and again.

When Stringer led the Mississippi NAACP, Pruitt regularly photographed him. This allowed the dentist to send his portrait with press releases to newspapers in cities around the country where he would be speaking.

Stringer had grown up in the Mississippi Delta in Mound Bayou, an all-Black community. A World War II veteran, he came to Columbus in 1950 to set up a dental practice on Catfish Alley, where he practiced for forty-two years. When he arrived, he said, "race relations were not too good." It took two years for the county officials to agree to register him to vote. Stringer was, he said, the first Black man to register in Lowndes County since Reconstruction. When he went to register, his preacher, who led the Missionary Union Baptist Church, asked to accompany him. "He felt like they were going to try to hurt me if I had gone up there by myself." The preacher's intuition was well-founded. Stringer explained, "The Circuit Clerk told me: 'You'd better be careful. If not, you're gonna get your ass kicked.' It seemed that almost as soon as he said it, he was regretful. I said: 'Well, Mr. Cochran, I'm sorry you're speaking like that. You ask anybody in this town about me, white or Black, and ... they'll tell you that I'm a decent, honorable person.'"

Soon after registering, Stringer became the president of the Mississippi NAACP. He worked with civil rights leaders Medgar Evers, Fannie Lou Hamer, and Aaron Henry. Stringer developed a friendship with future U.S. Supreme Court justice Thurgood Marshall when Marshall pursued Mississippi civil rights cases. During that time, an Associated Press story in the *New York Times* quoted Stringer about how groups such as the all-white Citizens Councils targeted Blacks in campaigns against desegregation. When Stringer was president, he gave a speech that inspired Evers to apply to law school at the University of Mississippi. Evers was rejected. Later, Stringer helped James Meredith apply a second time to the university and successfully desegregate it in 1962.

Once, in Columbus, a white man spat on Stringer. When people saw the dentist walking on the street, Black and white alike sometimes would cross the street to avoid him, a racial "rabble rouser." He recalled, "I was coming out [of the post office on Main Street] one day, and this fellow was coming in and ... he ... deliberately stuck his foot out. I said, 'Oh, pardon me, sir.' He said, 'Oh, no, I'll tell you what, if you're not careful, you're gonna get hurt.'"

IMAGE, MEMORY, HISTORY

In 2003, through a story in the *Commercial Dispatch*, I announced I'd like to meet people Pruitt had photographed. I set up shop in the Columbus–Lowndes County Public Library. Several dozen people came. Two people in particular contacted me, wanting to see the lynching photographs. One was a Black woman; the other, a white man. Both were insistent.

The Black woman said she should have a copy of the photograph because the image belonged to the history of her community and church where the lynching occurred. "I just want a copy," she told me. "I don't know if I would ever look at it. I just have to have it." On the Sunday evening before the lynching, she said, her church was having a revival; the mob "broke up that service" and "forced some of them [church members] to watch." Her husband, who was about five years old then and lived near the church, had seen the bodies hanging from the tree.

I listened to her and explained that four friends, all white and natives of Columbus, and I wanted to uncover the aspects of life that Pruitt depicted, the beautiful and the horrific. None of us, I told her, had heard before about local lynchings and were surprised how these photographs revealed our naiveté.

Would you still like a copy of the lynching photograph? I asked after we had talked at length.

No, she said without explanation, she didn't need a copy anymore.

I met, too, with the white man who wanted a copy. He lived in the country, he said, in the house where the Wootens had lived when the lynching happened. The image, he said, belonged to the house's history. He'd seen the same picture before, once, he said, at the nearby house of a white man. I told him I was uncomfortable giving him a copy, that he could buy the book *Without Sanctuary*, which contained the Pruitt photograph—and scores more images of lynching postcards of the nineteenth and twentieth centuries. He left unsatisfied.

Many years later, in the twenty-first-century era of racist violence, I was scheduled to meet in Columbus with a young Black woman related to one of the two men who had been lynched. In the end, we didn't meet; her family didn't want her to talk about the lynching.

Sometime after, in 2019, I met with Mary Theo Burns, a white woman then ninety-one. For much of her working life, she had taught in Columbus public schools, teaching Black and white children in the same classroom. When she was seven years old in 1935, she said, her father had taken her to see the aftermath of the lynching, telling her he wanted her to see the results of mob violence. She recalled, decades later, the horror of seeing the two bodies, hanging against one another. She spoke, too, about her life growing up—going to Luxapalila Creek to watch Black baptisms of children she knew, or working at the white movie theater where Blacks could sit only in the balcony.

Her father, she said, was a barber his whole life. When men came into his shop and wanted a shave or a haircut, he never asked them if they were members of the Ku Klux Klan. Her father, she said, did not want to know the answer to that question.

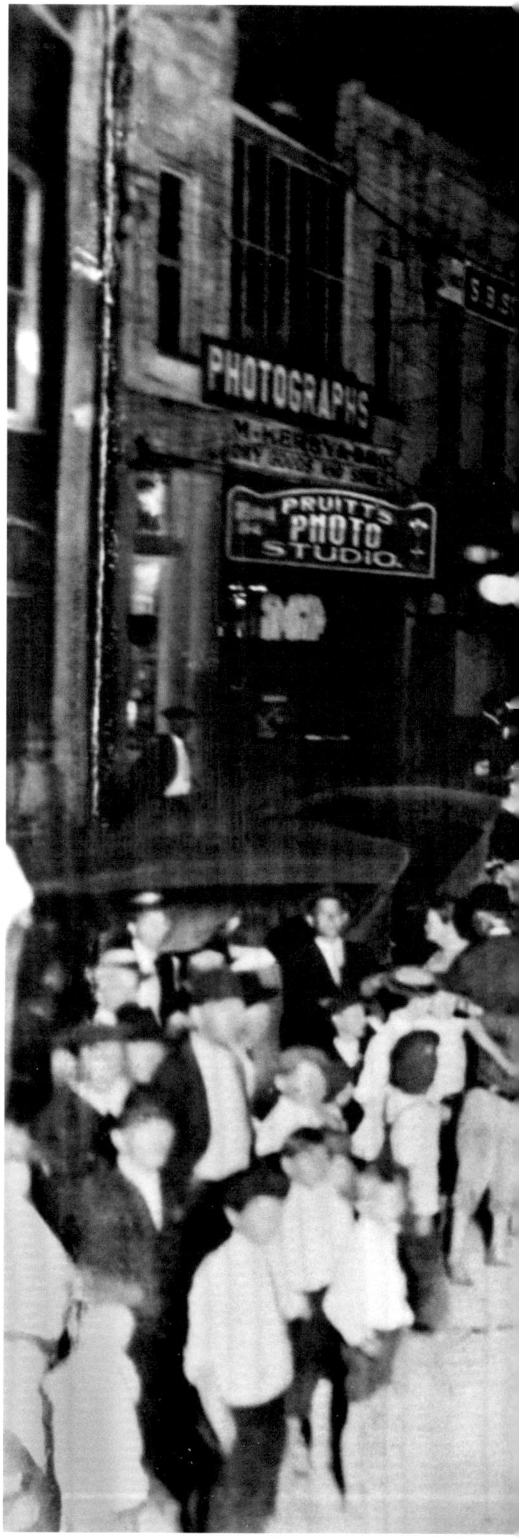

Ku Klux Klan march, Main Street in front of Pruitt's studio, circa 1922.

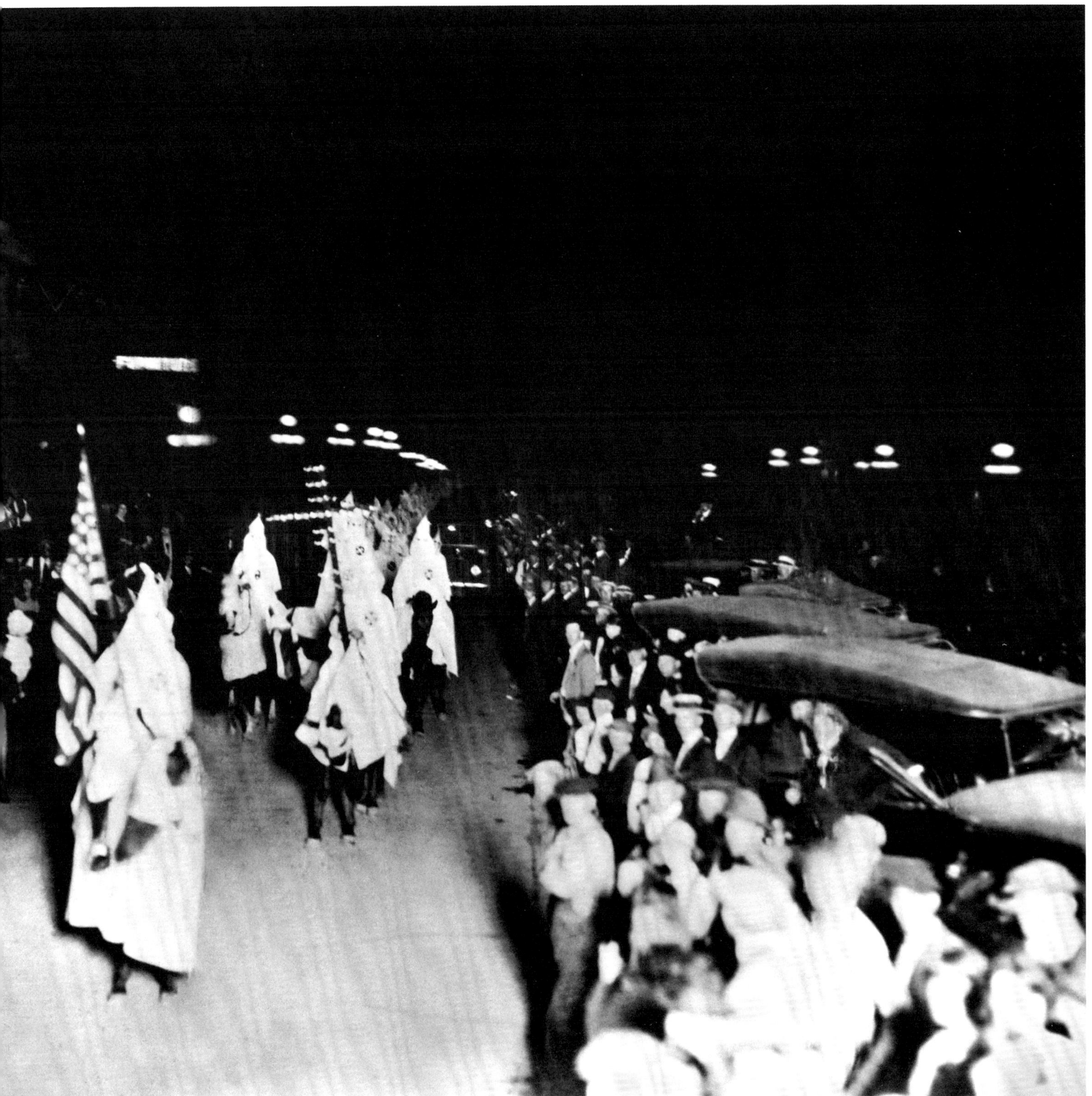

Execution of James Keaton, Lowndes County Courthouse, May 25, 1934.

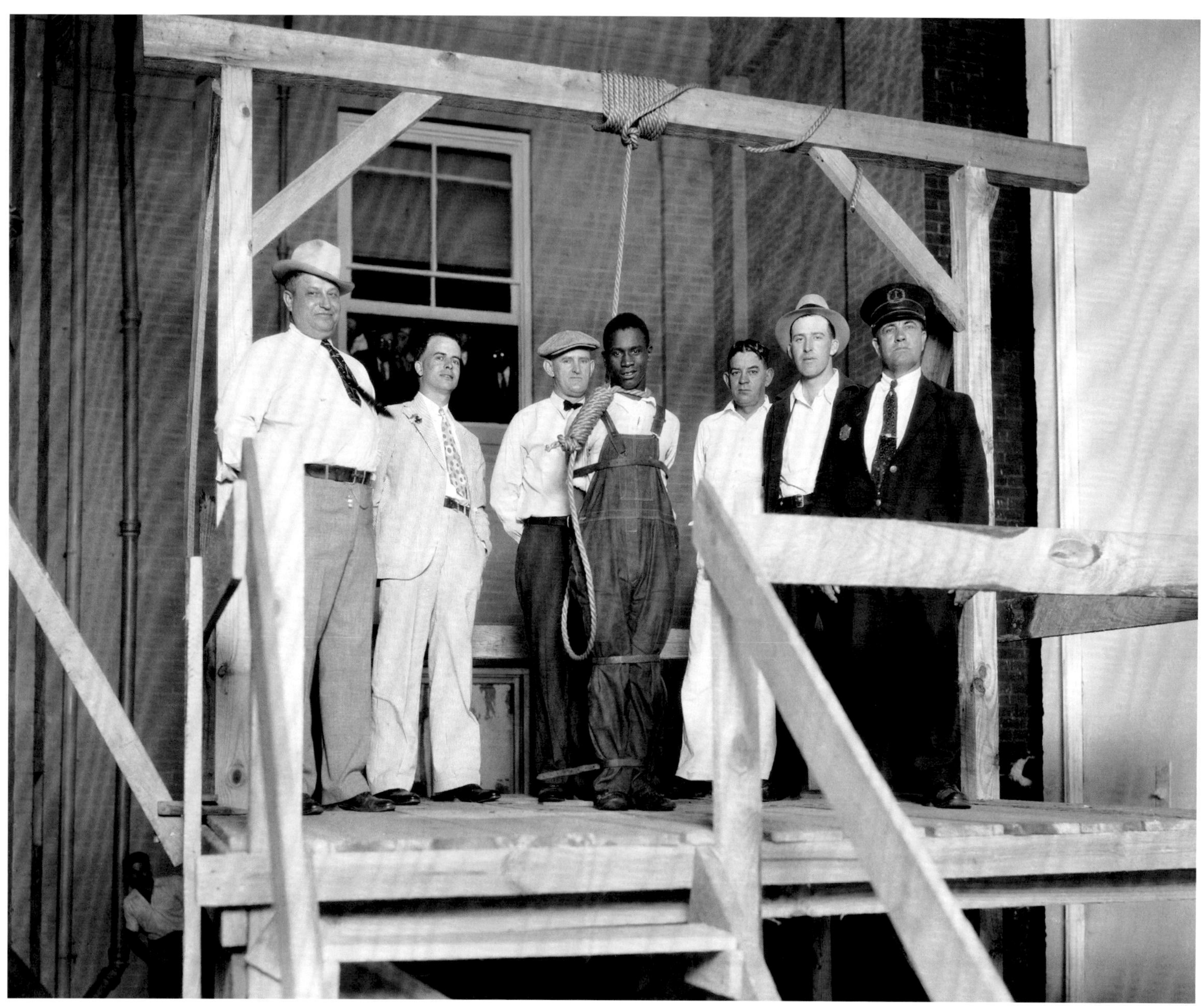

(opposite) *After the lynching of Bert Moore and Dooley Morton, July 1935.*

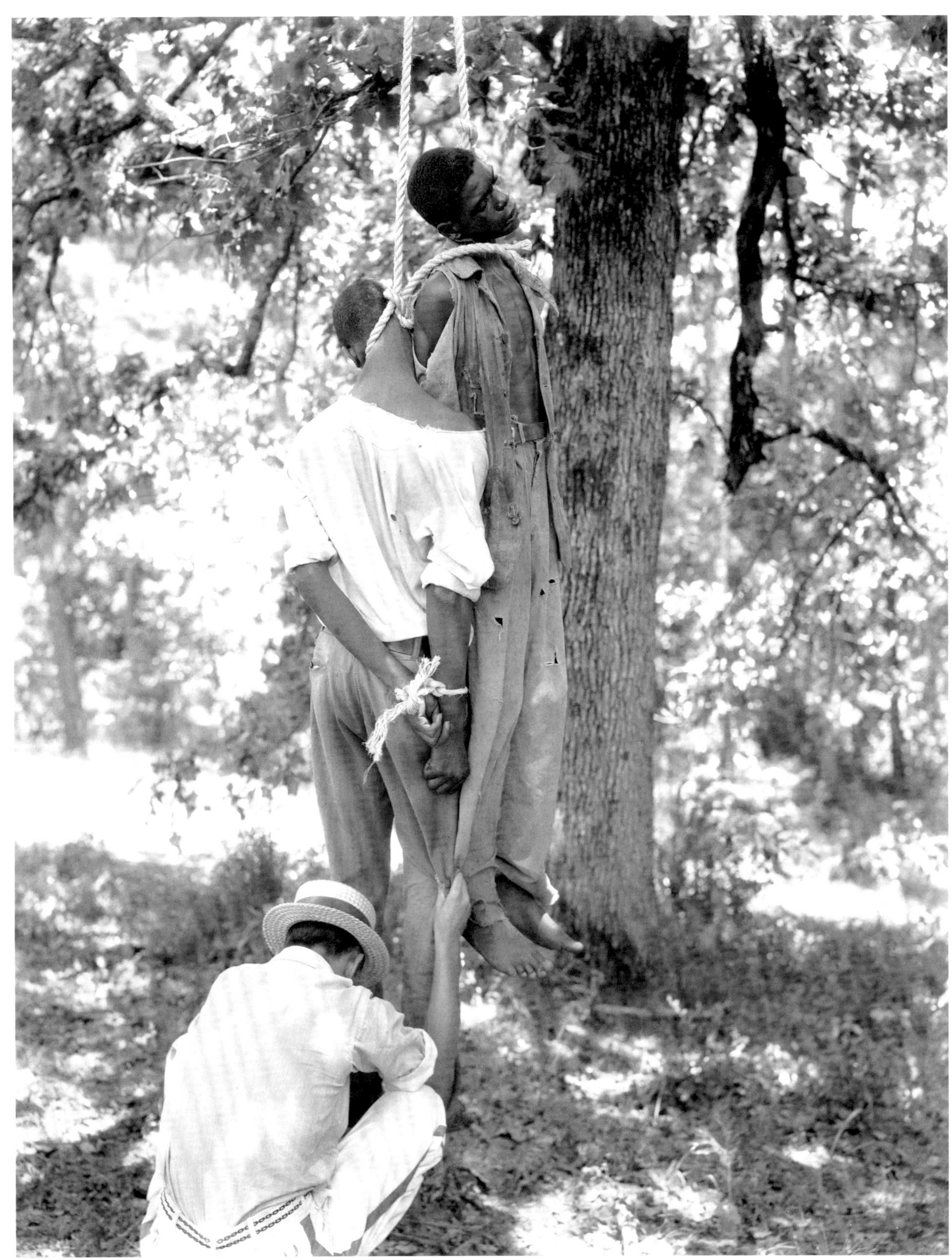

Death certificate for Dooley Morton, with cause of death "lynched by mob," Vital Records, Mississippi State Department of Health, July 15, 1935.

STATE OF MISSISSIPPI

MISSISSIPPI STATE DEPARTMENT OF HEALTH
VITAL RECORDS

BUREAU OF VITAL STATISTICS

STANDARD CERTIFICATE OF DEATH

State File No. 10900

MISSISSIPPI STATE BOARD OF HEALTH

1. PLACE OF DEATH
County Lowndes Registered No. 40
Voting Precinct Old Zion or Village Dist 2
or City ... No. ... St., ... Ward
(If death occurred in a hospital or institution, give its NAME instead of street and number)
Length of residence in city or town where death occurred ... yrs. ... mos. ... ds. How long in U. S. if of foreign birth? ... yrs. ... mos. ... ds.

2. FULL NAME Dooley Morton (Christy) (Write or Print Name Plainly)
(a) Residence: No. Columbus Miss St., ... Ward.
(Usual place of abode) (If nonresident give city or town and State)

PERSONAL AND STATISTICAL PARTICULARS

3. SEX Male
4. COLOR OR RACE Colored
5. Single, Married, Widowed, or Divorced (write the word) Single
5a. If married, widowed, or divorced HUSBAND of (or) WIFE of
6. DATE OF BIRTH (month, day, and year)
7. AGE 17 Years
8. Trade, profession, or particular kind of work done, as spinner, sawyer, bookkeeper, etc. Farming
9. Industry or business in which work was done, as silk mill, saw mill, bank, etc.
10. Date deceased last worked at this occupation (month and year) July 10 1935
11. Total time (years) spent in this occupation
12. BIRTHPLACE (city or town) (State or country) Lowndes Co Miss
FATHER 13. NAME Christie Morton
14. BIRTHPLACE (city or town) (State or country) Thomas Place Lowndes Co Miss
MOTHER 15. MAIDEN NAME
16. BIRTHPLACE (city or town) (State or country) Adaline Morton Pickens Co Ala
17. INFORMANT (and Address)
18. BURIAL, CREMATION, OR REMOVAL Place At Place of Date Death
19. UNDERTAKER (and) Address Buried by County
20. FILED July 15 1935 Annie B. Shackelford Registrar
J. H. Atkins, Coroner

MEDICAL CERTIFICATE OF DEATH

21. DATE OF DEATH (month, day and year) July 14 1935
22. I HEREBY CERTIFY, That I attended deceased from ..., 19... to ..., 19...
I last saw h... alive on ..., 19... Death is said to have occurred on the date stated above, at ... m.
The principal cause of death and related causes of importance in order of onset were as follows: Lynched by mob
Date of onset
Contributory causes of importance not related to principal cause:
Name of operation (if any was done) ... Date of ...
What test confirmed diagnosis? ... Was there an autopsy?
23. If death was due to external causes (violence) fill in also the following: Accident, suicide, or homicide?
Date of injury ..., 19...
Where did injury occur? (Specify city or town, county, and State)
Specify whether injury occurred in industry, in home, or in public place
Manner of injury
Nature of injury
24. Was disease or injury in any way related to occupation of deceased? ... If so, specify ...
(Signed) No Physician M. D.
(Address)

Very important. See instructions on back of certificate. Exact statement of OCCUPATION is very important, so that it may be properly classified.

THIS IS TO CERTIFY THAT THE ABOVE IS A TRUE AND CORRECT COPY OF THE CERTIFICATE ON FILE IN THIS OFFICE

Brian W. Amy, MD, MHA, MPH
STATE HEALTH OFFICER

APR 23 2007

Judy Moulder
STATE REGISTRAR

MISSISSIPPI STATE BOARD OF HEALTH

WARNING: A REPRODUCTION OF THIS DOCUMENT RENDERS IT VOID AND INVALID. DO NOT ACCEPT UNLESS EMBOSSED SEAL OF THE MISSISSIPPI STATE BOARD OF HEALTH IS PRESENT. IT IS ILLEGAL TO ALTER OR COUNTERFEIT THIS DOCUMENT.

THE FACE OF THIS DOCUMENT HAS A COLORED BACKGROUND ON WHITE PAPER. THIS IS WATERMARKED PAPER. DO NOT ACCEPT WITHOUT FIRST HOLDING TO LIGHT TO VERIFY WATERMARK.

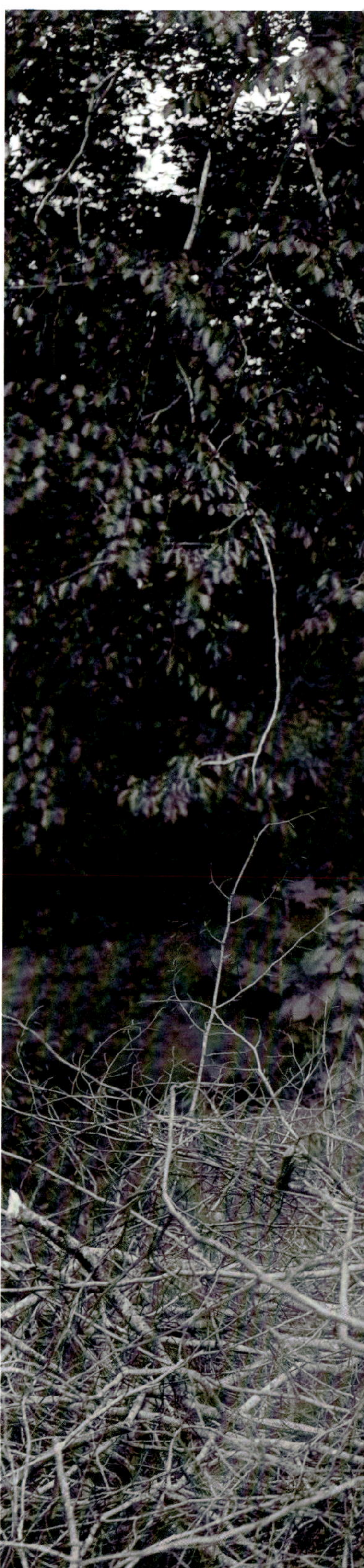

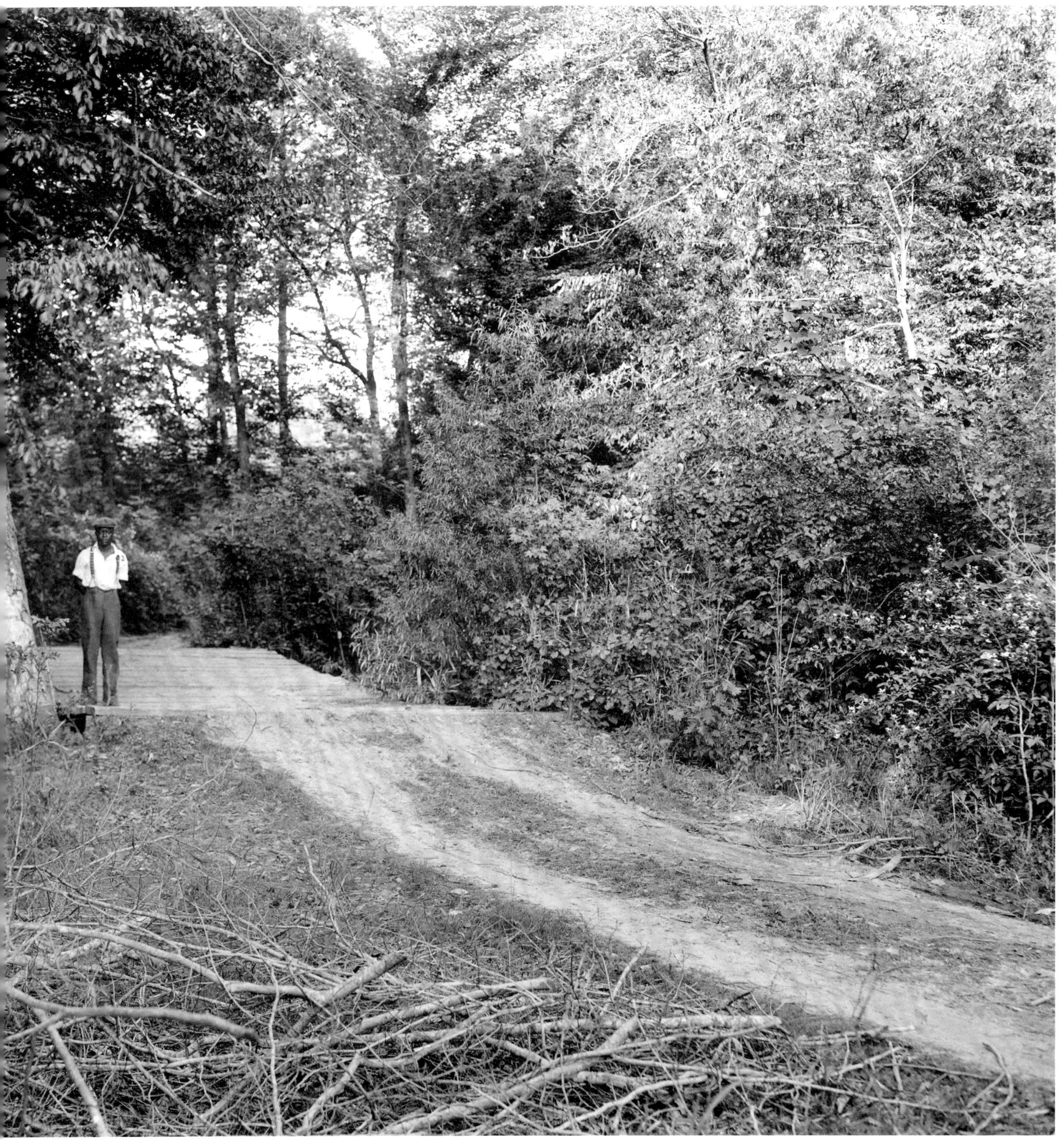

A SPUNKY FOLK HERO

A Farmer Named Sylvester Harris, 1934

In the Pruitt archives in 1987, nestled amid other prints, was a picture of a man in overalls standing next to a mule. In the background is a wooden frame house, known as a T-house because of its shape as an expansion of the traditional dogtrot house. There was no name, date, or description with the print; no negative matched with it. Why did Pruitt make this picture?

After seven years of searching, I found the answer in bound volumes of the *Commercial Dispatch*, and its front page on March 8, 1934. The caption with Pruitt's picture read, "Sylvester Harris, negro of Lowndes County, Miss., has plenty to be happy about. Recently he telephoned President Roosevelt in a plea to save his home from mortgage foreclosure, and a few days later an extension was granted on the mortgage. Here's Sylvester, with his mule, in front of his farmhouse near Columbus, Miss."

Inspired by the fireside chats of President Franklin D. Roosevelt, Harris had traveled to Columbus to call the White House on February 19, 1934. It took Harris ninety minutes on the phone, but he succeeded. The mainstream white press brought the story to the nation's attention, but the Black press celebrated Harris as a savvy folk hero. Harris, in today's parlance, went viral. So did Pruitt's photograph that the Associated Press distributed. A media chain reaction of newspaper stories, cartoons, songs, preacher's sermons, political speeches, and folklore sprang forth from Harris's call to Roosevelt. As a thank-you, until the president died in 1945, Harris annually shipped a Thanksgiving turkey to the Little White House in Warm Springs, Georgia.

Two decades ago, with the help of W. G. "Bit" Thompson, a member of the Lowndes County

Board of Supervisors who knew Harris and his relatives, I found his kinfolk living in two modest houses on the land where Harris and his brother Mason had farmed 140 acres of cotton, along with a garden patch where they raised their own food. One day in January 2003, Harris's relatives told me how Harris called the president. A great niece relished the fact that Harris was a bold man in every way. He once ignored a state highway patrol blockade, she said, and successfully rode around it, in order to get cotton he was carrying to the gin in Columbus before it closed for the day.

Another relative at a nearby house, Charley Will Harris, brought out a yellowed page from a magazine to explain how his great uncle Sylvester had called the president. Like his relatives, Charley Will, known as Sweet Man, had always been a farmer. In addition he had worked at the toilet seat factory in town for thirty-five years until his recent retirement. Harris sat in the living room of his white wood-frame house on the land where his great uncle Sylvester farmed. He did not know what magazine the scrap had come from. A relative had given it to him years ago. He unfolded the deteriorating page with great care, as if it were an ancient parchment. On both sides, midway through a magazine story, words and pictures told about Sylvester Harris.

One year later, in bound volumes of *Ebony* magazine, I found the full story in the March 1957 issue with this headline: "The Forgotten Man and the Mule: Hero of Depression Still Lives on Farm Saved by Direct Call to President Roosevelt." Below the 1934 Pruitt photograph of a smiling Harris and his mule, the story begins, "Twenty-three years ago, the man in the picture above was a living legend. From Maine to Mississippi his name was synonymous with the New Deal. Men without jobs or meat to sustain themselves invoked his name and took courage. In the darkest hour of the worst crisis in American history, Sylvester Harris and his mule, Jesse, were symbols of light and hope."

Indeed, Harris inspired a weary nation, including blues singer Memphis Minnie in her "Sylvester and His Mule Blues":

> Sylvester went out in his lot, and he looked
> at his mule,
> And he decided, he would send the
> president some news.
> Sylvester walked out across his field, begin to
> pray and moan,
> He cried, "Oh, Lord, believe I'm gonna
> lose my home."

Jazzman Ben Bernie wrote a song he performed on his New York City radio show. A Fox Movietone newsreel crew came to Columbus to record Harris's story, as did a Paramount Studios newsreel crew. Millions of people, including movie theatergoers in New York City's Times Square, would see the newsreel interviews with Harris outside his farmhouse.

An editorial cartoon in the *Chicago Defender*, however, pointed out the contrast in the plight of Harris and that of Blacks under siege from lynch mobs. This cartoon by Leslie Rogers was divided into two parts. On the top left-hand side, Harris is shown with a telephone. A caption reads, "Mr. President, I'm about to lose my land!" On the upper right President Roosevelt answers the phone: "Sylvester, I'll investigate!" On the bottom half, a Black man runs toward a telephone and away from a white mob that brandishes a hangman's noose. A caption says, "If he could but reach the President by phone."

Harris traveled to Chicago and gave speeches for Democrat Arthur W. Mitchell, who defeated Republican Oscar DePriest in a campaign for a U.S. congressional seat. Both Mitchell and DePriest were African American. Recounting that event, the 1957 *Ebony* story said, "history records that the farmer thus helped start a dynasty of Democratic congressmen from Illinois' First Congressional District."

The news treatment of Harris opens a window into the 1930s representation of African Americans. In some respects, Harris was portrayed as "colorless." In other treatments, in the Black or white press, he was "raced"—whether referred to as a "Negro" with a capital *N*, "negro" with a lowercase *n*, "colored," or, as he referred to himself in speaking to Roosevelt and was recorded on one newsreel, "a n—— way down here in Mississippi."

With a conservative racial viewpoint, the white press originated the Harris story. This was true in Harris's local newspaper, where he was presented as a spunky hometown hero who was Black; in regional newspapers that relied on wire service reports; or in national newspapers such as the *New York Times*, where the coverage had a slightly less racial overtone than in Deep South white newspapers. The white press cast Harris as an unlettered rural southern Black farmer who sought help from a powerful white authority figure, President Roosevelt. The Black press treated Harris not as an oddity who spoke in Black dialect but as someone more akin to a family member with the feistiness and courage to solve his financial problem in an innovative way. Pruitt's photograph played a role in that. The *Chicago Defender* published the photograph, headlined, "This Is Sylvester Talking!" The caption did not identify his race but described him only as a farmer, using an honorific when referring to him: "Mr. Harris' success in getting action from the White House is another indication that a different spirit of democracy now exists than appeared to exist there during the previous administration."

The photograph offers as good an example as any in the Pruitt Collection of the critical role of the caption, as John Berger conceived it. With a caption, the man and mule transcend the boundaries of a workmanlike photograph; they become symbols of light and hope in a story to be told over generations.

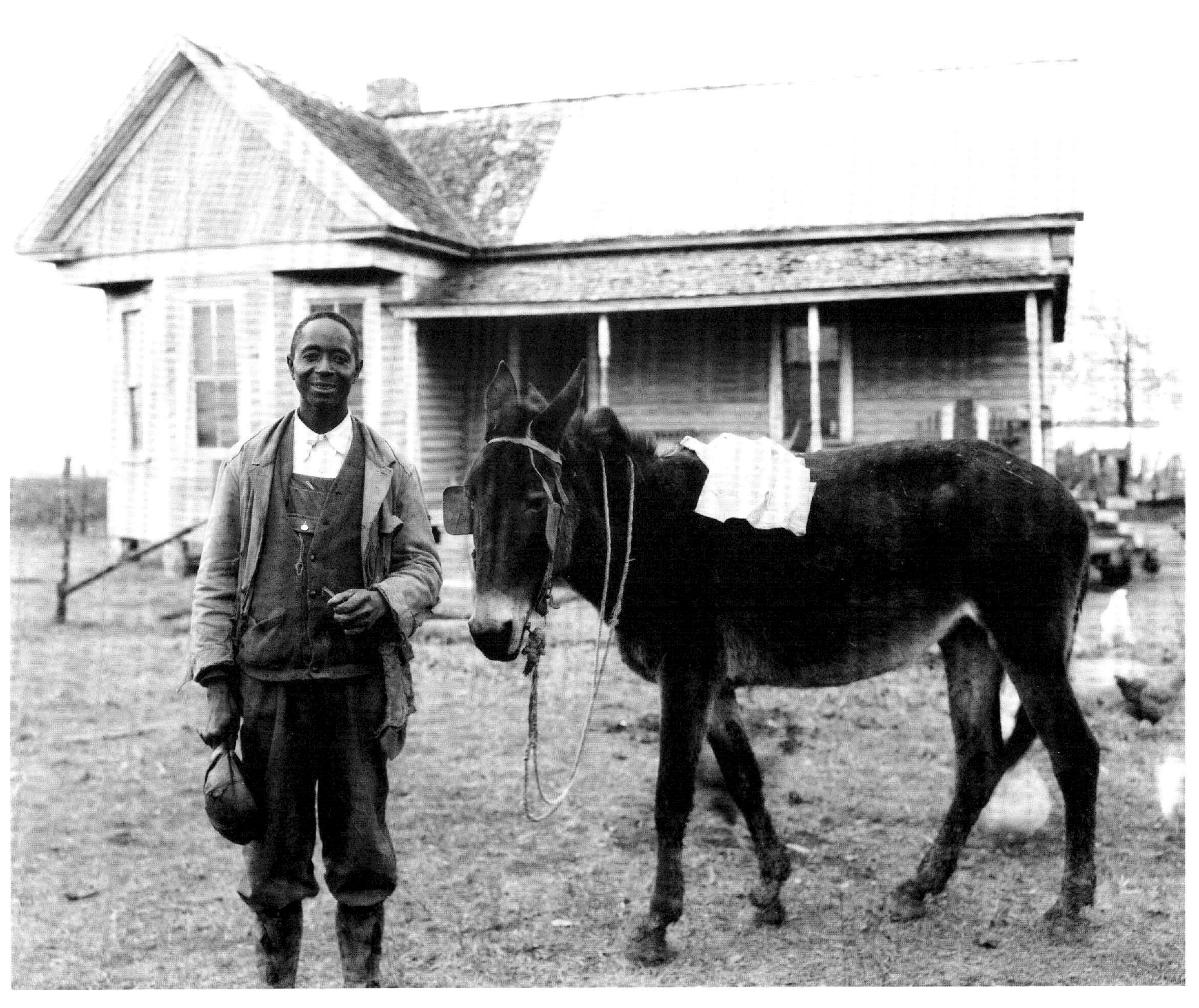

Lowndes County farmer Sylvester Harris with mule Jesse outside his home in Plum Grove community, February 1934. President Franklin D. Roosevelt helped Harris save his farm from foreclosure after Harris called Roosevelt on the phone and asked for assistance.

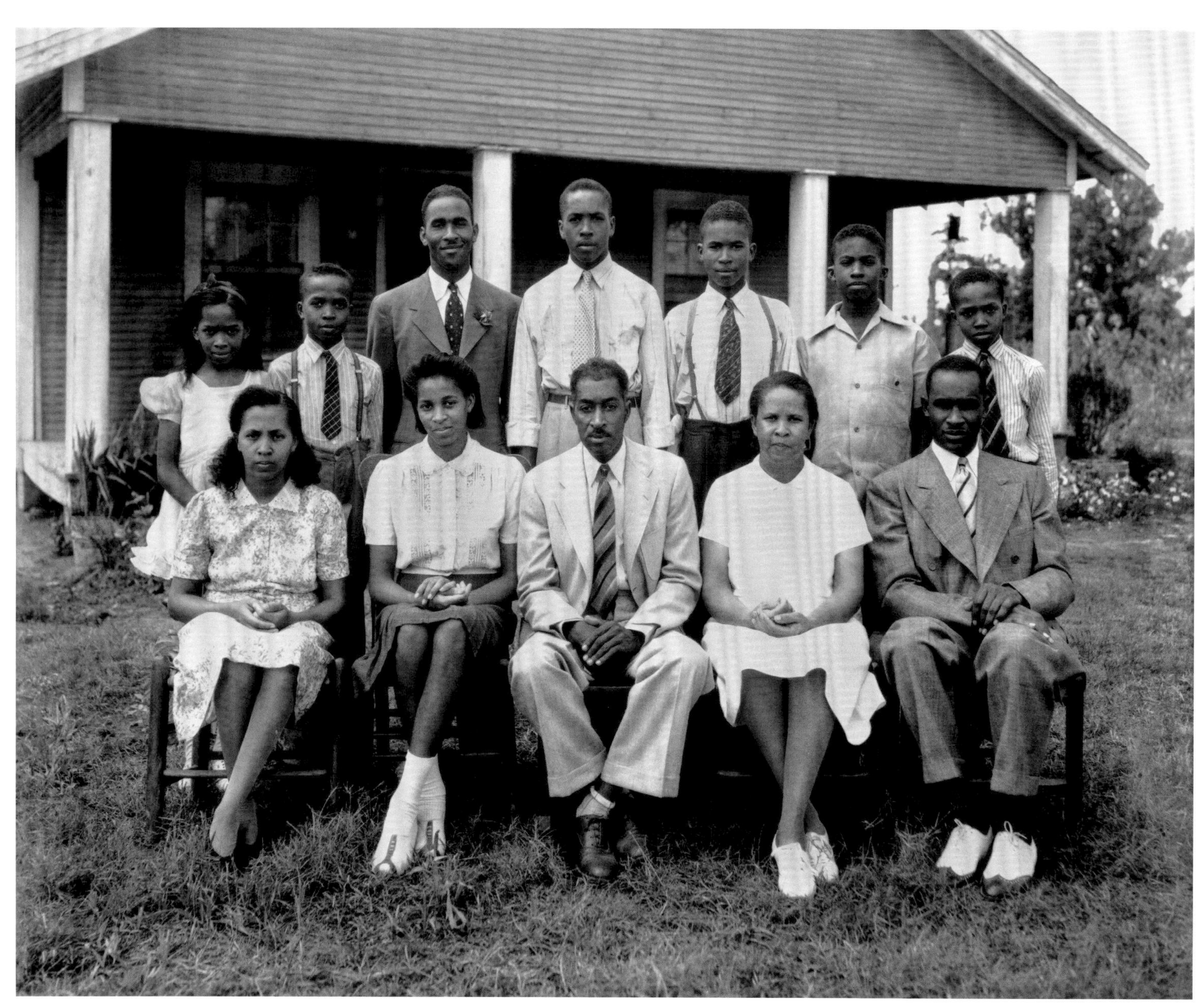

James Mann family portrait, 1948.

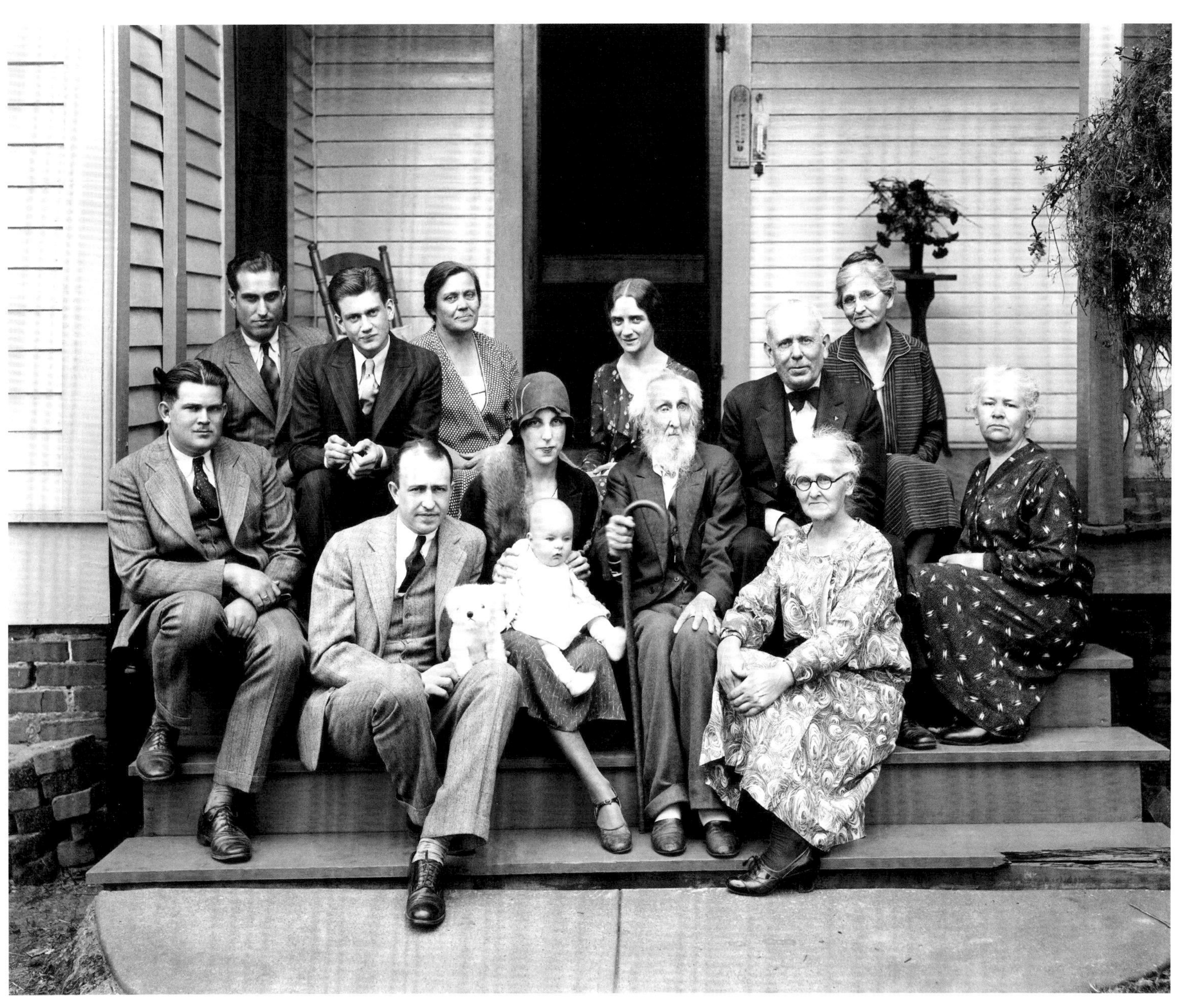

Family portrait. Mrs. Mary Stokes is in second row, far right.

BOXER JACK DEMPSEY, TRUMAN CAPOTE'S PARENTS, THE "EGYPTIAN MARVEL" OF THE GREAT PASHA, AND MADAME FLOZELLA, 1930

In November 1930, early in the Great Depression, former world heavyweight champion Jack Dempsey came to Columbus from Los Angeles to rendezvous with a "buried-alive" carnival act managed by Truman Capote's father.

At one point, on the outskirts of town at the Lake Norris Fishing Club, they posed for Pruitt around a grave dug into the earth, encircled by tall pines and swamp cypress. A dozen or so people surround an upturned wooden coffin in which stood the turbaned Great Pasha, dressed in white robes and accompanied by his similarly robed assistant, Madame Flozella. Capote's father, Arch Persons, a graduate of the Washington and Lee University law school, served as manager of the carnival act. Capote's mother, Lillie Mae Persons, also came to town and was photographed next to the champ with her husband, likely leaving Truman, age six, with relatives in Monroeville, Alabama.

The entourage had arrived to help celebrate "Dempsey Day" and "Columbus Dollar Days," designed to lure shoppers and boxing fans from hundreds of miles away. Dempsey had been scheduled to referee a series of boxing matches. However, a rainstorm washed out that event the day before Pasha's burial. Pruitt recorded the assemblage as it moved through town and countryside, visually telling a story that evokes themes of celebrity, carnival, fantasy, and clairvoyance in an age of economic uncertainty.

Some months before, in 1930 or 1929, Lillie Mae had met Dempsey on a train trip. She and young Truman were traveling from Memphis to St. Louis. An assistant for Dempsey walked up the train aisle and spotted Lillie Mae. He asked her and her son if they would like to meet the champ. After they met Dempsey, the boxer's assistant took Truman to the observation car for a Coca-Cola, while Lillie Mae and the champ got acquainted in his compartment. Capote's Aunt Tiny Rudisill writes, "Lillie Mae as a married woman felt free to indulge her passions. The sight of an attractive, well-dressed man ... put goose bumps up and down the inside of Lillie Mae's thighs."

That, in part, perhaps explains how Dempsey, Pasha, and Flozella came to Columbus. Lillie Mae, it seems, was the go-between for Dempsey, her husband, and Columbus, which wanted to stir up local business sales during the Great Depression.

At the Lake Norris event, fifty male guests feasted on Brunswick stew, lamb, and pork "barbecued to please the taste of any champion," according to a *Commercial Dispatch* story. They also ate what the *Dispatch* called a "famous Columbus dish," Hobbly-Cobbly, a southern-style chutney made of onions, bell pepper, vinegar, salt, sugar, and Louisiana hot sauce. It is served with dishes such as peas or greens.

Ten days before Dempsey arrived, Pasha and Flozella had already been entertaining the community. The *Dispatch* recounted, "After driving blind folded around town for an hour, Pasha was placed in an air-tight coffin and buried six feet underground for more than two hours. At four o'clock, he was taken from the grave and revived at Montgomery Ward and Company. Hundreds marveled at the dual sensations, but none could advance a solution as to how he did it, even after watching him."

Columbus resident Billy Thompson, then eighteen, recalled it this way seventy years later: "The promoters went to the Gilmer Hotel and all got drunk while [Pasha] was buried alive. They like to have kept him in the ground too long."

In a literary sense, the spirit of the Great Pasha and Madame Flozella lived again in a short story written by Truman Capote. In June 1945, when he was twenty, *Mademoiselle* published one of his first short stories, "Miriam." That prompted an inquiry from a *Harper's Bazaar* editor. In October 1949, almost two decades after Pruitt had photographed the "buried-alive" gathering, *Harper's* published "A Tree of Night."

Capote's story takes place in the American South in the 1920s. A train rumbles its way from New Orleans and into the night through Mississippi and Alabama on its way to Atlanta. A college coed named Kay is returning from an uncle's funeral. The train is crowded. Kay has found a seat next to a strange couple, a zombie-like man and a short woman wearing too much makeup and smelling of gin. The couple is a "buried-alive" carnival act.

At one point during the train ride, Capote's Flozella character says to Kay, "I've got something here I wanna show you, honey."

> What she passed to Kay was a handbill.... In fragile, overly fancy lettering, it read:
>
> LAZARUS
> The Man Who Is Buried Alive
> a miracle
> see for yourself
> *Adults, 25¢—Children, 10¢*

Kay said, "You mean you're with a circus or a side-show or something like that?"

"Nope, us alone," said the woman.... "We've been doing it for years and years—played every tank town in the South: Singasong, Mississippi—Spunky, Louisiana—Eureka, Alabama.... After the hymn, after the sermon we bury him."

"In a coffin?"

"Sort of. It's gorgeous, it's got silver stars painted all over the lid."

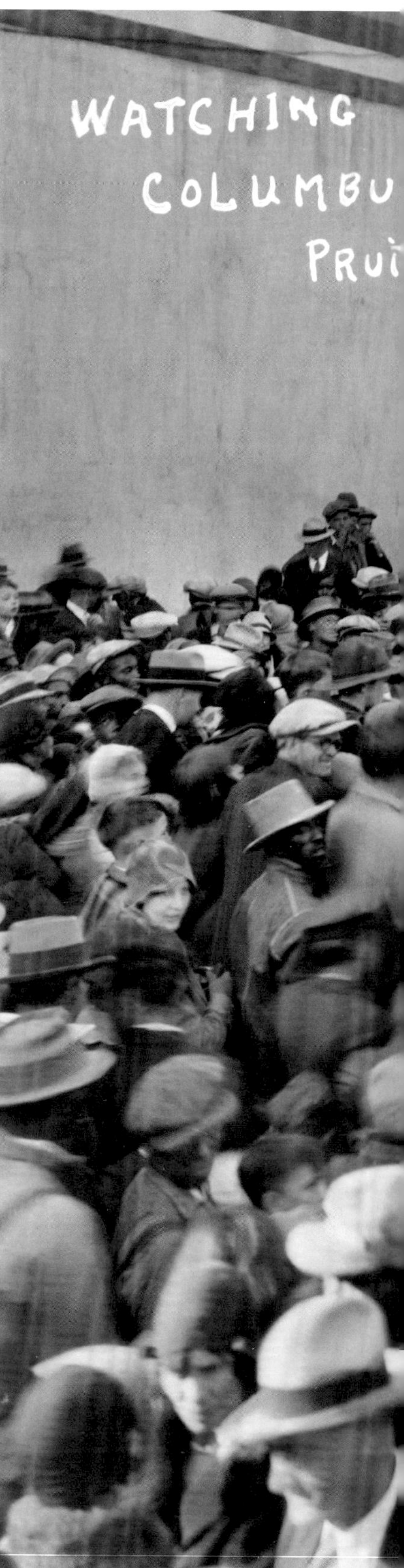

"Watching Pasha Buried Alive" next to the Commercial Dispatch *building on Main Street, November 1, 1930.*

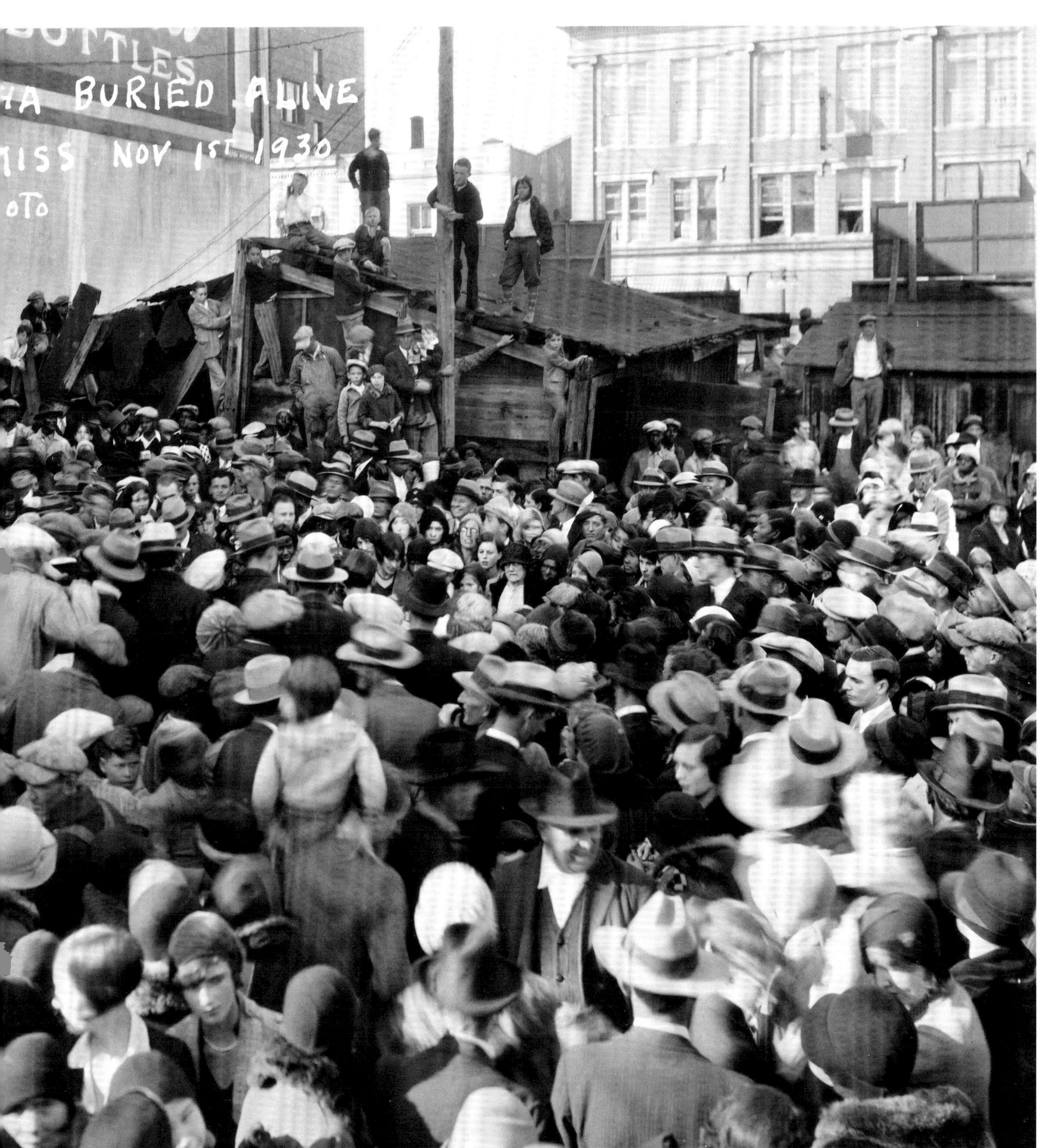

BURIED ALIVE
NOV 1ST 1930

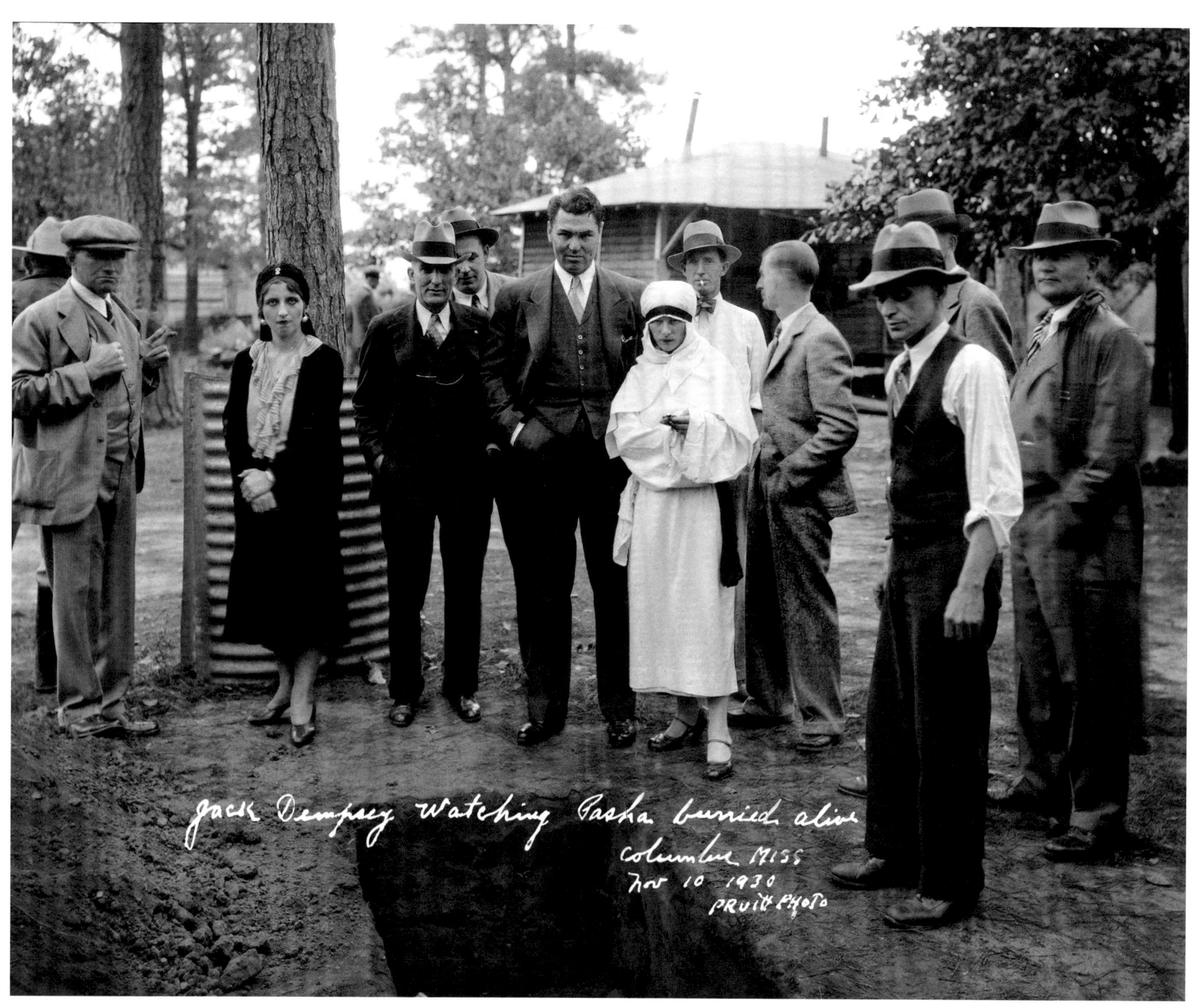

Boxing champion Jack Dempsey (center and hatless) *with Madame Flozella and Truman Capote's mother, Lillie Mae Faulk Persons (dressed in black), by grave dug at the Lake Norris Fishing Club, November 10, 1930.*

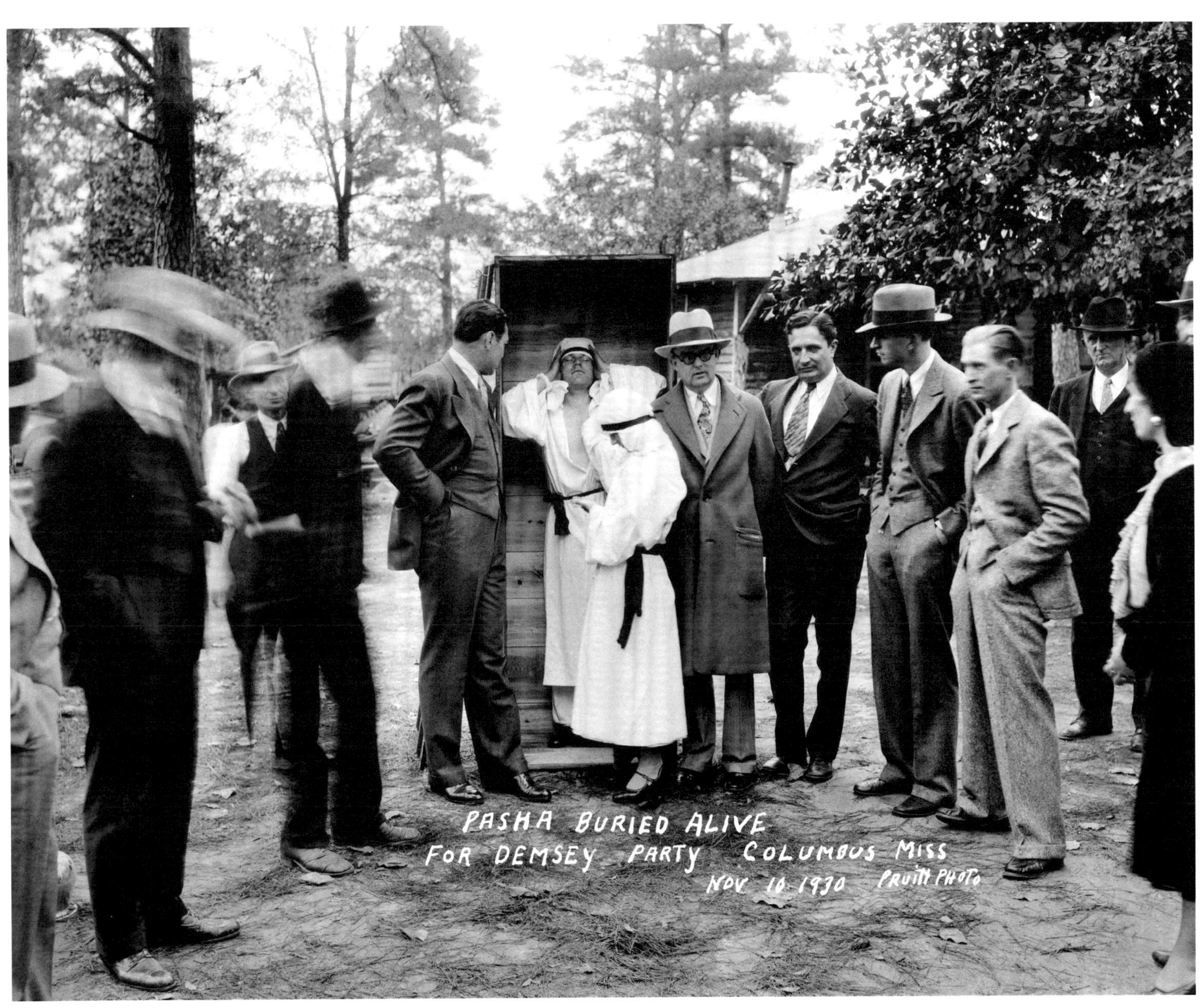

Boxing champion Jack Dempsey (left of coffin) *with the Great Pasha; Madame Flozella; "Buried Alive" act's manager, Arch Persons* (in white hat and glasses), *Truman Capote's father; and Lillie Mae Faulk Persons, Truman Capote's mother* (far right), *Lake Norris Fishing Club, November 10, 1930.*

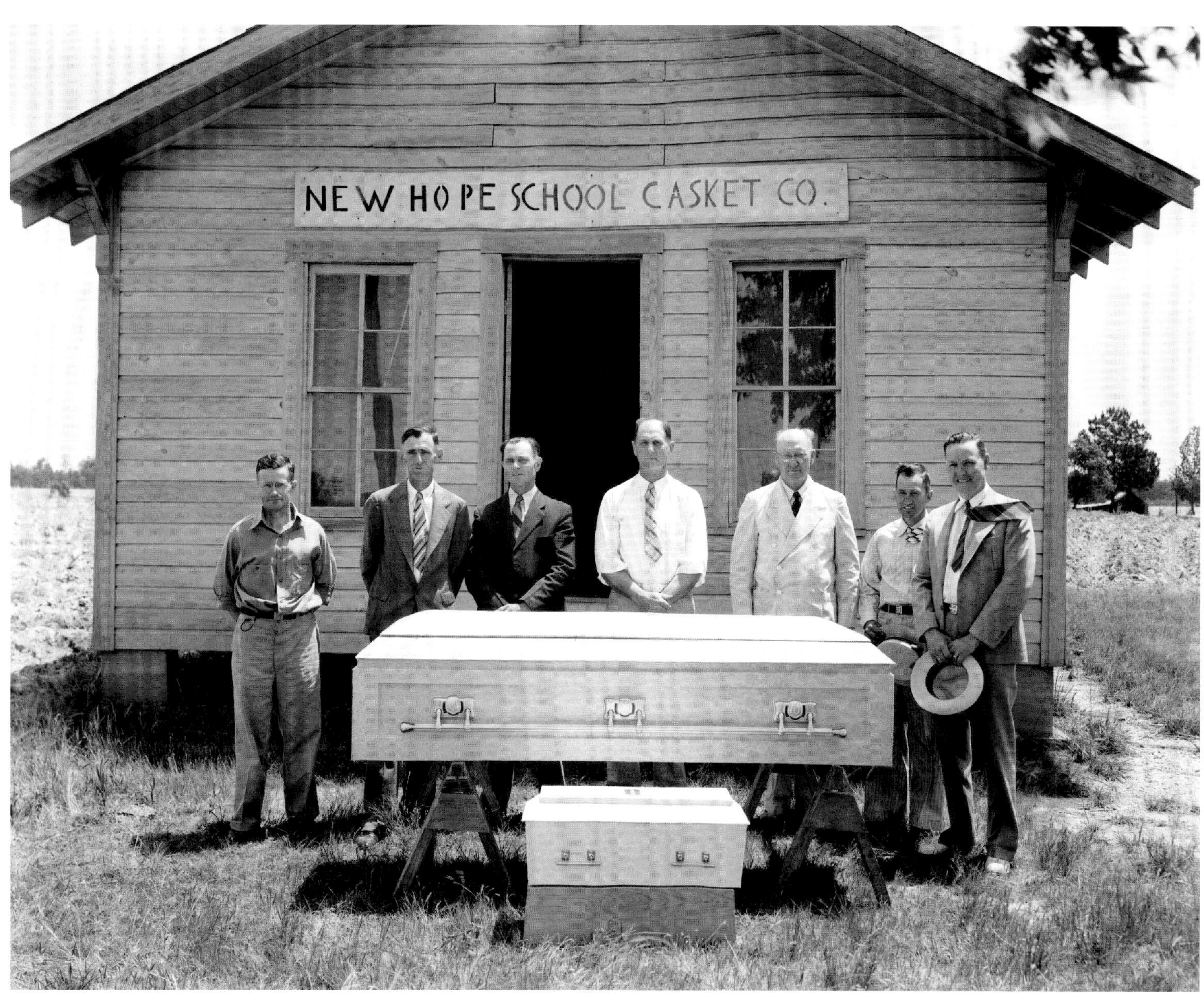
NEW HOPE SCHOOL CASKET CO.

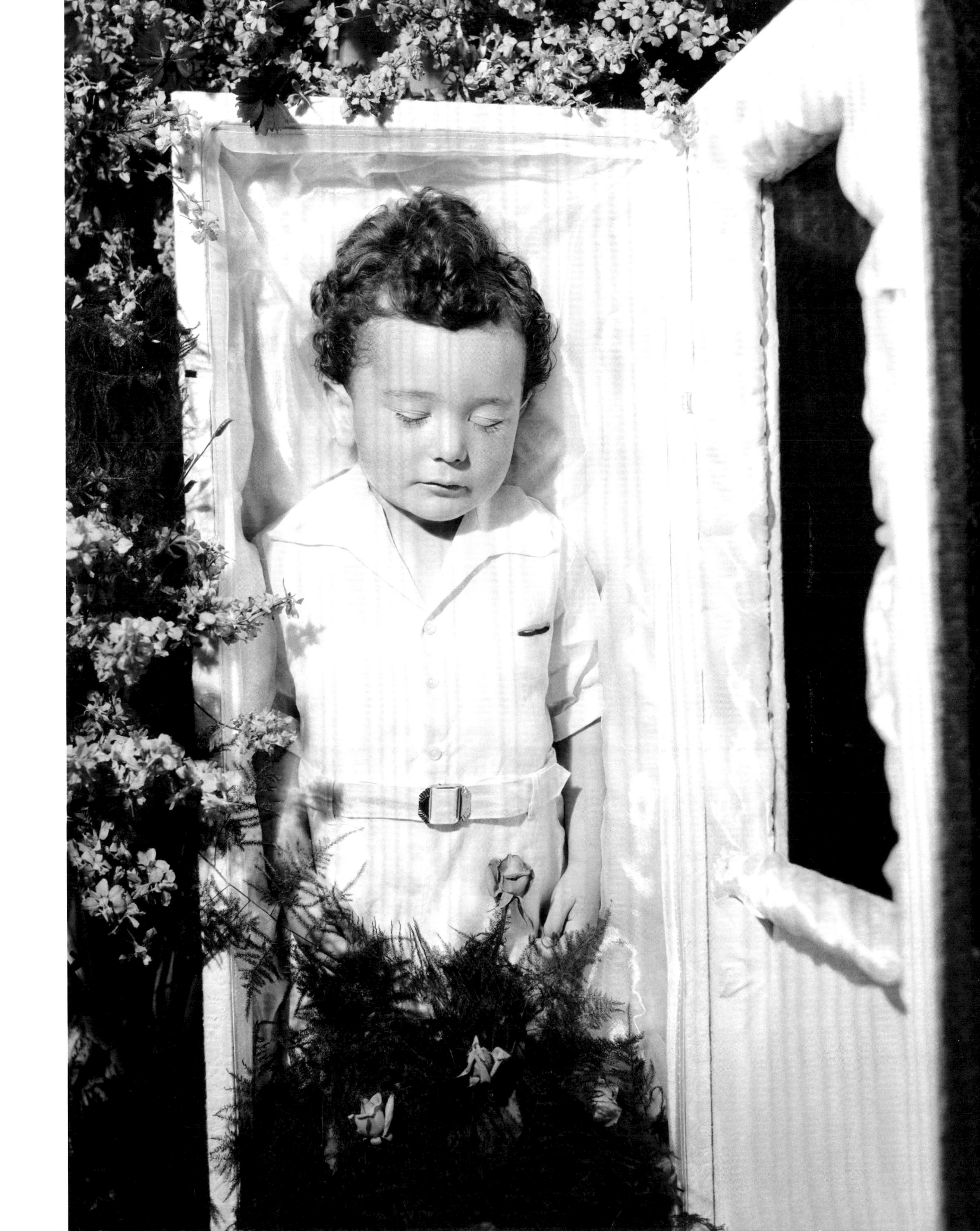

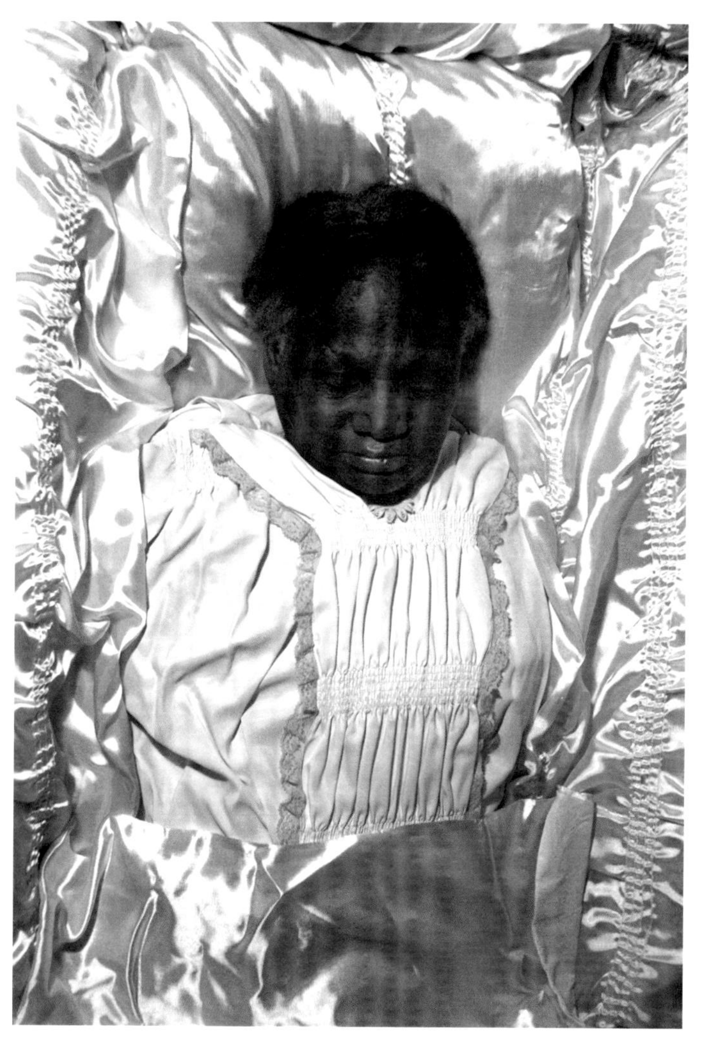

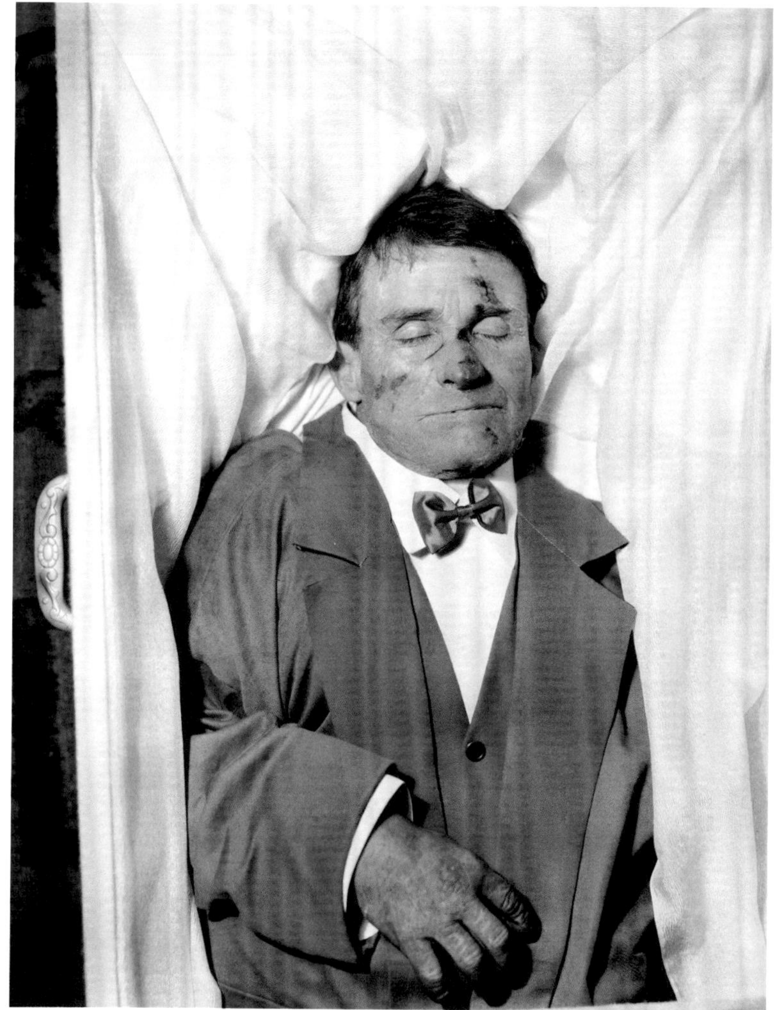

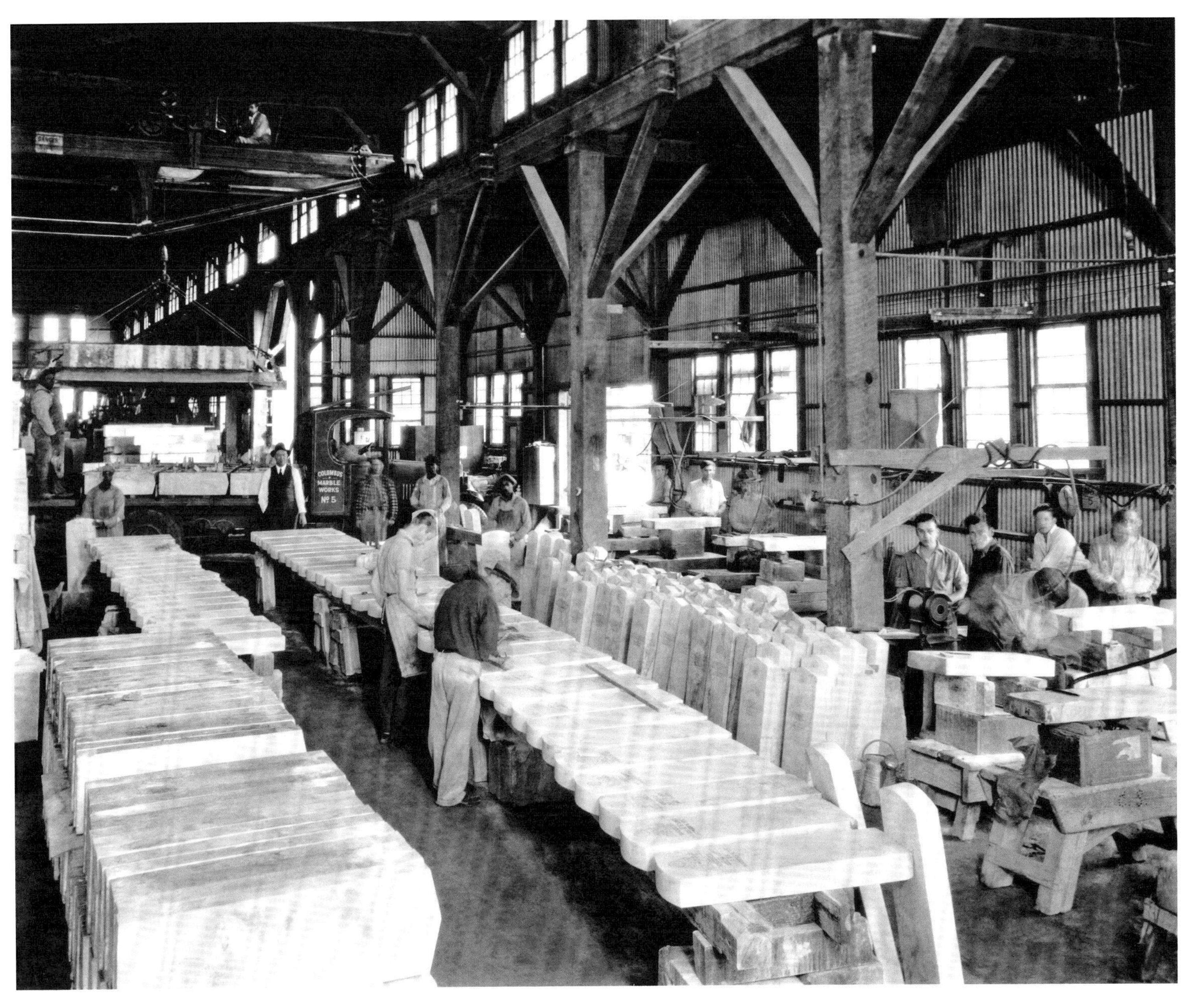

Columbus Marble Works, tombstone and monument manufacturers, established 1846, circa 1930s–40s.

SUNDAY-GO-TO-MEETING

In the buckle of the Bible Belt, Columbus and Lowndes County residents, both white and Black, long have practiced with fervor their Judeo-Christian faiths. Pruitt documented that, testifying in a singular way to the importance of spiritual life in northeast Mississippi, where religion and spirituality wove themselves into the quilt patchwork of the fibers of community life. It is nearly impossible to find an edition of the *Commercial Dispatch* in the first half of the twentieth century that does not mention churches or the Bible. Editorials often extolled Bible-reading.

The voluminous federal Works Progress Administration history of Lowndes County addresses the importance of religion. During the Great Depression, the white women working for the WPA project uncovered the story of a bold African American preacher during Reconstruction. Although the WPA version doesn't answer all of the questions about what happened, the anecdote is instructive about faith, race, and conflict.

The minister, known as Brother Bowler and described as a "mulatto," preached fiery sermons. In doing so, he ran afoul of *Columbus Index* editor James A. Stevens, a white supremacist who wrote editorials criticizing Bowler. At Stevens's urging, the sheriff arrested the preacher and brought him to the county jail. With that, Brother Bowler reminded the jailhouse denizens of the New Testament: "Mr. Jailer, bear in mind that bolts and bars did not prevail against Paul and Silas." The jailer replied, "God Almighty is not running this jail; as long as [Sheriff] Lawson Wolliford is in charge, he will put you where he will find you in the morning."

Although during Pruitt's era the dominant faiths were Protestant, Jewish and Roman

Catholic congregations also flourished. Many of the latter dated from the early and mid-nineteenth century; the first rabbi arrived in 1881. By 1930, Lowndes County had more than eighty churches. Some, such as First Baptist Church, counted as many as 1,500 members. Over the decades, choirs played a vital role, and Pruitt photographed them in white and Black churches. One of the most popular choirs in the 1920s and 1930s was directed by Annie Will Alexander, a teacher at the all-Black Union Academy. She led a countywide group of African Americans, often with 125 voices singing gospel and spirituals. The WPA history acknowledges the power of these groups, saying, "It is conceded that the only true American music is the Negro Folk Song or Spiritual. These native folk songs originated in the heart of the South." *Sacred Harp* singings, and regional, statewide, and national church denominational conventions were held in Columbus. Newspaper stories alerted the public to church solicitations for food to fill baskets for the poor at Thanksgiving and Christmas, encouraged church membership, and announced prayer meetings, as well as women's and men's church group get-togethers.

Pruitt, who regularly attended the First Methodist Church, photographed moments related to all this and more: births, christenings, baptisms, weddings (including ones in the Jewish synagogue), funerals, and revivals. He took pictures of countless Sunday school and church groups, Black and white.

Lula May Williams recalled how on June 28, 1942, Pruitt photographed her and her church—the only time Pruitt ever took her picture. She pointed to a framed panorama on a wall in her compact living room. Three feet long and eight inches tall, the picture shows rows upon rows of a hundred church members in their Sunday-go-to-meeting clothes. This image depicts the installation day of a new pastor, Rev. R. M. Prowell, and the officers of the auxiliary groups of Shiloh Missionary Baptist, the oldest African American church in Columbus, founded in 1861.

On that day in 1942, when Williams was about thirty-five and a member of the Missionary Society, she was dressed in the society's traditional clothing: all white shoes, dress, gloves, and hat. "We helped set the [sacrament] table, took care of the sacrament things, and visited the sick and things like that. On the first Sunday we serve the sacrament." She is on the second row, fourth from the left. Her three daughters and one son are also pictured. Pruitt was about the only photographer in town then, she said. He had no reservation about taking pictures of African Americans: "All you had to do was to pay him."

As for so many photographed by Pruitt in church groups, Lula May Williams's treasuring of the photograph testifies to the power of an image to carry forth the memory of faith and faithfulness. Pruitt took the picture he was paid to take; the subjects of the photograph paid the price he asked and then put on the wall or on a table a framed picture to reinforce their belief in something spiritual, something they considered priceless.

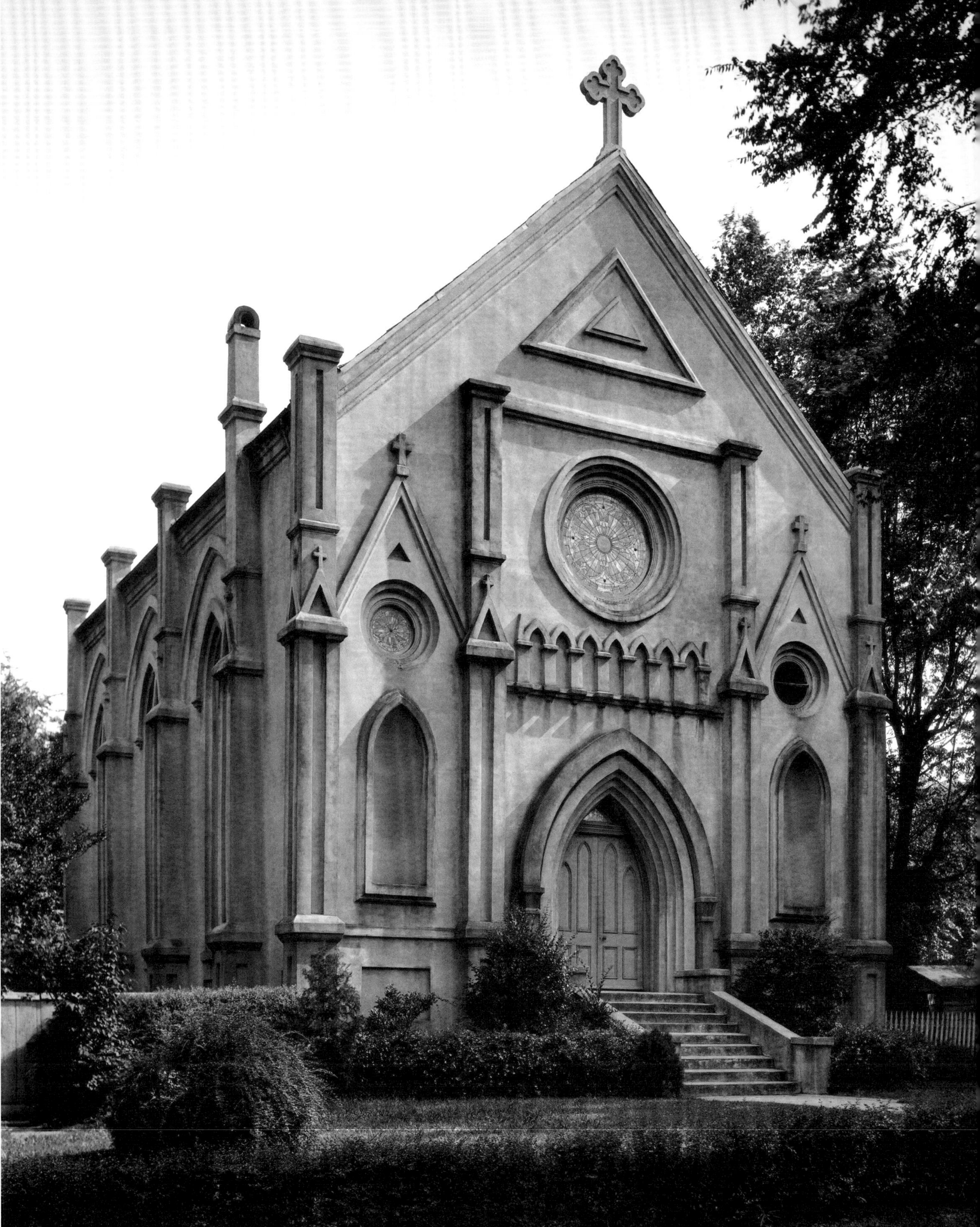

Young woman dressed for Jewish ceremony, Congregation B'nai Israel.

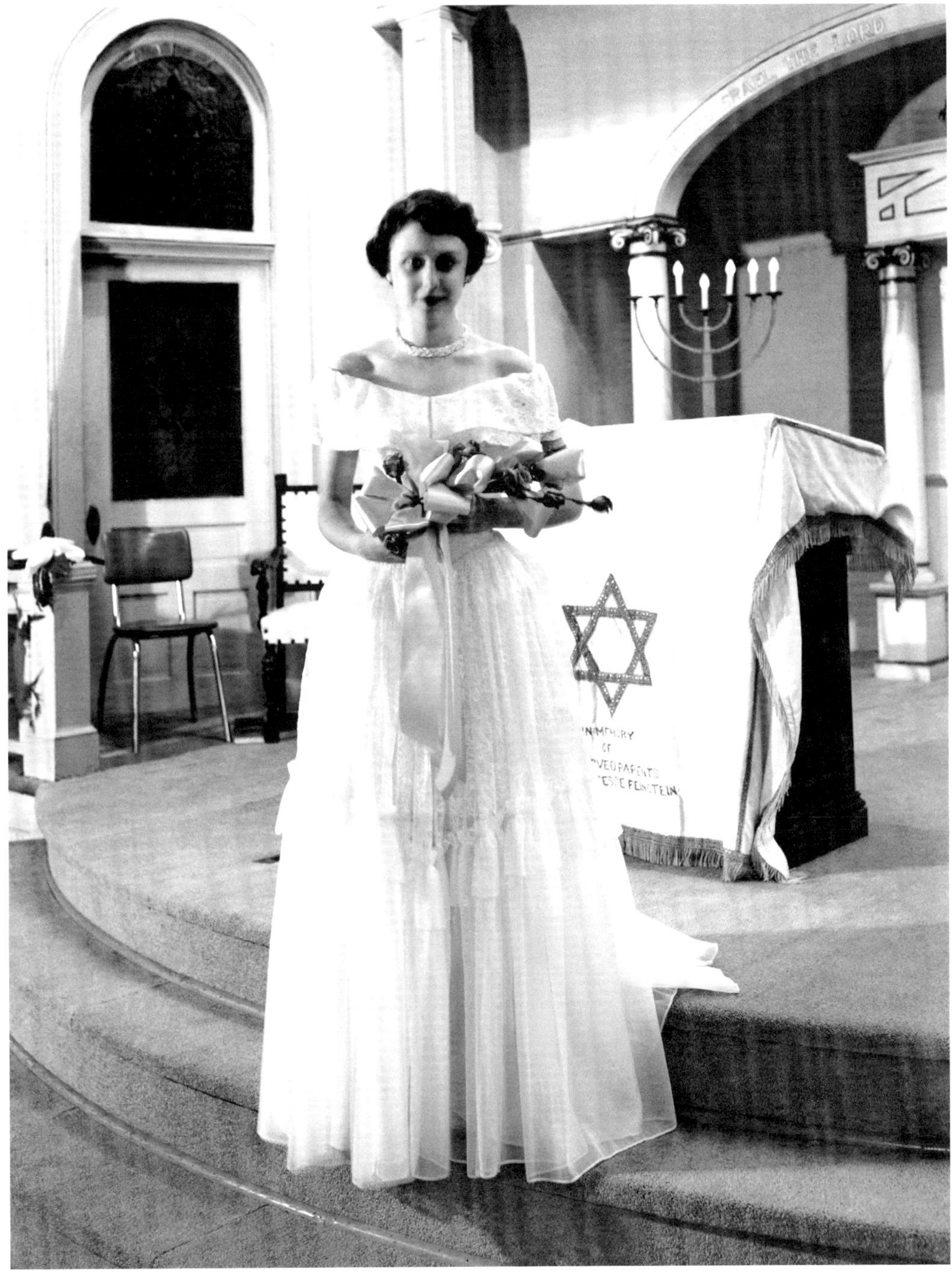

(opposite) *Annunciation Catholic Church.*

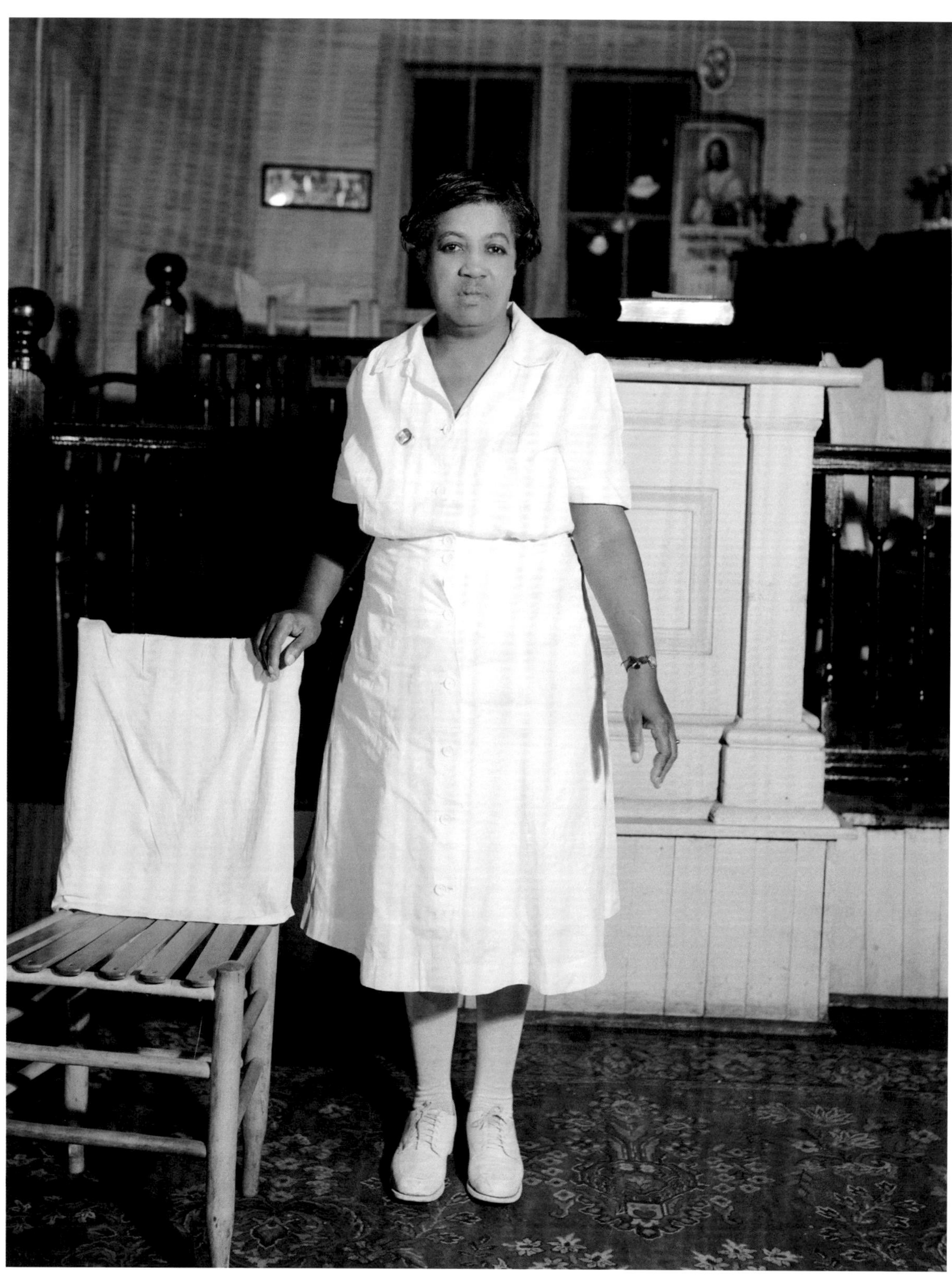

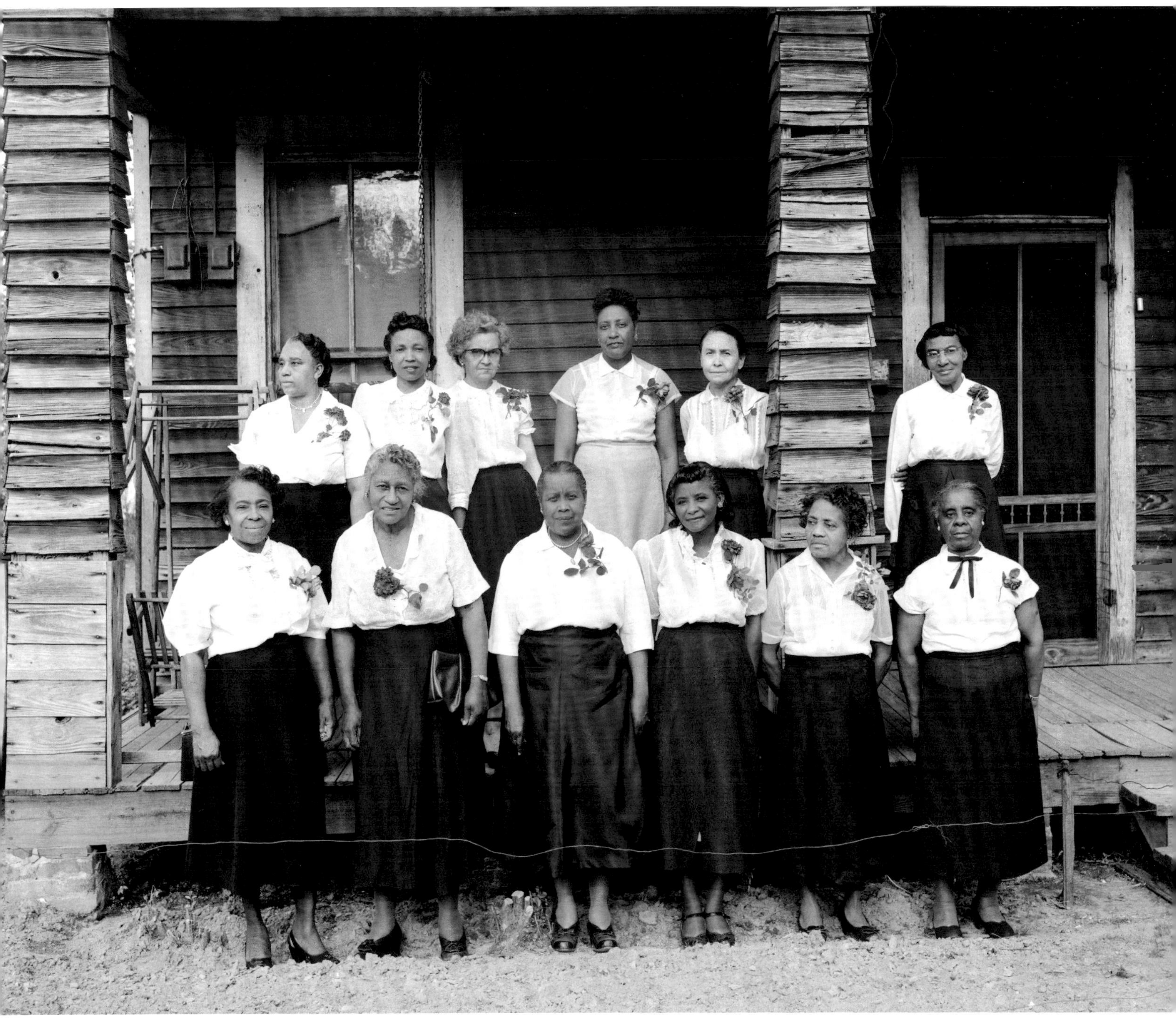

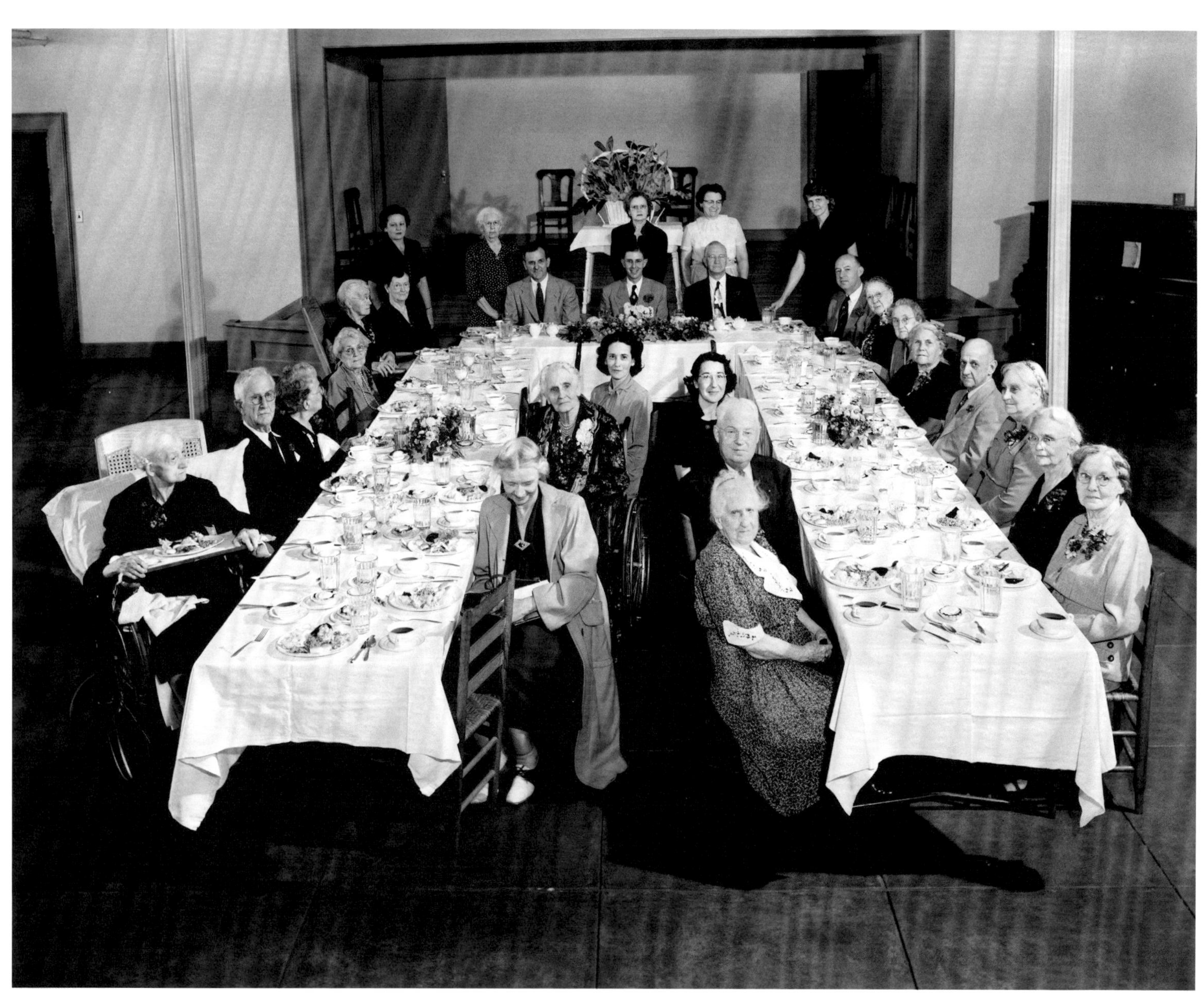

First Methodist Church's "Old Women's Dinner," October 15, 1952.

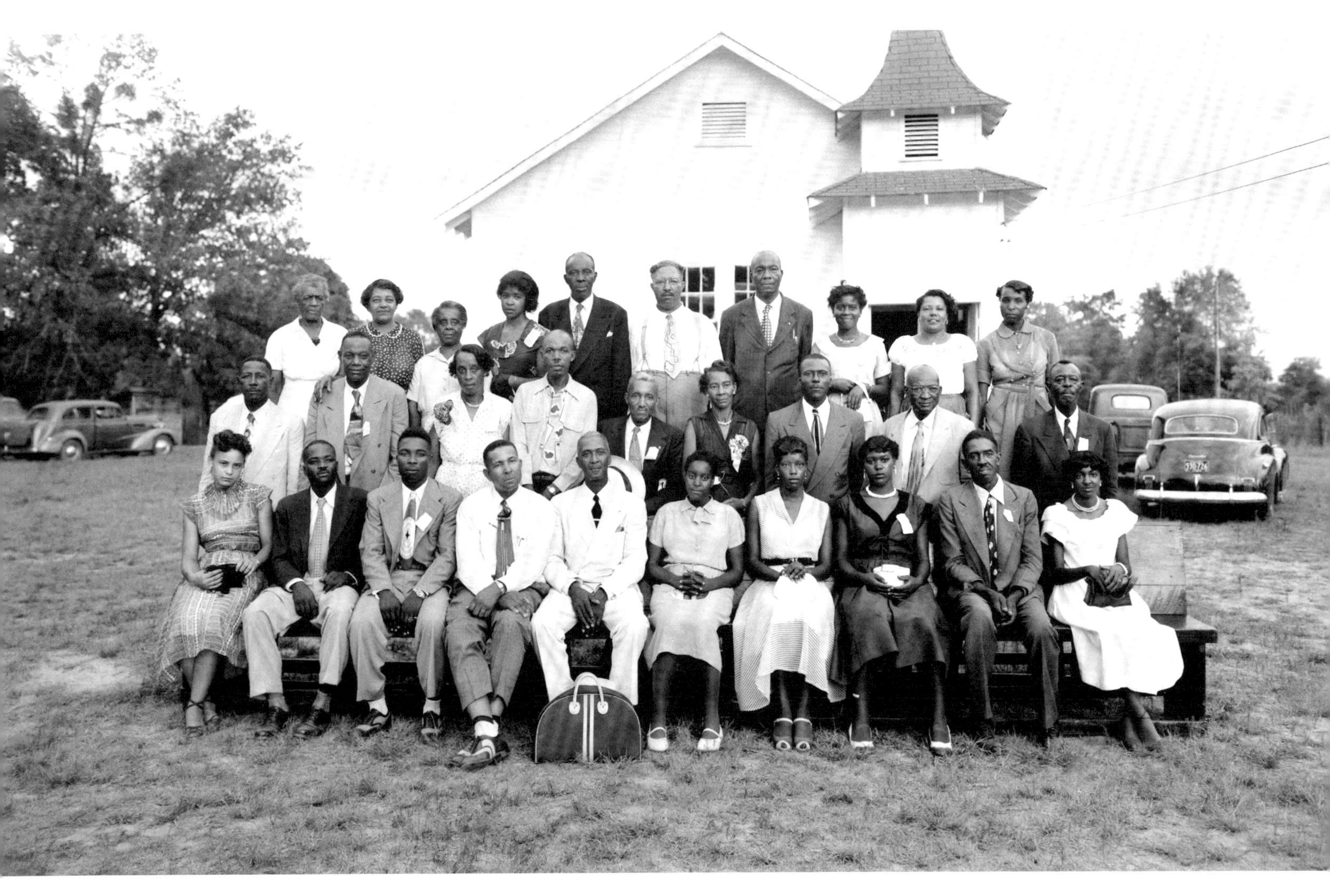

"Missionary Baptist Sunday School and B.T.U. Convention," July 18, 1952.

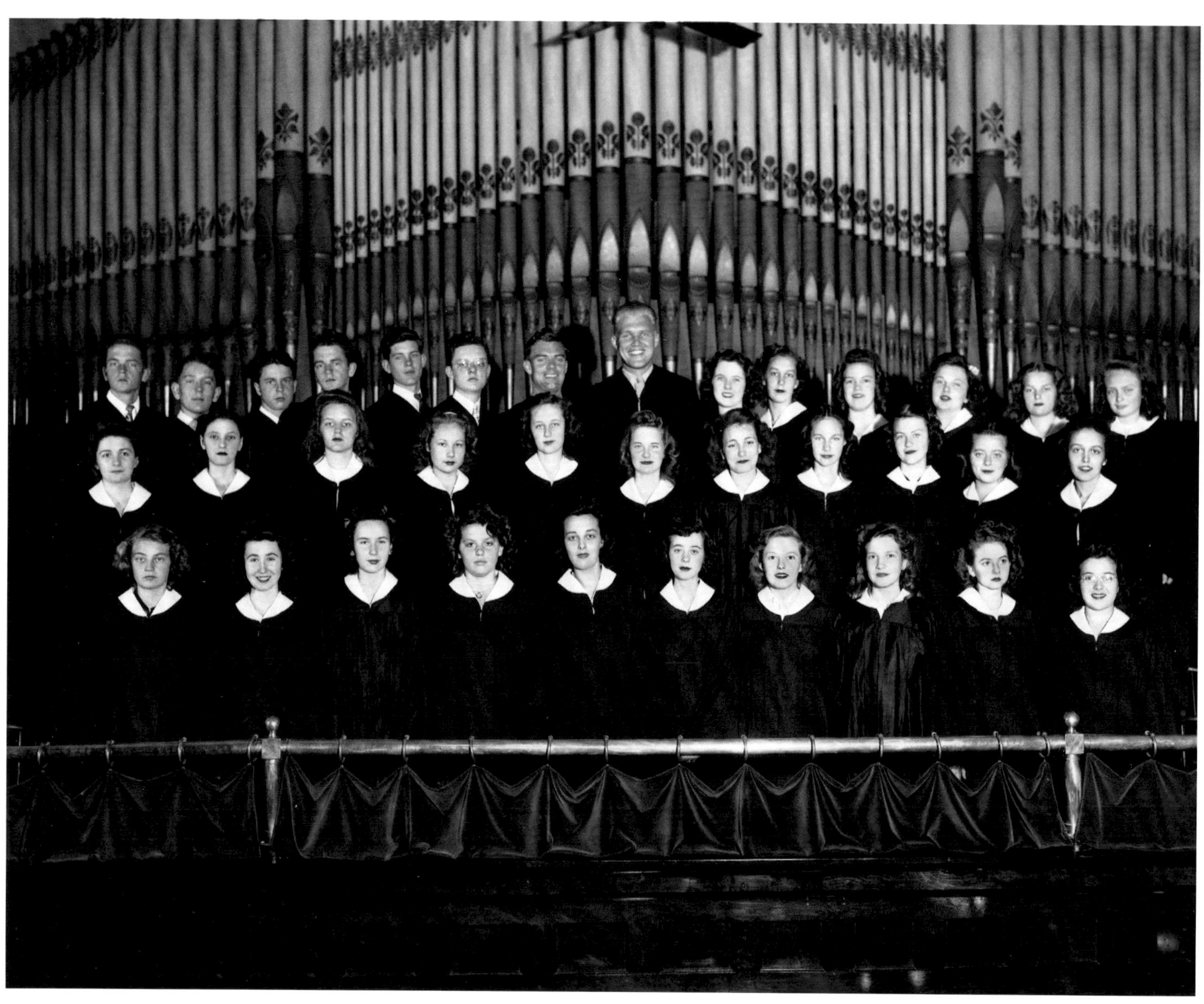

First Baptist Church choir.

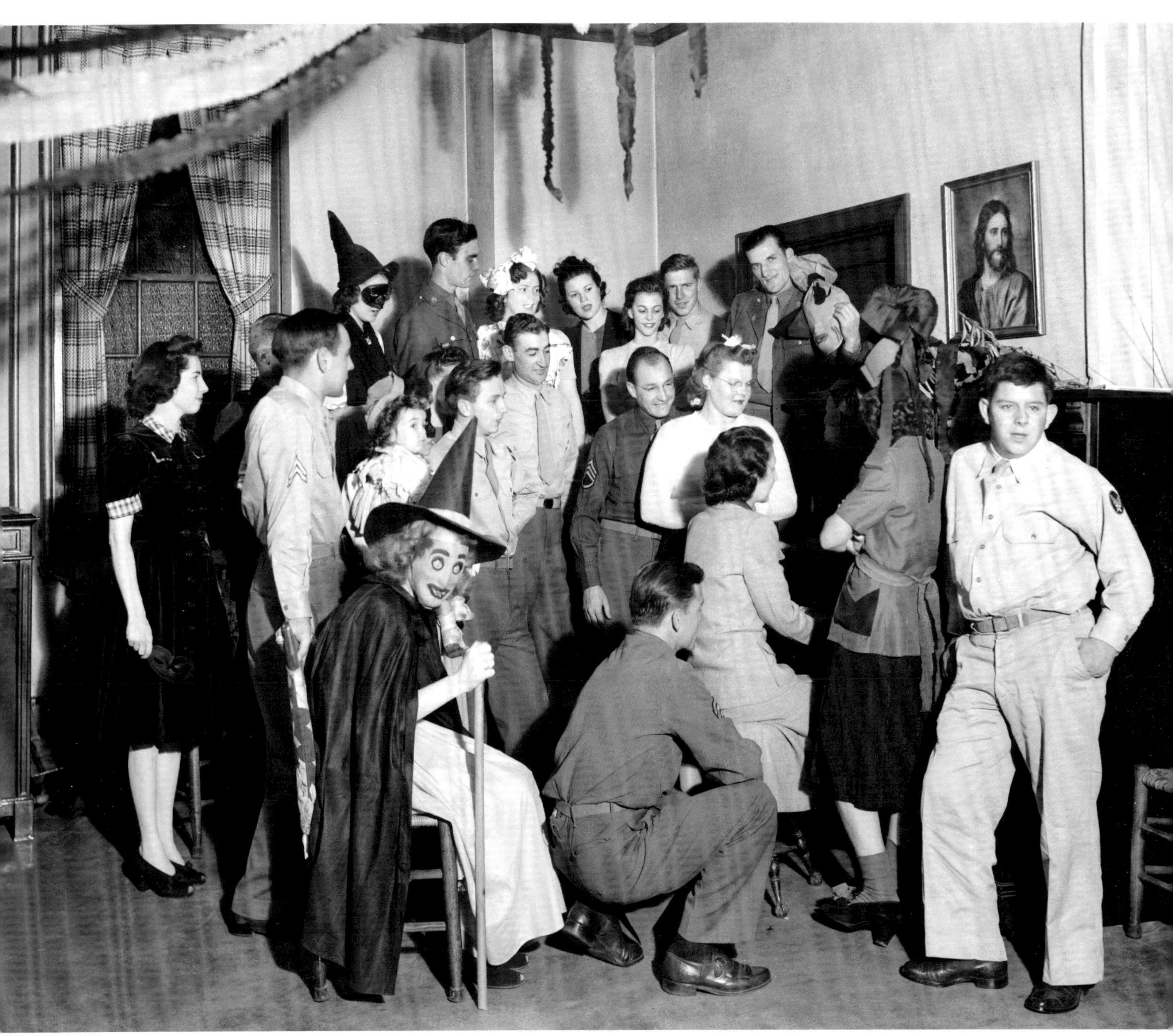

Church Halloween party during World War II.

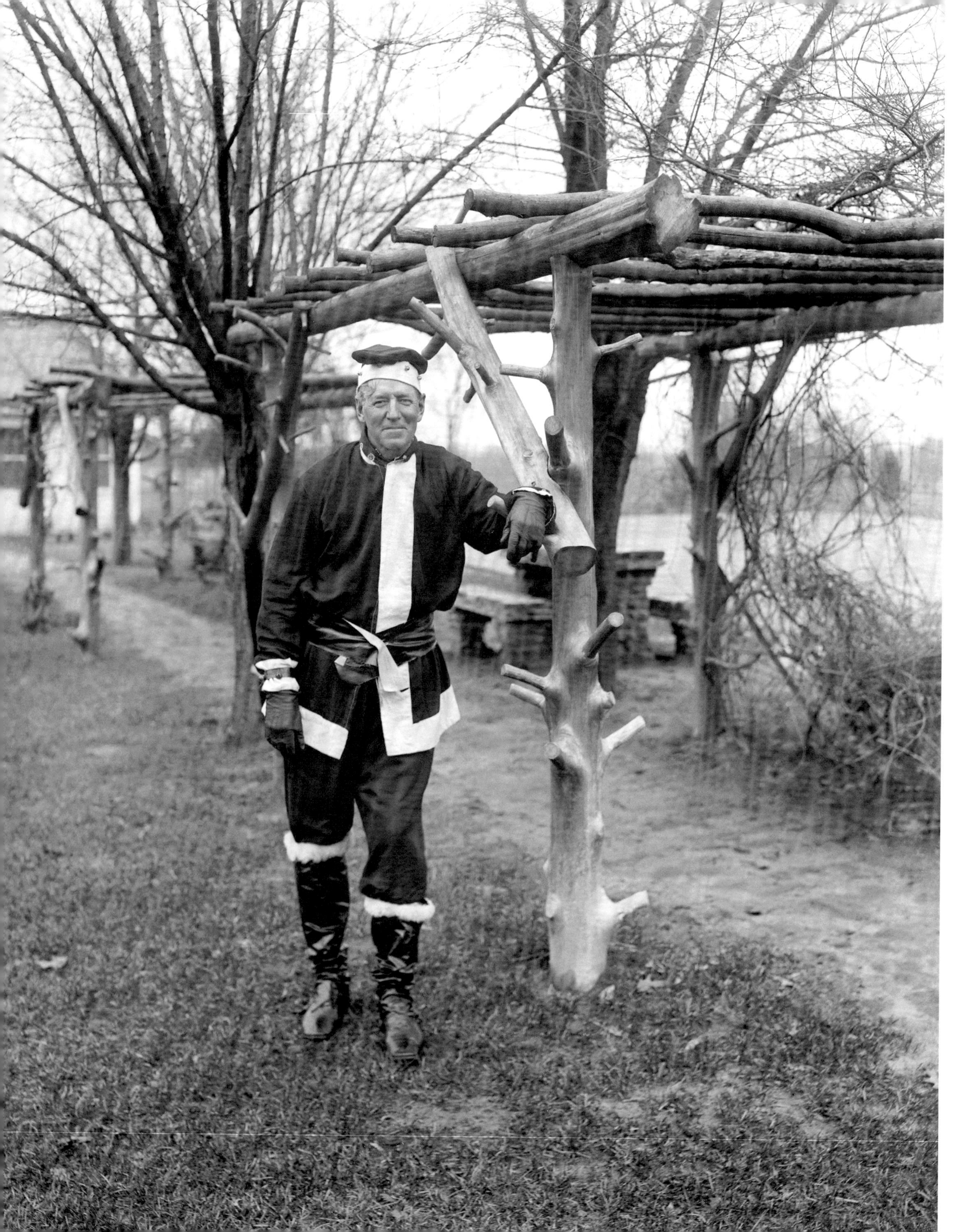

BAPTISMS, CIRCA 1930S

Thus, you are buried with Him in baptism,
And raised to walk in a newness of life.
—Spoken by a Southern Baptist preacher during a baptismal service

Baptism serves as a central practice in the Christian faith. So it is not surprising that Pruitt, working in the Bible Belt, would photograph such an important ritual in northeast Mississippi. What is extraordinary is that Pruitt photographed a common occurrence in the 1920s and 1930s in Columbus: both a white church group and a Black church group baptizing in the Tombigbee River at the same time. It is not clear whether the white group made the Black group wait until after the whites were baptized. What is clear is that Pruitt documented an unusual biracial religious practice, according to religious studies scholar Charles R. Wilson of the University of Mississippi. The photographs astonished him, he said, since these events happened in a time of racial apartheid and racial violence.

During that era, baptisms took place mainly in spring and summer. "Nearly all the negroes around Artesia are Baptists and hold their baptizing in stock pools over the prairies," the Works Progress Administration history of Lowndes County noted. The ordinance of baptism carries with it a detailed ritual, given vigor by the minister, candidates for baptism, and the congregation. The power of the sacrament, considered part of one's "public profession of faith," is lost on neither those most involved in the ritual nor outsiders who might witness or photograph it. The WPA account reported that "a lady from New York City" attended an early twentieth-century baptism presided over by Cornelius Williams, a country preacher in Mayhew, a farm community west of Columbus, and "was greatly impressed by his zeal, his voice, his power, and his earnestness."

The Pruitt baptismal pictures capture this. Although there is little astonishing technically, the photographs contain remarkable elements: a mixture of whites and Blacks together, as separate but equals and as witnesses for each other, at a baptismal site. Baptisms were a spectator event as well as an event for the individual, marking his or her badge of entry into the flock of followers of Jesus Christ.

The people in the photographs are engaged in a ceremony dating from nearly two millennia ago when John baptized Jesus. For the Baptists (or "baptizers"), whose roots grew in England as a reaction against infant baptism, immersion is essential. Rivers, creeks, lakes, and ponds replicate a biblical body of water—the Jordan River—distant in time and place but close to the hearts of Christian faithful in a Mississippi town. Baptism played a crucial role in the life of southern Blacks beginning in the late eighteenth and early nineteenth centuries, as Christianity found new faithful among enslaved Africans. Part of the appeal was the ritual. By the mid-twentieth century, two-thirds of Blacks who were Christian called themselves Baptists. Pruitt's pictures capture in an exceptional way a rite of initiation and a significant moment where a measure of racial harmony or at least accommodation existed in a sacred space along the Tombigbee River. The photographs function as a testament, one noticeably missing in other written or published sources. In the best Christian sense of the word, the Pruitt pictures testify.

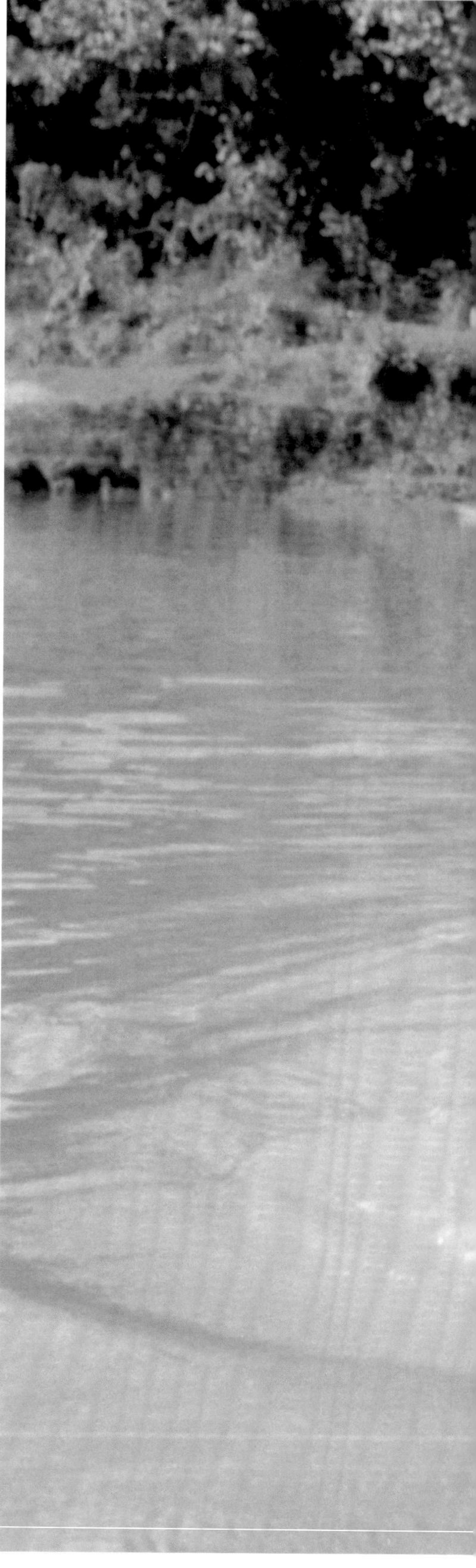

Tombigbee River baptism, circa 1930s.

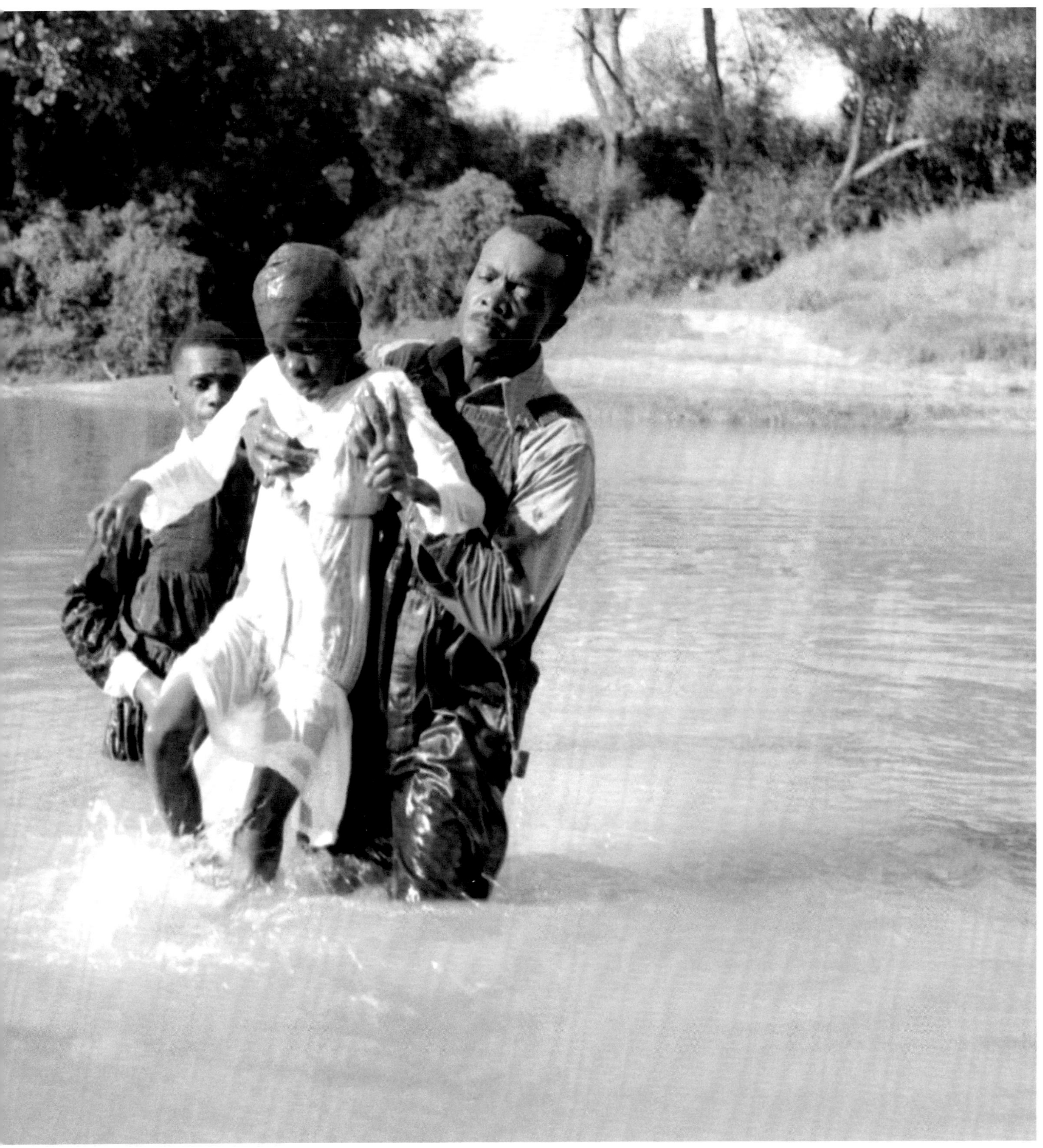

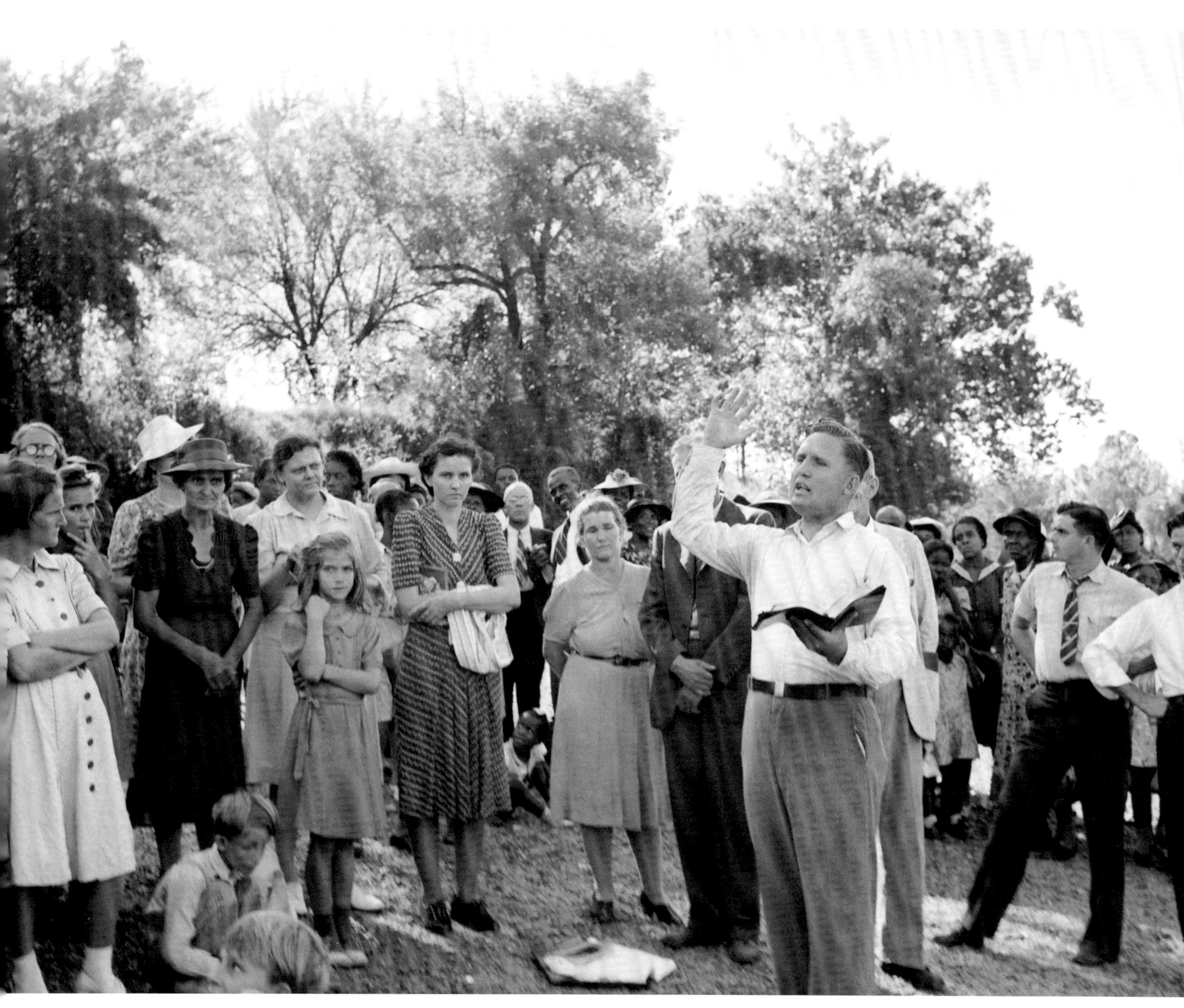

Preacher with baptismal group, Tombigbee River, circa 1930s.

Preacher with baptismal group, Tombigbee River, circa 1930s.

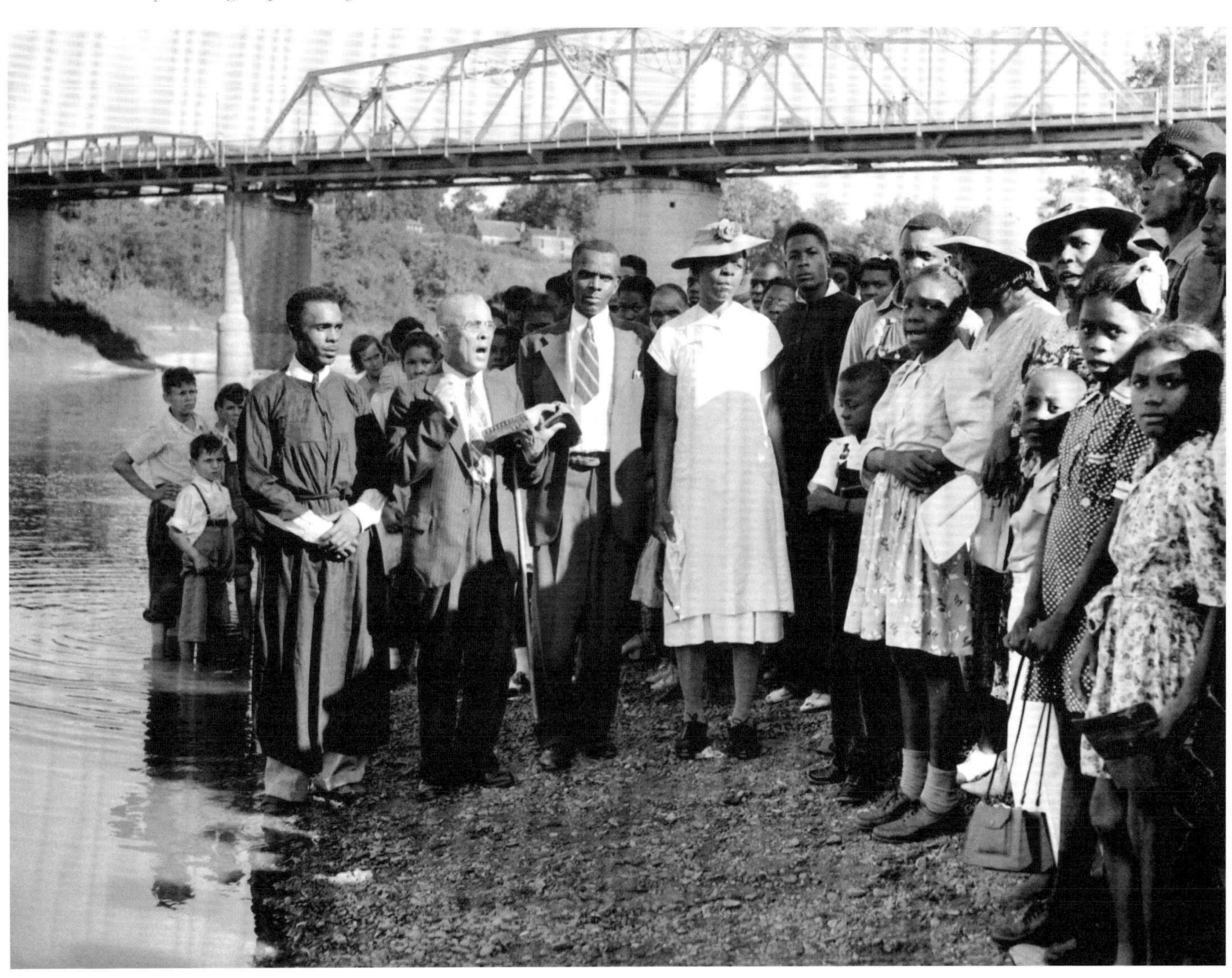

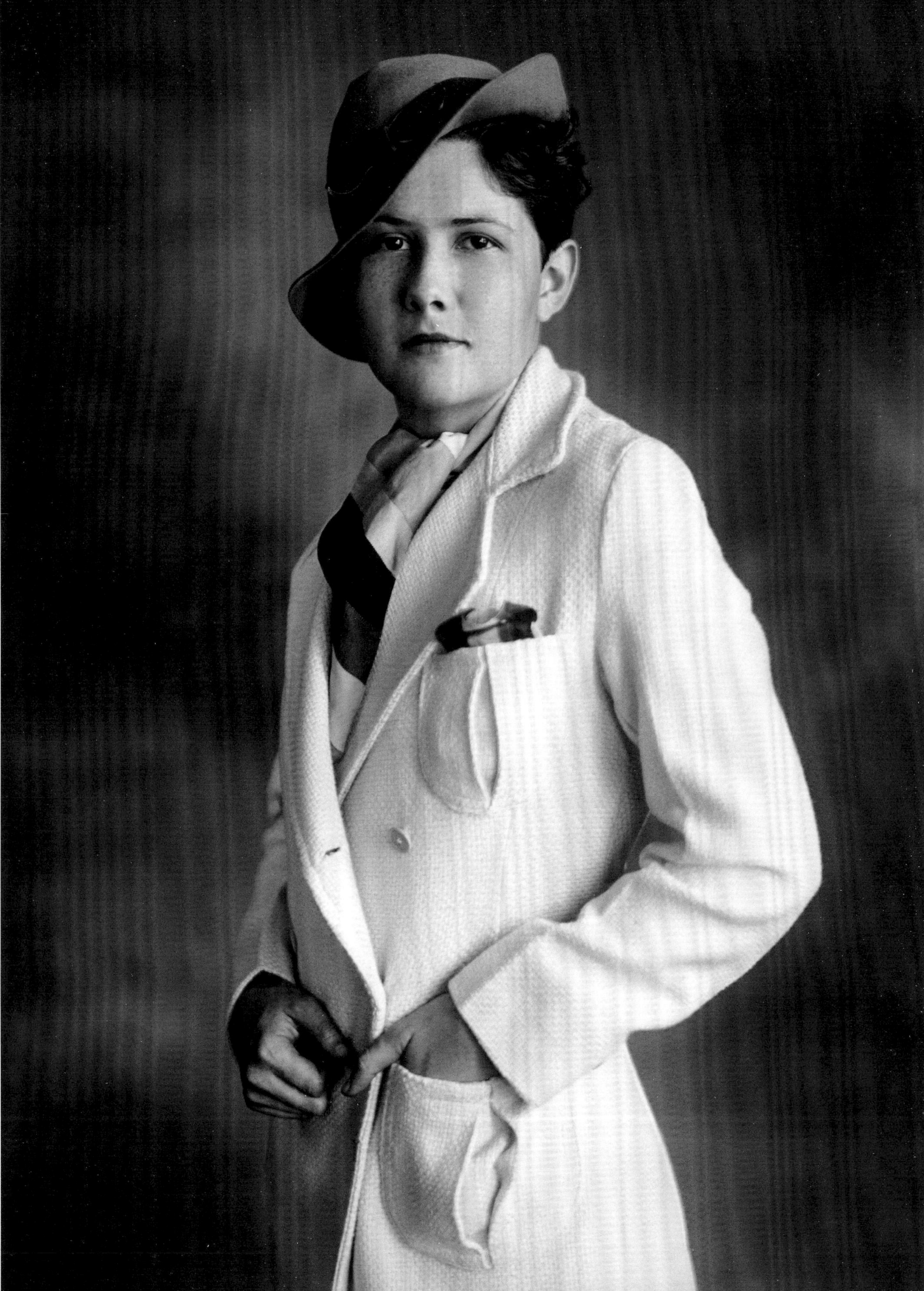

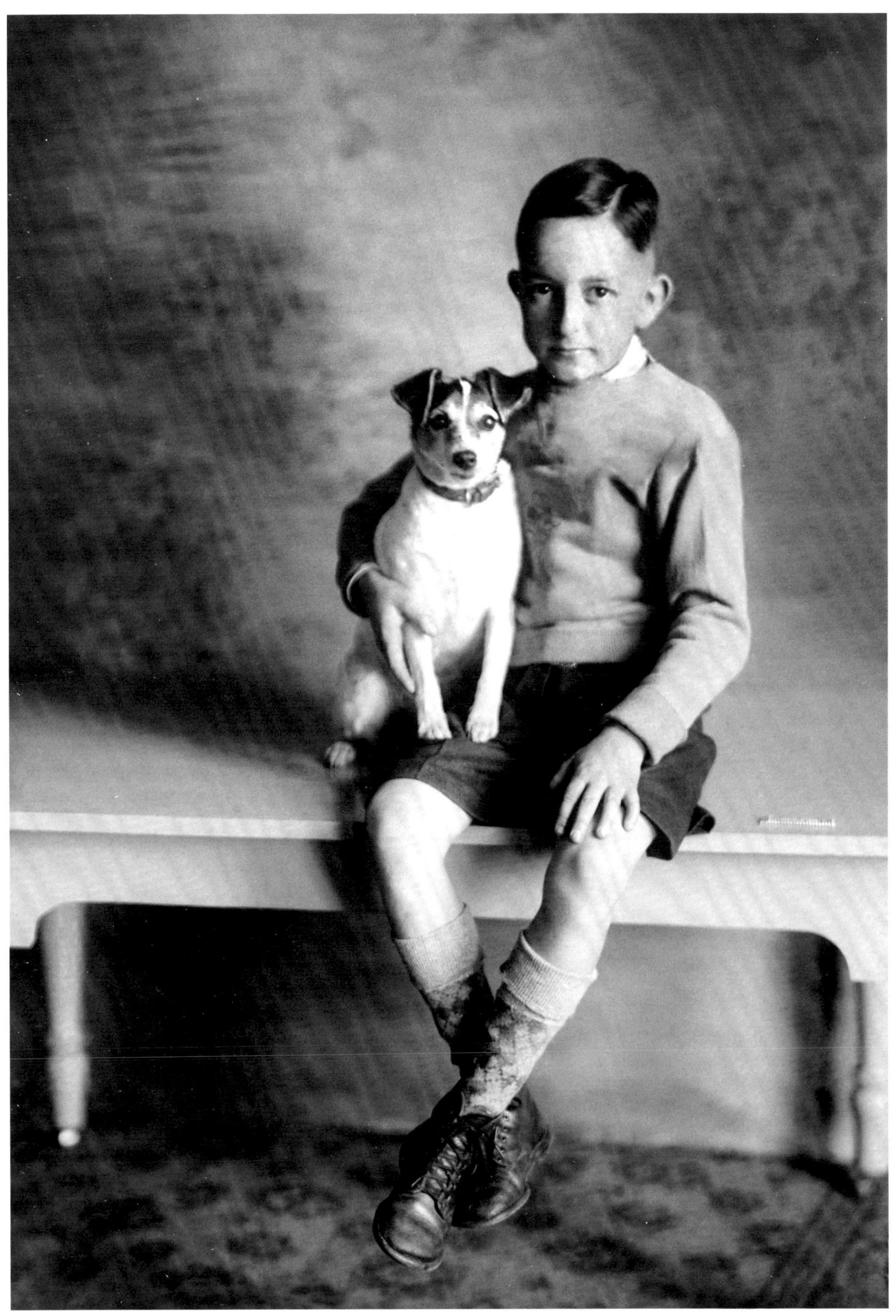

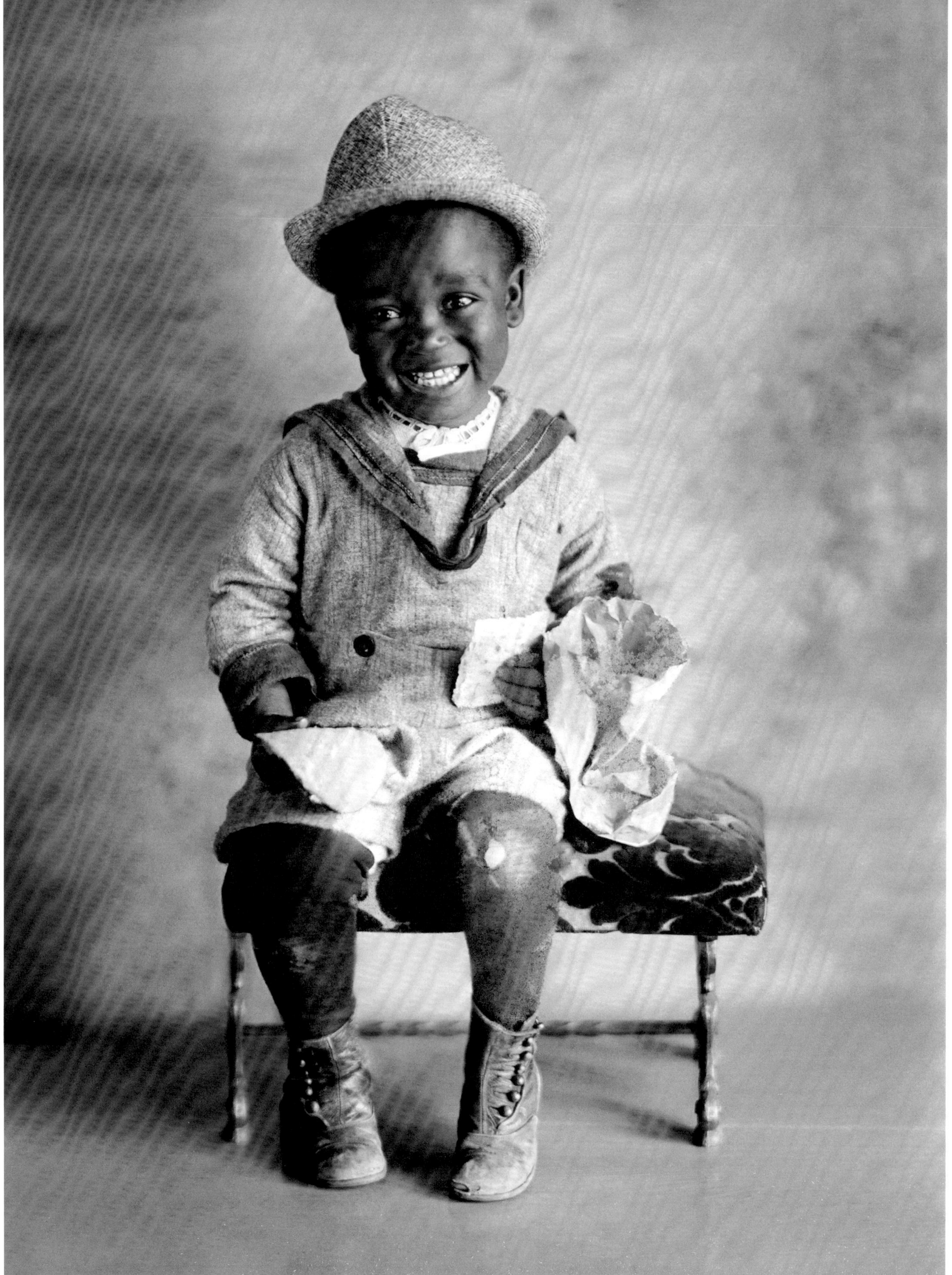

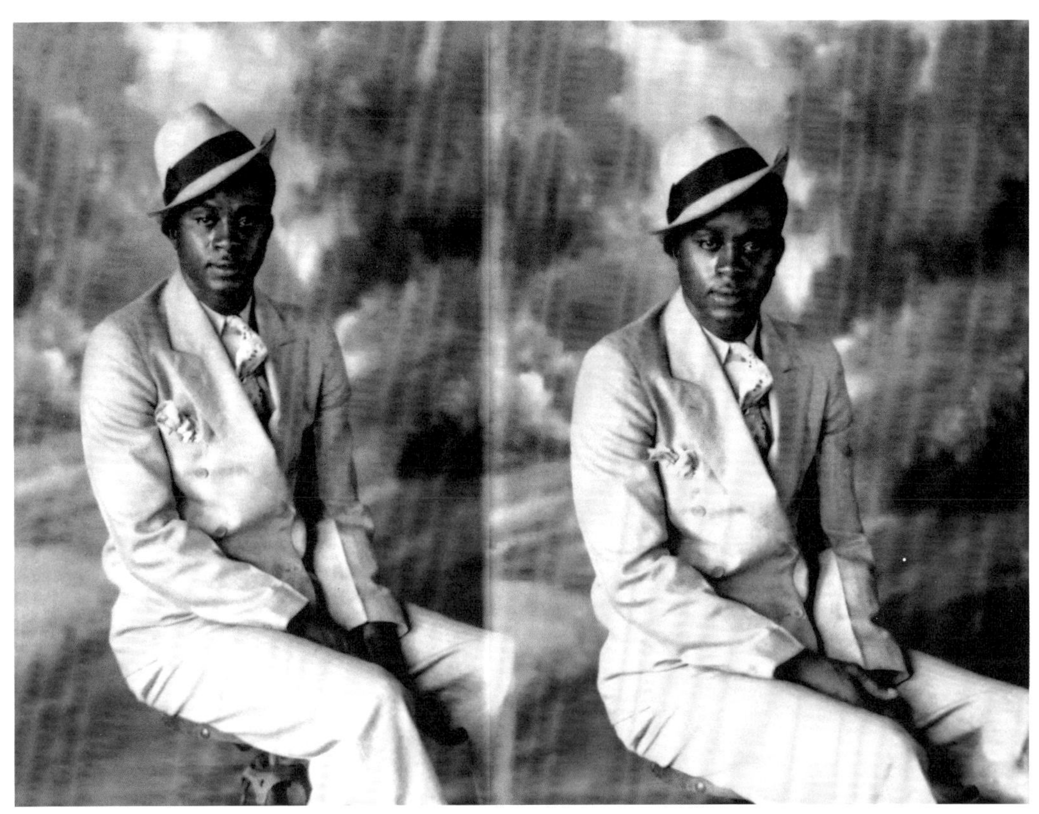

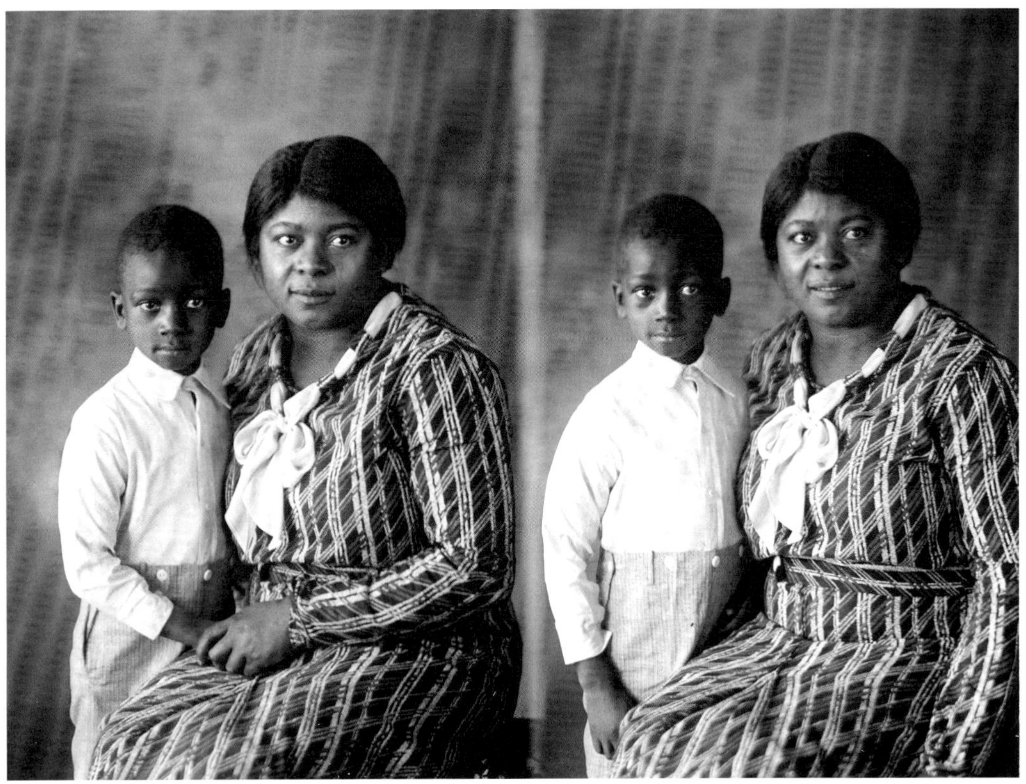

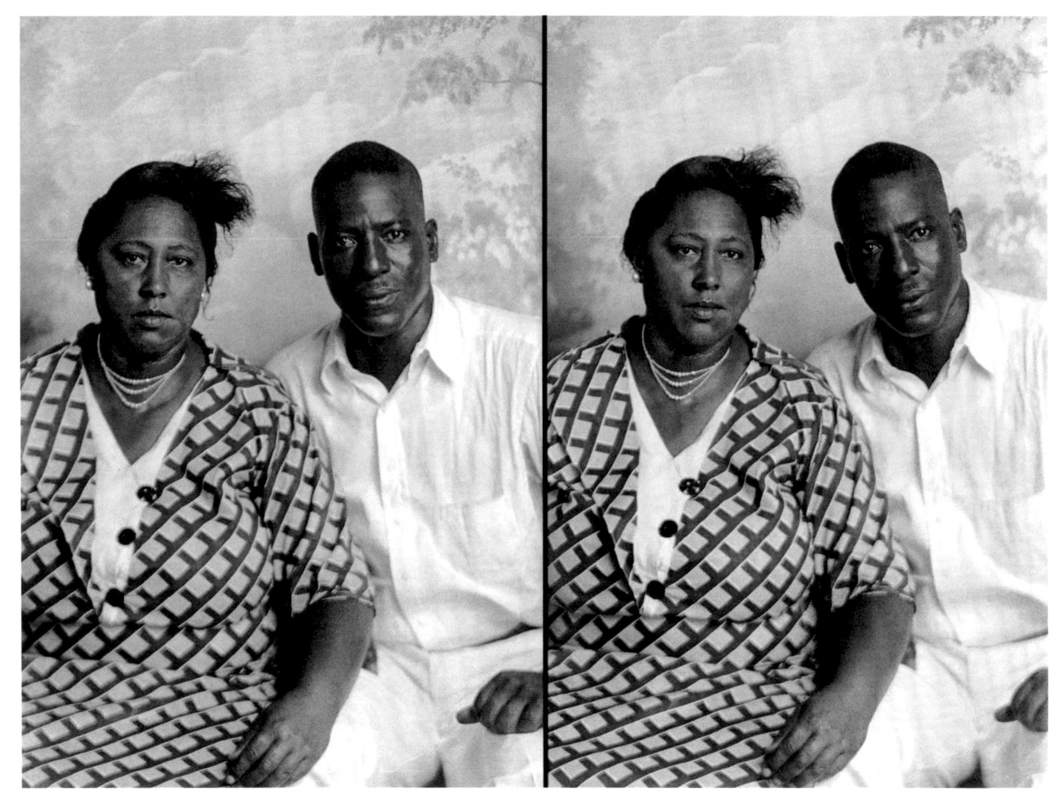

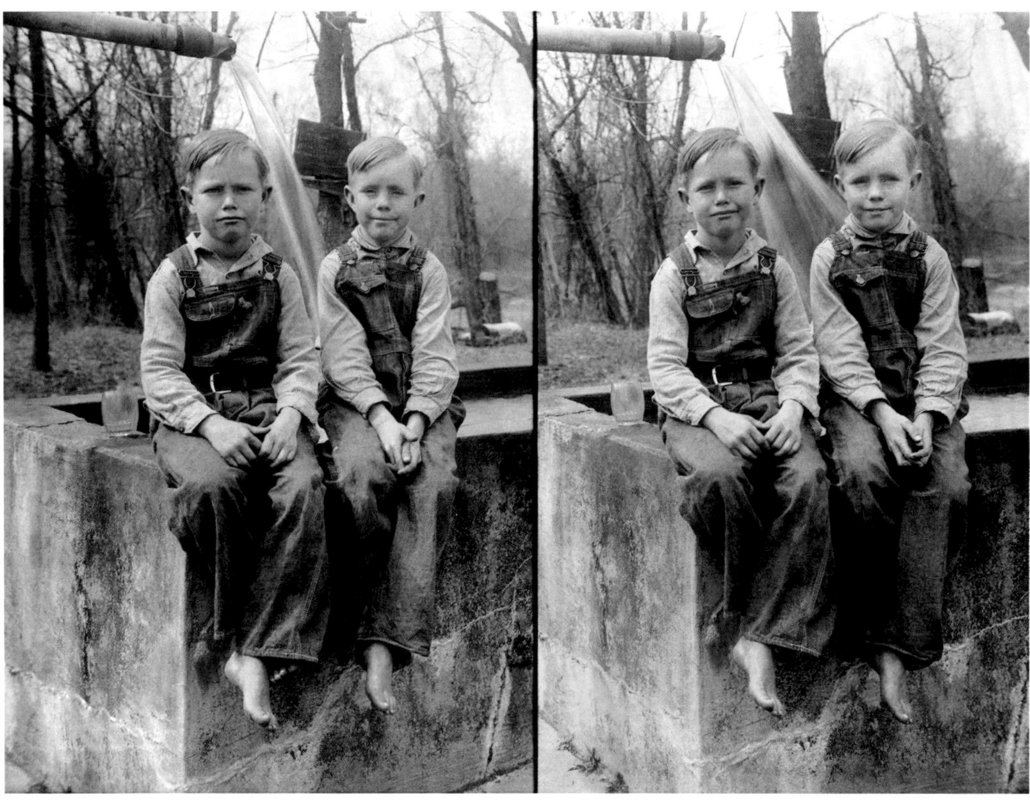

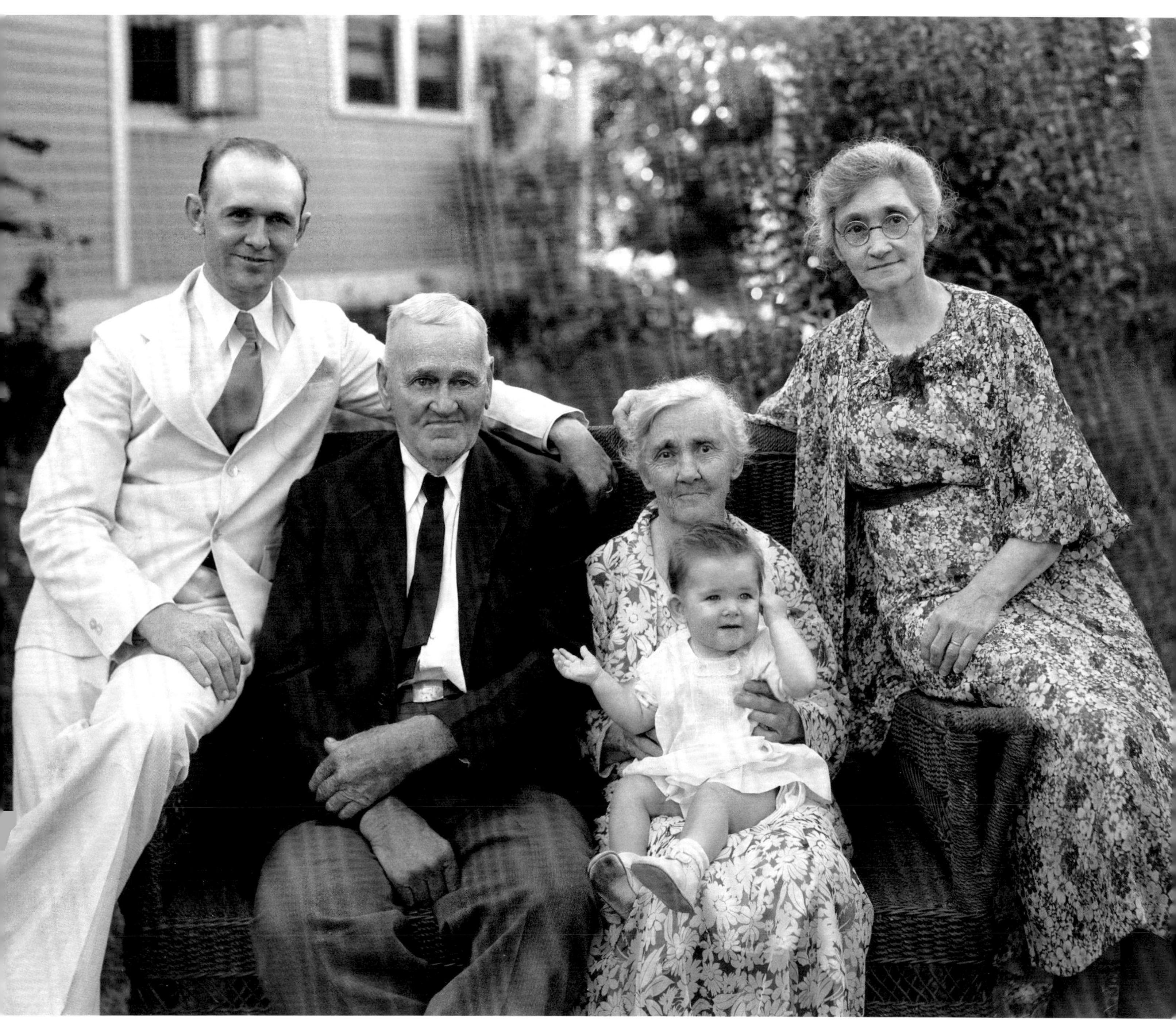

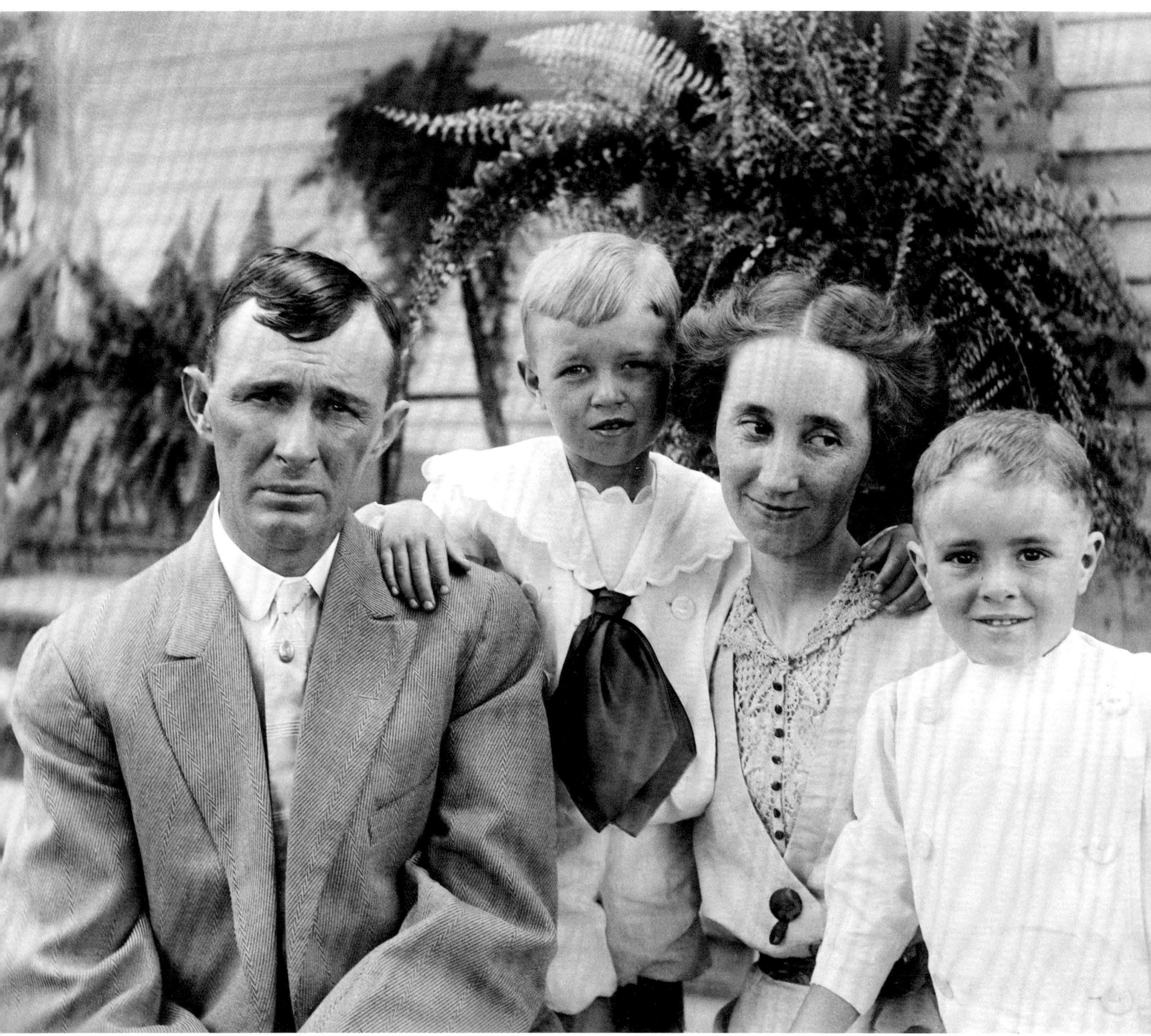

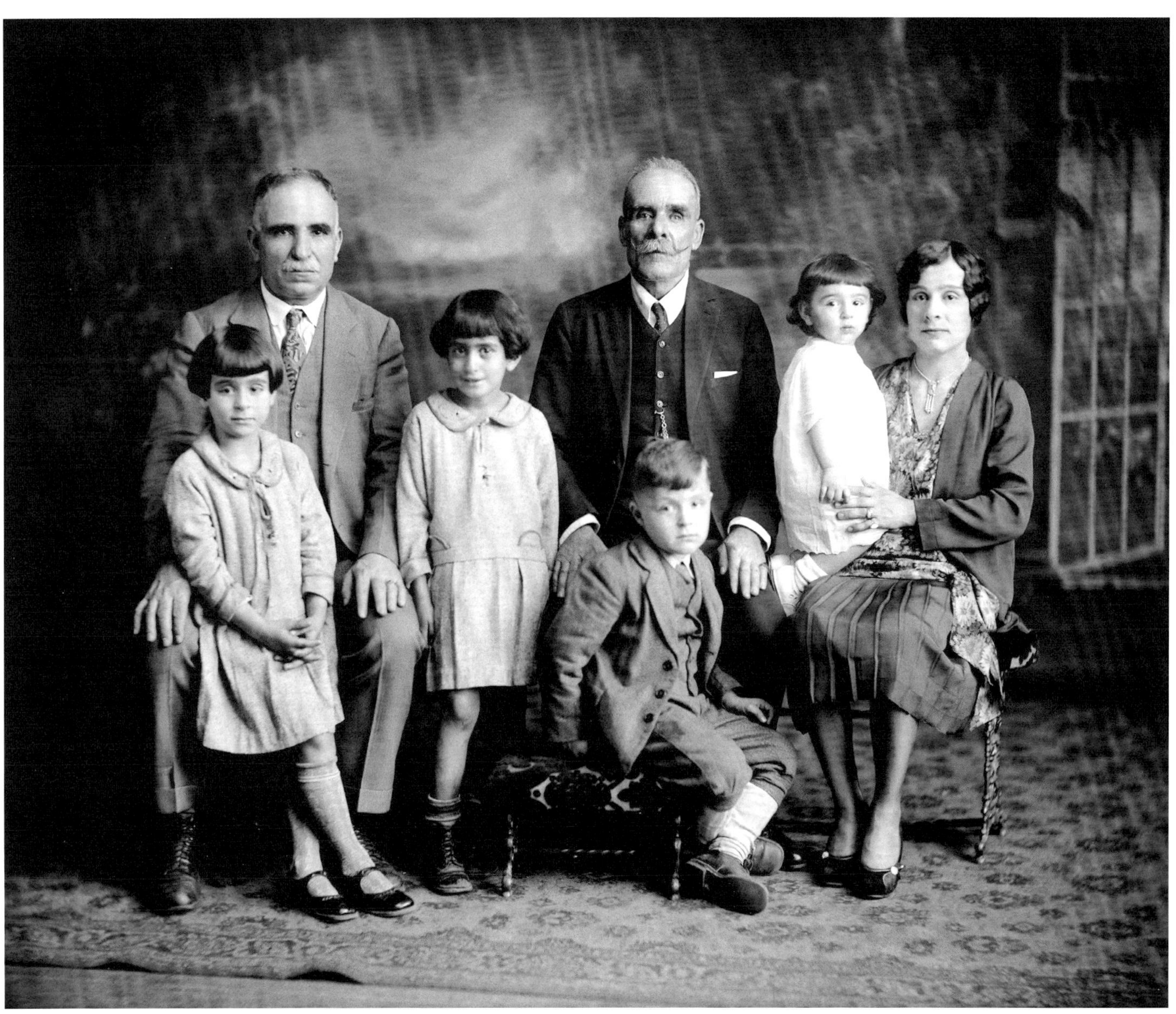

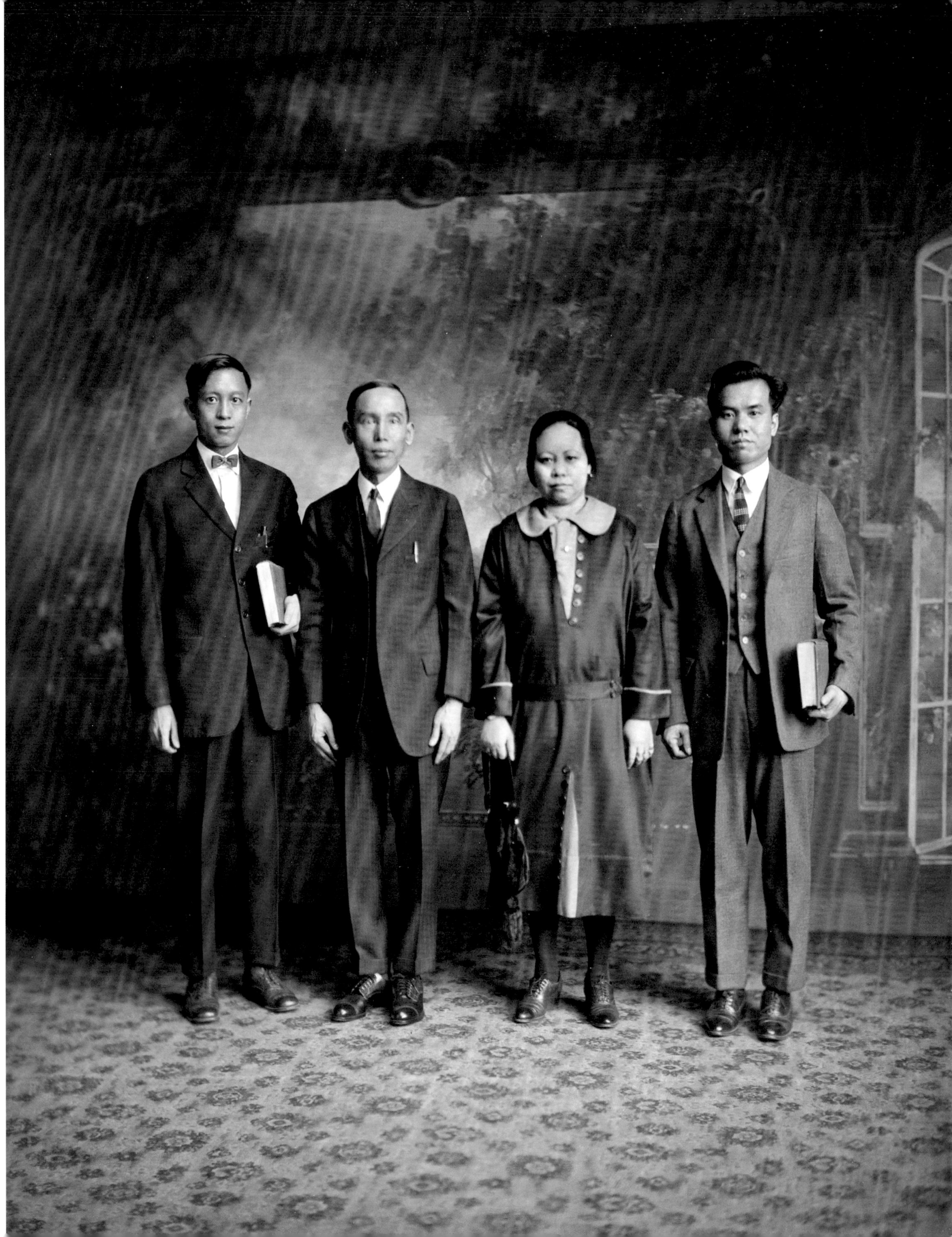

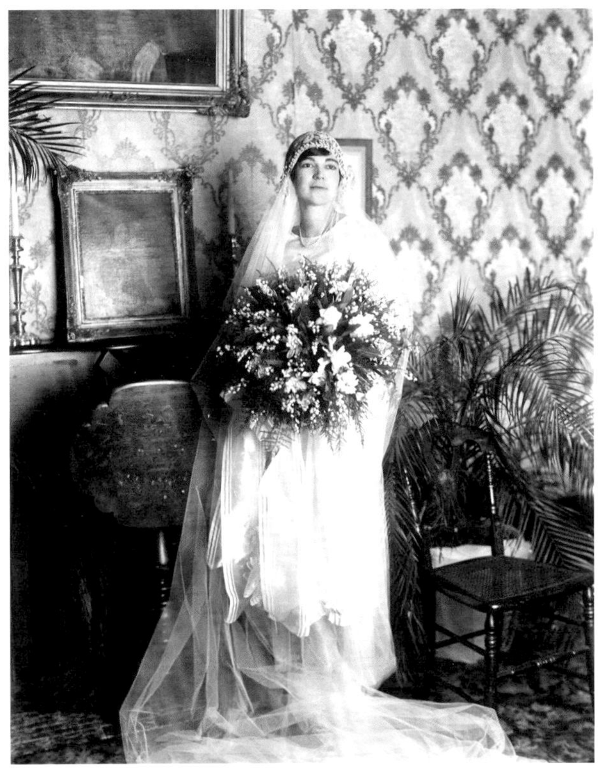

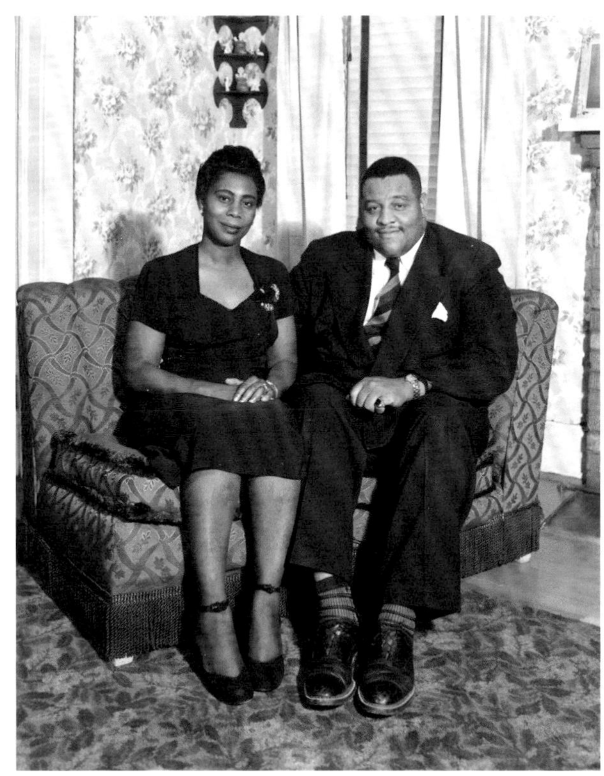

Robinson family portrait.

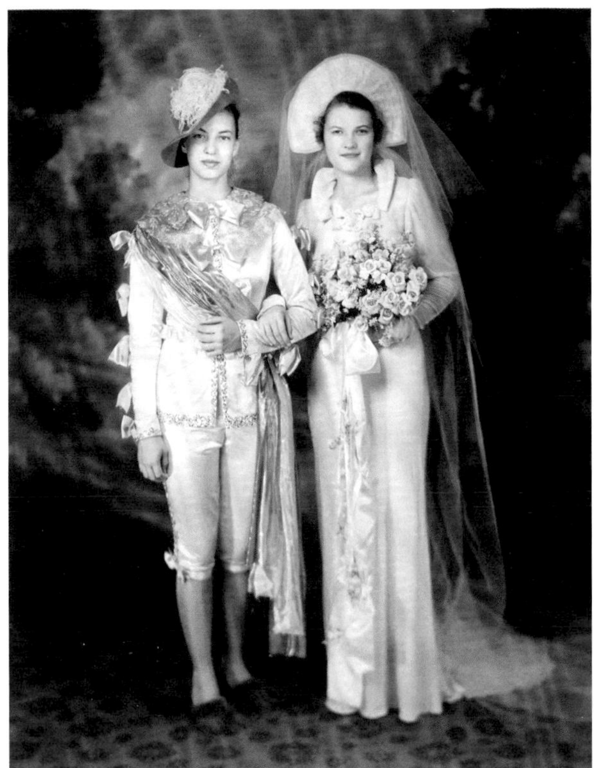

Junior-Freshman "wedding" at the event held each autumn at Mississippi State College for Women, late 1930s.

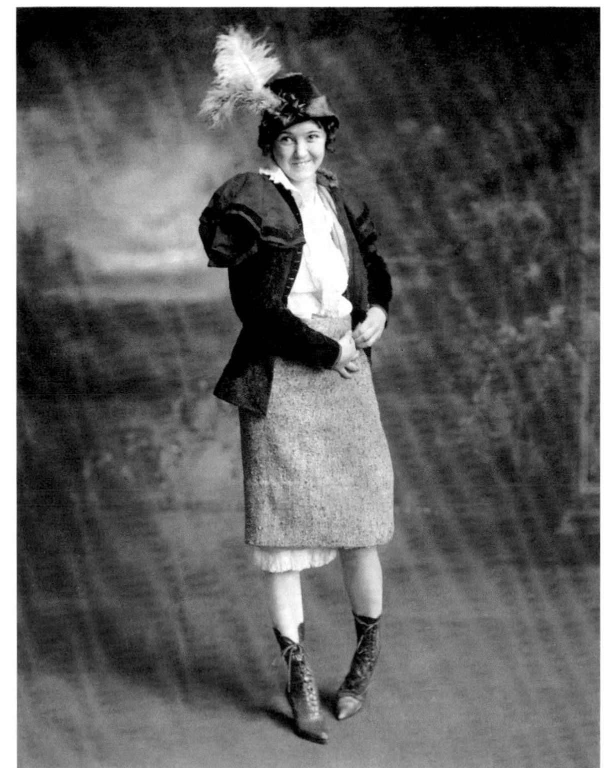

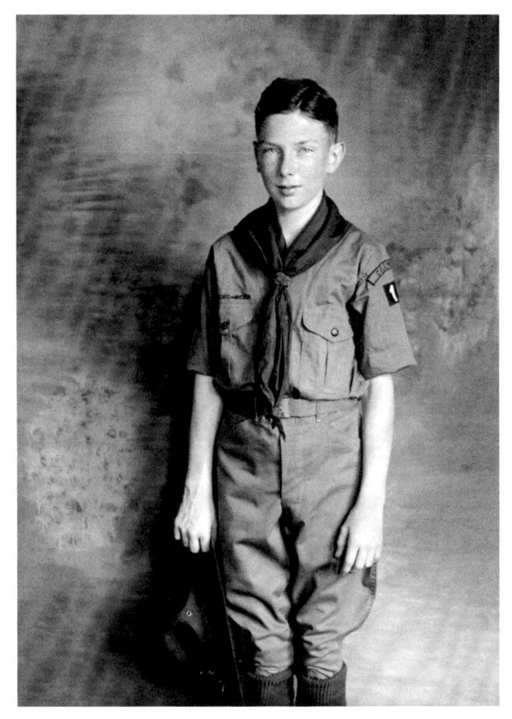

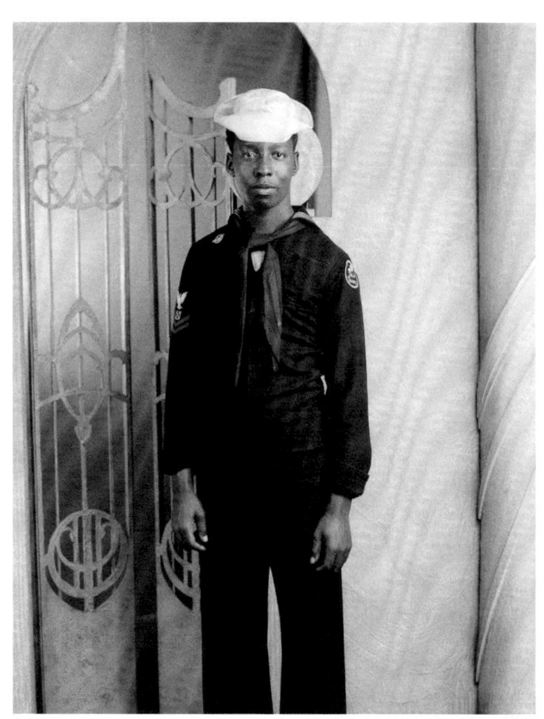

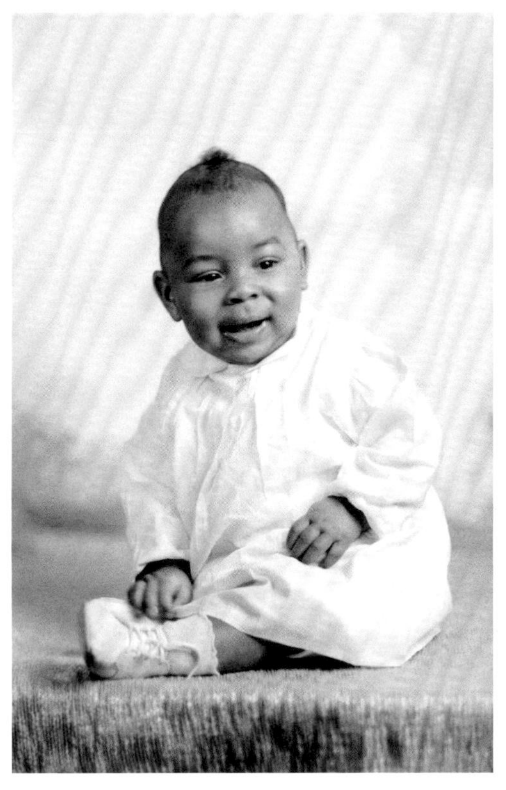

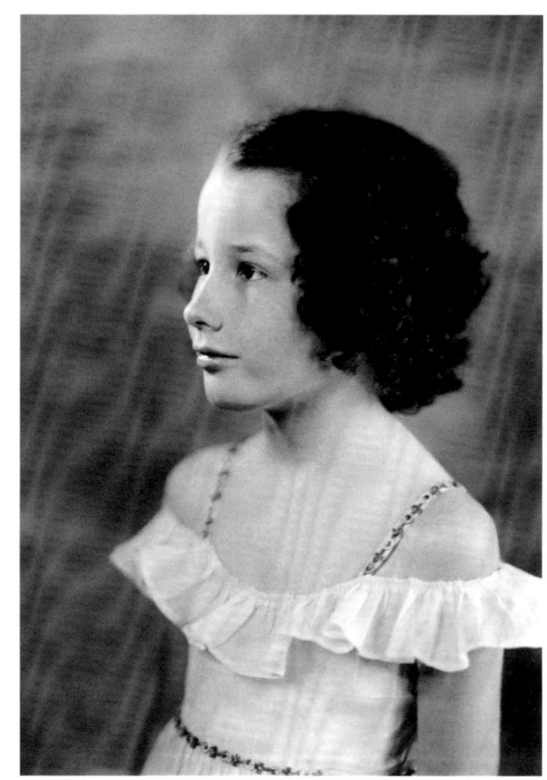

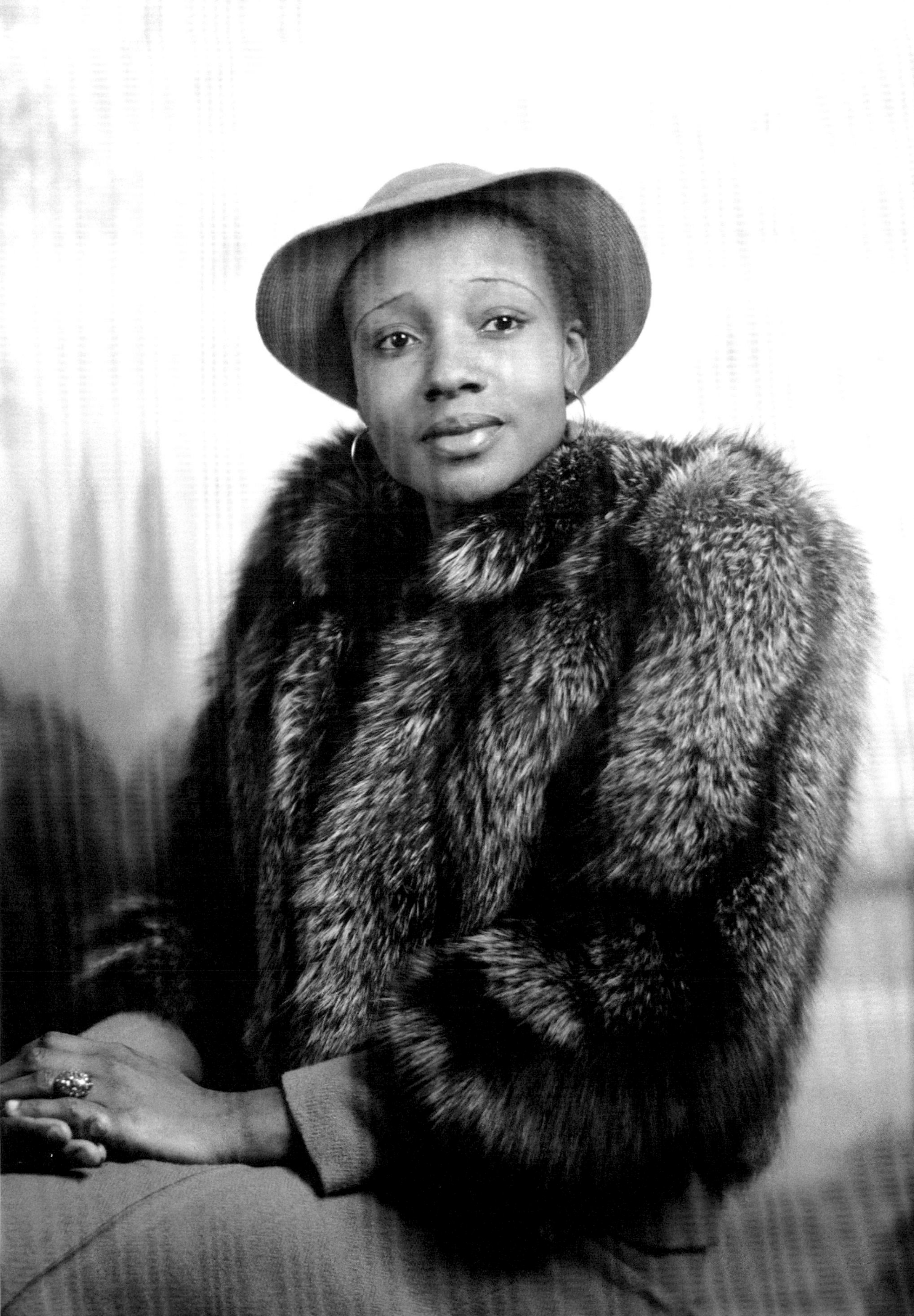

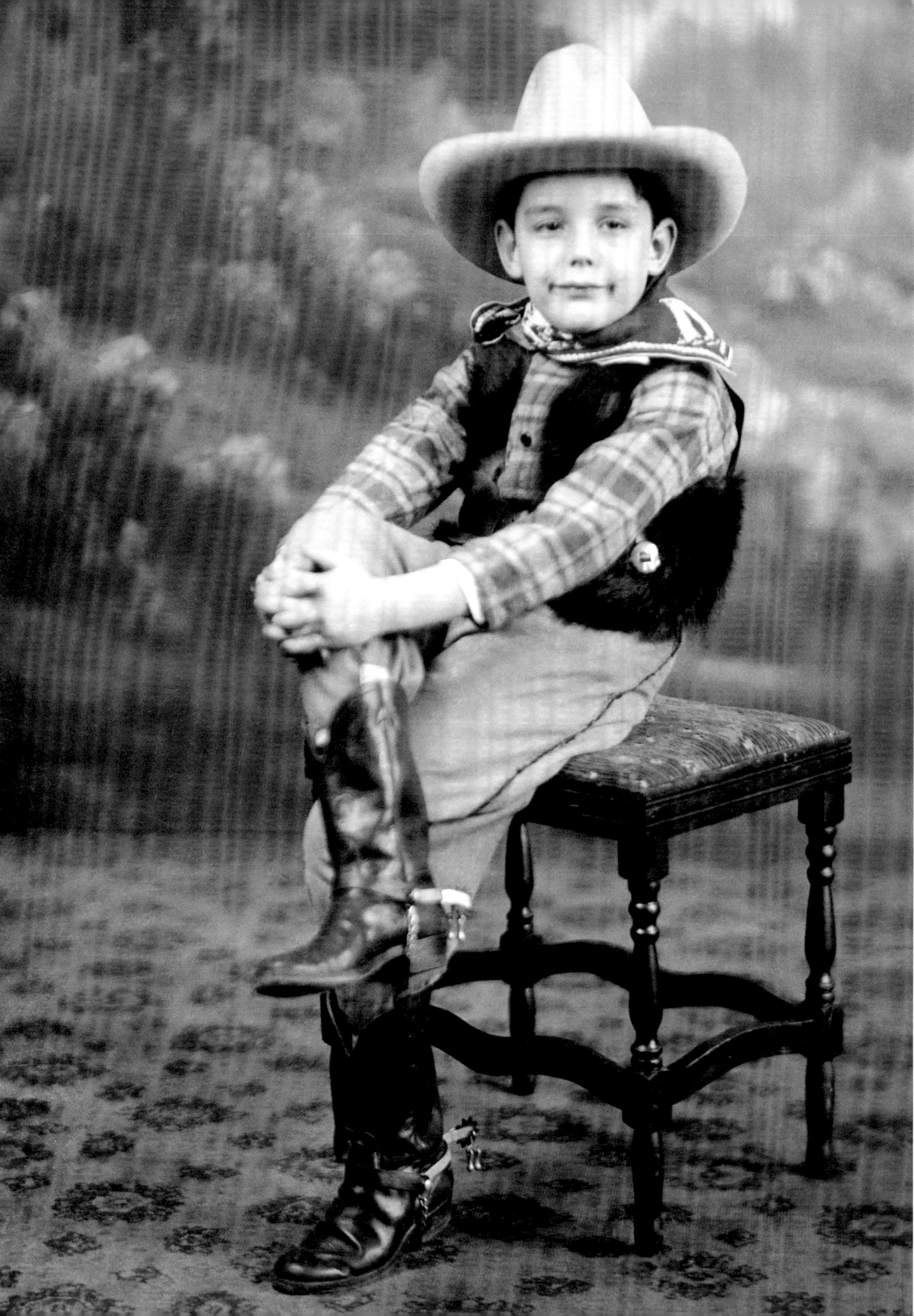

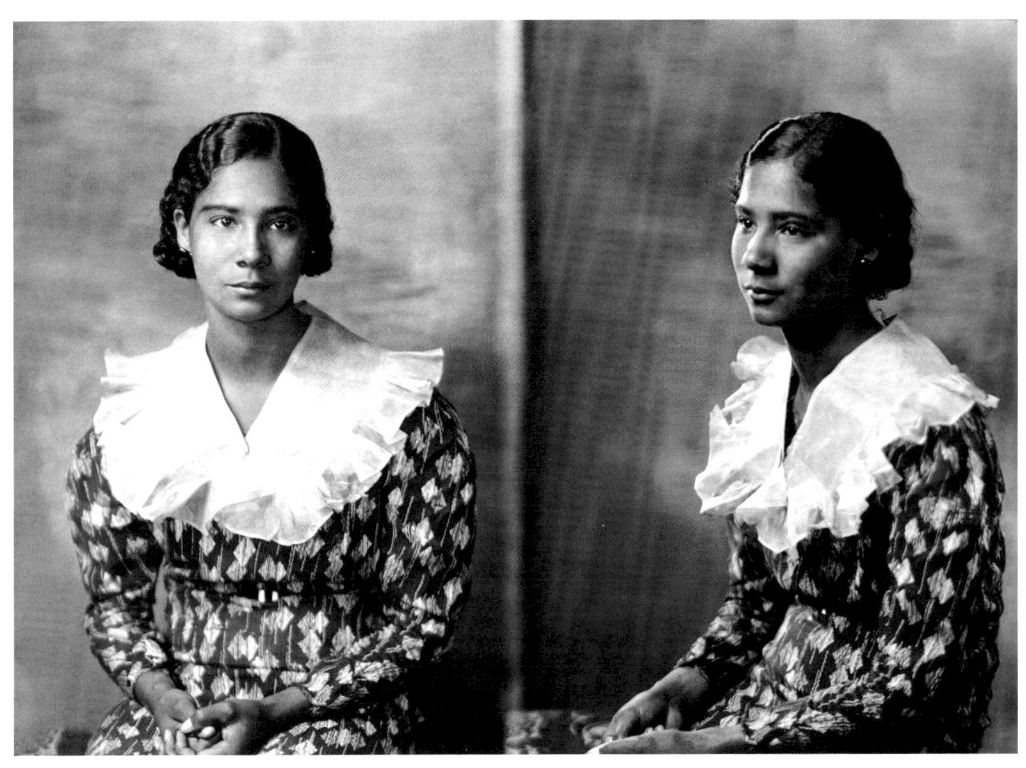

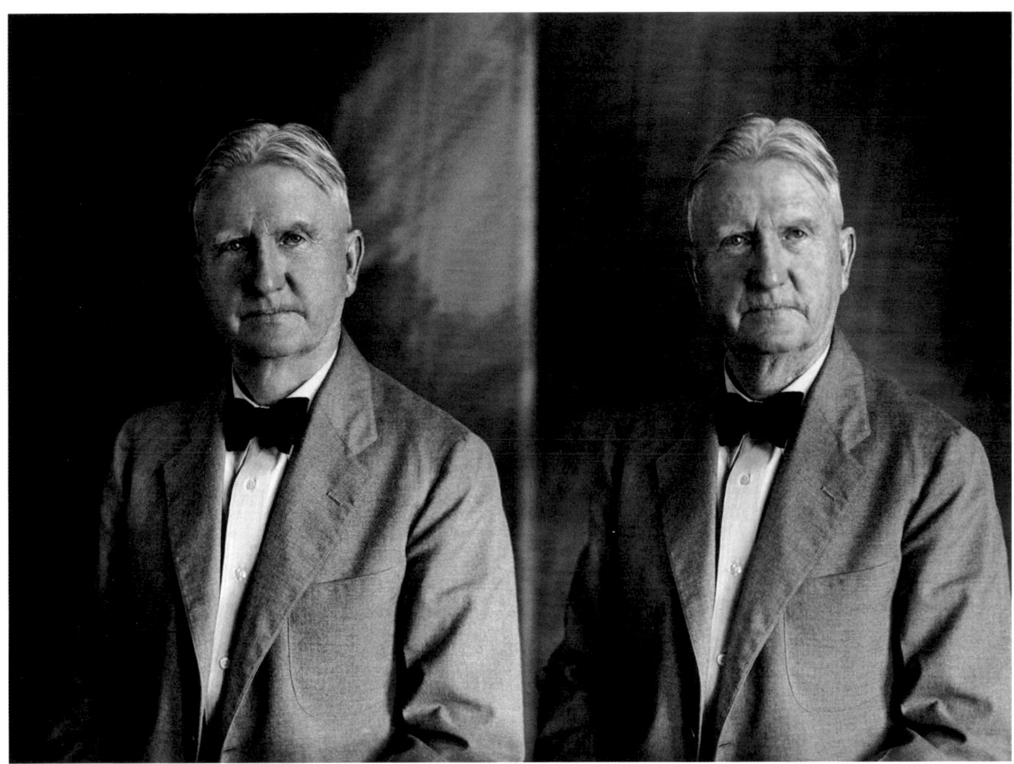

READING PRUITT

A Bibliographic Essay

Every image of the past that is not recognized by the present as one of its own concerns threatens to disappear irretrievably.

—Walter Benjamin, 1940

Once, in suburban Los Angeles, I had the good fortune to meet with photographic scholar Alan Trachtenberg of Yale University. His book *Reading American Photographs: From Mathew Brady to Walker Evans* had appeared nearly a decade earlier, in 1989, and was becoming a classic. William R. Ferris, my mentor and once a Yale colleague of Alan's and Walker Evans's, had connected us.

Alan, now a research fellow at the Huntington Library in San Marino, California, had invited me to lunch at a nearby Mexican restaurant. As we sat at an outside table in golden sunshine, we looked at print after print of Pruitt pictures. Alan marveled at the range of images, a Mississippi world away, and he helped me to understand the layers of possible meanings and how the pictures connect to history, culture, and life anywhere. Another time Alan invited me to the house the Huntington had provided him in the San Gabriel foothills. Inside, he showed me how he set up his large format Deardorff camera to survey the Arroyo Seco vistas. We talked about the meditative patience that kind of camera work requires, an attribute he shared with Pruitt and other photographers. From Alan, I learned that "to read an image is to write upon it, to incorporate it into story."

As a journalist turned media historian, I have learned the value of making scholarship accessible to everyone. In lieu of endnotes that might overwhelm a reader's experience of looking at the visual evidence, here I provide a research roadmap that buttresses the stories Pruitt and his subjects tell us—if we slow down to look, each in our own way. In my process of slowing down, surprises about Pruitt have greeted me. I've scanned through rolls of microfilm and sheets of microfiche. I've looked at thousands of Pruitt negatives made of glass and of film. I searched through yellowed, tattered pages in bound volumes of Columbus's newspaper, the *Commercial Dispatch*. I've read African American newspapers—the *Chicago Defender*, *Atlanta World*, and *Pittsburgh Courier*—and the NAACP's magazine the *Crisis*, and looked through volumes of *Harper's*, *Ebony*, *Jet*, *Billboard*, and *Variety*. For the last twenty years, I've exchanged ideas about Pruitt at academic conferences in Yamhill, Oregon; New York City; Atlanta; San Francisco; Banff, Alberta; Sandpoint, Idaho; Dresden, Germany; Columbia, South Carolina; and Washington, D.C. Once, in Seoul, South Korea, where I referenced Eric Lott's *Love and Theft* (1993), Pruitt images of blackface minstrelsy reminded an Israeli scholar of Middle East stage productions in which Jews in brownface mimicked Arabs.

PHOTOGRAPHIC AND DOCUMENTARY STUDIES

I've sought answers from hundreds of photography books, filling my bookcases with the works of Shelby Lee Adams, Bob Adelman, Henry Clay Anderson, Diane Arbus, and Eugène Atget, as well as Eudora Welty, Deborah Willis, Garry Winogrand, Ernest Withers, and Bayard Wootten.

Although I never met Museum of Modern Art photographic curator John Szarkowski, his books *Looking at Photographs* (1973) and *Photography Until Now* (1989) have taught me much. In 1991, he visited in Birmingham, Alabama, with three of my Pruitt partners—Jim Carnes, Mark Gooch, and Birney Imes—who showed him Pruitt photographs. He declared that, like a fine bottle of wine, over time the images would age with increasingly rich and complex flavors. With the years, Szarkowski said, the photographs would only become more fascinating to the viewer.

In the mid-1990s, I spoke at length on the telephone with photographic scholar Michael Lesy. His books have long assisted me, especially *Wisconsin Death Trip* (1973). Two decades ago, when Deborah Willis served as a visiting professor at both Duke University and the University of North Carolina, she taught me about the history of photography.

Her groundbreaking book *Reflections in Black* (2000) had been published the same year she was named a MacArthur Fellow. With her, I discussed the ideas of bell hooks, Shawn Michelle Smith, Roland Barthes, Jacques Lacan, Frantz Fanon, Robert Coles, Michel Foucault, Stuart Hall, John Berger, and Susan Sontag. We looked at photographs by Carrie Mae Weems, Clarissa Sligh, Charles "Teenie" Harris, the Scurlocks, and P. H. Polk. She taught me about visual representation and identity—using Robert Mapplethorpe and Madonna as well as Saartjie Baartman, the Hottentot Venus of South Africa—but above all in Pruitt.

In 2002, Willis, as a Black woman and a photographic historian, said I should go to an Emory University conference that included a panel on racial violence. As a white man I felt ambivalent about what role I might play in researching lynching images. She helped me to understand that the Pruitt Collection provides a rare context to understand not only racial violence but also the life of a community where a white photographer made images of everyday beauty as well as photographing brutality. In a transformative way for me, I spoke at Emory about the Pruitt pictures. Panelists included James Allen, whose book *Without Sanctuary* (2000) published a Pruitt image of the 1935 lynching of Bert Moore and Dooley Morton; and Amy Louise Wood, author of *Lynching and Spectacle: Witnessing Racial Violence in America, 1890–1940* (2009). High Museum curator of photography Thomas Southall was the moderator. The conference keynote speaker was David Levering Lewis, who won two Pulitzers in history: for *W. E. B. Du Bois: Biography of Race, 1868–1919* (1993) and *W. E. B. Du Bois: The Fight for Equality and the American Century, 1919–1963* (2000).

In graduate school, I studied with cultural anthropologist Catherine Lutz, who detailed for me her process with Jane L. Collins in researching their book *Reading National Geographic* (1993). Another professor, mass communication scholar Don Shaw, suggested that the Pruitt pictures were a "photobiography" of Mississippi. Later, I sought out curator Trudy Wilner Stack, who told me that the Pruitt pictures represent the history of a place in a way that only photographs can. This fit into the ideas of media historian James Carey, who one August day in 2004 at a Toronto conference took me on a walking conversation: we discussed how Pruitt connected with Carey's ideas in his landmark book, *Communication as Culture* (1989).

SOUTHERN HISTORY AND CULTURE

Arguably, my research process started in the 1950s at the Columbus–Lowndes County Public Library, a white wooden antebellum house behind St. Paul's Episcopal Church. The library was jammed with books and magazines. My mother and I would go there, three blocks from our home, and read. I read *Life*, the *Saturday Evening Post*, or *Time* while she searched for a stack of books to bring home. Even though my mother despised Faulkner's use of what she called blasphemous language, she encouraged me to read him, because he was from Mississippi and had won a Nobel Prize. So, I read him, beginning in junior high with "The Bear." She encouraged me to read other Mississippi journalists and writers: Eudora Welty and her "Petrified Man," "Why I Live at the P.O.," and *Losing Battles* (1970), with its cemetery scene. She told me about journalists Hodding Carter Jr., Bill Minor, Turner Catledge, and Hazel Brannon Smith. She led me to Willie Morris's *North toward Home* (1967), James Silver's *Mississippi: The Closed Society* (1964), and Russell Barrett's *Integration at Ole Miss* (1965). Several years after Barrett's book was published, he became one of my professors, and eventually as an Ole Miss student I would meet James Meredith, who had racially integrated our university, and his mentor James Silver. And even now as a primary source, for Pruitt's images of baptisms and more, I read my worn King James version of the Bible.

My mother never suggested reading Mississippi's Black authors to understand Pruitt's world, writers such as Richard Wright (*Black Boy*, 1945, and *Native Son*, 1940) and Ida B. Wells-Barnett (*The Red Record*, 1895). Nor did she discuss Leontyne Price of the Metropolitan Opera, composer William Grant Still, or bluesmen from northeast Mississippi's Black Prairie of the Tombigbee River: Big Joe Williams, Howlin' Wolf, or Bukka White and his "Columbus, Mississippi Blues." Eventually, I would discover them along with their Mississippi literary descendants who speak deeply of race, gender, class, religion, history, and identity: Ralph Eubanks, Kiese Laymon, Natasha Tretheway, Anthony Walton, Margaret Walker, Jesmyn Ward, and Etheridge Knight, especially his *Belly Song and Other Poems* (1973). I've read them to better understand Pruitt's pictures.

Although the Pruitt Collection had few notations about his subjects, I patched together threads of people, places, and stories with the help of the *Works Progress Administration Historical Research Project for Mississippi: Lowndes County*, volume 46, parts 1 and 2, *1936–1938*. These are in the Billups-Garth Archives of the Columbus–Lowndes County Public Library. Additionally, the Library of Congress's digitized collections have been invaluable, as has *Mississippi: The WPA Guide to the Magnolia State* (1988). What I sorely missed finding over the years was the Black newspaper published in Columbus in the late nineteenth and early twentieth centuries, the *New Light*.

Some of the most compelling Pruitt photographs were made in the 1920s and 1930s. During this period between World War I and World War II, the Civil War lingered in palpable ways as Jim Crow laws regulated what historian Joel Williamson calls a "rage for racial order." While the Great Depression bore down on the agrarian American South, Pruitt made portraits for people who did not own a camera and had never been photographed before. Historians of the American South such as David Blight, Jacquelyn Dowd Hall, John Hope Franklin, Leon Litwack, C. Vann Woodward, and Grace Hale provide guidance to explain the Confederacy's defeat and how that influenced daily life in the era of the Lost Cause, which included racial violence. Seeking connections with Pruitt's photographs of that violence, in June 1994 in Columbus, I interviewed Parker George, a mechanic, whom I'd known my whole life and who had worked with my father. When we spoke, he was ninety years old. He had seen the lynched bodies of Moore and Morton in 1935. He told me that Adolf Hitler and the Nazis tried to capitalize on the Columbus lynching as an example of American cruelty. Twelve years after that interview and after finding a *New York Times* mention of Nazi propaganda referring to the Columbus lynching, I went to Germany to visit the newspaper archives of the Staatsbibliothek zu Berlin, one of Europe's largest libraries. I leafed through bound volumes of 1930s German newspapers. It was riveting. I found no reference to Pruitt's depiction of a lynching, but I did find other examples, including a 1934 photograph of the lynching of Claude Neal in Marianna, Florida.

On another occasion, at the University of North Carolina at Chapel Hill, I walked to my library carrel, where I had 200 books. As I passed through the stacks—when Google in its infancy could help little—I spied black-bound volumes with names of Confederate states. I pulled down volume 12, *Testimony Taken by the Joint Select Committee to Inquire into the Condition of Affairs in the Late Insurrectionary States: Mississippi*. During Reconstruction, the struggle for political, economic, and social stability often became violent. When a congressional committee convened in Washington, D.C., witnesses testified to the Ku Klux Klan's upsurge and white brutality against Blacks. Later committee representatives gathered testimony throughout the American South. Dozens of pages from November 1871 focused on Columbus and Lowndes County.

A Lowndes County plantation worker, Joseph Turner, identified as "colored," testified that twenty Klan members—carrying pistols and sticks, dressed in white with horns on their heads, and riding on disguised horses—dragged him out of his house and took him down the road and beat him. And he testified about two men he knew who had been killed: "When they whipped Dick Halliday, they made him run naked and made him get down and pray, and then they made him take sacrament with them; they had bread in their pockets, and they made him eat bread."

The landscape of northeast Mississippi where that happened has always guided this project. I've sought confirmation and connections in buildings, homes, and neighborhoods, rich and poor. I've gone to churches, stores, the Lowndes County Courthouse, Friendship Cemetery—dating from the nineteenth century and the repose of many whites—and to a Black graveyard, Sandfield Cemetery. As I go, I hear snippets of a poem by New York judge Francis Miles Finch and published in the *Atlantic Monthly* in 1867 to commemorate Friendship as a burial site of Union and Confederate soldiers: "Under the sod and the dew, / Waiting the judgement day; / Love and tears for the Blue, / Tears and love for the Gray." In that era's spirit of reconciliation among whites, the poem explores the nation's grief. Yet the Decoration Day ceremonies neglected the unacknowledged trauma and torture wrought by human bondage.

ORAL HISTORY, ETHNOGRAPHY, AND FOLKLORE

In her novel *Mama Day* (1988), Gloria Naylor illustrates a key issue with which I've wrestled. Reema's boy, an ethnographer of sorts, has grown up and come back home from college to Willow Springs, a sea island off the Georgia and South Carolina coast where the Gullah people live. He, who knows little of the bone and marrow of his own home, wants everyone to tell him their stories about this magical place. In the novel's beginning, two older women sit on a front porch and talk about how Reema's boy could not handle their stories if they told them. Someone who does not know how to ask, one woman said to the other, would not know how to listen. The stories that Reema's boy missed hearing are a grand and harrowing set of tales. So, as folklorist Glenn Hinson has schooled me, I continue to ask and to listen to the tales the Pruitt pictures tell.

ACKNOWLEDGMENTS

The Firebird, as the folktale goes, drops a feather onto the forest floor. A naive sojourner picks up that golden feather, unaware of doom—and boons—to follow. As with that sojourner, I picked up a camera in Mississippi. I had four boyhood friends who loved pictures and the place we call home. We discovered a trove of photographs by O. N. Pruitt and decided to preserve, research, publish, and exhibit the images. Now, more than three decades later, comes this companion for a nationally traveling exhibit sponsored by the National Endowment for Humanities.

If I list all who helped, I'd need Hollywood film credits. To those allies I've omitted and for other omissions or errors, I apologize, noting, as writer Don Murray taught me, that "revision is a process."

That said, I thank the four boyhood friends—Jim Carnes, David Gooch, Mark Gooch, and Birney Imes—and their families. Your visions shape this book. I offer special thanks to Beth, John, Peter, and Tanner Imes and to the *Commercial Dispatch*, Mississippi's last family-owned daily, where I served as a carrier boy and in whose building the former WCBI-AM studios still provide me a Mississippi retreat loft.

In this book's bibliographic essay I reference scholars. Here I emphasize three: William Ferris, former chairman of the National Endowment for the Humanities (NEH), serves as my Pruitt polestar. Tom Rankin is true as a sharpened shovel digging into Mississippi Delta earth. Deborah Willis taught me to look in shadows, real and imagined, and to ask who made a photograph and whose images are included or excluded.

I offer appreciation to former NEH chairman Jon Parrish Peede and NEH advisor Carolina Cortina. I am grateful for my NEH humanities scholars: Rachel Boillot, LaGarrett King, Paul Litton, David Rees, Kristin Schwain, Stephanie Shonekan, Lynden Steele, Rufus Ward, Willie Williams, Charles R. Wilson, and Charles Yarborough.

Librarians and archivists have served as my bedrock: First came Joe Hewitt, the epitome of the Carolina Way and UNC Chapel Hill's head librarian, and then came Larry Alford, Robert Anthony, Patrick Cullom, Maria Estorino, Stephen Fletcher, Bryan Giemza, Nicholas Graham, Sarah Michalak, Rich Szary, Jason Tomberlin, Matthew Turi, Tim West, and Elaine Westbrooks. At the University of Missouri, Dorothy Carner and Sue Schuermann provided exquisite service. So did Erin Busbea and Mona Vance-Ali at Mississippi's Columbus-Lowndes Public Library.

Although I've lost touch with some University of Mississippi friends, I have a Goo-Goo Cluster who still help: Claiborne and Marian Barksdale, Joe Boggess, Lisa and Richard Howorth, A. J. Jaeger, Sparky Reardon, Curtis Wilkie, and Kathy and Dan Woodliff. Ole Miss professors Robert Haws, Jere Hoar, Will Norton Jr., and David Sansing ever boosted my spirits. In head and heart, I carry my Columbia University professors and classmates, particularly Marvin Barrett, Eduardo Cue, Fred Friendly, Phyl Garland, Johnny Greene, Lloyd Kramer, Jonathan Maslow, Mel Mencher, Lawrie Mifflin, Chip Scanlan, John Schultz, Don Shanor, Zachary Sklar, and Steve Wisch.

Coast-to-coast support flowed from Keven Barrett, Allison Bingeman, Noah Blough, Gene Call, Lisa Cremin, Deborah Davidson, Owen Dodge, Randy Eiken, Steve Gates, Robbin Gehrke, Scherrie Goettsch, Bruce Harlan, Patrick Kane, Mark Kramer, Dan Lefevre, Martin Love, Dave Maestrejuan, Polina Malkin, Margo McBane, Ann and David Mehr, Rob Moses, Gus Reininger, Louise Steinman, Paul Sturtz, Hoyt and Katie Taylor, Beth Thielen, Collins Walker, and David Wilson. Storytellers of the Blue Mountain Group and Robert and Jeannine Beekman enfolded me.

With colleagues, I saw sunrises and sunsets at the *Bulletin* in Bend, Oregon; the *Providence Journal* in Rhode Island, and the *Los Angeles Times*. I'm glad Carol McCabe taught me to accept a compliment.

My first grant came from the Freedom Forum Professors Publishing Program when I taught at California State University–Los Angeles. Then a Park Foundation Fellowship allowed me to immerse in Pruitt research at UNC–Chapel Hill, where I received support from the Center for the Study of the American South. The Council on Library Information Resources assisted the Pruitt-Shanks Collection. Funding came from the American Journalism Historians Association, the Cherng Program in Honors, the University of Missouri and the University of Missouri System, Mizzou Advantage, the Peace Studies Endowment, and the Southeastern Conference. I treasure the beneficence from the Sally and Dick Roberts Coyote Foundation, the Houston Jewish Community Fund, and the Martha and Spencer Love Foundation. Additionally, the Mississippi Humanities Council and Missouri Humanities Council contributed.

At Cal State LA, Judith Hamera and Carl and Carol Selkin encouraged my research. So did CSLA alum Felix Gutierrez. Soulmates in Jack Grapes's Los Angeles workshops, and mythopoetic friends in the California crucibles of Mendocino, Malibu, and Sierra Madre shaped my thinking. Thank you: Hector Aristizabal, Dan Attias, Robert Bly, John Densmore, Jory Farr, Jess Foster, James Hillman, Wayne Liebman, Michael Meade, Luis Rodriguez, Malidoma Somé, and Eric Lloyd Wright.

I'm blessed to have "friends of photography" with the Visual Communication Conference and Bobby Alter, Anne Barry, Gillian Brown, Richard Campbell, Michael Carlebach, Lisa De Lima, Craig Denton, Dennis Dunleavy, David Eason, Shane Epping, David T. Hanson, Paul Lester, Larry Mullen, Julie Newton, Erik Palmer, and Robert Sagerman. Likewise, Providence's East Side potluck—with Barnaby Evans, Liz Harden, Dennis Hlynsky, Karen Hlynsky, Denny Moers, Gail Porter, and Jon Sharlin—provided a sumptuous table. Additionally, my meditation, running, and tennis friends exhibit continual generosity.

At UNC Chapel Hill and Duke, I was nurtured by Deb Aikat, Margaret Blanchard, Tom Bowers, Jane Brown, Doug Cumming, Tori Ekstrand, Frank Fee, Barbara Friedman, Philip Gura, Trudier Harris, Glenn Hinson, Anne Johnston, Susan King, Tom Linden, Catherine Lutz, Phil Meyer, Toril Moi, David Paletz, Donald Shaw, Chuck Stone, Ruth Walden, Harry Watson, and Joel Williamson.

Scholars Tom Chaffin, Pete Daniel, James Early, Rex Ellis, Stetson Kennedy, and Allen Tullos posed incisive questions for me.

A host of University of Missouri scholars valued this research including those with the Faculty Council, Missouri School of Journalism, Peace Studies Faculty, and Race Relations Committee, especially Noor Azizan-Gardner, Jacqui Banaszynski, Alex Barker, Jackie Bell, Mary Kay Blakely, Bill Bondeson, J. D. Bowers, Liz Brixey, Brian Brooks, Alexander Cartwright, Mun Choi, Kathryn Chval, Mike Cook, Juanamaria Cordones-Cook, Fritz Cropp, Ken Dean, Keona Ervin, John Fennell, Elisa Glick, Keith Greenwood, Michael Grinfeld, Kristopher Hagglund, Joanna Hearne, Andrea Heiss, Chuck Henson, Sara Hiles, Amanda Hinnant, Mike Jenner, George Kennedy, Ted Koditschek, Brian Kratzer, Lynda Kraxberger, Gary Kremer, Dave Kurpius, April Langley, Clarence Lo, Bowen Loftin, Ed McCain, Amy McCombs, Kevin McDonald, Mark McIntosh, Julie Middleton, Dean Mills, Cristina Mislan, Daryl Moen, Jeimmie Nevalga, Pat Okker, Earnest Perry, Randy Picht, Latha Ramchand, Don Ranly, Rita Reed, Steve Rice, Craig Roberts, Jen Rowe, Janet Saidi, Rick Shaw, Randy Smith, Zoe Smith, Jim Spain, Jo Stealey, Brian and Marty Steffens, Ron Stodghill, Esther Thorson, Ben Trachtenberg, Ron Turner, Michael Ugarte, Nadège Uwase, Tom Warhover, Steve Weinberg, and Nancy West. Above all, I'm thankful for Jan Colbert; fellow Mississippian Michael Middleton, and magazine faculty assistant Kim Townlain, who solved problems with her farmer's pragmatism.

Mizzou students, including my Honors College visual tutorial and *Vox* magazine editors, helped me uncover sadness and joy in Pruitt pictures: Delia Cai,

Abby Callard, Dan Christian, Sal Cochran, Bailey Conard, Carlos Cortes Martinez, Bea Costa Lima, Brenda Edgerton-Webster, Sarah Everett, John Farmer de la Torre, Julien Gorbach, Seth Graves, Hany Hawasly, Ginger Hervey, Beck Jaeckels, Yehun Kim, Damian Kostiuk, Liz Lance, Robert Langellier, Cary Littlejohn, Chris Long, Megan Madden, Annika Meerilees, Beatriz Wallace Metts, Jordan Novet, Katie Parkins, Greg Perrault, Liz Pierson, Emmalee Reed, Zach Reger, Sangeeta Shastry, T. J. Thomson, Vivien Kim Thorp, Dariya Tsyrenzhapova, Kelsey Whipple, Nick Wyer, and Jieyang Zheng.

Financial, grant, legal, and tech shepherds are Matt Bader, Dan Brady, Joe Collins, Steve Edds, Justin Giles, Ann Harris, Carolyn Jackson, Scot Kirkpatrick, Christine Montgomery, Pat Muck, John Meyer, Lisa Schwartz, Cheryl Spang, and David Steine.

Lauren Steele, whom I met as a Mizzou undergrad straight-from-the-farm, now is a savvy Pruitt coordinator with help from Anne Geissinger, Emma Geissinger Cutchins, and Jennifer Mosbrucker.

From Mizzou students Jonathan Butler, Reuben Faloughi, and Corie Wilkins, and from Bryan Stevenson, I've learned to reckon with painful histories of race relations. I am grateful my history intersected with Lee High School classmates and First Baptist Church denizens Deborah Prince Blanchard, Kenny Bozeman, Milford Hough, and Jim Lollar. Years later, I met Tom Mayfield, who shared his love of Columbus history.

I'm delighted this book found a home with UNC Press's partnership with Duke University's Center for Documentary Studies. For this I sing praises of Kim Bryant, Mary Caviness, Alexa Dilworth, Cate Hodorowicz, and Mark Simpson-Vos. Intertwined with that effort is the Pruitt exhibition by Curatorial in Pasadena, California, led by Graham Howe and Phillip Prodger and enlivened by Remington Annetta, Bjarne Bare, Jeremy Bigalke, Viviana Carlos, Natalia Leal Delgado, Marika Lundeberg, and Alexis Sutcliffe.

A steward extraordinaire of children's literature, Lloyd E. Cotsen guided Neutrogena Corporation and, along with his librarian Ivy Trent, taught me philanthropy's real value in preserving archives for posterity.

I thank my Fraser first cousins photographed by Pruitt: Marge Fitzsimmons, Merle Fraser, Ginger Hite, and Ann Williams.

Lastly, I thank my wife, dearest friend and storyteller Milbre Burch. She *knows* stories, including the Firebird. The best stories we've fashioned are the ones of daughters Katy Blake Burch-Hudson and Elizabeth Travis Walker Burch-Hudson. Their exuberant spirits buoy me, an all-day talker when it comes to Pruitt.

SELECTED BIBLIOGRAPHY

INTERVIEWS

All interviews were conducted by the author in Columbus, Mississippi, unless otherwise noted.

Chebie Gaines Bateman, January 2003
Hawley Knox Brown, April 2000
Ed Bush, interview by Mark Gooch, November 1974 and January 1975
Thomas Caldwell, Fairfield, Ohio, May 2001
James A. Carnes, January 2003
Virginia Shelley Dornan, April 2000
Marjorie Baugh Doster, January 2003
Billy Frates, September 2000
Parker George, June 1994
Mary Alice Gibson, June 2000
Joe Hanna, interview by Mark Gooch, November 1974 and January 1975
Selma Hanna, interview by Mark Gooch, November 1974 and January 1975
Charlie Harris, Trinity community, Lowndes County, Mississippi, January 2003
Laura Harris, Trinity community, Lowndes County, Mississippi, January 2003
Lee Harris, Trinity community, Lowndes County, Mississippi, January 2003
Mason Harris, Trinity community, Lowndes County, Mississippi, January 2003
Willie Harris, Trinity community, Lowndes County, January 2003
Charles Hayslett, September 2002
Eva Byrd (Fraser Hudson) Heard, August 2002
Russell Hudson, 1983 and 2003
Bonnie Kimbrell, interview by Mark Gooch, November 1974
Jessie Koonce, January 2003
Oscar Lang, August 2000
Sara Lusk, June 1994
Ben Owen, June 1994
Helen Randolph, January 2003
Irene Pruitt Caldwell Raper, interview by James P. Carnes, October 1991
Claudia Locke Rhett, January 2003
Dottie Richards, January 2003
Oren Richardson, January 2003
Rachel Shute, April 2000
Nannie Kate Smith, June 1994
Wilbern Sprayberry, June 1994
Clyde Stokes, January 2003
Emmett J. Stringer, June 1994
Tammy Taylor, March 2003
Billy Thompson, April 2000
W. G. "Bit" Thompson, January 2003
Lloyd Vaughan, January 2003
Edwina R. Williams, January 2003
Lula May Williams, June 1994

PUBLISHED SOURCES

Agee, James, and Walker Evans. *Cotton Tenants: Three Families*. Edited by John Summers. Boston: Melville House, 2013.

Als, Hilton. "GWTW." In *Without Sanctuary: Lynching Photography in America*, edited by James Allen. 38–45. Santa Fe, N.M.: Twin Palms, 2000.

Asim, Jabari. The N Word: Who Can Say It, Who Shouldn't, and Why. Boston: Houghton Mifflin, 2007.

Baker, Ray Stannard. *Following the Color Line: American Negro Citizenship in the Progressive Era*. New York: Doubleday, Page, 1908.

Bannos, Pamela. *Vivian Maier: A Photographer's Life and Afterlife*. Chicago: University of Chicago Press, 2017.

Barber, Red, and Robert Creamer. *Rhubarb in the Catbird Seat*. Garden City: Doubleday, 1968.

Barnwell, Marion, ed. *A Place Called Mississippi: Collected Narratives*. Jackson: University Press of Mississippi, 1997.

Barry, John M. *Rising Tide: The Great Mississippi Flood of 1927 and How It Changed America*. New York: Simon & Schuster, 1998.
Barthes, Roland. *Camera Lucida: Reflections on Photography*. Translated by Richard Howard. New York: Hill and Wang, 1981.
Behar, Ruth. *The Vulnerable Observer: Anthropology That Breaks Your Heart*. Boston: Beacon, 1996.
Benjamin, Walter. *Illuminations*. Edited and with an introduction by Hannah Arendt. Translated by Harry Zohn. London: Pimlico, 1999.
Berger, John. *About Looking*. New York: Pantheon, 1980.
Blight, David. *Race and Reunion: The Civil War in American Memory*. Cambridge, Mass.: Harvard University Press, 2001.
Bloom, Lisa, ed. *With Other Eyes: Looking at Race and Gender in Visual Culture*. Minneapolis: University of Minnesota Press, 1999.
Bodgan, Robert. *Freak Show: Presenting Human Bodies for Amusement and Profit*. Chicago: University of Chicago Press, 1988.
Broderick, Janice. "Charles Elliott Gill: Ozark Life through the Lens of an Early Photographer." *Missouri Historical Society* 35, no. 2 (1979): 83–91.
Brundage, W. Fitzhugh. *The Southern Past: A Clash of Race and Memory*. Cambridge, Mass.: Belknap Press of Harvard University Press, 2005.
Bunkers, Suzanne L. ed. *The Diary of Caroline Seabury, 1854–1863*. Madison: University of Wisconsin Press, 1991.
Campbell, James T., and Elaine Owens. *Mississippi Witness: The Photographs of Florence Mars*. Jackson: University Press of Mississippi, 2019.
Capote, Truman. *"The Grass Harp" and "A Tree of Night" and Other Stories*. New York: Vintage, 1993.
Carby, Hazel. *Race Men*. Cambridge, Mass.: Harvard University Press, 1998.
Cash, W. J. *The Mind of the South*. New York: Knopf, 1941.
Chafe, William H., Raymond Gavins, and Robert Korstad, eds. *Remembering Jim Crow: African Americans Tell About Life in the Segregated South*. New York: New Press, 2001.
Chambi, Martín. *Martín Chambi: Photographs, 1920–1950*. Washington, D.C.: Smithsonian Institution Press, 1993.
Clarke, Gerald. *Capote: A Biography*. New York: Ballantine, 1989.
Cobb, James C. *The Most Southern Place on Earth: The Mississippi Delta and the Roots of Regional Identity*. Oxford: Oxford University Press, 1992.
Coles, Robert. *Doing Documentary Work*. Oxford: Oxford University Press, 1997.
Commission on Interracial Cooperation. *The Mob Still Rides: A Review of the Lynching Record, 1931–1935*. Documentary History of the Franklin D. Roosevelt Presidency, 1936.
Cone, James H. *The Cross and the Lynching Tree*. Maryknoll, NY: Orbis Books, 2011.
Cotton, Jerry W. *Light and Air: The Photography of Bayard Wootten*. Chapel Hill: University of North Carolina Press, 1998.
Crunk, Hardy. "A Legend in His Time: Hunter, Bird Dog Trainer and Author Er M. Shelley Earned Fame on Two Continents; Though Dead for 40 Years, His Legend Endures." *Commercial Dispatch* (Columbus, Miss.), December 13, 1998.
Daniel, Pete. *The Shadow of Slavery: Peonage in the South, 1901–1969*. Urbana: University of Illinois Press, 1972.
Disfarmer, Mike. *Disfarmer*. Text by Julia Scully. Santa Fe, N.M.: Twin Palms, 2000.
Dittmer, John. *Local People: The Struggle for Civil Rights in Mississippi*. Chicago: University of Illinois Press, 1994.
Dray, Philip. *At the Hands of Persons Unknown: The Lynching of Black America*. New York: Random House, 2002.
Dugan, Ellen, ed. *Picturing the South: 1860 to the Present*. San Francisco: Chronicle, 1996.

Dundes, Alan, ed. *Mother Wit from the Laughing Barrel: Readings in the Interpretation of Afro-American Folklore*. Jackson: University Press of Mississippi, 1990.

Dyer, Richard. *White*. New York: Routledge, 1997.

Ellison, Ralph. *Invisible Man*. New York: Random House, 1952.

Enyeart, James, ed. *Decade by Decade: Twentieth-Century American Photography from the Collection of the Center for Creative Photography*. Boston: Bullfinch, 1989.

Evans, Walker. "Photography." In *Quality: Its Image in the Arts*, edited by Louis Kronenberger, 169–211. New York: Atheneum, 1969.

Fanon, Franz. *Black Skin, White Masks*. New York: Grove, 1967.

Faulkner, William. *Light in August*. New York: Random House, 1932.

Ferris, William. *Give My Poor Heart Ease*. Chapel Hill: University of North Carolina Press, 2009.

Ferris, William, and Charles Reagan Wilson, eds. *Encyclopedia of Southern Culture*. Chapel Hill: University of North Carolina Press, 1989.

Fleischhauer, Carl, and Beverly W. Brannan, eds. *Documenting America, 1935–1943*. Los Angeles: University of California Press, 1988.

Fox-Genovese, Elizabeth. *Within the Plantation Household: Black and White Women of the Old South*. Chapel Hill: University of North Carolina Press, 1988.

Franklin, John Hope, and Alfred A. Moss Jr. *From Slavery to Freedom: A History of African Americans*. New York: Knopf, 2000.

Giltner, Scott E., and P. S. E. Giltner. *Hunting and Fishing in the New South*. Baltimore: Johns Hopkins University Press, 2008.

Greene, Johnny. "Selling Off the Old South." *Harper's*, April 1977.

Gubar, Susan. *Racechanges: White Skin, Black Face in American Culture*. Oxford: Oxford University Press, 1997.

Hale, Grace Elizabeth. *Making Whiteness: The Culture of Segregation in the South, 1890–1940*. New York: Vintage, 1999.

Hall, Jacquelyn Dowd. *Revolt against Chivalry: Jessie Daniel Ames and the Women's Campaign against Lynching*. New York: Columbia University Press, 1993.

Harris, Trudier. *Exorcising Blackness: Historical and Literary Lynching and Burning Rituals*. Bloomington: Indiana University Press, 1984.

Hawthorne, Ann, ed. *The Picture Man: Photographs of Paul Buchanan*. Chapel Hill: University of North Carolina Press, 1993.

Hendrickson, Paul. *Sons of Mississippi: A Story of Race and Its Legacy*. New York: Vintage, 2003.

Hirsch, Marianne. *Family Frames: Photography, Narrative and Postmemory*. Cambridge, Mass.: Harvard University Press, 1997.

Holditch, Kenneth, and Richard Freeman Leavitt. *Tennessee Williams and the South*. Jackson: University Press of Mississippi, 2002.

Hudson, Berkley. "A Mississippi Negro Farmer, His Mule, and President Franklin D. Roosevelt: Racial Portrayals of Sylvester Harris in the Black and White 1930s." *Journalism History* 32, no. 4 (Winter 2007): 201–12.

———. "O. N. Pruitt's Possum Town: The 'Modest Aspiration and Small Renown' of a Mississippi Photographer." *Southern Cultures* 13, no. 2 (Summer 2007): 52–77.

Hughes, Langston. *The Collected Poems of Langston Hughes*. New York: Knopf, 1994.

Imes, Birney. *Juke Joint*. Introduction by Richard Ford. Jackson: University Press of Mississippi, 1990.

———. *Partial to Home (Photographers at Work)*. Washington, D.C.: Smithsonian Institution Press, 1994.

———. *Whispering Pines*. Jackson: University Press of Mississippi, 1994.

Johnson, Dinah. *All around Town: The Photographs of Richard Samuel Roberts*. New York: Henry Holt, 1998.

Jussim, Estelle. "The Eternal Moment: Essays on the Photographic Image." *Aperture*, 1989.

Kahn, Roger. *A Flame of Pure Fire: Jack Dempsey and the Roaring 20s*. San Diego: Harcourt Brace, 1999.

Kaye, Samuel, Rufus Ward, Jr. and Carolyn B. Neault. *By the Flow of the Inland River: The Settlement of Columbus, Mississippi to 1825*. Columbus, Miss.: N.p., 1992.

Kelley, Robin D. G. Foreword to *Reflections in Black: A History of Black Photographers 1840 to Present*. New York: Norton, 2000.

Kennedy, Randall. *nigger: The Strange Career of a Troublesome Word*. New York: Pantheon, 2002.

Klarman, Michael J. "The Racial Origins of Modern Criminal Procedure." *Michigan Law Review* 99, no. 1 (October 2000): 48–97.

Lamunière, Michelle. *You Look Beautiful Like That: The Portraits Photographs of Seydou Keïta and Malick Sidibè*. Cambridge, Mass.: Harvard University Art Museums, 2001.

Lipscomb, William Lowndes. *A History of Columbus, Mississippi during the 19th Century*. Birmingham, Ala.: Press of Dispatch Printing, 1909.

Litwack, Leon F. *Trouble in Mind: Black Southerners in an Age of Jim Crow*. New York: Knopf, 1998.

Malcolmson, Scott L. *One Drop of Blood: The American Misadventure of Race*. New York: Farrar, Straus and Giroux, 2000.

Matthews, Scott L. *Capturing the South: Imagining America's Most Documented Region*. Chapel Hill: University of North Carolina Press, 2018.

McCandless, Barbara. *Equal before the Lens: Jno. Trilica's Photographs of Granger, Texas*. College Station: Texas A&M University Press, 1992.

McMillen, Neil R. *Dark Journey: Black Mississippians in the Age of Jim Crow*. Champaign: University of Illinois Press, 1989.

Moltke-Hansen, David. "Seeing the Highlands, 1900–1939: Southwestern Virginia through the Lens of T. R. Phelps." *Southern Cultures* 1, no. 1 (Fall 1994): 23–49.

Nathan, Hans. *Dan Emmett and the Rise of Early Negro Minstrelsy*. Norman: University of Oklahoma Press, 1962.

Nederveen Pieterse, Jan. *White on Black. Images of Africa and Blacks in Western Popular Culture*. New Haven, Conn.: Yale University Press, 1992.

Newhall, Beaumont. *The History of Photography*. Boston: Little, Brown, 1982.

Norfleet, Barbara. *The Champion Pig*. Boston: Godine, 1979.

O'Kain, Dennis. "Documenting the Deep South: William E. Wilson, Photographer." *Georgia Review* 33, no. 3 (1979): 662–80.

Oshinsky, David M. *Worse than Slavery: Parchman Farm and the Ordeal of Jim Crow Justice*. New York: Simon & Schuster, 1996.

Ownby, Ted, ed. *Black and White: Cultural Interaction in the Antebellum South*. Jackson: University Press of Mississippi, 1993.

Plimpton, George. *Truman Capote*. Edited by Nan Talese Doubleday. New York: Doubleday, 1997.

Puckett, Newbell Niles. *Folk Beliefs of the Southern Negro*. Chapel Hill: University of North Carolina Press, 1926.

Rankin, Tom. *One Place: Paul Kwilecki and Four Decades of Photographs from Decatur County, Georgia*. Edited by Iris Tillman Hill. Chapel Hill: University of North Carolina Press, 2013.

Ruby, Jay. *Secure the Shadow: Death and Photography in America*. Cambridge, Mass.: MIT Press, 1995.

Rudisill, Marie, and James C. Simmons. *Truman Capote: The Story of His Bizarre Boyhood by an Aunt Who Helped Raise Him*. New York: William Morrow, 1983.

Sander, August. *August Sander*. New York: Aperture Foundation, 1977.

Sartor, Margaret, and Alex Harris, eds. *Where We Find Ourselves: The Photographs of Hugh Mangum, 1897–1922*. Chapel Hill: University of North Carolina Press, 2019.

Scully, Julia. *Disfarmer: The Heber Springs Portraits, 1939–1946*. Danbury, N.H.: Addison House, 1976.

Severa, Joan. *Dressed for the Photographer: Ordinary Americans and Fashion, 1840–1900*. Kent, Ohio: Kent State University Press, 1995.

Shelley, Er M. *Bird Dog Training Today and Tomorrow*. New York: G. P. Putnam's Sons, 1947.

Smith, R. T. "Special Collections: Girl with a Canebrake Rattlesnake." *Georgia Review*, Fall 2010.

Sontag, Susan. *Regarding the Pain of Others*. New York: Farrar, Straus and Giroux, 2003.

Stevenson, Bryan. *Just Mercy*. New York: Spiegel & Grau, 2014.

Stott, William. *Documentary Expression and Thirties America*. Oxford: Oxford University Press, 1973.

Thomason, Michael V. R. "Two Alabama Photographers Who Recorded History: Erik Overbey and Draffus Hightower." *Alabama Review* 55, no. 3 (July 2002): 163–80.

Trachtenberg, Alan. *Reading American Photographs: From Mathew Brady to Walker Evans*. New York: Hill & Wang, 1989.

Tucker, Toba Pato. *Heber Springs Portraits: Continuity and Change in the World Disfarmer Photographed*. Introductory essay by Alan Trachtenberg. Albuquerque: University of New Mexico Press, 1996.

Turitz, Leo E., and Evelyn Turitz. *Jews in Early Mississippi*. Jackson: University of Mississippi Press, 1983.

Van Rijn, Guido. *Roosevelt's Blues: African American Blues and Gospel Songs on FDR*. Jackson: University Press of Mississippi, 1997.

Ward, Jason Morgan. *Hanging Bridge: Racial Violence and America›s Civil Rights Century*. New York: Oxford University Press, 2016.

War Memories, 1861–1865. Columbus, Miss.: Stephen D. Lee Chapter No. 34, United Daughters of the Confederacy, 1961.

Wells-Barnett, Ida. *The Red Record: Tabulated Statistics Alleged Causes of Lynching in the United States*. Chicago: Donohue & Henneberry Printers, 1894.

Wiencek, Henry. *The Hairstons: An American Family in Black and White*. New York: St. Martin's Press, 1999.

Wilkerson, Isabel. *The Warmth of Other Suns: The Epic Story of America's Great Migration*. New York: Random House, 2010.

Williams, Edwina Dakin. *Remember Me to Tom*. As told to Lucy Freeman. New York: Putnam's Sons, 1963.

Williamson, Joel. *The Crucible of Race*. New York: Oxford University Press, 1984.

Willis, Deborah, and Barbara Krauthamer. *Envisioning Emancipation: Black Americans and the End of Slavery*. Philadelphia: Temple University Press, 2013.

Wilson, Charles Reagan. *Judgment and Grace in Dixie*. Athens: University of Georgia Press, 1995.

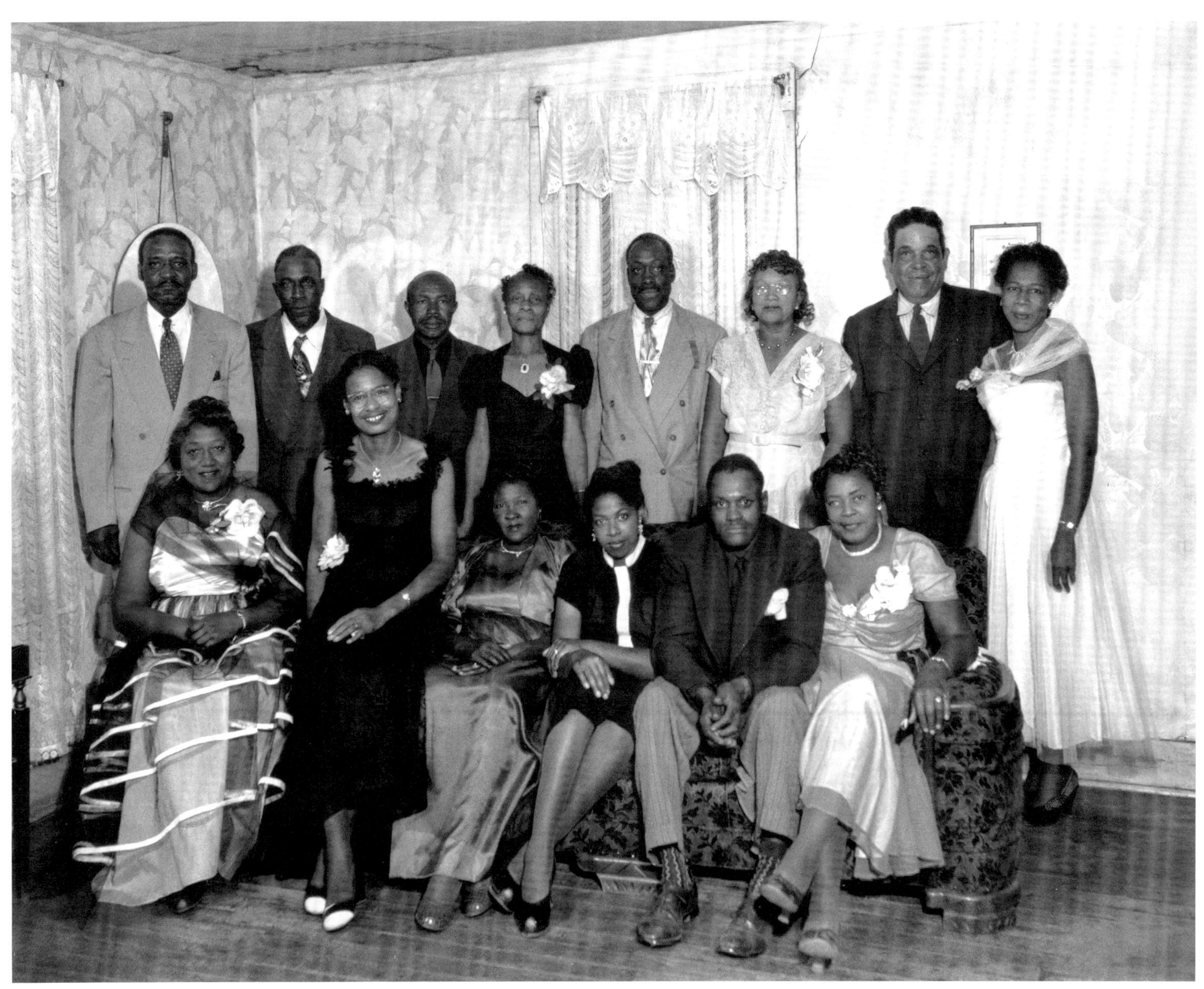

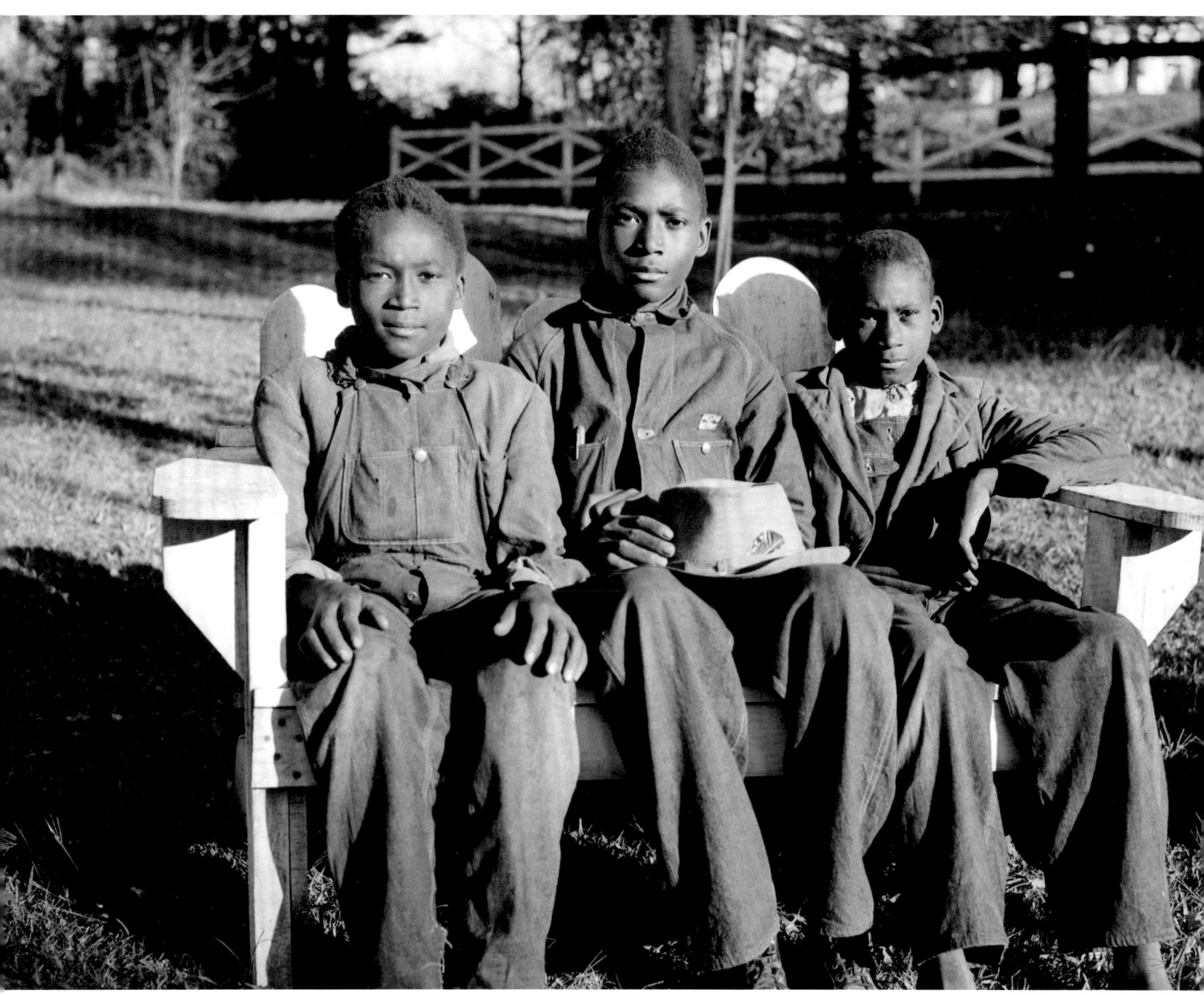

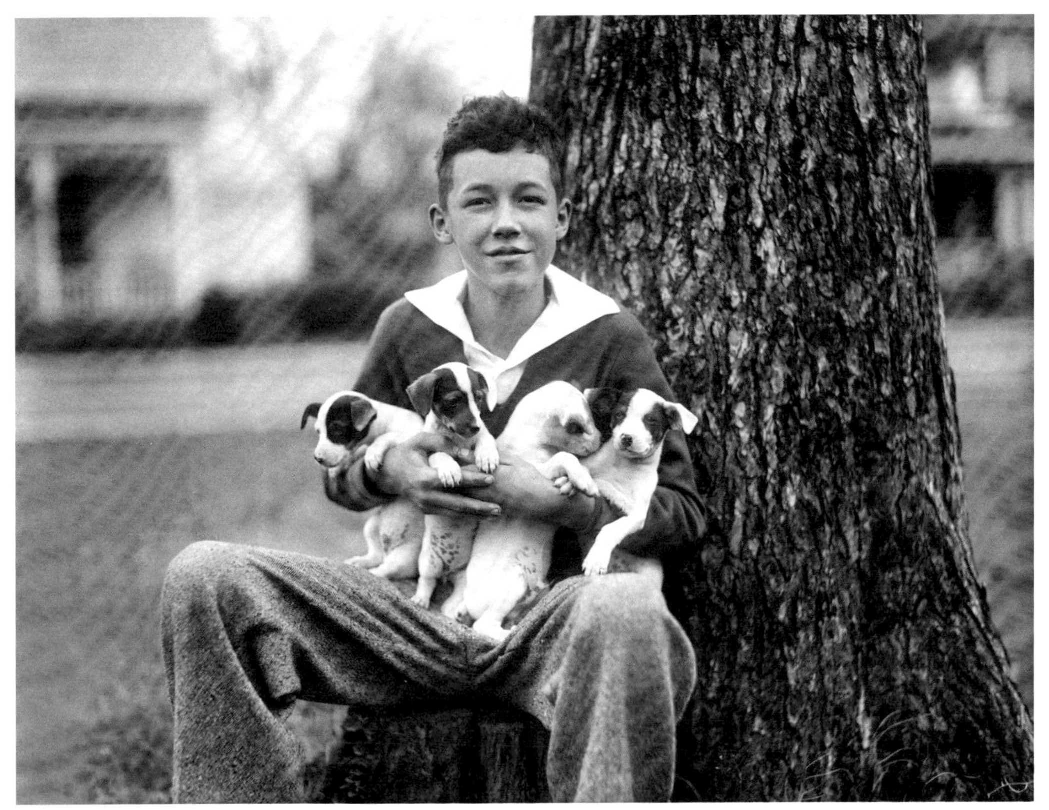

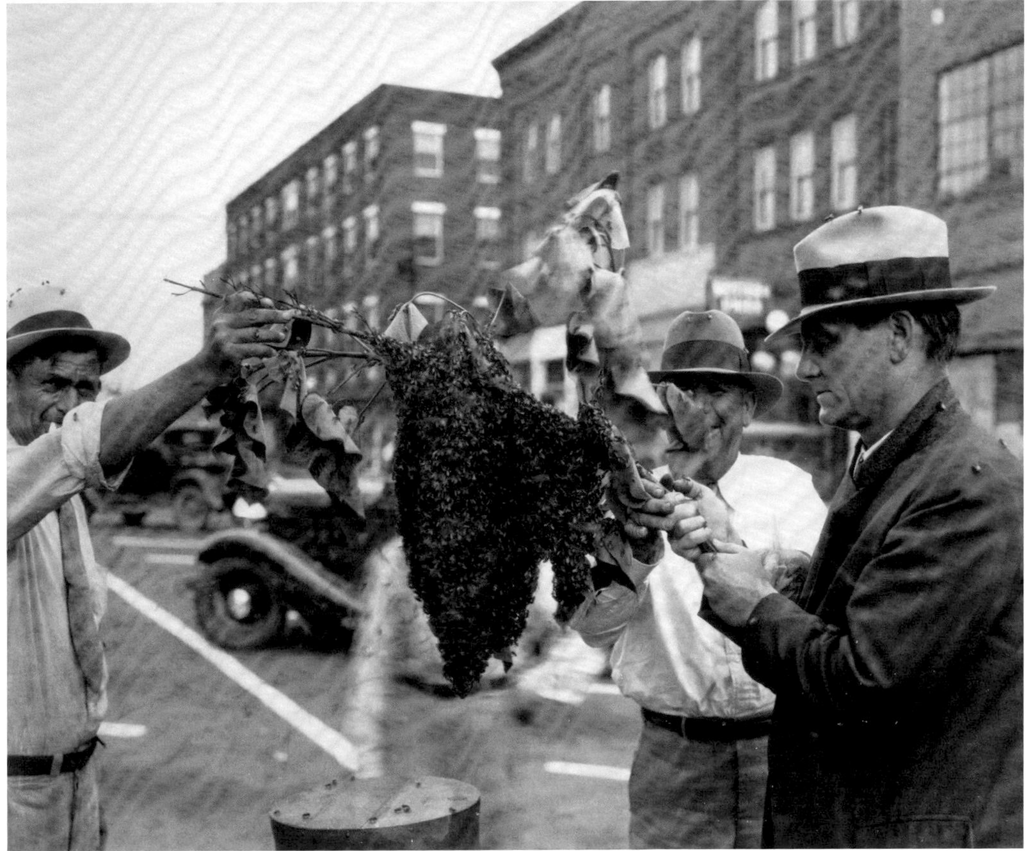

Swarm of bees, Main Street, circa 1930s.

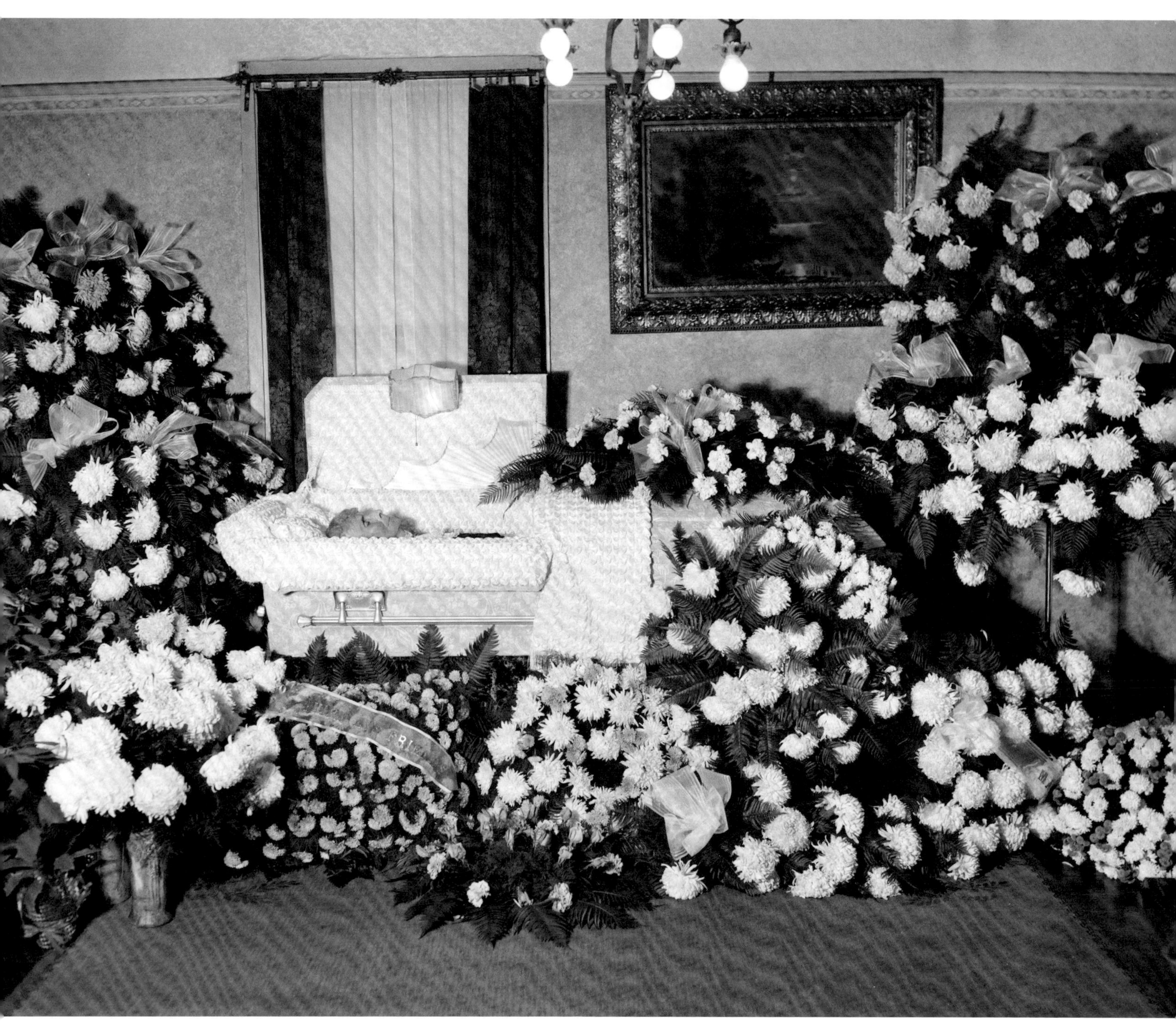

(opposite) *Works Progress Administration construction of Magnolia Bowl stadium, 1933.*

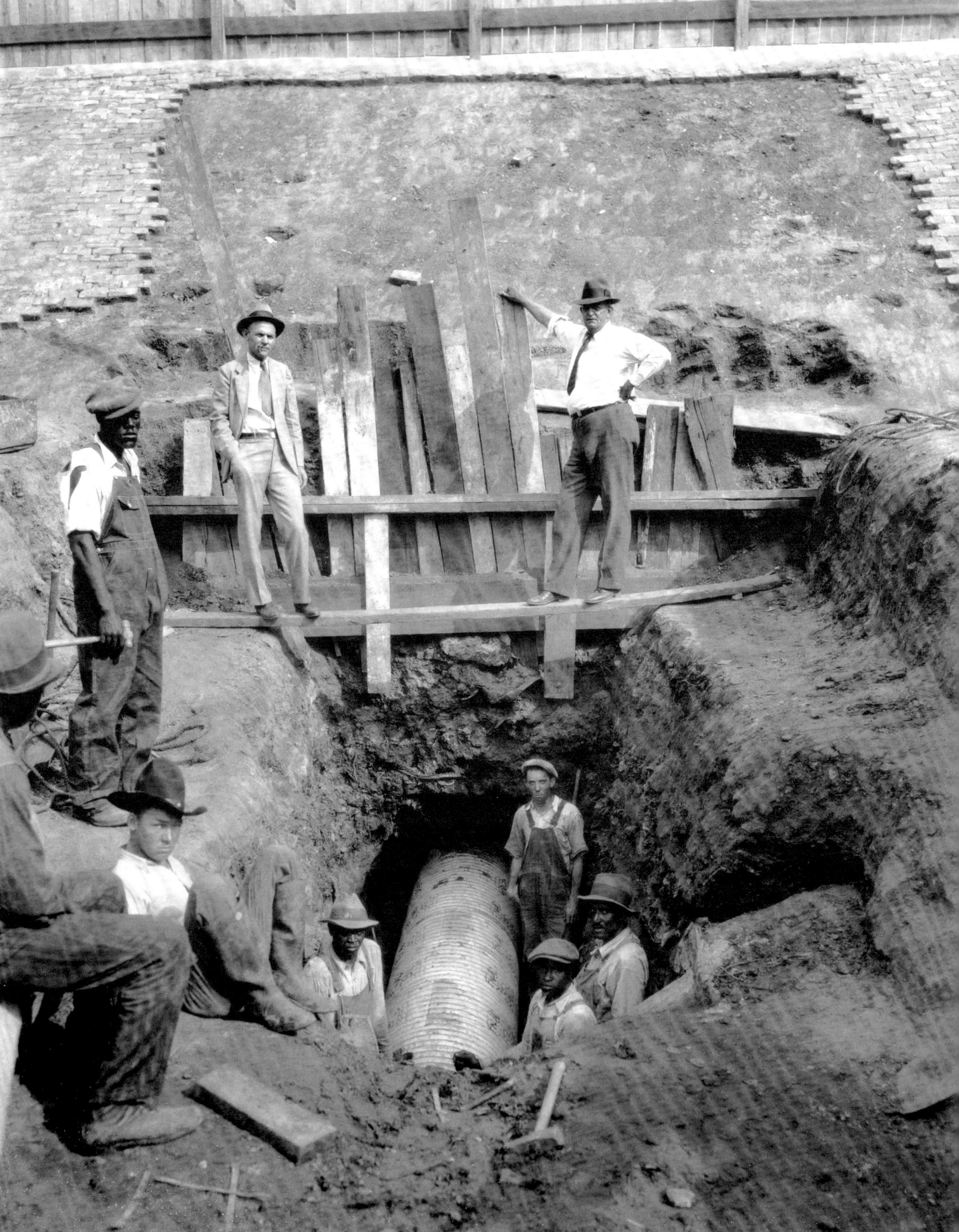

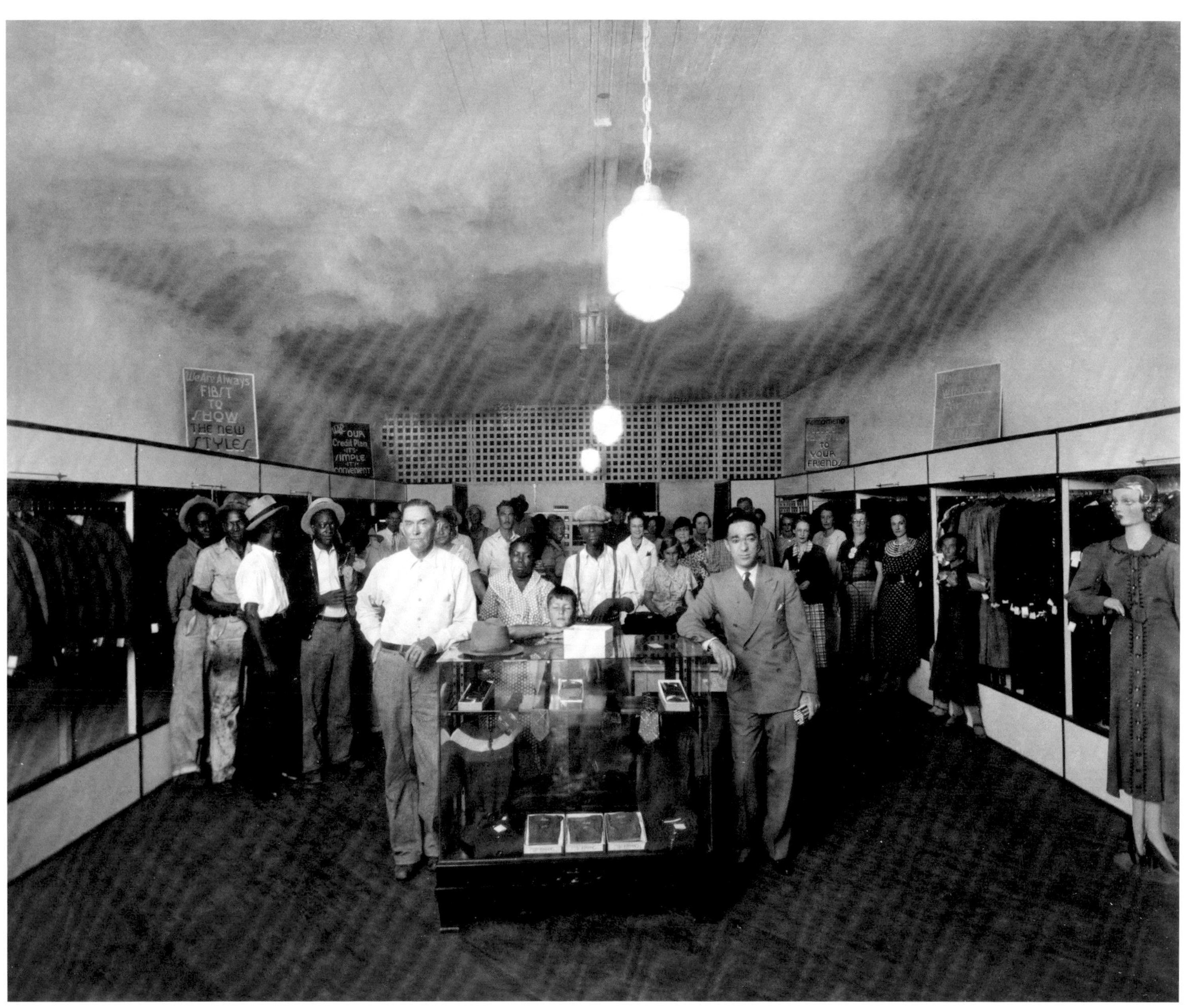
We Are Always
FIRST
TO
SHOW
THE NEW
STYLES
OUR
Credit Plan
IT'S
SIMPLE
IT'S
CONVENIENT
Recommend
TO
YOUR
FRIENDS

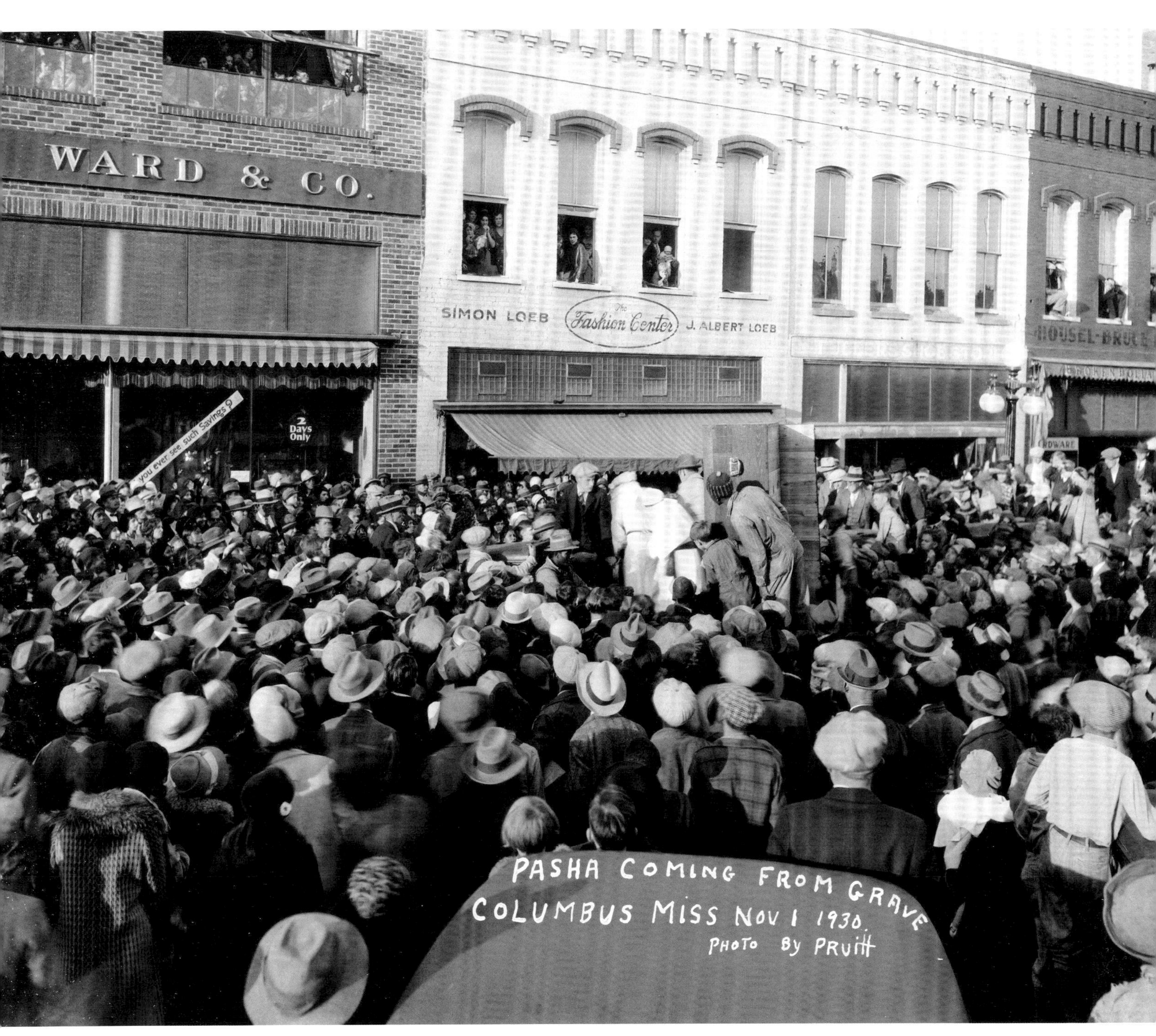

The Great Pasha coming out of coffin, intersection of Main and Market Streets, November 1, 1930.

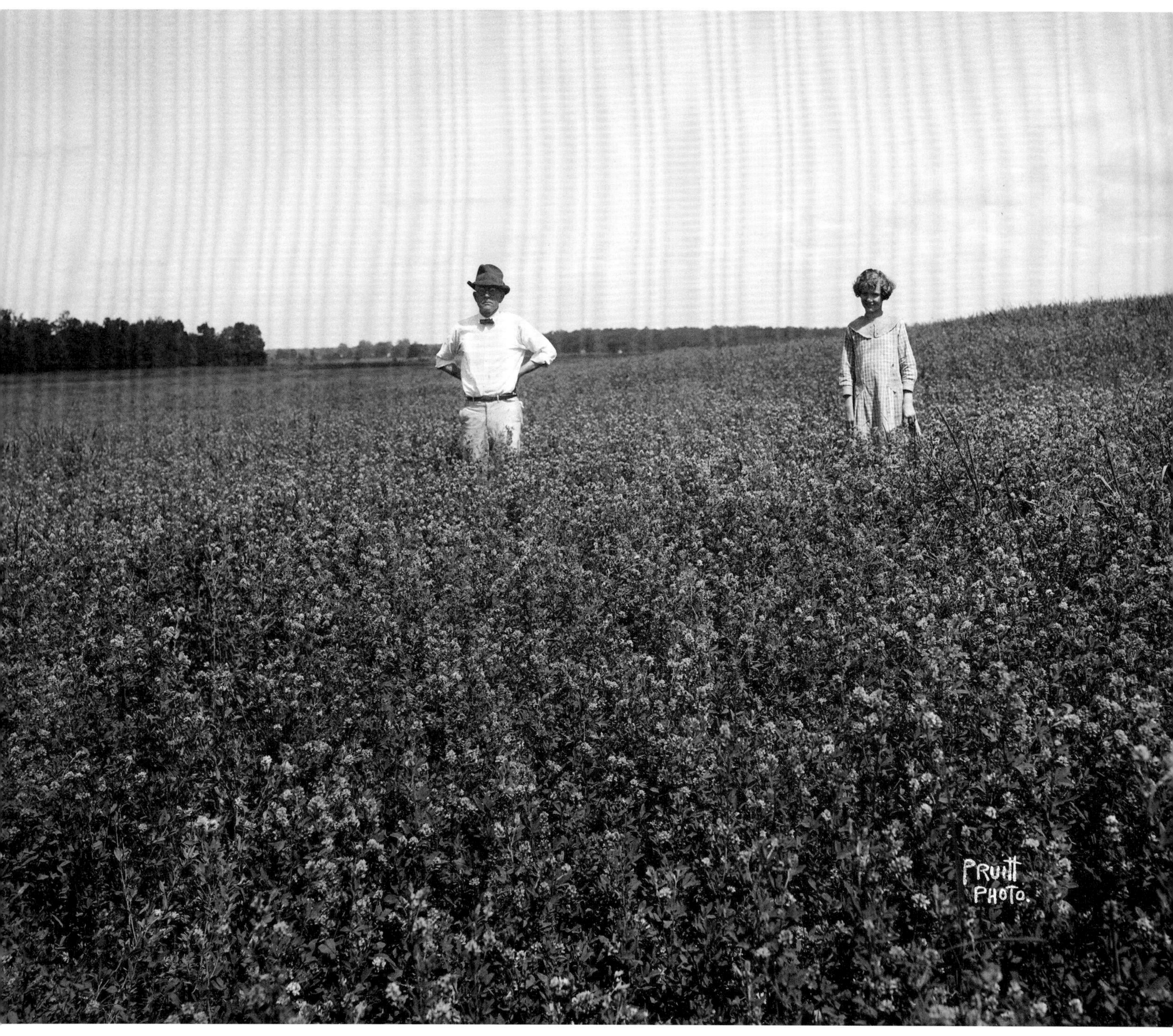
PRUITT
PHOTO.

LIST OF PHOTOGRAPHS AND ILLUSTRATIONS

The photographs in this book generally depict Columbus, Mississippi, and surrounding Lowndes County and, in some cases, the northeast Mississippi counties of Noxubee, Clay, Lee, Monroe, and Oktibbeha, and western Alabama. The list below contains identification numbers from the archives of the Pruitt-Shanks Collection at the Wilson Library's Southern Historical Collection at the University of North Carolina at Chapel Hill. The overall collection is identified with the number 05463. Numbers immediately following that can be used to find a specific photograph. Any photographs below without those numbers are still being processed from among the collection's approximately 140,000 images.

Front endsheet
top left
Studio portrait of woman, circa 1920s–30s.
5 × 7 glass negative. Glass plate box 08. 05463/02465.

top middle
Studio portrait of boy on bench with ball.
5 × 7 glass negative. Glass plate box 011. 05463/02727.

top right
Studio portrait of family.
5 × 7 glass negative. Glass plate box 013. 05463/02793.

bottom left
Studio portrait of woman.

bottom middle
Studio portrait of woman with child (*left*) and man (*right*).

bottom right
Studio portrait of older man.

Page i
Church of Christ tent revival, circa 1955. Oliver Murray, preacher, seated to right of tent pole.
8 × 10 black-and-white sheet film. Black and white film box 24. 05463/01408.

Page ii
Five women on porch, circa 1920s–30s.
8 × 10 glass negative. Glass plate box 06. 05463/02566.

Page iii
Studio portrait of woman, circa 1920s–30s.
Two images on 5 × 7 glass plate. Glass plate box 08. 05463/02470.

Page iv
Businessman Thomas J. Locke Jr., "Catch at Locke's Lodge," at his lake retreat, zoo, and lodge, south of Friendship Cemetery, by Tombigbee River, August 18, 1934.
8 × 10 black-and-white sheet film. Black and white film box 35. 05463/02890.

Page v
Men in cornfield, circa 1950s.
8 × 10 black-and-white sheet film. Black and white film box 02. 05463/00182.

Page vi
Fifteen people alongside railroad tracks with engine and train cars, circa 1925–30.

Page vii
Young person and baby.
5 × 7 glass negative. Two 2.5 × 3.5 images on plate. Glass plate box 08. 05463/02500.

Page viii
Girl with live canebrake rattlesnake, circa 1920s–30s. See fictionalized account in R. T. Smith poem, "Special Collections: Girl with Canebrake Rattlesnake," *Georgia Review* (Fall 2010).
5 × 7 glass negative. Glass plate box 09. 05463/02590.

Page ix
Woman sitting on porch steps.
4 × 5 black-and-white sheet film. Black and white film box 37. 05463/02495.

Page x
Boy with bloodied nose.
3 × 4 black-and-white sheet film. Black-and-white film box 15. 05463/01485.

Page xi
Florist and nurseryman Herman Owen (*at left*) with his 1937 Ford V8 and an unidentified man in a field of oats, circa 1938–39.
8 × 10 black-and-white sheet film. Black-and-white film box 35. 05463/02668.

Page xii
Bethel Presbyterian Church in the Black Belt Prairie, Lowndes County. Erected 1844–45. Destroyed by 2002 tornado.
4 × 5 black-and-white sheet film. Black-and-white film box 15. 05463/01248.

Page 4
Fraser family with Berkley Hudson in mother's lap (*front row*) and matriarch Gaddy (*center*), Third Street South, Christmas Day 1953.
8 × 10 black-and-white sheet film. Black-and-white film box 35. 05463/02589.

Page 10
Studio portrait of O. N. Pruitt.

Page 13
"Photographs Live Forever." Advertisement in *Commercial Dispatch* for Pruitt's studio with reproduction of nineteenth-century daguerreotype, April 4, 1941.

Page 14
O. N. Pruitt (*right*) with his son Lambuth (*left*) and Pruitt's brother Jim. Lambuth later worked as a photographer in Jackson as did Jim in nearby Starkville, circa 1925.
8 × 10 black-and-white photographic prints. Print box 3. 05463/02690.

Page 15
"Equipment Our Hobby If You Want It Photographed We Can Do It." O. N. Pruitt (*left*) and unidentified man with car and photography equipment, circa early 1920s.
8 × 10 black-and-white glass plate. Glass plate box 01. 05463/00939.

Page 16
O. N. Pruitt by artesian well, Lake Norris Fishing Club, circa 1920s. Artesian wells once flowed freely in northeast Mississippi.

Page 17
Studio portrait of O. N. Pruitt with twelve-gauge shotgun and squirrels, circa 1925. Pruitt loved to hunt and fish and built his own fishing lake.
8 × 10 black-and-white sheet film. Black-and-white film box 35. 05463/02691.

Page 21
A farmers' hay market where pigs, chickens, and sorghum and cane syrup also were sold, Main Street at Catfish Alley intersection, circa 1927.

Page 22
Columbus Drug Company, northwest corner of Main Street at Market Street intersection, late 1940s.
8 × 10 black-and-white sheet film. Black-and-white film box 02. 05463/00398.

Page 23
Grocery store interior.
5 × 7 black-and-white sheet film. Black-and-white film box 06. 05463/00697.

Page 24
Newsstand with employee behind counter, May 1933.
5 × 7 black-and-white sheet film. Black-and-white film box 05. 05463/00883.

Page 25
Artesia, west of Columbus in Lowndes County, Mississippi.

Page 26
Beer joint with beer can walls on exterior and interior, circa 1930s–40s.

Page 27
Auction, circa late 1920s to 1930s. Black-and-white film box 35. 8 × 10 black-and-white sheet film. 05463/02369.

Page 28
Grand champion cow, 1946.
8 × 10 black-and-white sheet film. Black-and-white film box 02. 05463/00115.

Page 29
Two men on a turkey farm, circa 1930s–40s.
8 × 10 black-and-white sheet film. Black-and-white film box 03. 05463/00187.

Pages 30–31
Panorama from atop Gilmer Hotel at Main Street intersection with Catfish Alley, late 1920s.
"Street Sc. So. Side of Main 300–500 Blocks," black-and-white film box 43. Rolled circuit negatives (2).

Page 32
Potato farmers with politician-farmer Johnny Williams (*left foreground*), Caledonia, Mississippi, circa 1930s.
8 × 10 black and white sheet film. Black-and-white film box 03. 05463/00197.

Page 33
Mr. Gaynes's chickens.
8 × 10 black-and-white sheet film. Black-and-white film box 02. 05463/00190.

Page 34
Men with log trucks, from Taylor Machine Works, Louisville, Mississippi. The timber may be from quite sizable bald cypress.

Page 35
Farmer bending in field.
4 × 5 black-and-white sheet film. Black-and-white film box 34. 05463/02414.

Page 36
Man with tomato plants and basket of large tomatoes, circa 1920s–30s.
8 × 10 black-and-white glass plate. Glass plate box 01. 05463/00184.

Page 37
Man with fish in cornfield.
4 × 5 black-and-white sheet film. Black-and-white film box 34, 10 images. 05463/02414.

Page 38
County fair produce exhibit.
8 × 10 black-and-white sheet film. Black-and-white film box 03. 05463/00217.

Page 41
Mississippi gathering of statewide fox hunting association, circa 1945.

Pages 42–43
Renowned hunting dog breeder and trainer Er M. Shelley with his wife, Lucille, and three dog trainers, circa 1930.
"Mr. Shelley's dogs." Black-and-white film box 43. Rolled circuit negatives (2).

Page 44
Four men in suits and vests and wearing hats.
8 × 10 black-and-white sheet film. Black-and-white film box 35. 05463/02785.

Page 45
Children on American Legion Auxiliary horse-drawn float.
8 × 10 black-and-white sheet film. Black-and-white film box 17. 05463/01505.

Page 46
Newspaper carrier boys, known as "Little Merchants," for *Commercial Dispatch*, outside Main Street office, circa 1928. A celebrated "Little Merchant" of the 1920s was Joshua "Catfish" Meador, who became a painter and distinguished animator for Walt Disney Studios, helping to win an Oscar in 1954 for *20,000 Leagues Under the Sea*.
8 × 10 black-and-white glass plate negative. Glass plate box 02. 05463/01701.

Page 49
L. W. Richardson Wholesale Groceries, with Oren Richardson, young boy with women on left, circa 1925.
8 × 10 black-and-white sheet film. Black-and-white film box 11. 05463/00702.

Page 50
Three dozen women outside F. W. Woolworth store, Market Street, circa 1920s.
8 × 10 glass. Glass plate box 02. 05463/01263_01.

Page 53
Studio portrait of Oscar West, circa 1930.
8 × 10 glass negative. Glass plate box 06. 05463/02448.

Page 54
Wood frame house with woman on porch swing.

Page 55
Kitchen, circa 1920s.

Page 58
Waverly Plantation, built 1852, on Tombigbee River's western side in Clay County, September 3, 1939. Pruitt made this photograph for inclusion in a brochure of the first Pilgrimage of antebellum homes, in 1940.
8 × 10 black-and-white sheet film. Black-and-white film box 27, 05463/02059.

Page 59
Motorized parade float as part of Decoration Day ceremonies at Friendship Cemetery, circa 1925. The parade was part of an annual ritual to commemorate when flowers were first placed in 1866 on Friendship graves of Confederate and Union soldiers. The bodies had been buried there after the Civil War's Battle of Shiloh in 1862. Controversy lingers even today about whether Columbus's Decoration Day served to inspire what became Memorial Day (Columbus, Georgia, and Waterloo, New York, also make claims for that). Additionally, Decoration Day over the years took on a Lost Cause focus. Still, President Barack Obama spoke in his Memorial Weekend address in 2010 about the Columbus women who placed flowers on Confederate graves and saw no one there to laurel the Union graves, "so [the women] decided to lay a few stems for those men, too, in recognition not of a fallen Confederate or a fallen Union soldier, but a fallen American."

Page 60
Teenage "hostesses" in hoopskirts for annual spring Pilgrimage of antebellum homes, circa 1955. *From left*, Marjorie Baugh, Emily Fletcher, Paula Harmond, Elizabeth Banks, and Mary Ann Betts. A decade earlier, *Life* magazine photographer Alfred Eisenstaedt visited Columbus to photograph antebellum homes for the feature "Life Goes to Southern Hoopskirt Party for Air Cadets," published March 8, 1943. He made photographs at Riverview, circa 1847, and Whitehall, circa 1843.
8 × 10 black-and-white sheet film. Black-and-white film box 36. 05463/02875.

Page 61
Monument honoring Union and Confederate soldiers who died in the 1864 Battle of Tupelo, circa 1940s.

Page 65
Playwright Tennessee Williams (*right*) and his maternal grandfather, Reverend Walter Dakin, during a visit to Columbus, where Williams was born, with Davis Patty (*left*) at Patty's home on Seventh Street South, May 1952. Reverend Dakin had been rector at St. Paul's Episcopal Church. Davis Patty, a banker, was a lay leader of the church.
Black-and-white 120 roll film. Black-and-white film box 29. 05463/02003 to 02007.

Page 66
Singer with Mutual Broadcasting System banner hanging from WCBI radio microphone.

Page 67
Studio portrait of man with Lucas brand accordion.
8 × 10 glass negative. Glass plate box 10. 05463/02649.

Page 68
Three vaudeville performers (man and two women) in costume.
8 × 10 black-and-white sheet film. Black-and-white film box 25. 05463/01642.

Page 69
Zeke's Wabash Five, circa 1920s–30s.
8 × 10 black-and-white sheet film. Black-and-white film box 17. 05463/01649.

Page 70
Country music band with Mid-South Network banner hanging on microphone.

Page 71
Dancers and instrumentalists.
8 × 10 black-and-white sheet film. Black-and-white film box 25. 05463/01605.

Page 72
Studio portrait of Mississippi State College for Women students, circa 1920s.
8 × 10 glass negative. Glass plate box 06. 05463/02597.

Page 73
Young woman dancer in top hat.
8 × 10 black-and-white sheet film. Black-and-white film box 35. 05463/02537.

Page 74
Studio portrait of five young dancers, circa 1920s.
8 × 10 glass negative. Glass plate box 06. 05463/02524.

Page 75
Rotary Club band in front of Pruitt's studio, circa 1920s.
8 × 10 black-and-white glass plate negative. Glass plate box 02. 05463/01660.

Page 76
"Marie's Dancing Beauties" carnival sideshow.
8 × 10 black-and-white sheet film. Black-and-white film box 35. 05463/02658.

Page 78
Studio portrait of member of Miller's Travelling Museum.
5 × 7 glass plate

Page 80
"Miller[']s Travelling Museum. World Fair Freaks."
8 × 10 black-and-white sheet film. Black-and-white film box 35. 05463/02392.

Page 81
Boy with toys, circa 1925.
8 × 10 glass negative. Glass plate box 06. 05463/02518.

Page 82
Two boys with pony outside an electric supply company.
8 × 10 black-and-white sheet film. Black-and-white film box 09. 05463/00579.

Page 86
Irene Locke (*center*), daughter of Thomas J. Locke Jr., on camel at Locke's Zoo, circa 1925.
8 × 10 glass negative. Glass plate box 06. 05463/02530.

Page 89
War bond rally during World War II at Princess Theatre, Market Street.
8 × 10 black-and-white sheet film. Black-and-white film box 10. 05463/00930.

Page 90
Princess Theatre, Market Street, circa 1930s–40s.

Page 91
Teenage girls at Luxapalila Creek swimming hole, circa 1925. Hawley Knox is center with hand on chin.

Page 92
Alligator Lake, circa 1930s. Jim Wilder (*center*) holds a spoonbill catfish. William Jimmison is at far left.
8 × 10 black-and-white sheet film. Black-and-white film box 35. 05463/02894.

Page 93
Fireworks.
8 × 10 black-and-white photographic prints. Print box 2. 05463/02578.

Page 94
From left: Hubert Holmes, T. C. Billups, unidentified mechanic, and pilot Jess Windham with two-seater biplane, circa 1920s–30s.
8 × 10 glass negative. Glass plate box 06. 05463/02296.

Page 95
Woman, man, and boy on crutches on front porch.
4 × 5 black-and-white sheet film. Black-and-white film box 34. 05463/02414.

Page 96
Woman caretaking a woman in bed.
4 × 5 black-and-white sheet film. Black-and-white film box 34. 05463/02414.

Page 97
Macon's Dramatic Club; image labeled "Teatime in the country."
8 × 10 black-and-white sheet film. Black-and-white film box 35. 05463/02405.

Page 98
Boy by backyard pond with lily pads.
8 × 10 black-and-white photographic copy prints. Print box 3. 05463/02859.

Page 99
Young woman in backyard.
4 × 5 black-and-white sheet film. Black-and-white film box 37. 05463/02509.

Page 100
Man in front passenger side of car with open doors.
4 × 5 black-and-white sheet film. Black-and-white film box 34. 05463/02786.

Page 101
WCBI-AM radio announcer interviews a Soap Box Derby participant holding a rabbit, circa 1950s.

Page 102
Boy and girl with watermelons in front of Vaughan Bros. grocery.
8 × 10 black-and-white sheet film. Black-and-white film box 36. 05463/02353.

Page 103
Main Street barbershop, circa 1930s.
5 × 7 black-and-white sheet film. Black-and-white film box 05. 05463/00274 (275-276?).

Page 104
Beauty shop.

Page 105
Young woman in garden.
4 × 5 black-and-white sheet film. Black-and-white film box 34. 05463/02459.

Page 106
Man and woman in office, circa 1950s.

Page 107
Man shakes hand of young woman wearing "Miss Air Express" sash in window display with two female mannequins.

Page 108
"Hold That Waist Line," Egger's Department Store window display.

Page 111
Catfish Alley fire, circa 1940.

Page 112
Tornado aftermath, Tupelo, Mississippi, April 4, 1936. This tornado often is referred to as the second deadliest in the United States, killing more than 200. Research determined that official records undercounted the deceased Black residents, whose neighborhoods were devastated by the cyclone. Minrose Gwin's novel *Promise* (2019) explores the complexities of that and uses a Pruitt image of a makeshift morgue where African American bodies were laid out. The tornado did not kill one particular toddler, Elvis Presley. In 1985, Nick Cave and the Bad Seeds paid tribute in the song "Tupelo": "Distant thunder rumble / Rumble hungry like the Beast / The King will walk on Tupelo / And carry the burden of Tupelo."
5 × 7 black-and-white sheet film. Black-and-white film box 37. 05463/02924.

Page 113
Tombigbee River flooding, with men in boat by house.
Black-and-white film box 34 or 35. 02375 through 02380.

Page 114
Men in front of doors that say "Office."
8 × 10 black-and-white sheet film. Black-and-white film box 35. 05463/02785.

Page 115
"U.S. Postal Employes [*sic*]," circa 1935.
8 × 10 black-and-white sheet film. Black-and-white film box 17. 05463/01500.

Page 116
Schoolroom with mural that includes advertisement for Pruitt's studio on lower right.
8 × 10 black-and-white photographic copy print. Print box 3. 05463/02899.

Page 117
Union Academy, circa 1930s–40s. Founded December 1865 as the first school for freed Blacks in Columbus in a building that originally was a Confederate hospital. One of the most popular choirs in the 1920s and 1930s was directed by Annie Will Alexander, a Union Academy teacher. She led a countywide group of African Americans, often with 125 voices singing gospel and spirituals.

Page 118
Jack and Jill Kindergarten, circa May Day 1958. Joy Dill (*center*) wears a flowered headband.
8 × 10 black-and-white sheet film. Black-and-white film box 25. 05463/01620.

Page 119
Hunt High School girls basketball team, circa 1950s. Built as an all-Black school in 1954 and consolidated with white S. D. Lee High School in 1970.

Page 120
Macon High School girls basketball team, circa 1930s.

Page 121
Columbus Redbirds baseball team.

Page 122
Hunt High School baseball team, circa 1950s.

Page 123
Hunt High School library.

Page 124
Springtime Zouave exercise demonstrations, Mississippi State College for Women, late 1930s.

Page 125
Mississippi State College for Women students dancing "Grecian-style" by pool, circa 1920s.
8 × 10 glass negative. Glass plate box 6. 05463/02592.

Page 128
Gilmer Hotel bellhops, circa 1930. Manager J. O. Slaughter is seated. Guests of the whites-only hotel of that era included boxer Jack Dempsey and Nobel Laureate William Faulkner. Standing, second from the right, is Ed Bush, prominent Catfish Alley businessman who in the late 1940s renovated and operated the Queen City Hotel with his wife, Bessie Bush. The Queen City was listed in the *Negro Travelers' Green Book*. Black musicians B.B. King, Count Basie, Marian Anderson, and baseball player Jackie Robinson were guests.
8 × 10 black-and-white sheet film. Black-and-white film box 12. 05463/00685.

Page 129
Men at work.

Page 130, top
Bakery.

Page 130, bottom
Columbus Meat Packing Co.
8 × 10 black-and-white sheet film. Black-and-white film box 35. 05463/02660.

Page 131
Men field dressing deer.
4 × 5 black-and-white sheet film. Black-and-white film box 34. 05463/02784.

Page 132
Men cooking barbecue, most likely at Magowah Gun and Country Club, as named when it was founded in 1906 as a place for trap and skeet shooting. It catered to elite whites in the fertile western Lowndes County area known as the Black Belt Prairie and where antebellum plantations had been established. Ben Harris, possibly pictured right, was among the fabled Black pit masters of Magowah barbecues.
4 × 5 black-and-white sheet film. Black-and-white film box 15. 05463/01785/03.

Page 133, top
Teenagers at picnic likely at Magowah.
4 × 5 black-and-white sheet film. Black-and-white film box 15. 05463/01785/01.

Page 133, bottom
Woman fishing from boat.
4 × 5 black-and-white sheet film. Black-and-white film box 34. 05463/02871.

Page 136
Birney Imes Sr., editor and publisher of the *Commercial Dispatch*, with statue representing a Native American, 1931.
8 × 10 black-and-white sheet film. Black-and-white film box 35. 05463/02616.

Page 137
Men with crane extracting horse stuck in mud.

Page 138
Ed "Sonny" Edmondson with raccoon, circa 1950.
8 × 10 black-and-white sheet film. Black-and-white film box 36. 05463/02541.

Page 139
Turkey hunter with gun and turkey.

Page 140
Three young equestrians astride horses.
8 × 10 black-and-white glass plate negative. Glass plate box 04. 05463/01854.

Page 141
Woman before vanity with mirror.
8 × 10 black-and-white sheet film. Black-and-white film box 36. 05463/02860.

Page 142
Two women in work uniforms.
4 × 5 black-and-white sheet film. Black-and-white film box 34. 05463/02414.

Page 143
Blind man with cane and tin cup whistles on southwest corner of Main and Market Streets, soliciting donations, circa 1950s.

Pages 144–45
Picking cotton, likely at Harris Hardy farm in Black Belt Prairie of southwest Lowndes County, circa 1920s–30s.
Black-and-white film box 43. Rolled circuit negatives (2).

Page 146
Cotton bales at Williams Cotton Warehouse, circa 1930s. By 1860, Lowndes County produced 50,000 bales of cotton and 1 million bushels of corn annually. For at least another century, agriculture played a key role in northeast Mississippi.
5 × 7 black-and-white sheet film. Black-and-white film box 05. 05463/00126.

Page 149
White school children as minstrels in blackface, circa 1920s.
8 × 10 black-and-white sheet film.
Black-and-white film box 35.
05463/02526.

Page 150
Kiwanis Club blackface minstrel show at Gilmer Hotel, circa 1940s–50s.
4 × 5 black-and-white sheet film.
Black-and-white film box 15.
05463/01573.

Page 159
Ku Klux Klan march, Main Street in front of Pruitt's studio, circa 1922.
4 × 5 black-and-white sheet film.
Black-and-white film box 15.
05463/01583.

Page 160
Execution of James Keaton, Lowndes County Courthouse, May 25, 1934.
4 × 5 black-and-white sheet film.
Black-and-white film box 41.
05463/02940.

Page 161
After the lynching of Bert Moore and Dooley Morton, July 1935.
8 × 10 black-and-white sheet film. Black-and-white film box 41.
05463/02941.

Page 162
Death certificate for Dooley Morton, with cause of death "lynched by mob." Vital Records, Mississippi State Department of Health, July 15, 1935.

Page 163
Man standing along gravel road in woods.

Page 167
Lowndes County farmer Sylvester Harris with mule Jesse outside his home in Plum Grove community, February 1934. President Franklin D. Roosevelt helped Harris save his farm from foreclosure after Harris called him asking for assistance.
8 × 10 black-and-white sheet film.
Black-and-white film box 35.
05463/02612.

Page 168
James Mann family portrait outside of home, 1948.
8 × 10 black-and-white photographic copy print. Print box 2. 05463/02423.

Page 169
Family portrait on porch steps. Mrs. Mary Stokes is in second row, far right.
8 × 10 black-and-white photographic copy print. Print box 2. 05463/02570.

Page 173
"Watching Pasha Buried Alive" next to *Commercial Dispatch* building on Main Street, November 1, 1930.
8 × 10 black-and-white sheet film.
Black-and-white film box 35. Sheet film 05463/02387/03.

Page 174
"Jack Dempsey watching Pasha buried alive." Boxing champion Jack Dempsey (*center and hatless*) with Madame Flozella and Truman Capote's mother, Lillie Mae Faulk Persons (dressed in black), by grave dug at the Lake Norris Fishing Club, November 10, 1930.
8 ×10 black-and-white sheet film.
Black-and-white film box 35.
05463/02387/02.

Page 175
"Pasha buried alive for Demsey [*sic*] Party." Boxing champion Jack Dempsey (*left of coffin*) with the Great Pasha; Madame Flozella; "Buried Alive" act's manager, Arch Persons (*in white hat and glasses*), Truman Capote's father; and Lillie Mae Faulk Persons, Truman Capote's mother (*far right*), Lake Norris Fishing Club, November 10, 1930.
8 × 10 black-and-white sheet film.
Black-and-white film box 35.
05463/02387/01.

Page 176
New Hope School Casket Company.
8 × 10 black-and-white photographic copy prints. Print box 2. 05463/02337.

Page 177
Body of boy in coffin.

Page 178, left
Body of woman in coffin.
5 × 7 black-and-white sheet film.
Black-and-white film box 34.
05463/02507.

Page 178, right
Body of man with visible injuries in coffin.
8 × 10 black-and-white sheet film.
Black-and-white film box 35.
05463/02538.

Page 179
Columbus Marble Works, circa 1930s–40s. Founded in 1846, the tombstone and monument company grew into one of the nation's principal suppliers for veteran's markers at sites such as Arlington National Cemetery. For at least a dozen Mississippi towns including Brandon, Cleveland, Greenwood, Oxford, Philadelphia, Port Gibson, and Tupelo, the firm made Confederate monuments in the early twentieth century to memorialize, as the *Columbus Dispatch* reported at the time, "heroes of the Lost Cause." In 2021, as part of a national reckoning with the Civil War's legacy, Columbus's monument was removed from the Lowndes County Courthouse grounds and was scheduled to be placed in Friendship Cemetery's section with graves of Confederate soldiers.
8 × 10 black-and-white sheet film.
Black-and-white film box 03.
05463/00464.

Page 182
Annunciation Catholic Church.

Page 183
Young woman dressed for Jewish ceremony at Congregation B'nai Israel. 8 × 10 black-and-white sheet film. Black-and-white film box 18. 05463/01269.

Page 184
Woman in church.
4 × 6 black-and-white sheet film. Black-and-white film box 15. 05463/01323.

Page 185
Women's church group.
8 × 10 black-and-white sheet film. Black-and-white film box 36. 05463/02508.

Page 186
First Methodist Church's "Old Women's Dinner," October 15, 1952.
8 × 10 black-and-white sheet film. Black-and-white film box 24. 05463/01315.

Page 187
"Missionary Baptist Sunday School and B.T.U. Convention," July 18, 1952.

Page 188
First Baptist Church choir.
8 × 10 black-and-white sheet film. Black-and-white film box 19. 05463/01296.

Page 189
Church Halloween party during World War II.
8 × 10 black-and-white sheet film. Black-and-white film box 19. 05463/01392.

Page 190
Man dressed as Santa Claus, circa 1930s.

Page 193
Tombigbee River baptism, circa 1930s.
4 × 5 black-and-white sheet film. Black-and-white film box 15. 05463/01404.

Page 194
Preacher with baptismal group, Tombigbee River, circa 1930s
4 × 5 black-and-white sheet film. Black-and-white film box 15. 05463/01405.

Page 195
Preacher with baptismal group, Tombigbee River, circa 1930s.
4 × 5 black-and-white sheet film. Black-and-white film box 15. 05463/01405.

Page 196
Studio portrait of young woman in white tailored coat with scarf and hat.

Page 197
Studio portrait of boy with dog on bench.
Possibly 4 × 5 black-and-white sheet film. Black-and-white film box 34. 05463/02610.

Page 198
Studio portrait of boy with food on bench.

Page 199, top
Man in white suit and hat, circa 1920s–30s.
5 × 7 glass negative. Two 2.5 × 3.5 images on plate. Glass plate box 07. 05463/02455.

Page 199, bottom
Studio portrait of woman with boy.
5 × 7 glass negative. Glass plate box 08. 05463/02503.

Page 200, top
Studio portrait of man and woman.
5 × 7 black-and-white sheet film. Black-and-white film box 37. 05463/02422.

Page 200, bottom
Two boys at well.
5 × 7 glass negative. Glass plate box 09. 05463/02519.]

Page 201
Family portrait outdoors.
8 × 10 black-and-white sheet film. Black-and-white film box 35. 05463/02544.

Page 202
Family portrait outdoors.

Page 203
Studio portrait of family.
8 × 10 glass negative. Glass plate box 06. 05463/02564.

Page 204
Studio portrait of three men and one woman.
Black-and-white film box 35. 8 × 10 black-and-white sheet film. 05463/02532.

Page 205, top left
Woman in wedding dress.
8 × 10 glass negative. Glass plate box 010. 05463/02864.

Page 205, top right
Robinson family portrait.
8 × 10 black-and-white sheet film. Black-and-white film box 36. 05463/02698.

Page 205, bottom left
Studio portrait of Junior-Freshman "Wedding" held each autumn at Mississippi State College for Women, late 1930s.
8 × 10 black-and-white sheet film. Black-and-white film box 35. 05463/02595.

Page 205, bottom right
Studio portrait of girl with feather in hat.
8 × 10 black-and-white sheet film. Black-and-white film box 35. 05463/02595.

Page 206, top left
Studio portrait of Boy Scout in uniform.
5 × 7 glass negative. Glass plate box 09. 05463/02517.

Page 206, top right
Studio portrait of young man in navy uniform.
8 × 10 black-and-white sheet film. Black-and-white film box 36. 05463/02445.

Page 206, bottom left
Studio portrait of baby.
8 × 10 glass negative. Glass plate box 010. 05463/02719.

Page 206, bottom right
Studio portrait of young girl.

Page 207
Studio portrait of woman.
4 × 5 black-and-white sheet film. Black-and-white film box 34. 05463/02459.

Page 208
Studio portrait of boy in cowboy hat and boots.

Page 209, top
Studio portrait of woman.
5 × 7 glass negative. Glass plate box 08. 05463/02497.

Page 209, bottom
Studio portrait of man in suit wearing bow tie.

Page 223
"The Willing Working Club" portrait of fourteen members, October 24, 1952.
8 × 10 black-and-white sheet film. Black-and-white film box 25. 05463/01673.

Page 224
Three boys in overalls on a bench outside.
4 × 5 black-and-white sheet film. Black-and-white film box 34. 05463/02414/07.

Page 225, top
Boy with puppies.
5 × 7 glass negative. Glass plate box 09. 05463/02520.

Page 225, bottom
Men on Main Street with swarm of bees, circa 1930s.
8 × 10 black-and-white sheet film. Print box 35. 05463/02677.

Page 226
Body of woman in casket with portable light to illuminate it.

Page 227
Works Progress Administration construction of Magnolia Bowl stadium, 1933.
8 × 10 black-and-white sheet film. Black-and-white film box 35. 05463/02670.

Page 228
Store interior with clerks and customers.

Page 229
"Pasha Coming from Grave," intersection of Main and Market Streets, November 1, 1930.
8 × 10 black-and-white sheet film. Black-and-white film box 35. 05463/02386.

Page 230
Man and girl in field, circa 1920s.
8 × 10 black-and-white glass plate. Glass plate box 01. 05463/00170.

Back endsheet
top left
Studio portrait of woman, circa 1920s–30s.
5 × 7 glass negative. 2 images on 5 × 7 piece of glass. Glass plate box 08. 05463/02467.

top middle
Studio portrait of girl posing as older woman holding fan.
5 × 7 glass negative. Glass plate box 09. 05463/02596.

top right
Studio portrait of man.
5 × 7 glass negative. Glass plate box 012. 05463/02779.

bottom left
Studio portrait of woman.

bottom middle
Studio portrait of two girls.

bottom right
Studio portrait of man.

INDEX

Page numbers in italics refer to photographs and photograph captions.

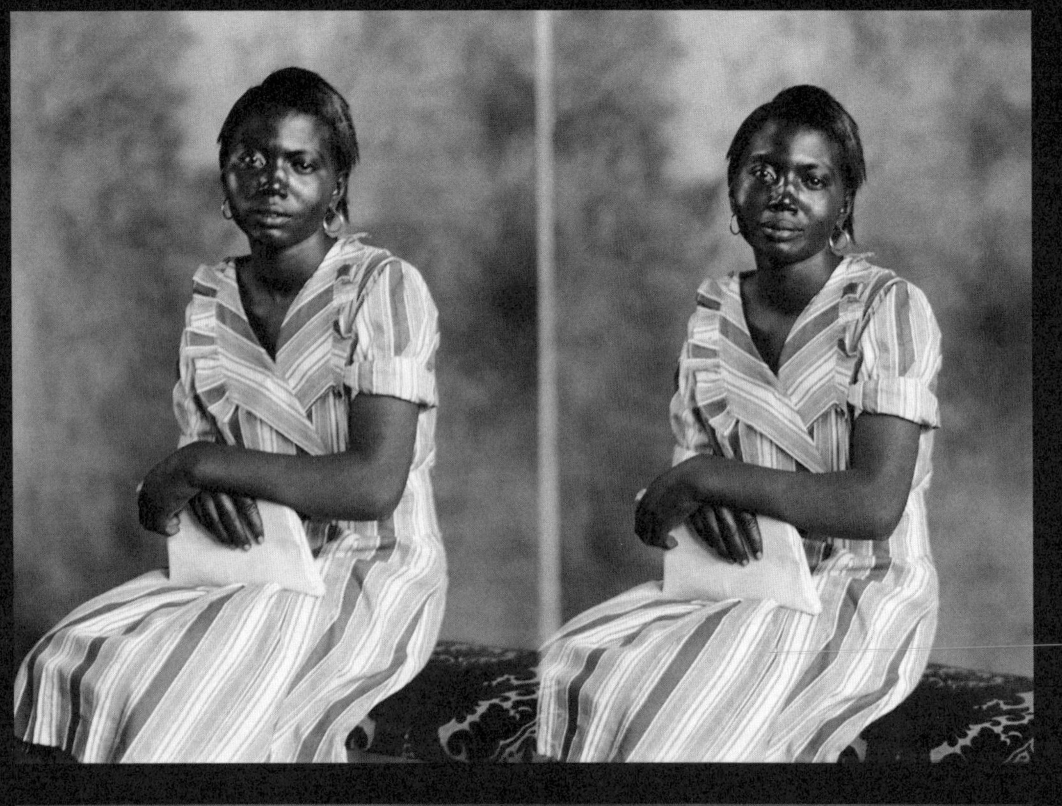
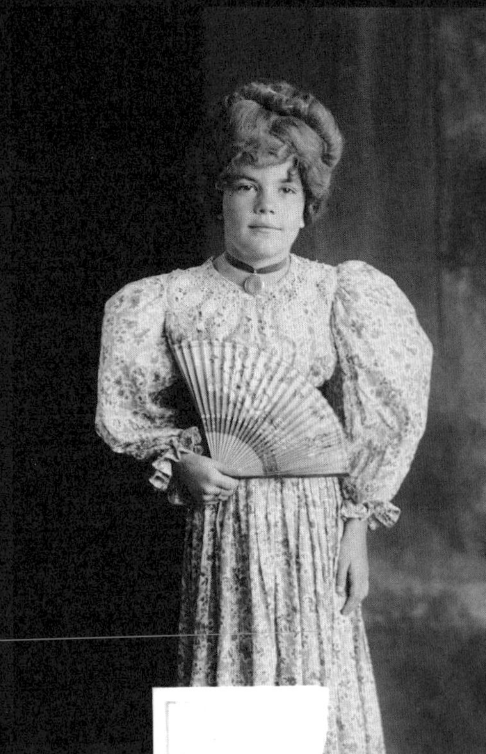
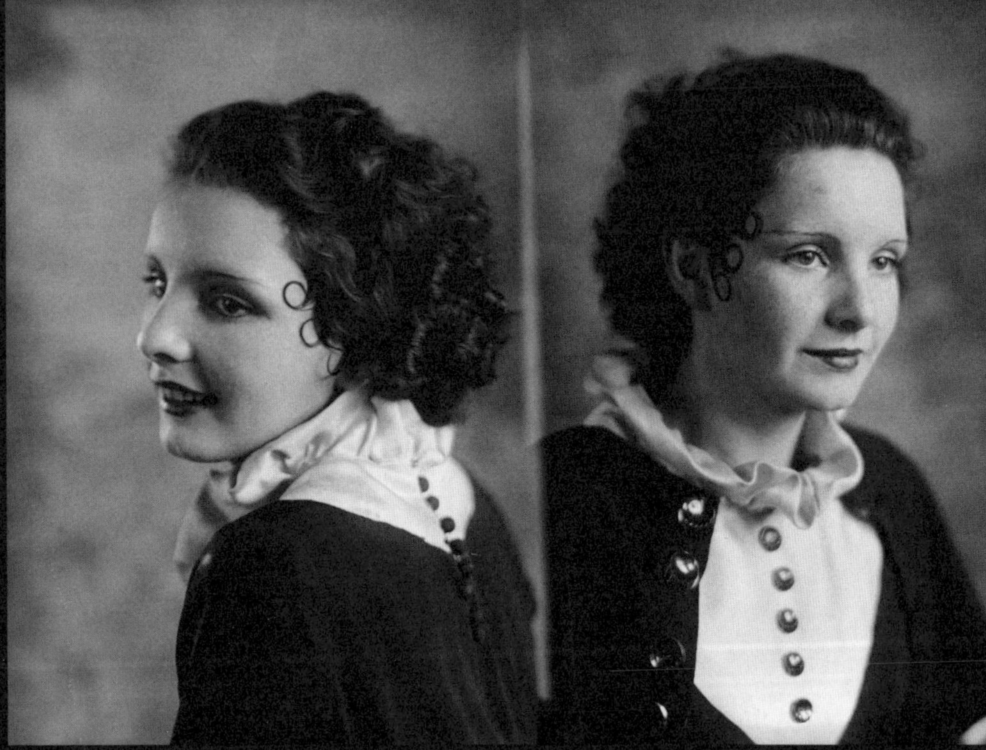
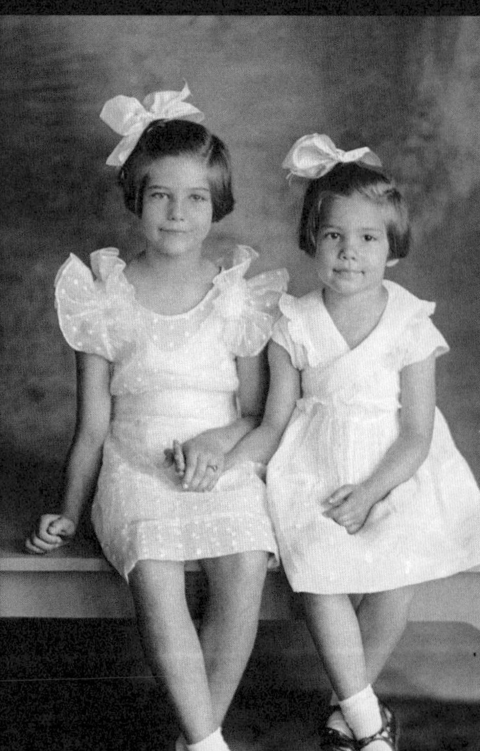